MCA
Microsoft® Office Specialist Complete Study Guide
(Office 365 and Office 2019)

Word Exam MO-100, Excel Exam MO-200, and PowerPoint Exam MO-300

Eric Butow

SYBEX®
A Wiley Brand

Published by John Wiley & Sons, Inc., Hoboken, New Jersey.
Published simultaneously in Canada.

ISBN: 978-1-119-71849-9
ISBN: 978-1-119-71851-2 (ebk.)
ISBN: 978-1-119-71850-5 (ebk.)

Library of Congress Control Number: 2021938302

Cover Image: © Getty Images Inc./Jeremy Woodhouse
Cover Design: Wiley

SKY10027259_052621

To my family and friends

Acknowledgments

I have many people to thank, starting with my literary agent, Matt Wagner. He connected me with Sybex to write this book and managed our relationship well. Next, I want to give a shout out to my excellent editing team: Gary Schwartz, Barath Kumar Rajasekaran, Christine O'Connor, and Senior Acquisitions Editor Kenyon Brown.

And, as always, I want to thank my family and friends for their everlasting support. I couldn't write this book without them.

—Eric Butow

About the Author

Eric Butow is the owner of Butow Communications Group (BCG) in Jackson, California. BCG offers website development, online marketing, and technical writing services. Eric is a native Californian who started working with his friend's Apple II Plus and Radio Shack TRS-80 Model III in 1980 when he lived in Fresno, California. He learned about programming, graphic design, and desktop publishing in the Fresno PC Users Group in his professional career, and when he started BCG in 1994.

Eric has written 40 other technical books as an author, co-author or, in one case, as a ghostwriter. Most of Eric's works were written for the general book market, but some were written for specific clients including HP and F5 Networks. Two of his books have been translated into Chinese and Italian. Eric's most recent books are *Programming Interviews for Dummies* (For Dummies, 2019) with John Sonmez, *Ultimate Guide to Social Media Marketing* (Entrepreneur Press, 2020) with Herman, Liu, Robinson, and Allton, and *Instagram for Business for Dummies Second Edition* (For Dummies, 2021) with Jennifer Herman and Corey Walker.

Upon his graduation from California State University, Fresno in 1996 with a master's degree in communication, Eric moved to Roseville, California, where he lived for 13 years. Eric continued to build his business and worked as a technical writer for a wide variety of businesses from startups to large companies including Intel, Wells Fargo Wachovia, TASQ Technology, Cisco Systems, and Hewlett-Packard. Many of those clients required their technical writers to know Microsoft PowerPoint, which Eric has used since the early 1990s. From 1997–1999, during his off-time, Eric produced 30 issues of *Sacra Blue*, the award-winning monthly magazine of the Sacramento PC Users Group.

When Eric isn't working in (and on) his business or writing books, you can find him enjoying time with friends, walking around the historic Gold Rush town of Jackson, and helping his mother manage her infant and toddler daycare business.

About the Technical Editor

Kristen Merritt is an experienced technical editor who has reviewed books for several publishers, including Wiley and Microsoft Press. Kristen spent 12 years in technical sales, and she is currently employed as a digital marketer.

Contents at a Glance

Contents

Chapter 16 Applying Transitions and Animations 589

Appendix Answers to Review Questions 627

Table of Exercises

Introduction

Welcome to this book about becoming a Microsoft Certified Office Specialist for the Microsoft 365 suite of productivity applications to which you can subscribe. You can also use this book with the one-time purchase version of Office, which Microsoft calls Office 2019.

Microsoft 365 allows you to use different versions on many platforms, including Windows, macOS, iOS, iPadOS, and Android. You can even use the free online version of Microsoft 365. This book, however, talks about using the most popular version of Microsoft 365 on the most popular operating system, which happens to be the Word, Excel, and PowerPoint applications in Microsoft 365 running on Windows 10.

You may already know about a lot of Word, Excel, and PowerPoint features by working with it, but no matter if you use Word, Excel, and PowerPoint for your regular documentation tasks, or if you're new to the application, you'll learn a lot about the power that Word, Excel, and PowerPoint gives you to create all kinds of documents.

Who Should Read This Book

If you want to prepare to take one or all the Microsoft Office Specialist exams, which will help you become a certified specialist in Word, Excel, and/or PowerPoint, and hopefully increase your stature, marketability, and income, then this is the book for you. Even if you're not going to take the exam, but you want to learn how to use Word, Excel, and PowerPoint more effectively, this book will show you how to get the most out of using Word, Excel, and PowerPoint based on features that Microsoft believes are important for you to know.

What You'll Learn from this Book

What you learn in this book hews to the topics in the Microsoft Office Specialist exams, because this book is designed to help you learn about the topics in the exam and pass it on the first try.

After you finish reading the book and complete all the exercises, you'll have an in-depth understanding of Word, Excel, and PowerPoint that you can use to become more productive at work and at home (or in your home office).

Hardware and Software Requirements

You should be running a computer with Windows 10 installed, and you should have Word, Excel, and PowerPoint for Microsoft 365 or Word, Excel, and PowerPoint 2019 installed and running too before you dive into this book. Either version of Word, Excel, and PowerPoint contains all of the features that are documented in this book so that you can pass the exam.

How to Use this Book

Start by taking the Assessment Test after this introduction to see how well you know Word, Excel, and PowerPoint already. Even if you've been using Word, Excel, and PowerPoint for a while, you may be surprised at how much you don't know about it.

Next, read each chapter and go through each of the exercises throughout the chapter to reinforce the concepts in each section. When you reach the end of the chapter, answer each of the 10 Review Questions to test what you learned. You can check your answers in the appendix at the back of the book.

If you're indeed taking the exam, then there are two other pedagogical tools that you can use: Flashcards and a Practice Exam. You may remember flashcards from when you were in school, and they're useful when you want to reinforce your knowledge. Use the Flashcards with a friend or relative if you like. (They might appreciate learning about Word, Excel, and PowerPoint, too.) The Practice Exam will help you further hone your ability to answer any question on the real exam with no worries.

How to Contact Wiley or the Author

If you believe you have found an error in this book, and it is not listed on the book's web page, you can report the issue to our customer technical support team at support.wiley .com.

You can email the author with your comments or questions at eric@butow.net. You can also visit Eric's website at www.butow.net.

How this Book Is Organized

Part I: Word Exam MO-100

Chapter 1: Working with Documents   This chapter introduces you to navigating within a document, how to format a document so that it looks the way you want, saving a document, sharing a document, and inspecting a document before you share it, so that all of your recipients can read it.

Chapter 2: Inserting and Formatting Text   This chapter follows up by showing you how to add text into a document, how to format text and paragraphs in your document using Word tools, including Format Painter and styles, as well as how to create and format sections within a document.

Chapter 3: Managing Tables and Lists   This chapter shows you how to use the built-in table tools to create tables of information, convert the table to text (and vice versa), as well as modify the table to look the way that you want. You'll also learn how to create bulleted and numbered lists in your text.

Chapter 4: Building References   This chapter tells you about how to add and format reference elements in a document including footnotes, endnotes, bibliographies, citations in those bibliographies, as well as a table of contents.

Chapter 5: Adding and Formatting Graphic Elements   This chapter covers all of the ins and outs of adding various types of graphic elements in a document. Word comes with plenty of stock shapes, pictures, 3D models, and Microsoft's own SmartArt graphics. What's more, you'll learn how to add text boxes that sit outside of the main text in the document, such as for a sidebar.

Chapter 6: Working with Other Users on Your Documents   This chapter wraps up the book with a discussion about how to use the built-in Comments and Track Changes features when you share a document with others. The Comments feature allows you to add comments outside of the main text for easy reading, and the Track Changes feature shows you which one of your reviewers made changes and when.

Part II: Excel Exam MO-200

Chapter 7: Managing Worksheets and Workbooks   This chapter introduces you to importing data into workbooks, navigating within a workbook, how to format worksheets and workbooks so that they look the way you want, customizing Excel options and views, saving a workbook, sharing a workbook, and inspecting a workbook before you share it, so that all of your recipients can read it.

Chapter 8: Using Data Cells and Ranges   This chapter follows up by showing you how to manipulate your data in a worksheet to show the data that you want to see, how to format cells and ranges in a worksheet using Excel tools, including Format Painter and styles, define and reference cell ranges, as well as how to summarize your data with Sparklines and conditional formatting.

Chapter 9: Working with Tables and Table Data   This chapter shows you how to use the built-in table tools to create tables of information, convert the table to a cell range (and vice versa), as well as modify the table to look the way that you want. You'll also learn how to sort and filter text in a table.

Chapter 10: Performing Operations by Using Formulas and Functions   This chapter tells you how to insert references into a cell formula, perform calculations, count cells, execute conditional operations, as well as format text using a variety of built-in Excel functions.

Chapter 11: Managing Charts   This chapter covers how to create charts within a worksheet and on a separate worksheet, how to modify a chart to show the data you want, how to format a chart with layouts, styles, and add alternative text to a chart so that everyone who sees the chart will know what it's about.

Part III: PowerPoint Exam MO-300

Chapter 12: Creating Presentations   This chapter introduces you to managing presentations including how to modify slide masters, handout masters, and note masters, change presentation options and views, configure print settings for your presentation, configure and present slideshows, and prepare presentations for collaboration with others.

Chapter 13: Managing Slides   This chapter follows up by showing you how to insert slides including from Word and other presentations, insert Summary Zoom slides, modify slides including inserting slide headers and footers, as well as how to order and group slides.

Chapter 14: Inserting and Formatting Text, Shapes, and Images   This chapter shows you how to format and apply styles to text in a slideshow, insert links, insert and format images, insert and format graphic elements including shapes and text boxes, as well as order and group objects on slides.

Chapter 15: Inserting Tables, Charts, SmartArt, 3D Models, and Media   This chapter tells you how to insert and format tables, charts, SmartArt graphics, 3D models, audio and video clips, and screen recordings into a slideshow.

Chapter 16: Applying Transitions and Animations   This chapter covers how to apply and configure transitions between slides, animate content within a slide, and set timing for slide transitions.

Interactive Online Learning Environment and TestBank

Learning the material in the *MCA Microsoft® Office Specialist Complete Study Guide (Office 365 and Office 2019)* is an important part of preparing for the Microsoft Office Specialist exams, but we also provide additional tools to help you prepare. The online TestBank will help you understand the types of questions that will appear on the certification exam.

The Sample Tests in the TestBank include all the questions in each chapter as well as the questions from the Assessment Test. In addition, there is a Practice Exam containing 150 questions. You can use this test to evaluate your understanding and identify areas that may require additional study.

The Flashcards in the TestBank will push the limits of what you should know for the certification exam. The Flashcards contain 300 questions provided in digital format. Each flashcard has one question and one correct answer.

The online Glossary is a searchable list of key terms introduced in this Study Guide that you should know for the Microsoft Office Specialist exams.

To start using the test bank to study for the Microsoft Office Specialist exams, go to www.wiley.com/go/sybextestprep and register your book to receive your unique PIN. Once you have the PIN, return to www.wiley.com/go/sybextestprep, find your book, and click register, or login and follow the link to register a new account or add this book to an existing account.

Exam objectives are subject to change at any time without prior notice and at Microsoft's sole discretion. Please visit the Microsoft Certifications website (https://docs.microsoft.com/en-us/learn/certifications/) for the most current listing of exam objectives.

Objective Map

Assessment Test

1. How big of a table can you create using the Table grid in the Insert menu ribbon?

    A.   12 columns and 10 rows

    B.   10 columns and 8 rows

    C.   10 columns and 10 rows

    D.   12 columns and 12 rows

2. What search option do you use to find all words in a document that start with the same three letters?

    A.   Match Suffix

    B.   Match Prefix

    C.   Use Wildcards

    D.   Sounds Like (English)

3. What menu option do you click to create a new comment in a document?

    A.   Insert

    B.   References

    C.   Review

    D.   Home

4. What are the three reference elements that you can add to a document?

    A.   Citation, source, and bibliography

    B.   Caption, table of figures, cross-reference

    C.   Footnote, endnote, citation

    D.   Table of contents, table of figures, table of authorities

5. You need to have a link on page 30 of your document that goes back to page 1. What menu option do you click on to get there?

    A.   Home

    B.   References

    C.   View

    D.   Insert

6. Where can you find pictures to add into a Word document? (Choose all that apply.)

    A.   On a drive connected to your computer

    B.   On the Internet

    C.   Stock images

    D.   Office.com

7. When you need to indent a paragraph, where can you do this? (Choose all that apply.)

   A. In the Home menu ribbon

   B. In the Insert menu ribbon

   C. In the Layout menu ribbon

   D. Using the Tab key

8. Your customers want an easy way to see what's in your document and go to a location quickly. How do you do that?

   A. Add links.

   B. Add a bibliography.

   C. Add a table of contents.

   D. Add a bookmark.

9. How can you quickly change the format of selected text?

   A. By using the Insert menu ribbon

   B. By using the Layout menu ribbon

   C. By moving the mouse pointer over the selected text and selecting formatting options from the pop-up menu

   D. By selecting the style in the Home ribbon

10. What do you have to do before you cite a source?

    A. Select the writing style guide to use.

    B. Add a bibliography.

    C. Add the source to the document.

    D. Add a table of contents.

11. How does Word allow you to sort in a table?

    A. By number and date

    B. By text, number, and date

    C. By text and number

    D. Text only

12. You need to send your document to several coworkers for their review. How do you make sure that you see all their additions, changes, and deletions?

    A. Click the Show Comments icon in the Review menu ribbon.

    B. Add a comment at the beginning of the document.

    C. Click Read Mode in the View menu ribbon.

    D. Turn on Track Changes.

13. Your boss wants you to convert a Word document and share it as a PDF file. How can you do that?

    A. Print to a PDF printer.

    B. Use the Send Adobe PDF For Review feature.

    C. Use Adobe Acrobat.

    D. Use the Home menu ribbon.

14. How do you go to each comment in your document? (Choose all that apply.)

    A. By using the View menu ribbon

    B. By using the Review menu ribbon

    C. By scrolling through the document to read them

    D. By using the Find And Replace dialog box

15. Your boss wants you to create a nice-looking organization chart for the company. What do you use to create one in Word?

    A. Pictures

    B. Shapes

    C. SmartArt

    D. Screenshot

16. What are the two types of lists that you can add to a document?

    A. Cardinal and ordinal

    B. Roman and alphabetical

    C. Bulleted and numbered

    D. Symbol and picture

17. How do you select all of the text in a document?

    A. Click the first word in the document and then hold and drag until all of the words are selected.

    B. Press Ctrl+A.

    C. Use the Home menu ribbon.

    D. Use the View menu ribbon.

18. What category of paragraph styles does Word look for when you create a table of contents?

    A. Title

    B. Subtitle

    C. Strong

    D. Heading

19. What WordArt styles can you add to text within a text box? (Choose all that apply.)

   A. Text Fill

   B. Text Direction

   C. Text Alignment

   D. Text Outline

20. Why would you change a number value in a numbered list?

   A. Word gets confused as you add more entries.

   B. You have one list separated by other text or images.

   C. You need to add a number value manually for each entry in the list.

   D. You can't change a number value in a numbered list.

21. What wrapping style do you use to get an image to sit on a line of text?

   A. Square

   B. Tight

   C. In line with text

   D. Top and bottom

22. How do you check a document so that you can make sure everyone can read it before you share it with others?

   A. Look through the entire document.

   B. Use Find and Replace.

   C. Use the Document Inspector.

   D. Use the spell checker.

23. How do you change the color for each reviewer in a document?

   A. You can't.

   B. Use the Review menu ribbon.

   C. Add different styles with different text colors.

   D. Show all comments.

24. How do you start a new section on a new page?

   A. Add a page break.

   B. Add a continuous page break.

   C. Add an even or odd page break.

   D. Add a next page break.

25. How do you add descriptive information to an image or graphic?

   A. By selecting the appropriate style in the Home menu ribbon

   B. By adding Alt text

   C. By typing the description above or below the text

   D. By using the Insert menu ribbon

26. What does the header row do in a table? (Choose all that apply.)

  A. It tells you what the columns are about.

  B. It allows you to sort data in a column.

  C. It sets apart the table from the rest of the worksheet.

  D. It allows you to filter data in a column.

27. When you copy a cell, what's the fastest way of copying it?

  A. Clicking Copy in the Home ribbon

  B. Right-clicking the cell and then clicking Copy in the context menu

  C. Pressing Ctrl+C

  D. Adding the Copy icon to the Quick Access Toolbar

28. What are ways in which you can identify data in a chart? (Choose all that apply.)

  A. Axes

  B. Legend

  C. Table

  D. Titles

29. What are the three reference types that you can add in a formula? (Choose all that apply.)

  A. Relative

  B. Absolute

  C. Numeric

  D. Mixed

30. What two types of files can you import into an Excel workbook? (Choose all that apply.)

  A. Word

  B. Text

  C. CSV

  D. PowerPoint

31. How can you select a chart element in your chart? (Choose all that apply.)

  A. Click the chart element.

  B. Click within the chart.

  C. Click the Chart Area box in the Format ribbon.

  D. Click Select Data in the Chart Design ribbon.

32. What option do you use to rotate text but not make the text itself change its orientation?

  A. Rotate Text Up

  B. Align Center

  C. Vertical Text

  D. Rotate Text Down

33. What does the SUM() function do?

   A. Adds all of the numbers in selected cells

   B. Summarizes the numbers in selected cells

   C. Calculates the average of all numbers in selected cells

   D. Counts all of the selected cells that have numbers in them

34. What drop-down list box do you select when you want to find information in an entire workbook?

   A. Search

   B. Look In

   C. Within

   D. Find What

35. What function do you use in a new cell to have Excel return the first few characters in a cell that contains text?

   A. MID()

   B. UPPER()

   C. LEN()

   D. LEFT()

36. What information can you show and hide in a table style? (Choose all that apply.)

   A. Header row

   B. First column

   C. Filter button

   D. Banded rows

37. Why would you assign a name to a range of cells?

   A. You don't have to because cells automatically have row numbers and column letters.

   B. You need to do this before you save the workbook.

   C. You can't find cells in a worksheet without naming them.

   D. You want to find groups of cells in a worksheet more easily.

38. What is the default row height in an Excel worksheet?

   A. 10 points

   B. 15 points

   C. One inch

   D. 72 points

39. How does the COUNTA() function differ from the COUNT() function?

   A. COUNTA() counts all the blank cells in a selected range.

   B. You can count specific numbers in the COUNTA() function.

   C.   COUNTA( )allows you to only count text, not numbers.

   D.   The COUNTA( ) function counts selected cells that are not empty.

40. What does Excel call a chart created in a new worksheet?

   A.   Chart sheet

   B.   Chart1

   C.   Whatever you decide the new worksheet should be

   D.   Excel creates a new workbook and then you must give it a name.

41. When you need to sort table data with text and numbers in it, what is the best way to sort?

   A.   In ascending order

   B.   Using the sort and filter buttons in the header row

   C.   A custom sort

   D.   In descending order

42. What is a Sparkline chart?

   A.   A chart format that lets you add graphic sparkles to your chart

   B.   A small chart that quickly summarizes what you see in a row

   C.   One of the built-in chart styles

   D.   Another term for a win-loss chart

43. When would you use the TEXTJOIN( ) function instead of the CONCAT( ) function?

   A.   When you want to ignore blank cells in the selected range

   B.   You don't have to because TEXTJOIN( ) replaces CONCAT( ) in the latest version of Excel.

   C.   To add a space between text in each cell

   D.   When you don't want to type in the cell references within the formula

44. What does an error bar in a chart show? (Choose all that apply.)

   A.   How inaccurate the data is in the chart

   B.   Margins of error

   C.   Standard deviation

   D.   How much you can change the numeric value in a cell formula

45. When you format a table style, what formats can you change? (Choose all that apply.)

   A.   Font

   B.   Alignment

   C.   Border

   D.   Fill color and pattern

46. Your boss likes your chart but wants the background of the chart to be dark so that the text will stand out. How do you do this quickly?

    A. Apply a chart layout.

    B. Change the background color of the chart.

    C. Apply a different chart style.

    D. Tell your boss that there are no chart backgrounds other than white.

47. What are the minimum and maximum magnification views in a worksheet?

    A. 20 percent and 125 percent

    B. 10 percent and 150 percent

    C. 25 percent and 200 percent

    D. 5 percent and 300 percent

48. If you delete a row or column and immediately decide that you didn't want to do that, what do you do?

    A. Nothing

    B. Open the Home menu ribbon.

    C. Add the new row or column again.

    D. Press Ctrl+Z.

49. In the Paste Special dialog box, what button do you click to paste a number from one cell into a blank cell?

    A. Formats

    B. Values

    C. None

    D. Validation

50. What file formats can you save an Excel file to? (Choose all that apply.)

    A. XML

    B. Word

    C. PDF

    D. Excel

51. In what menu ribbon do you add a bulleted or numbered list?

    A. Design

    B. Home

    C. Insert

    D. Slide Show

52. When you want to add a slide from another presentation, what option do you select in the New Slide drop-down list?

    A. Duplicate Selected Slides

    B. The custom theme slide

    C. Reuse Slides

    D. Slides from Outline

53. What are the two ways to configure animation paths in a slideshow? (Select all answers that apply.)

    A. Motion paths

    B. The Animation Pane

    C. The Transitions ribbon

    D. Morph

54. What are the four table row and column insertion types?

    A. Row, Column, Header Row, First Column

    B. Top, Bottom, Left, Right

    C. Above, Below, Left, Right

    D. Left End, Right End, Top, Bottom

55. What do you have to do to add information into a slide?

    A. Add a theme

    B. Add a new slide master

    C. Modify the slide master content

    D. Click in a placeholder area

56. Why do you add a link to a slide? (Select all answers that apply.)

    A. To link to an email address

    B. To connect with a website

    C. To create a new slide

    D. To link to another slide

57. What options do you have when selecting a footer? (Select all answers that apply.)

    A. Date and Time

    B. Company

    C. Don't Show on Title Slide

    D. Copyright information

58. When you want to add a SmartArt graphic, which menu option do you click?

    A. Design

    B. Slide Show

C. Insert

D. Home

59. What view do you use when you want to see thumbnail-sized images of slides?

A. Notes Page

B. Reading view

C. Slide Sorter

D. Outline view

60. What are some of the audio and video formats that you can add into a PowerPoint slideshow? (Select all answers that apply.)

A. MPEG

B. OGG

C. WAV

D. FLV

61. From what sources can you insert an image? (Select all answers that apply.)

A. Office.com

B. Web images

C. Stock images

D. JPEG format images

62. What slide content can you animate? (Select all options that apply.)

A. Text

B. 3D Models

C. Pictures

D. SmartArt graphics

63. What menu option do you click to print a slideshow?

A. Home

B. View

C. File

D. Design

64. What can you move when you modify the order of slides? (Choose all that apply.)

A. Master slides

B. One or multiple slides

C. Sections

D. Layouts

65. What is the term for the effect that occurs when you move from one slide to another in your slideshow?

A. Animation

B. Morph

C. Transition

D. Effect

66. What are the three ways to change the text appearance in a shape or text box? (Select all answers that apply.)

A. Convert to SmartArt

B. Text Direction

C. Text Effects

D. Align Text

67. When you change your mind immediately after setting a new slide background, what do you do? (Select all answers that apply.)

A. Change the slide background back to what it was.

B. Press Ctrl+Z.

C. Close the slideshow without saving it and then reopen it.

D. Click the Undo icon.

68. What are some of the elements that you can modify within a chart? (Select all answers that apply.)

A. Numbers

B. Legend

C. Gridlines

D. Lines

69. Your boss wants you to create a slideshow that runs automatically for the big tradeshow coming up. What do you do to set the transition time between each slide?

A. Set the duration in the Animations ribbon.

B. Use the tools in the View ribbon.

C. Select the After check box in the Transitions ribbon.

D. Change the theme in the Design ribbon.

70. How do you get a good idea where PowerPoint places objects in a slide? (Select all answers that apply.)

A. An object snapping to a point within the slide

B. Gridlines

C. The mouse pointer

D. Guides

71. After you add a transition, how do you add an effect to it?

    A. Change the theme in the Design ribbon.

    B. Change the view to Slide Sorter in the View ribbon.

    C. Click Effect Options in the Transitions ribbon.

    D. Add a new slide in the Insert ribbon.

72. What are the types of custom slideshows that you can create? (Select all answers that apply.)

    A. Simple

    B. Multi-Slide

    C. Hyperlinked

    D. Timing

73. Where can you find 3D models to insert into a slide? (Select all answers that apply.)

    A. The Insert ribbon

    B. Stock models

    C. On your computer

    D. The Illustrations section in the Insert ribbon

74. Where do you modify the slide order in the PowerPoint window?

    A. The Design ribbon

    B. Right pane

    C. The View ribbon

    D. Left pane

75. What are the two ways that you can keep others from editing a slideshow? (Select all answers that apply.)

    A. Mark the slideshow as final.

    B. Email the users to tell them not to edit the slideshow.

    C. Add a slide that tells the users not to edit the slideshow.

    D. Use a password.

Answers to Assessment Test

1. B. The Table grid has enough cells for 10 columns and 8 rows. See Chapter 3 for more information.

2. C. When you open the Find and Replace box, click More, click Use Wildcards, and then add the asterisk (*) to the end of the search term. See Chapter 2 for more information.

3. C. Add a new comment by clicking the New Comment icon in the Review menu ribbon. See Chapter 6 for more information.

4. C. You can add a footnote on a page, an endnote at the end of the document, and citations on a page. See Chapter 4 for more information.

5. D. Click the Insert menu option, and then click the Link icon in the ribbon. See Chapter 1 for more information.

6. A, C, D. Word makes it easy to add pictures from your computer, stock images installed with Word, and images from Office.com. See Chapter 5 for more information.

7. A, C. You can add a one-half indent in the Home menu ribbon and add more precise indent spacing in the Layout menu ribbon. See Chapter 2 for more information.

8. C. You can create a table of contents (TOC) easily so that readers can get a summary of what's in your document and click the entry they want in the table to go to the section on the appropriate page. See Chapter 4 for more information.

9. C. A pop-up menu appears after you move the mouse pointer on the selected text so that you can change the format including the font style, font size, styles, and more. See Chapter 1 for more information.

10. C. You need to add the source to a document so that Word can find it and cite it. See Chapter 4 for more information.

11. B. You can sort by text, number, and date in a table column. See Chapter 3 for more information.

12. D. Track Changes adds information to your document so that you can see the changes that reviewers have made. See Chapter 6 for more information.

13. B. Word allows you to convert a Word document after you click File ➤ Share ➤ Send Adobe PDF For Review. See Chapter 1 for more information.

14. B, C. You can scroll through the document, or you can click the Previous and Next icons in the Review menu ribbon. See Chapter 6 for more information.

15. C. SmartArt is a set of custom diagrams, including organizational charts, which you can add and edit quickly. See Chapter 5 for more information.

16. C. You can add bulleted and numbered lists in a variety of styles. See Chapter 3 for more information.

17. B. You select all text in a document quickly by pressing Ctrl+A. See Chapter 2 for more information.

18. D. Word adds text with Heading styles as entries in a table of contents. See Chapter 4 for more information.

19. A, D. Text Fill and Text Outline are two WordArt styles that you can apply. See Chapter 5 for more information.

20. B. You may need to have the numbered list continue from the entry in the previous list, or you may need the second numbered list reset to 1. You can do both in Word. See Chapter 3 for more information.

21. C. When you wrap an object in line with text, the object is added to the document at the cursor point. See Chapter 5 for more information.

22. C. The Document Inspector checks your document to ensure that people of all abilities and Word versions can open and read your document. See Chapter 1 for more information.

23. A. Word assigns colors to each reviewer automatically. See Chapter 6 for more information.

24. D. A next page break ends the current section and creates a new section on the next page. See Chapter 2 for more information.

25. B. Alt text attaches descriptive information that appears when the user moves the mouse over the object. See Chapter 5 for more information.

26. B, D. Each cell in the header row contains a button that allows you to sort and filter data in the column. See Chapter 9 for more information.

27. C. Press Ctrl+C to copy all the information in one cell into an empty cell. See Chapter 8 for more information.

28. B, C. You can add a legend, a data table, as well as data labels to a chart to help you and others understand what the chart represents. See Chapter 11 for more information.

29. A, B, D. Excel can create relative, absolute, and mixed reference types in a cell formula. See Chapter 10 for more information.

30. B, C. You can import files with the TXT and CSV formats into an Excel workbook. See Chapter 7 for more information.

31. A, C. You can click on various elements within the chart. When you click the down arrow next to the Chart Area box in the Format ribbon, you see a drop-down list with all of the chart elements so that you can select an element easily. See Chapter 11 for more information.

32. C. When you click Vertical Text in the Orientation drop-down menu in the Home ribbon, Excel makes the text vertical, but it does not change the orientation so that each letter in the text appears in a separate line. See Chapter 8 for more information.

33. B. The SUM() function summarizes all selected cells that have numbers in them. See Chapter 10 for more information.

34. C. When you click the Within box, which shows the default Sheet option, a drop-down list appears so that you can select the Workbook option. See Chapter 7 for more information.

35. D. The LEFT() function tells Excel to read the first few characters of text and show that text in a new cell. See Chapter 10 for more information.

36. A, C. You can hide and show the header row in a table as well as filter buttons within a header row. See Chapter 9 for more information.

37. D. Naming a range of cells helps you find groups of cells in the same worksheet or a different worksheet in a workbook. See Chapter 8 for more information.

38. B. The default row height is 15 points. See Chapter 7 for more information.

39. D. The COUNTA() function counts cells in the selected range that are not empty, and the COUNT() function tells you how many cells have numbers. See Chapter 10 for more information.

40. A. You can move a chart to a separate worksheet, which Excel calls a chart sheet. See Chapter 11 for more information.

41. C. You need to create a custom sort so that you can decide if you want to sort first by text or by number. See Chapter 9 for more information.

42. B. A Sparkline chart summarizes all of the numerical data in other columns within a row. See Chapter 8 for more information.

43. C. The TEXTJOIN() function adds a delimiter of your choosing, including a space, between text in two or more cells that you combine with TEXTJOIN(). See Chapter 10 for more information.

44. B, C. An error bar can show both a margin of error and standard deviation. See Chapter 11 for more information.

45. A, C, D. You can change the font, border, and the fill color and/or pattern in the style. See Chapter 9 for more information.

46. C. Two of the built-in chart styles have dark backgrounds. See Chapter 11 for more information.

47. C. Excel has five magnification levels from 25 percent to 200 percent. See Chapter 7 for more information.

48. D. Press Ctrl+Z to bring back the deleted row or column and all of its data. See Chapter 9 for more information.

49. B. When you click the Values button in the Paste Special dialog box, you paste the value but not the formula from the copied cell into the blank cell. See Chapter 8 for more information.

50. A, C, D. You can save to XML, PDF, and Excel (with the extension .xlsx) versions. You can also save to older versions of Excel. See Chapter 7 for more information.

51. B. You add a bulleted or numbered list using the tools in the Home ribbon. See Chapter 14 for more information.

52. C. Select Reuse Slides from the bottom of the drop-down list to select a slide from another slideshow to insert into your slideshow. See Chapter 13 for more information.

53. A, D. You can add motion paths to animate an object within a slide and use the Morph feature to animate objects between slides. See Chapter 16 for more information.

54. C. You can add a row above or below a selected table cell, as well as a column to the left or right of the selected cell. See Chapter 15 for more information.

55. D. When you want to add information into a specific slide, you click in the appropriate placeholder area, such as the area for the slide title, and then add your text and/or object(s). See Chapter 12 for more information.

56. A, B, D. PowerPoint allows you to add various types of links, including to an email address, website, and another slide within your slideshow. See Chapter 14 for more information.

57. A, C. You can add a date and time and slide number, and you can also choose not to show the footer on the title slide in a slideshow. See Chapter 13 for more information.

58. C. Click the Insert icon to add a SmartArt graphic in the Illustrations section in the Insert ribbon. See Chapter 15 for more information.

59. C. The Slide Sorter view shows thumbnail-sized images of all slides in your slideshow for your review. See Chapter 12 for more information.

60. A, C. You can add audio and video MPEG files, WAV audio files, and many other audio and video file formats. See Chapter 15 for more information.

61. A, C. You can insert images from Office.com, PowerPoint stock images, and images stored on your computer. See Chapter 14 for more information.

62. A, B, D. You can animate text, 3D models, and SmartArt graphics in a slide. See Chapter 16 for more information.

63. C. Print a document by clicking the File menu option and then clicking Print in the menu on the left side of the File screen. See Chapter 12 for more information.

64. B, C. You can move one or multiple slides as well as all slides in a section. See Chapter 13 for more information.

65. C. A transition is the effect that happens when the slideshow moves from one slide to another. See Chapter 16 for more information.

66. A, B, D. You can convert text to a SmartArt graphic, change the text direction, and change the text alignment. See Chapter 14 for more information.

67. B, D. You can press Ctrl+Z or click the Undo icon in the Quick Access Toolbar. See Chapter 13 for more information.

68. B, C. You can change the legend, view gridlines, and modify many other elements in a chart. See Chapter 15 for more information.

69. C. After you select the After check box in the Transitions ribbon, you can set the time for each slide transition. See Chapter 16 for more information.

70. B, D. You can get visual cues of where PowerPoint places objects in a slide with gridlines, guides, and rulers. See Chapter 14 for more information.

71. C. After you add a transition, click Effect Options in the Transitions ribbon to view all effects that you can set for that transition. See Chapter 16 for more information.

72. A, C. You can create a simple custom slideshow that you create for a specific audience, as well as a hyperlinked slideshow that contains links to custom slides for different audiences. See Chapter 12 for more information.

73. B, C. When you add 3D models in the Illustrations section in the Insert ribbon, you can add stock models installed with PowerPoint or 3D models stored on your computer. See Chapter 15 for more information.

74. D. You modify the order from within the list of thumbnail-sized slides in the left pane. See Chapter 13 for more information.

75. A, D. PowerPoint allows you to mark a slideshow as final and add a password to your slide-show file. The latter is more effective at keeping reviewers from editing your presentation. See Chapter 12 for more information.

Word
Exam MO-100

Chapter

1

Working with Documents

MICROSOFT EXAM OBJECTIVES COVERED IN THIS CHAPTER:

✓ **Manage documents**

- Navigate within documents
  - Search for text
  - Link to locations within documents
  - Move to specific locations and objects in documents
  - Show and hide formatting symbols and hidden text
- Format documents
  - Set up document pages
  - Apply style sets
  - Insert and modify headers and footers
  - Configure page background elements
- Save and share documents
  - Save documents in alternative file formats
  - Modify basic document properties
  - Modify print settings
  - Share documents electronically
- Inspect documents for issues
  - Locate and remove hidden properties and personal information
  - Find and correct accessibility issues
  - Locate and correct compatibility issues

You're reading this book because you want to study for and pass the MO-100 Microsoft Word (Word and Word 2019) exam and become a certified Microsoft Office Specialist: Word Associate. I hope you have your favorite beverage nearby, you're comfortable, and you have Word fired up so that you can go through the exercises in this chapter.

Before embarking on a road trip, we often refer to the directions provided by our favorite map app before we leave. In this chapter, I'll show you how to work with documents, including navigating within documents so that you can edit them easily. Next, I'll show you how to format documents to make them look the way you want.

When you know how to control your documents, I'll show you how to save them in the format you want and share them with other people. Finally, I'll show you how to *inspect* your documents so that you can find and remove hidden properties as well as fix any issues with accessibility and compatibility.

I'll have an exercise at the end of every section within this chapter so that you can practice doing different tasks. Then, at the end of this chapter, you'll find a set of review questions that mimic the test questions you'll see on the MO-100 exam.

Navigating Within Documents

It's easy just to fire up Word and start writing. But, of course, you're doing more than just writing. You inevitably need to start moving around the document and making changes to it, and in this section I talk about the tools Word gives you to do those tasks.

Microsoft has added a lot of powerful *search* features to Word so that you can find the text you're looking for pretty easily. You can access these tools through menu options and their associated ribbons, as well as by using keyboard shortcuts.

If you want to move quickly from one location in a long document to another so that you don't have to keep scrolling up and down a lot of pages, Word makes it easy to add a *link* within your document. You can also use tools in the ribbon, as well as keyboard shortcuts, to go to different spots in your document.

Word also has a lot of hidden formatting symbols that you can show. What's more, you can hide text that you don't want to see cluttering your document, but Word also makes it easy to reveal *hidden text* whenever you want to see it.

Searching for Text

Unless you have only a small amount of text in your document, you'll find that you need help locating the words that you want. Word has you covered with tools not only to find words in your document, but to replace them easily as well.

Using the Search Bar

The Search bar appears within the Word window's title bar to make it more conspicuous. Type one or more search terms in the Search box, and then click the terms within the Find In Document area in the drop-down list. The Navigation pane opens on the left side of the Word window and displays a list of results (see Figure 1.1).

FIGURE 1.1   Navigation pane

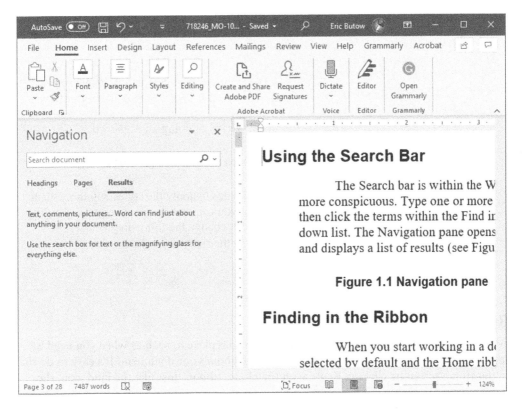

Finding in the Ribbon

When you start working in a document, the Home menu option is selected by default and the Home ribbon appears underneath. Within the Home ribbon, icons appear separated into several sections. On the right side of the ribbon, the Editing section contains the Find icon.

After you click the icon, the Navigation pane appears. Within the pane, type your search term(s) in the Search box and then Word shows you a list of results, as shown in Figure 1.2. Word also takes you to the first instance of the search term(s) in the document itself.

Microsoft places the titles of each section within a ribbon at the bottom center of the section instead of the top.

FIGURE 1.2   List of search results

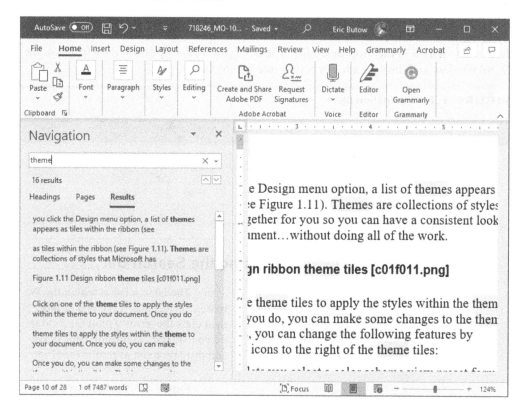

Replacing in the Ribbon

Sometimes, you may want to find a word in order to replace it, such as when you need to replace a product name with an updated one throughout your document. It's easy to do this in the Home screen by clicking Replace on the Home ribbon. Just like the Find icon, the Replace icon appears in the Editing section.

After you click the Replace icon, the Find And Replace dialog box appears with the Replace tab open (see Figure 1.3). This dialog box is probably familiar to you if you've used previous versions of Word because it's been a standard feature (literally) for decades.

Type the existing text you want to find in the Find box. In the Replace box, type the replacement text. Now you can click one of three buttons:

- Click Next to have Word find and highlight the next instance of text in the document.

- Click Replace to have Word replace the next instance of existing text with the replacement text but not replace any other instance. To do that, you need to click the Replace button every time.

- Click Replace All to replace all instances of the existing text in the document with the Replacement text.

FIGURE 1.3   Find And Replace dialog box

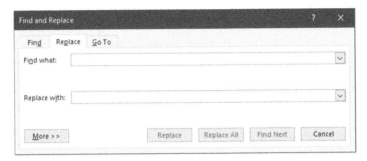

When you click Replace All, Word searches the document after the point where your cursor is located within the document. Once Word reaches the end of the document, a dialog box appears that asks if you want to continue searching from the beginning of the document. If you click Yes, Word continues searching and replaces any other existing text it finds. When Word finishes finding and replacing, a dialog box opens and tells you how many changes it made within the document.

Opening the Navigation Pane

I said earlier in this chapter that you can open the Navigation pane by clicking Find in the Home ribbon. The Navigation pane stays active until you close it by clicking the Close icon in the upper-right corner of the pane.

However, you don't need to click the Find icon in the Home ribbon every time you need to open the Navigation pane. Click the View menu option, and then click the Navigation Pane check box in the View ribbon. It's in the Show section, as you see in Figure 1.4. You can close the pane again whenever you want.

You may need to click the Show icon in the ribbon and then click the Navigation Pane check box from the drop-down menu if your window is too small for the ribbon to show the check box.

Replacing with the Keyboard

Word has had support for keyboard shortcuts since the first version of Word for Windows was released in 1989. (Windows 2.0 had much better keyboard support than its predecessor, fortunately.)

It's easy to open the Navigation pane using the keyboard—just press Ctrl+F. If you want to open the Find And Replace dialog box, use the same key combination that Word has used for decades: Ctrl+H.

FIGURE 1.4   The Navigation Pane check box

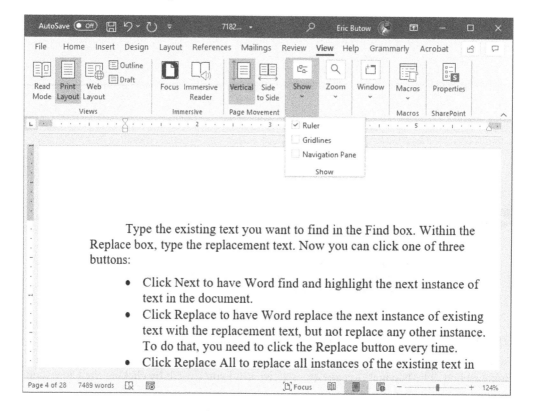

Linking to Locations Within Documents

You can put in a link in one place in your document that links to another place, such as a link on page 27 that will take you to the beginning of the document. Here's how to do it:

1. Click the word in the document that you want to use in the link.
2. Click the Insert menu option.
3. Within the Insert ribbon, click the Link icon.
4. Click Insert Link in the drop-down menu.
5. In the Insert Hyperlink dialog box shown in Figure 1.5, click the Place In This Document option under Link To.
6. Click what you want to link to. From the Select A Place In This Document list box, click Top Of The Document, for example.
7. Click OK.

   Now the link appears in your text.

FIGURE 1.5 Hyperlink dialog box

Moving to Specific Locations and Objects in Documents

Word makes it easier (I didn't say easy) to move to a specific location or an object. Start by clicking the Home menu option if it isn't already open.

Within the ribbon, click the down arrow to the right of Find (it's in the Editing section). Click Go To in the drop-down menu.

Now you see the trusty Find And Replace dialog box, but the Go To tab is selected, as shown in Figure 1.6. Scroll up and down in the Go To What list, and then click on what you want to go to. It can be a location, such as a page in your document, or an object, such as a graphic.

What you see next depends on what you select. The default place to go is on a page in your document, so type the page number and then click Next to go to that page. You click an object in the list and then select an object by clicking in the Any Object list to view the list of options. When you click one, click Next to move the cursor to it.

FIGURE 1.6 Go To tab

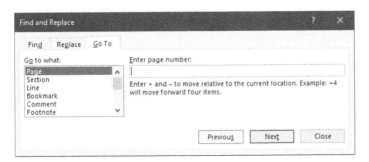

Showing and Hiding Formatting Symbols and Hidden Text

Word adds a bunch of formatting symbols like paragraph marks in your document, but Microsoft is nice enough not to clutter your document with them by default. You can also hide text such as comments within the document that most people who read it in Word don't need to see.

Formatting Symbols

It's easy to view formatting symbols from within the Home ribbon. In the Paragraph section, click the Show/Hide ¶ icon that looks, of course, like a paragraph mark (see Figure 1.7).

FIGURE 1.7 Show/Hide ¶ icon

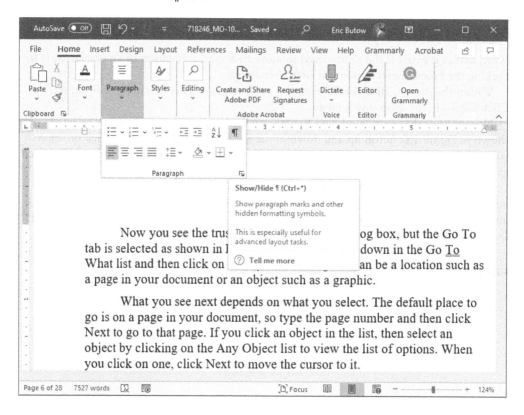

Now you see all the paragraph marks and other symbols, like a square dot that denotes a space. When you're done, click the icon again to turn off the formatting symbols.

If you want to turn formatting symbols on and off more quickly, press Ctrl+Shift+8 on your keyboard.

Hidden Text

You can hide text that you select within the document, and you can even hide text in the entire document.

Selected Text

Here's how to hide selected text (and show it again):

1. Select the text that you want to hide.

2. Right-click in the selection, and then click Font in the pop-up menu or press Ctrl+Shift+F on your keyboard.

3. In the Font dialog box, as shown in Figure 1.8, click the Hidden check box under Effects.

4. Click OK.

FIGURE 1.8   Font dialog box

Now the text is hidden and doesn't show up at all, which leaves you with the potential pitfall of accidentally deleting hidden text. So how do you show the text again?

You'll need to show hidden text for the entire document, as I'll describe in the next section. However, if you know where the hidden text is located, then select the text before and after the hidden text. Now you can repeat steps 2–4 and you'll see your text restored.

For the Entire Document

You can tell Word to hide text for the entire document and yet still view the hidden text (with some formatting). This is especially useful if you've lost track of your hidden text. Here's what to do:

1. Click the File menu option.

2. Click Options at the lower left of the File window.

3. In the Word Options dialog box, as shown in Figure 1.9, click Display in the menu at the left side.

4. Click the Hidden Text check box under "Always show these formatting marks on the screen" to show all text with hidden text formatting.

5. Click OK.

FIGURE 1.9 Word Options dialog box

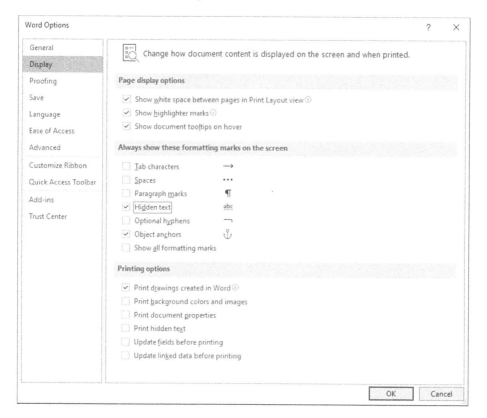

Now all of the hidden text in your document has a dotted black line underneath the hidden characters. If you share the Word document itself, the other person will be able to see the hidden characters. When you save the document to another format (like PDF) or print it, the hidden text doesn't appear.

Navigating and Modifying Text in a Document

1. Open an existing Word document, preferably one that has multiple pages.

2. Open the Navigation pane.

3. Search for a word and click one of the results in the list to have Word highlight the result on the page.

4. Replace the word you found by opening the Find And Replace dialog box.

5. Since the word you want to replace is already in the Find box, type the new word in the Replace box.

6. Replace all of the words in the document.

7. Continue by scrolling to the end of the document. An easier way to get to the end is to press Ctrl+End on your keyboard.

8. Add a new link to the bottom of the page that links to the top of the document.

9. Select a sentence within a paragraph and hide it.

10. Unhide the sentence.

Formatting Documents

Word uses a basic template, which Word calls the Normal template, for a new document, which Word calls a blank document. When you create a new document, you can also select from various built-in templates, such as a brochure.

However, if you want to format a document to fit your specific needs, you should start with a blank document and then set up your document pages. In this section, I'll tell you how to set up document pages as well as how to create and apply *styles* to text. Styles are a great way to apply *formatting* quickly to more than one block of text.

You may also want to create headers and footers that run at the top and bottom, respectively, of every page. For example, you can add a page number as a footer if you have a long document. I'll talk about those as well as how to create a *background* on each page, such as adding the word "DRAFT" to a document that you want to make sure your readers understand isn't final yet.

At the end of this section, I'll have an exercise for you so that you can learn for yourself how to use Word's tools to format your documents.

Setting Up Document Pages

When you open a blank document for the first time, document pages have a default size, margins, orientation, columns, and more. If you need to change any of your page settings, start by clicking the Layout menu option.

Now that you see the Layout ribbon, the Page Setup section shown in Figure 1.10 sports seven options that you can click to alter your document layout:

- Margins

- Orientation

- Size

- Columns

- Breaks (including page breaks)

- Line Numbers (which lets you add line numbers to your document)

- Hyphenation

FIGURE 1.10   Page Setup section

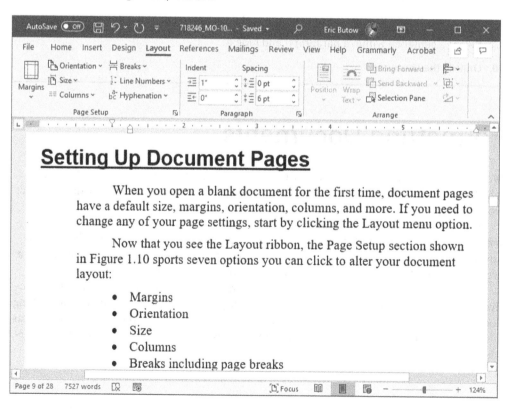

The Paragraph section is to the right of the Page Setup section. Here you can view and change the paragraph indent to the left and right, as well as the spacing before and after each paragraph.

The Arrange section is the last section in the ribbon. Here you can arrange a selected object on the page so that it appears where you want it.

 I'll talk more about page breaks and other formatting tools in Chapter 2, "Inserting and Formatting Text."

Applying Style Settings

Styles are a great way to save formatting information so that you can apply the style to selected text in your document.

When you select text, a pop-up menu appears above the selected text. In this menu, you can apply a style by clicking Styles in the list and then clicking a style tile. Each tile shows you what the text looks like with the style applied.

There are two other ways to find and apply styles: through the Design menu and in the Styles pane.

Design Menu

When you click the Design menu option, a list of themes appears as tiles within the ribbon (see Figure 1.11). Themes are collections of styles that Microsoft has put together for you so that you can have a consistent look and feel within your document. . .without doing all of the work.

Click one of the theme tiles to apply the styles within the theme to your document. Once you do, you can make some changes to the theme within the ribbon. That is, you can change the following features by clicking the icons to the right of the theme tiles:

Colors: This lets you select a color scheme and view preset formats within tiles in different colors.

Fonts: This allows you to select a font style and view preset formats within tiles in different fonts.

Paragraph Spacing: Use this to change paragraph spacing between elements.

Effects: This allows you to change effects for illustrations in your document.

Set As Default: Use this to set your theme or format as the default for all new documents.

FIGURE 1.11 Design ribbon theme tiles

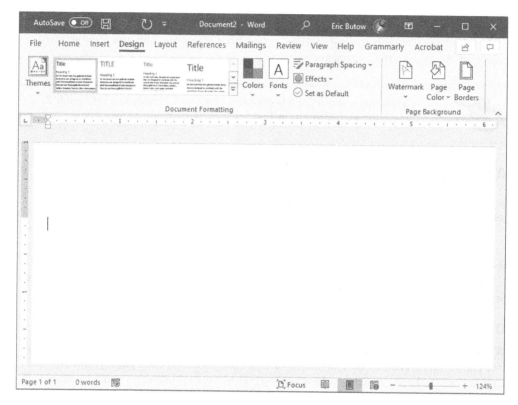

Styles Pane

The catch with using themes is that you have to like the major elements of the theme if you want to use it. A blank document comes with several styles already set up for you, such as heading text.

When you click the Home menu option, open the Styles pane in the ribbon by clicking the down arrow at the bottom right of the Styles area. The Styles list appears, as shown in Figure 1.12, so that you can scroll up and down the list (if needed).

There are two types of styles: paragraph and character. In the list, you see the paragraph mark to the right of the style name. A character style has the lowercase "a" symbol to the right of the name.

Apply the style by clicking the style name in the list. When you click a paragraph style, the style applies to the entire paragraph that you're writing. But when you click a character style, that style only applies either to selected text or to all text you type after you apply the style.

FIGURE 1.12   Styles pane

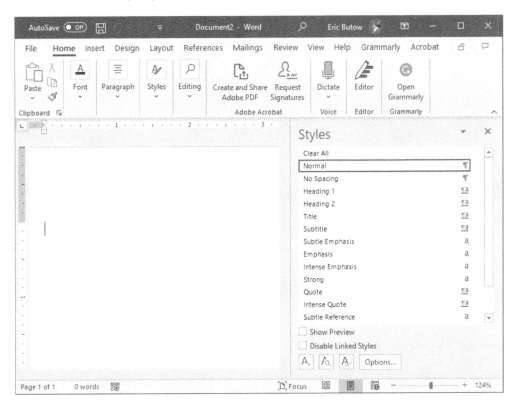

 You can also open the Styles pane using the keyboard by pressing
Ctrl+Alt+Shift+S. (You may need to use two hands.)

Inserting and Modifying Headers and Footers

Headers and *footers* can provide consistent information about a document on every page so
that you don't need to add it every time. One common way to use a header is as a chapter
or section name, and a common footer is (you guessed it) a page number.

You can insert a header or footer by clicking the Insert menu option. The Header &
Footer section contains icons for adding a header and footer. When you click the Header or
Footer icon, you see the same built-in options in the drop-down menu.

The Header and Footer menus are the same, and so are the design options, though the
options look a little different as headers and footers. Figure 1.13 shows the Header &
Footer menu.

FIGURE 1.13   Header & Footer menu

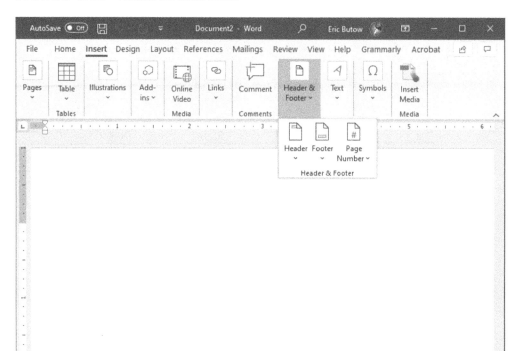

You can also get more header and footer styles from the Office.com website by moving the mouse pointer over either More Headers From Office.com or More Footers From Office.com in the menu and then selecting one of the styles from the submenu if one strikes your fancy.

After you click a design option, the header or footer appears at the top or bottom of the page, respectively. How much editing you can do depends on the option you selected. For example, if you selected the Blank option at the top of the menu, Word puts a placeholder header or footer so that you can edit it to your liking.

Configuring Page Background Elements

A *watermark* is lighter background text that reinforces the document's status to your readers. If you need to add a watermark, such as "DO NOT COPY" or "DRAFT," or you want the page to be a specific color and/or you want a border on the page, Word has you covered.

Start by clicking the Design menu option. At the right side of the Design ribbon, the Page Background section, as shown in Figure 1.14, contains three icons that change the look and feel of your background—and give you plenty of customization options.

Watermark Click Watermark to add a preselected watermark. You can add your own by clicking Custom Watermark and then adding a picture or text watermark from the Printed Watermark dialog box.

Page Color Click Page Color to select a color swatch from the Theme Colors drop-down box. You can also select from more colors or set your own by clicking More Colors. What's more, you can add fill effects like a gradient or texture by clicking Fill Effects.

Page Borders Click Page Borders to set the borders on all pages in the Borders And Shading dialog box. You can select the styles of the borders and where one or more borders appear on the page.

FIGURE 1.14 Page Background section

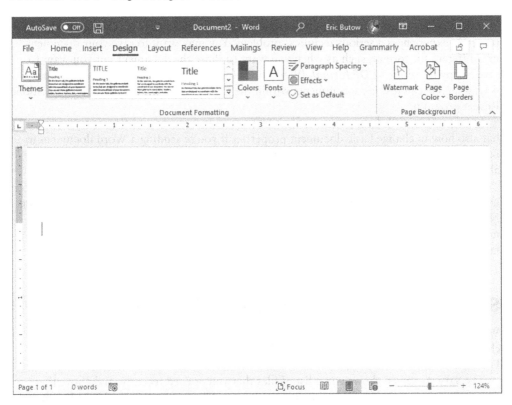

EXERCISE 1.2

Setting Up Your Document

1. Open a new document.

2. Change the margins of a page to the prebuilt Narrow setting.

3. Apply one of the existing themes to your document.

4. Add a header and footer to your document, and add your preferred built-in header and footer style.

5. Add a dark blue background page color from the Page Color drop-down list. After you add it, press Ctrl+Z to return to the default white background.

Saving and Sharing Documents

You should save your document regularly as you work on it in case your computer loses power or experiences a serious technical problem. You may want to save your document in a different file format, such as when you want to share the document but you want to save a copy in Adobe's *PDF format*. (PDF stands for Portable Document Format.) That way, someone can just leave comments within the PDF document using Adobe's free Adobe Reader program.

In this section, I'll show you not only how to save documents in different formats, but also how to change basic document properties if you're sending a Word document to other people and they need to see basic information like who wrote it and any comments about the file.

In case you plan to *print* your document to review and/or share with others, I'll tell you how to modify your print settings, such as how to tell Word what pages you want to print. Next, I'll show you Word's *sharing* tools so that you can send your document to one or more people as an email attachment, in PDF format, as a web page, in a blog, or even as a fax document.

Finally, I'll provide an exercise so that you can practice using these tools yourself.

Saving Documents in Alternative File Formatting

Word can save in any one of 16 file formats, including its native DOCX format. Start by clicking the File menu option and then click Save As in the menu on the left side of the File screen.

The Save As screen shows you a list of files that you opened recently, and above that list you can change the file folder, name, and format. When you click the Word Document (*.docx) box, as shown in Figure 1.15, the list of types appears in the drop-down menu. Once you select one, click Save to the right of the box.

FIGURE 1.15 Save As screen

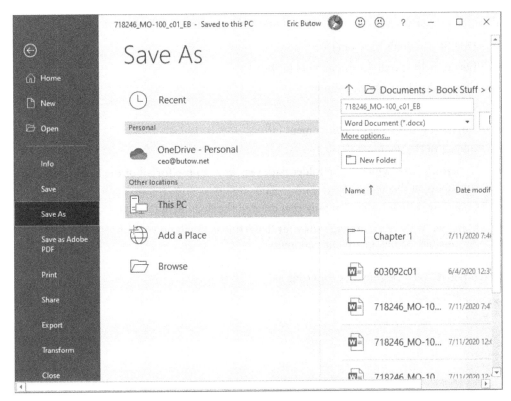

 NOTE After you save a file, what you see next depends on the format that you selected. For example, if you save to a plain text (.txt) file, you'll see the File Conversion dialog box so that you can tweak the conversion settings. If you save to a Word 97–2003 document, then Word immediately converts the file and shows that older version file in the document window with the words "Compatibility Mode" in the title bar. If you want to continue editing the original file that you created in Word in Office 365 or Word 2019, you need to close the currently open document (your older-version file) and open the original file.

Changing Basic Document Properties

There are standard *properties* and there are those that you can change to help you search for a document in Word and tell people more about the document if they need it.

Start by clicking the File menu option. Now click Info in the menu on the left side of the File screen.

The Info screen contains the Properties area that lists everything you need to know about the document. At the bottom of the list, click Show All Properties. Now you can see all of the properties (see Figure 1.16) and make changes in the following fields:

- Title (if you don't have one)

- Tags to help search for documents in Word

- Comments about the document

- Status of the document

- Categories into which the document falls

- Subject of the document

- *Hyperlink base*, which is the folder path you want to use for all of the hyperlinks that you create in this document

- Company, which is the company that created the document (if any)

- Manager, if there's a manager of your department to whom you report and who is responsible for the document's contents

FIGURE 1.16   Document properties list

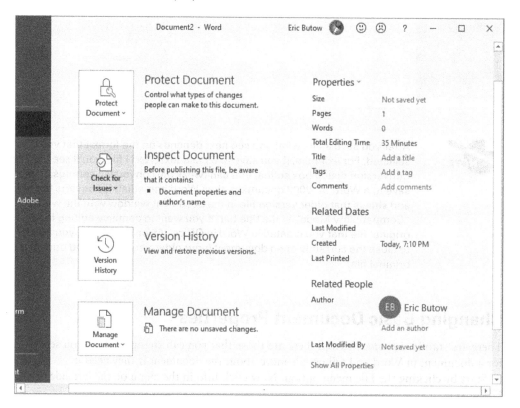

If you don't want to see as many properties the next time you open the Info screen, click Show Fewer Properties at the bottom of the list.

Modifying Print Settings

Word easily detects the default printer that you're using in Windows and lets you change the printer settings so that your document appears on paper the way you want.

Start by clicking the File menu option, and then click Print in the menu on the left side of the File screen. Now you see the Print screen, and the print preview area appears on the right side so that you have a good idea of what the document will look like on the printed page.

Between the menu area on the left and the print preview area, the settings menu you see depends on the printer you have.

In my case, as shown in Figure 1.17, I can change the printer to another one that I have installed in Windows. I can also change different settings for the selected printer, including how many pages to print, the page orientation, and if I should print on one or both sides of the paper.

FIGURE 1.17   Print screen

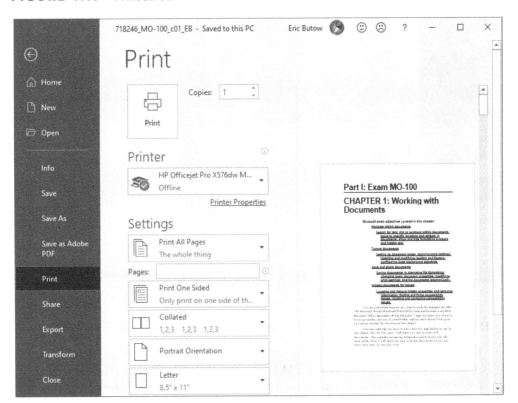

Sharing Documents Electronically

If you're sharing a document with other people and they expect to receive it in electronic form, such as an email attachment, Word gives you five different ways to send a file online directly within Word.

Start by clicking the File menu option. Now click Share in the menu on the left side of the File screen.

Within the Share screen, as shown in Figure 1.18, the Share With People option is selected in the Share menu. This option allows you to share your document to a OneDrive location by clicking the Save To Cloud button.

FIGURE 1.18   Share screen

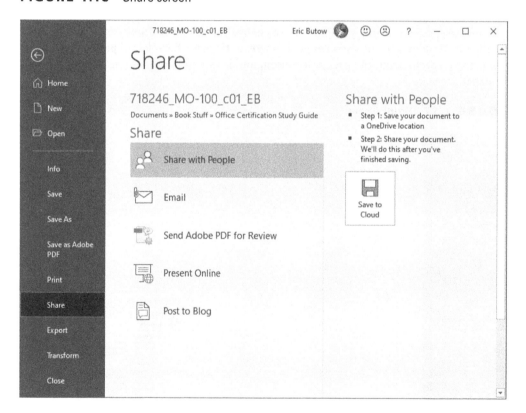

Here are the other four formats that Word supports to share your documents online:

Email   You can send your Word file as an email file attachment in native Word format or as a link to the file in a shared folder on a network. What's more, you can save the file in PDF or XPS format and attach it to an email message. You can even send the file to an online fax service.

If you're scratching your head and wondering what a "fax" is, the word "fax" is short for facsimile. You fax a document by using a device (either a computer or a stand-alone device called a fax machine) to scan the document and then transmit it electronically through telephone lines to your recipient's computer or fax machine. This technology is even older than you think—the first fax machine, called the Electric Printing Telegraph, was invented by Alexander Bain in 1843.

Send Adobe PDF For Review   Select this option if you only want to send a PDF file as an email attachment, place it on a shared folder, or share it on `Acrobat.com`.

Present Online   When you select this option, Word creates a link so that people can read the document on a web page. You need a Microsoft account, which you probably already have, especially if you're using Word as part of Microsoft 365.

Post To Blog   Word will create a new blog post from your document if your blog is on an intranet SharePoint server or on a public blog website that uses the WordPress, Telligent Community, or Typepad blog platforms. You need to register your blog account with Word the first time you use this feature.

 Real World Scenario

The Case for Sending a Document by Fax

When would you ever use a fax machine? Aren't we in the 21st century? Despite the fact that faxes have mostly been overtaken by email and secure file storage services like Dropbox, you may find in your job that a client in a certain industry requires that you send and receive files through fax. If you work in any of the following industries, don't be surprised if you receive a fax request:

- Health care
- Manufacturing
- Finance
- Government

All these industries have documents with really sensitive information, like medical records, so they require that the documents be sent securely through a fax machine over phone lines or that the sender use secure encryption on online fax services such as eFax, Fax.Plus, and HelloFax.

EXERCISE 1.3

Changing the File Type and Sharing Your Document

1. Open an existing document.

2. Save the file as a plain text (*.txt) document.

3. Close your plain text document, and reopen the Word format document that you opened in step 1.

4. Change your print orientation to landscape, and then print your document.

5. Share your document as an email attachment and send the email to someone else. Just be sure to tell the other person in your email message that this is a test document, unless the document is really something that you need to send to that person.

Inspecting Documents for Issues

If you have any problems with your document, or you just want to take a closer look at it to make sure that other people will (or won't) see the information in your shared document, Word has the tools you need.

I'll start by showing you how you can remove any hidden properties that may be causing problems, such as weird formatting and how to remove any personal information that you don't want to share. I'll also show you how to find and fix issues with document *accessibility* (for people who may have trouble reading your document) and *compatibility* issues with earlier versions of Word.

And as with all previous sections in this chapter, this section concludes with an exercise so that you can get a feel for these tools.

Locating and Removing Hidden Properties and Personal Information

Here's where to find properties and personal information and then use the built-in Document Inspector to remove them.

Start by clicking the File menu option. Click Info in the menu bar on the left side of the File window. Now that you're in the Info screen, click the Check For Issues button. Within the drop-down list, click Inspect Document.

Now you see the Document Inspector dialog box, as shown in Figure 1.19. Scroll up and down in the list of content that Windows will inspect.

FIGURE 1.19   Document Inspector dialog box

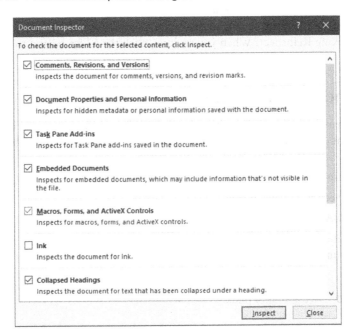

By default, the following check boxes next to the content category names are checked:

- Comments, Revisions, And Versions
- Document Properties And Personal Information
- Task Pane Add-Ins
- Embedded Documents
- Macros, Forms, And ActiveX Controls
- Collapsed Headings, which is text collapsed under a heading
- Custom XML Data
- Headers, Footers, And Watermarks
- Invisible Content, which is content that has been formatted as such but does not include objects covered by other objects
- Hidden Text

These check boxes mean that the Document Inspector will check content in all those areas. Click Ink, the only clear check box, if you want to check to see if someone has written in the document with a stylus, such as the Microsoft Surface Pen.

When you decide what you want Word to check out, click Inspect. When Word finishes its inspection, you can review all the results within the dialog box.

The results show all content categories that look good by displaying a green check mark to the left of the category name. If Word finds something that you should look at, you see a red exclamation point to the left of the category. Under the category name, Windows lists everything it found. Remove the offenders from your document by clicking the Remove All button to the right of the category name.

You can reinspect the document as often as you want, until you see all of the categories are okay, by clicking Reinspect. When you're done, click the Close button to return to the Info screen.

Finding and Fixing Accessibility Issues

If you plan to share your document with other users, Word makes it easy to check your document so that everyone of all abilities can not only read your document but edit it as well. Here's how:

1. Open the Info screen as you did in the previous section.

2. Click the Check For Issues button.

3. Click Check Accessibility in the drop-down menu.

The Accessibility panel appears at the right side of the Word window after Word checks your documents (see Figure 1.20). The panel displays your results in the Inspection Results list.

FIGURE 1.20   Accessibility panel

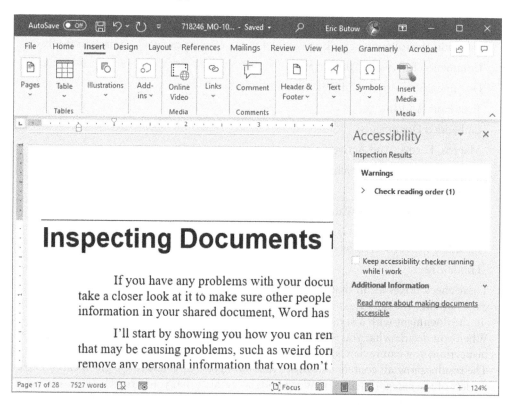

Click the warning to view each issue Word found. Click on the issue to view additional information and steps to fix the problem under the list. You can close the panel by clicking the Close icon in the upper-right corner of the panel.

> You can also open the Accessibility panel in the main document window by clicking the Review menu option and then clicking Check Accessibility in the ribbon.

Locating and Correcting Compatibility Issues

If you're going to share your document with others who use older versions of Word, and you're not sure if what you have in Microsoft 365 or Word 2019 will be readable, Microsoft has you covered.

Start by opening the Info screen as you did in the "Locating and Removing Hidden Properties and Personal Information" section earlier in this chapter. Click the Check For Issues button, and then click Check Compatibility in the drop-down menu.

Now you see the Microsoft Word Compatibility Checker dialog box with a list of any issues Word found in the Summary list (see Figure 1.21). The list includes the number of occurrences of each issue. If there are no issues, Word tells you at the top of the dialog box.

FIGURE 1.21   Microsoft Word Compatibility Checker dialog box

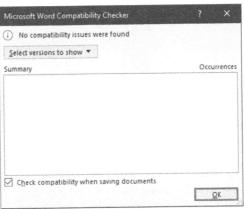

You can check for a specific version of Word someone else is using by clicking the Select Versions To Show button to view a drop-down list of Word versions to check compatibility. You can select from the previous three versions: Word 97–2003, Word 2007, and Word 2010.

What's more, you may find it unlikely that you'll have to open this feature from the Info screen because Word automatically checks compatibility with all three of those earlier versions. If Word finds something, the dialog box opens automatically.

If you don't want to check compatibility when you save a document so that you can check it manually, clear the Check Compatibility When Saving Documents check box.

Unfortunately, you have to remember what the problems are because you can't edit the document while the dialog box is open. Close the dialog box by clicking OK.

EXERCISE 1.4

Checking Out Your Document

1. Open an existing document.

2. Run the Document Inspector.

3. If the Document Inspector finds anything, click the Remove All button in that category.

4. When you're done inspecting your document, click the Close button.

5. Check your document for accessibility issues and make any changes that Word recommends.

6. Check your document for compatibility issues with previous versions of Word.

Summary

This chapter started by exploring the various ways you can navigate around the document to find text that you're looking for. You also learned how to add a link within a document to another place or object in your document. Then you learned how to hide formatting symbols in your document, hide text within your document, and show the hidden text again.

After I discussed how to move around your document, we moved on to learning how to set up your document so that it looks the way you want. Word gives you the power to change many document features, including the look and feel of the page; text setting styles you can apply to a paragraph or selected text; headers and footers; and page background elements, including the page color.

When you finish your document and save it, you can save it in one of 16 different formats in addition to the DOCX format that's native to Word 365 and Word 2019. You can change print settings in Word so that your printed document looks the way you want, and you can take advantage of Word's built-in sharing tools to send your document to others in various formats.

Finally, you learned about the built-in tools that Word gives you to inspect your document before you share it with others. These tools ensure that you don't share any sensitive information, that people of all abilities can read your document, and that people who have older versions of Word can read your document.

Key Terms

accessibility	Inspect
background	Link
compatibility	print
footers	properties
formatting	search
headers	sharing
hidden text	styles

Exam Essentials

Know how to find and link to text and objects as well as replace text in a document.   Understand how to search for text from the Word title bar, the Navigation pane, and the Find And Replace dialog box. Know how to add a link within the document to a different location in the document. You also need to know how to view and hide Word formatting symbols on the page.

Understand how to set up document pages.   Know how to change document page settings from within the Layout tab ribbon. Be able to apply a design template and page background elements.

Know how to apply a style.   Understand how to open the Styles pane and apply one of the built-in styles to a paragraph or selected text in your document.

Know how to add a header and footer.   Understand how to add a header and footer as well as how to select and apply a prebuilt header and footer style.

Understand how to save a document in different formats.   Know when you need to save a document in a different format and what happens after you save the document in a new format.

Be able to change document and print properties. Understand how to view all of your document properties before you share your document, as well as your printing properties, before you print your document.

Understand how to send documents electronically within Word. You need to know how to use the built-in sharing tools to share your documents electronically in email and on the web.

Understand how to inspect and fix document issues. Know how to use the Word Document Inspector to find any potential problems with your documents that you need to fix, including accessibility for all devices and readability for users with older versions of Word.

Review Questions

1. How can you replace text in multiple places within a document most quickly?

   A. Search for the text in the Word title bar and then change each one.

   B. Open the Navigation pane, search for the text, click on each result in the results list, and then change the text for each instance.

   C. Open the Find And Replace dialog box, type the text to find and replace in the Find and Replace fields, and then click the Replace All button.

   D. Scroll down through the document and change any instance of the word that you see.

2. Adding lighter background text to the background of a document is called what?

   A. Header

   B. Watermark

   C. Footer

   D. Style

3. What is the area above the text of a document called?

   A. Footer

   B. Top

   C. Margin

   D. Header

4. Which menu option do you click to inspect documents?

   A. Home

   B. Review

   C. File

   D. Help

5. How do you know a style applies to a paragraph?

   A. The paragraph marker appears to the right of the style name within the Styles pane.

   B. The name of the style

   C. The lowercase "a" appears to the right of the style name in the Styles pane.

   D. The Navigation pane shows that information.

6. What is the difference between a style and a theme?

   A. They're the same thing.

   B. Styles are in the Home ribbon and themes are in the Design ribbon.

   C. The lowercase "a" appears to the right of the style name in the Styles pane.

   D. A style is a collection of formatting settings, and a theme is a collection of styles.

7. Within the File screen, what menu option do you click on the left side of the screen to send a document to someone else?

   A. Info

   B. Share

   C. Save

   D. Export

8. How do you jump to a specific page in a document?

   A. Scroll down to that page.

   B. Search for text you know is on that page within the Navigation pane.

   C. Click the down arrow to the right of the Find icon in the Home ribbon and then click Go To.

   D. Type the page number in the Search box in the Word title bar.

9. How do you find out if a document may be hard for people of different abilities to read?

   A. Send the document to other people and ask if they have any trouble reading it.

   B. Search for accessibility in the Search box within the Word title bar.

   C. Save the document in a different format.

   D. Use the Accessibility Checker.

10. What does the Compatibility Checker answer about your document?

   A. If the document is compatible with the web

   B. If the document can be read in earlier versions of Word

   C. If the document can be exported to other file formats

   D. If you need to use a different word processing program

Chapter 2

Inserting and Formatting Text

MICROSOFT EXAM OBJECTIVES COVERED IN THIS CHAPTER:

✓ **Insert and format text, paragraphs, and sections**

- Insert text and paragraphs
    - Find and replace text
    - Insert symbols and special characters
- Format text and paragraphs
    - Apply text effects
    - Apply formatting by using Format Painter
    - Set line and paragraph spacing and indentation
    - Apply built-in styles to text
    - Clear formatting
- Create and configure document sections
    - Format text in multiple columns
    - Insert page, section, and column breaks
    - Change page setup options for a section

Chapter 1, "Working with Documents," contained high-level information about not only how to add text, but also how to find and replace text in your document. In this chapter, I will take a deeper dive into the various ways of finding and replacing text as well as how to insert special characters.

I will then show you how to format text and paragraphs by using text effects, using the *Format Painter*, and setting spacing and indents for both lines and paragraphs. Next, I will show you how to apply built-in *styles* to text, something I also touched on in Chapter 1, as well as to *clear* any formatting you've made within the text or after you've applied a style that you don't want anymore.

Then I will tell you how to format text in multiple columns as well as add *breaks* to create a new page, *section* of text, or *column*. Finally, I will show you how you can change your page setting options within a section. At the end of each section, I provide an exercise so that you can test yourself and see if you can apply what you've learned.

Adding and Replacing Text

When you open a new document, the cursor is blinking in the upper-left corner of the page. All you have to do to add text is just start typing.

When you need to replace a word, it's easy to replace text just by selecting the word and typing a new one. Yet, as your document grows, you'll find that replacing text this way is too cumbersome, which is why Word comes with a handy find and replace feature.

Finding and Replacing Text

Whenever you need to find text in a document (especially a long document), and possibly replace the text with some new text, Word has this basic function down cold.

Finding Text

There are several ways to find text in your document:

- In the Home ribbon, click Find in the Editing area.
- In the Navigation pane, the last word you entered is the default find term.
- Click in the Search box within the Word title bar, and then type the text that you want to find.

A couple of seconds later, Word lists all instances of the word in the Results list. How Word presents the results depends on the tool you use. For example, when you search for text in the Navigation pane, Word highlights all instances of the text it finds, and it takes you to the first instance of the text in the document (see Figure 2.1).

FIGURE 2.1   First instance of the word "AutoFit" highlighted

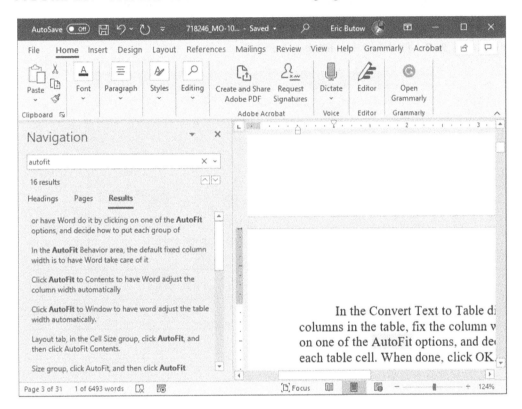

Using Advanced Find to Locate More than Just Text

Change your Find parameters by clicking the down arrow to the right of Find in the Home ribbon and then clicking Advanced Find. The Find And Replace dialog box appears so that you can find using different parameters, including case, the text format, and other *special characters* (such as an em dash) that you'll learn about in the next section.

Replacing Text

When you need to replace text, all you have to do is click the Home menu option (if it isn't selected already). In the Home ribbon, click Replace in the Editing area. The Find And Replace dialog box appears with the Replace tab open, as shown in Figure 2.2.

Replacing text is a two-step process. First, in the Find What text box type the text in the document that you want to replace. Next, in the Replace With text box type the replacement text.

FIGURE 2.2   Find And Replace dialog box

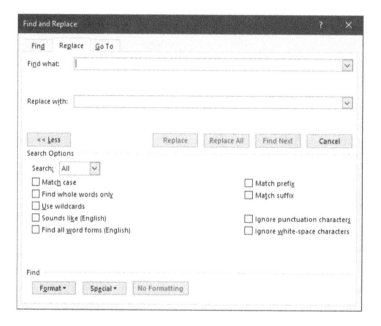

In the dialog box, you see several different options that you can choose to refine your search. When you set one or more options, the options that Word will apply appear underneath the Find text box.

Search   By default, the setting is All, which means that you search through the entire document. Click the All box, and then click Up in the drop-down list to search from your cursor to the beginning of the document or click Down to search from your cursor to the end of the document.

Match Case   Select this check box to find and replace words that match the specific capitalization you've typed in the Find What and Replace With text boxes.

Find Whole Words Only   Use this option to tell Word not to search for matches in a word. For example, if you want to change the word "one" to "four," clicking this check box will ensure that Word doesn't change entries like "anyone" to "anyfour."

Use Wildcards   Select this check box and then type an asterisk at the end of the part of the word that you want to find. For example, when you type **the*** in the Find What box, Word finds all words that start with the letters "the," such as "these" and "theory."

Sounds Like (English)   When you search in the English language, you can find and replace words that sound similar. (Word includes a database that knows what words sound like.) So, when you click this check box and search for the word "there," Word will also find the words "their" and "they're."

Find All Word Forms (English)   Word also has a database of verb tenses, so when you click this check box and search for the verb "wind," Word will also find the words "wound," "winds," and "winding."

Match Prefix   If you have a common prefix in your document, such as "pre," click this check box to find words with the prefix and replace them if you want.

Match Suffix   When you have a common suffix in your document, such as "est," click this check box to find words with that suffix so that you can replace them.

Ignore Punctuation Characters   Use this option to tell Word to ignore any punctuation in the text you're searching for.

Ignore White-Space Characters   Use this option to tell Word to ignore all spaces between characters.

Format Button   Search for and replace existing text or all text that has certain *formatting* attributes such as font types, colors, and paragraph alignment.

Special Button   Find and replace text elements such as a tab or white space. You can also find and replace a graphic in your document with text or a line, column, page, or section break.

No Formatting Button   Click this button to turn off all formatting options you set in the Find What and/or Replace With text boxes.

When you're ready to search for the term or format, click the Find Next button to go to the next instance of the search term.

Click the Replace icon to replace only the next instance of the text with your replacement. If you want to replace any other text that meets your criteria, click the Replace button again to go to the next instance and replace that.

Replace all instances of the text and/or formatting in the Find text box by clicking the Replace All button. If you search from the middle of your document to the end, then when Word finishes its search a dialog box appears and asks if you want to continue searching from the beginning of the document.

When Word completes its search, a dialog box appears in the middle of the screen and tells you how many changes it made. Close the dialog box by clicking OK.

If you just want to find text, click the Find tab in the dialog box.

Inserting Symbols and Special Characters

Sometimes you need to add *symbols* and special characters in a document that aren't keys on your keyboard. For example, you may need to insert the copyright symbol into a copyright statement.

It's easy to insert symbols and other special characters into your text. Start by placing your cursor where you want to insert the symbol and/or special character. Next follow these steps:

1. Click the Insert menu option.
2. In the ribbon, click the Symbol icon in the Symbols area.
3. Click More Symbols in the drop-down menu.

The Symbols dialog box appears and displays 20 common symbols in the drop-down menu. Add one of the symbols to your text by clicking it. If you want to view all the symbols and special characters that you can add, click More Symbols.

The Symbol window appears, as shown in Figure 2.3, and displays many more common symbols on the Symbols tab.

FIGURE 2.3   Symbol window

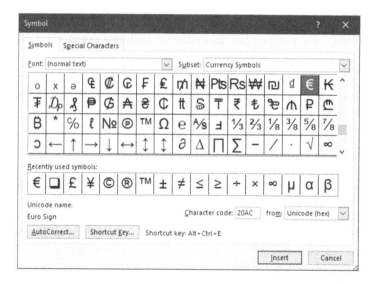

Scroll up and down the list of symbols. When you find the one you want, click it and select Insert.

Different font sets often have different symbols in them. You can change the font by clicking (Normal Text) in the Font box to choose the font set that you want to use from the drop-down list.

You can also choose from font subsets so you don't have to scroll through hundreds of symbols to find the right one. For example, subsets include currency, subscript, and super-script symbols. Click Currency Symbols in the Subset box to view all the subsets in the drop-down list. When you select a subset, the symbols in that subset appear in the dialog box so that you can select one.

Click the AutoCorrect button to add a word or phrase. You can type text within parentheses to insert a symbol or special character automatically. For example, when you type (c), AutoCorrect replaces that text with the © symbol.

Click the Shortcut Key button under the list of symbols to open the Customize Keyboard dialog box and tell Word to add the symbol when you press a combination of keys on your keyboard. Many symbols already have a shortcut key combination assigned to them. If one is assigned, the combination appears to the right of the Shortcut Key button.

Word also allows you to insert a variety of special characters. Click the Special Characters tab to view the list of characters. The list shows you what the character looks like (if applicable), the name of the character, and the corresponding shortcut key.

Click Insert to insert the symbol or special character where your cursor is positioned in the document. The dialog box stays open in the Word window so that you can insert multiple symbols and/or special characters if you want. When you're done, click the Close button.

EXERCISE 2.1

Finding and Replacing Text

1. Open a new document and type several paragraphs of text or open an existing document.

2. Move the cursor to the beginning of your document.

3. Open the Find And Replace dialog box.

4. Enter a word that contains at least one capital letter that you want to replace.

5. Enter the replacement word.

6. Match the case of the word that you want to replace from step 4.

7. Click the Replace All button.

8. Click OK in the dialog box that tells you how many changes Word made.

9. Save and close your document.

Formatting Text and Paragraphs

Word processors have always had the ability to format text and paragraphs from the time Michael Shrayer Software produced the program Electric Pencil in December 1976. As word processors have grown in ability and complexity over the years, especially on Windows and other *graphical user interfaces (GUIs),* you can create and apply all sorts of formatting that conveys the message you want to send in your documents.

Adding Text Effects

Word includes several text effects that not only ensure that your text appears the way you want it to, but that also apply graphical pizzazz to your text to make it stand out. Here's how to apply text effects:

1. Select the text that you want to change.
2. In the Home ribbon, click the Text Effects And Typography icon in the Font area.
3. Click one of the 15 text effects icons shown in Figure 2.4 to apply that effect.

FIGURE 2.4   Text Effects menu

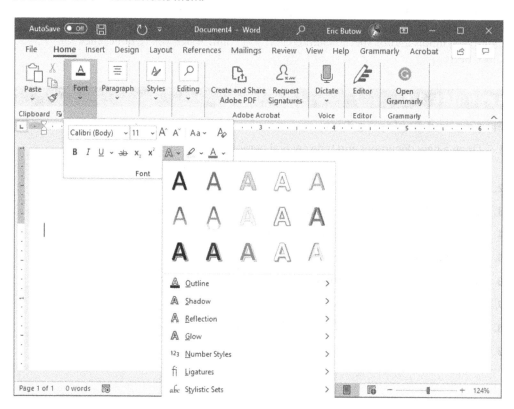

4. Move the mouse pointer over one of the following seven effects to customize each effect in the side menu before you apply them:

Outline: Sets outline colors, weights, and line styles

Shadow: Changes shadow settings

Reflection: Changes settings for a reflection, which is a drop shadow underneath the word that fades from top to bottom

Glow: Sets the glow type, colors, and other options

Number Styles: Sets one of five numbering format styles, such as proportional old-style numbering

Ligatures: Sets the ligature style for your text

Stylistic Sets: Selects one of the built-in style sets that come with your font

Applying Formatting by Using Format Painter

The Format Painter feature is a quick and easy way to apply formatting from selected text or an entire paragraph to another block of text or a paragraph. Follow this process to get started:

1. Select the text or click text in a paragraph that has the formatting you want to copy.
2. Click the Home menu option if it's not selected already.
3. In the Home ribbon, click the Format Painter icon in the Clipboard area, as shown in Figure 2.5.

The mouse pointer changes to a cursor icon combined with a paintbrush. Now you can select a block of text or click inside a paragraph. The text or paragraph that you selected now shows the format you copied.

This process works only once, but you can change the format of multiple blocks of text or paragraphs. After you select the text with the formatting you want to copy, double-click the Format Painter icon in the Home toolbar and then select the text and/or paragraphs. When you're done, press the Esc key.

Setting Line and Paragraph Spacing and Indentation

You may need to change *spacing* between lines and/or paragraphs for readability, or because of requirements from another company or people (like book editors).

FIGURE 2.5   Format Painter icon

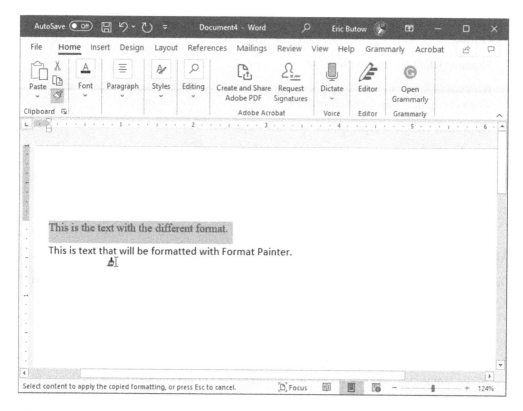

Line Spacing

When you want to set line spacing, place the cursor where you want to start the different line and paragraph spacing, or select the text that will have the different line spacing. In the Home ribbon, click the Line And Paragraph Spacing icon in the Paragraph area.

Now you can select one of the built-in line spacing amounts, as shown in Figure 2.6. For example, clicking 2.0 means that you will see double-spaced lines as you type.

Below the list of built-in line spacing amounts, click Line Spacing Options to open the Paragraph dialog box to set line and paragraph spacing (as well as indents).

Paragraph Spacing

You can change paragraph spacing from the Home and Layout menu ribbons.

Home Ribbon   If you want to look at a paragraph's spacing as you make changes, click Add Space Before Paragraph and/or Remove Space After Paragraph in the menu. Word adds a small space above or below so that you can see if you like it.

Layout Ribbon   In the Paragraph area, click the Before or After box to add spacing in points above or below the paragraph, respectively. You can also click the up or down arrow at the right of the boxes to increase or decrease the spacing by 6 points every time you click one of the arrows.

FIGURE 2.6   Line And Paragraph Spacing menu

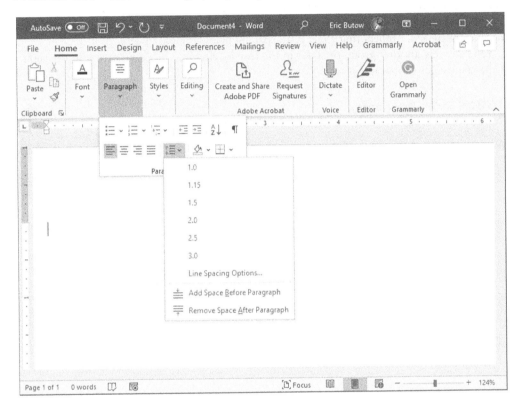

Indenting a Paragraph

When you need to *indent* the first line of a paragraph, you can make changes in the Home and Layout ribbons.

Home Ribbon   Click the Increase Indent icon in the Paragraph area to add a one-half inch indent. Click the Decrease Indent icon to remove the previous indent that you added.

Layout Ribbon   In the Paragraph area, click the Left or Right box to add spacing in points above or below the paragraph, respectively. You can also click the up or down arrow to the right of the boxes to increase or decrease the spacing by one-tenth of an inch every time you click one of the arrows.

Applying Built-In Styles to Text

When you open a new document, Word includes 16 different styles for you to apply to text. You can view and apply these styles to text by clicking the Home menu option if it's not already active.

In the Styles area in the Home ribbon, a row of built-in styles appears with a preview tile. Each tile shows you what the text will look like after you apply it, though some styles may look the same. For example, the Normal and No Spacing styles look the same, but the No Spacing tile can't reflect that there is no spacing below the paragraph.

You can view another group of styles in the row by clicking the down arrow to the right of the last tile, as shown in Figure 2.7.

FIGURE 2.7   Down arrow

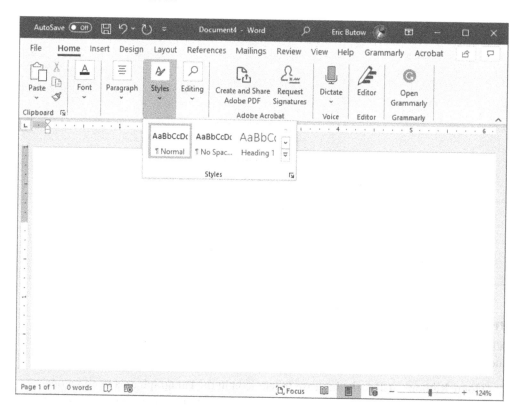

Click the up arrow to return to the previous group of styles. If you prefer to see all the style tiles (see Figure 2.8), click the More button below the down arrow.

FIGURE 2.8   Menu with all style tiles

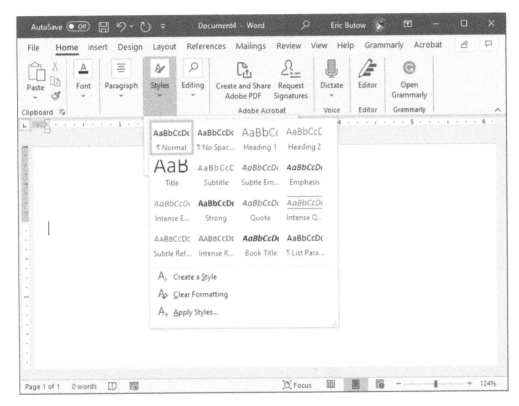

When you select text, you can apply a style from the pop-up menu that appears after you release the mouse button. In the menu, click Styles and then click the style tile in the drop-down list.

You can view the Styles list pane quickly by pressing Alt+Ctrl+Shift+S on your keyboard. Now you can view all the styles by scrolling up and down the list, if necessary. You can also change settings for a style by right-clicking on a style and clicking Modify in the drop-down menu.

Clearing Formatting

You can clear formatting in selected text or in one or more selected paragraphs.

In the Pop-Up Menu   Start by selecting text in a paragraph, placing your cursor in a paragraph, or selecting one or more paragraphs. In the pop-up menu, click Styles, and then click Clear Formatting in the drop-down menu, as shown in Figure 2.9.

FIGURE 2.9   Clear Formatting option

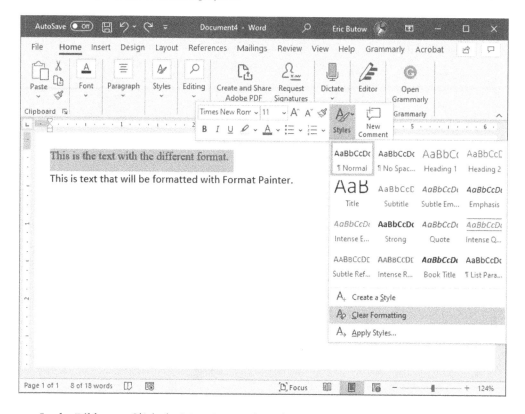

In the Ribbon   Click the More icon (a line above a down arrow) to the right of the row of style tiles, and then click Clear Formatting in the drop-down menu (see Figure 2.10).

If you select text in a paragraph, the text reverts to the style of that paragraph. When you select one or more paragraphs, then all the text in those paragraphs revert back to the default Normal paragraph style.

What if you want to clear the formatting of all the text? Press Ctrl+A to select all the text. In this case, you need to right-click on the selected text to see the pop-up menu.

FIGURE 2.10   More icon

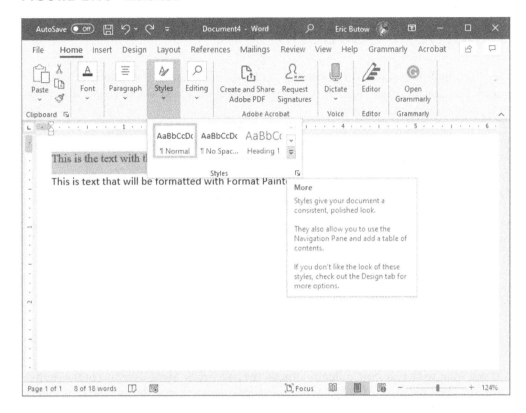

EXERCISE 2.2

Changing a Paragraph Format

1. Open a new document and type several paragraphs of text or open an existing document.

2. Select a paragraph of text.

3. Apply a blue text effect to the paragraph. (The effect tile is a plain blue A.)

4. Copy the format in the paragraph with the Format Painter and apply it to a word that you want to highlight in another paragraph.

5. Select another paragraph without any formatting and indent the first line.

6. Open the Styles menu and apply the Title style to the paragraph.

7. Clear the formatting in the paragraph.

8. When you're done, save and close the document.

Creating and Configuring Document Sections

Word has a built-in feature to create multiple columns on a page so that your text is easier to read. You can also place columns in a section, and Word allows you to create four different types of sections in a document.

You can have different settings in each section that you create. For example, you can change the columns in different sections. If you create a section on a new page, you can also change the margins, orientation, and size in that section page.

Formatting Text in Multiple Columns

If you want to put your text into more than one column, here are the steps to add multiple columns in Word:

1. Select the text that you want to change. If you want to change all the text, press Ctrl+A.

2. Click the Layout menu option.

3. In the Layout ribbon, click Columns in the Page Setup section.

4. Click the number of columns in the drop-down list. The default is One. You can select as many as Three, shown in Figure 2.11.

If you want to change how columns look on the page, click More Columns in the drop-down list. The Columns dialog box appears so that you can change the number of columns, the width of each column, and the spacing between each column.

 **Real World Scenario**

Creating Different Column Sections on One Page

Your boss has given you the task of creating a one-page marketing document that has one section at the top of the page for an introduction, a middle section for body text, and a third section with a conclusion. The introduction and conclusion sections have one column and the body text section has two.

How do you do this? In Word, the solution is easy. Type all the text that you have in the document. When you're done, select the text that will have more than one column. Now change the column number for the selected text to two.

Only your selected text appears in two columns. The text that you didn't select above and/or below your body text appears in one column. The area with columns may not appear even because you have less text in the second column than the first. In this case, you may have to add a column break, which you will learn about in the next section.

You can add space below the introduction by placing your cursor at the end of the introductory text and then pressing Enter as many times as you need or adding space below the paragraph, a task that you learned about earlier in this chapter. Add space between the body text and conclusion by placing the cursor at the beginning of the conclusion text and then pressing Enter or adding space above the paragraph.

Be careful, though, to keep all your text on one page. As you type in the second column of body text, you see the text that follows pushed down, perhaps to the next page. And as you type text in the introduction, then the body text and conclusion will be pushed farther down on the page.

FIGURE 2.11   Columns menu

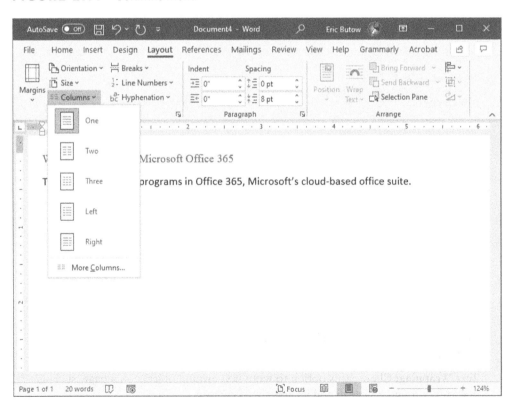

Inserting Page, Section, and Column Breaks

Word makes it easy to insert the page, section, or column break you need. Start by clicking the cursor at the place in your document where you want to add the break. In the Layout ribbon, click the Breaks icon in the Page Setup area, as shown in Figure 2.12.

FIGURE 2.12 Breaks icon

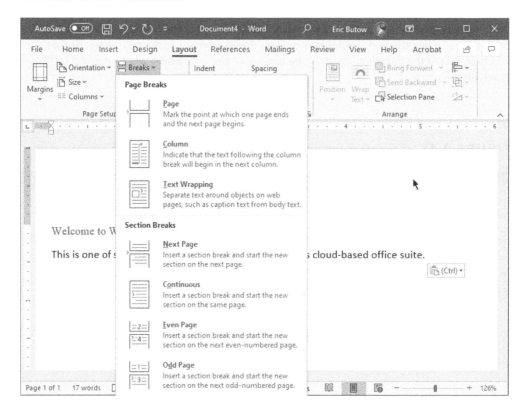

In the drop-down menu, click one of the following options:

Page: Use this option to leave the rest of the current page blank and enter new text on the next page.

Column: Select this option to have text following the current column continue in the next column.

Text Wrapping: Choose this option to wrap text around objects on a page, such as body text around a picture and its associated caption.

Next Page: Use this option to end the current section and create a new section on the next page.

Continuous: Select this option to end the current section and create a new section on the same page.

Even Page: Choose this option to end the current section and create a new section on an even-numbered page. For example, if you're on page 2 and you create a new even-numbered page section, then the next page will have the page number 4.

Odd Page: Use this option to end the current section and create a new section on an odd-numbered page. For example, if you're on page 1 and you create a new odd-numbered page section, then the next page will have the page number 3.

Changing Page Setting Options for a Section

When you add a section on a new page, you can change the page settings only in that section. So, you can have a document that includes one page in portrait orientation with one column and another page in landscape orientation with three columns.

After you create a new page section, your cursor appears on the new page. Now follow these steps to change the page settings:

1. Click the Layout menu option if it isn't open already.

2. In the Layout ribbon, click Margins in the Page Setup section (see Figure 2.13), and then click one of the default margin types in the drop-down menu. If you want a custom margin setting, click Custom Margins at the bottom of the menu.

FIGURE 2.13 Page Setup options

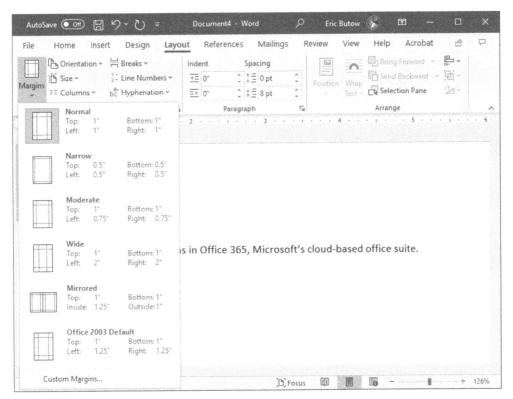

3. Click Orientation to select between Portrait and Landscape page orientation for all the text in the section.

4. Change the number of columns in the section by clicking Columns and then selecting the number of columns, as you learned to do earlier in this chapter.

5. Add page numbering by clicking the Insert menu option.

6. In the Insert ribbon, click Page Number in the Header & Footer section.

7. In the drop-down menu, as shown in Figure 2.14, move the mouse pointer over the position of the page number in the menu and then select the page number style in the side menu.

FIGURE 2.14   Page Number menu

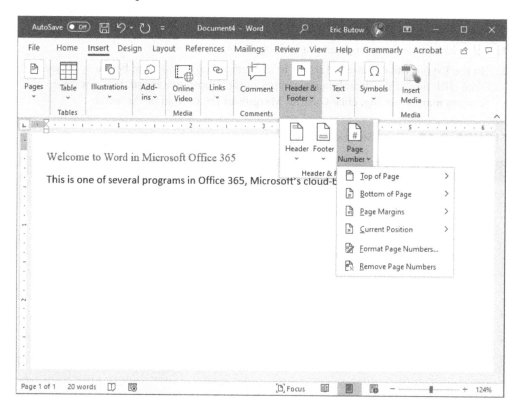

8. Add a border to the page containing your section by clicking the Design menu option.

9. In the Design ribbon, click Page Borders in the Page Background area.

10. Create the border in the Borders And Shading dialog box (see Figure 2.15); when you finish, click OK.

FIGURE 2.15   Borders And Shading dialog box

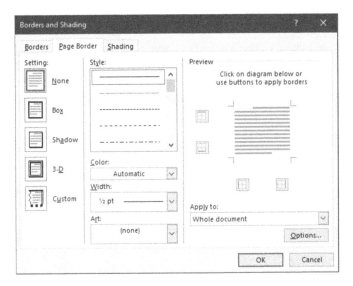

11. Add a header or footer by clicking the Insert menu option.

12. In the ribbon, click Header or Footer in the Header & Footer area. Select the built-in style for the header or footer in the drop-down menu.

After you click a header or footer, the page that has your section displays the header and/or footer. Figure 2.16 shows one of the built-in footer styles.

EXERCISE 2.3

Inserting Sections

1. Open a new document and type some text or open an existing document.

2. Add a next page section break at the end of your document.

3. In your new section, create two columns.

4. Open the Borders And Shading dialog box, select the Box border type, and then click OK.

5. Create a new header and footer, both with the built-in Facet style.

6. When you're done, save and close your document.

FIGURE 2.16   Built-in footer style

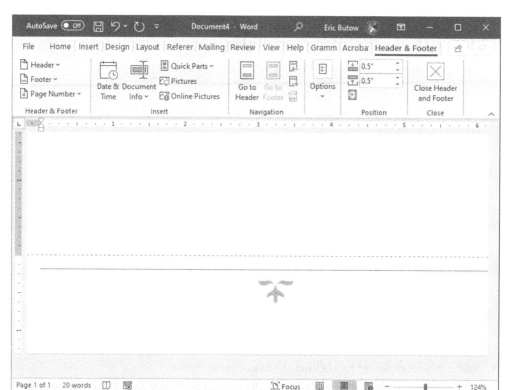

Summary

In Chapter 1, I talked about finding and replacing text, and I started this chapter by going into greater detail. I followed up by showing you how to insert one or more symbols or special characters into your documents.

Next, you learned about how to format text and paragraphs using built-in effects, as well as applying formats using Format Painter. Then I dove deeper into line and paragraph spacing as well as indentation that followed up on what I discussed in Chapter 1.

You also learned more about applying styles that Word provides automatically in new documents, which build on what I discussed in Chapter 1. I finished that section by telling you how to clear all your formatting and start fresh without losing your text (and your time).

Finally, you learned about how to create and configure breaks and sections in a document. I talked a little bit about these in Chapter 1. In this chapter, however, you learned much more, including changing page settings in a section.

Key Terms

break	indent
Clear	Section
Column	Spacing
Format Painter	special characters
formatting	Styles
graphical user interfaces (GUIs)	symbols

Exam Essentials

Understand how to find and replace text in a document.　Know the different ways to find text, how to find and replace text, and how to customize your search by setting different search and formatting options.

Understand how to add one or more symbols and special characters.　Know how to add symbols and special characters that aren't on the keyboard and how to add symbols or special effects by creating a shortcut key.

Understand how to add text effects.　Understand how to access the Text Effects And Typography area to select a preexisting effect and create your own effects in the Text Effects And Typography menu.

Know how to apply formatting using Format Painter.　Understand how to use the Format Painter feature to copy and apply formatting from one paragraph to another in a document.

Be able to change spacing between lines, as well as change paragraph spacing and indentation.　Know how to change spacing between lines and between paragraphs and how to indent a line and remove an indent in a paragraph.

Know how to apply styles to, and clear styles from, document text.　Understand how to apply styles in your document to selected text, as well as a paragraph, and how to clear all formatting.

Understand how to add breaks for pages, sections, and columns.　Know what the differences are between pages, sections, and columns and how to add breaks to change your document layout between all three layout types.

Understand how to change page settings in a section.　Know how to change section page settings, including margins, borders, headers, and footers.

Review Questions

1. When you want to find something in your document using the Find feature, how do you change the find parameters?
   - **A.** The options are available in the Navigation pane.
   - **B.** Click the Find icon in the Home ribbon.
   - **C.** Click the down arrow to the right of the Find icon in the Home ribbon and then click Advanced Find.
   - **D.** Use the Search box in the Word title bar.

2. How do you find and replace words that match only specific capitalization?
   - **A.** You can do this in the Navigation pane.
   - **B.** Open the Find And Replace dialog box and then click the Match Case check box.
   - **C.** Click Find in the Home ribbon.
   - **D.** Scroll through the document and make the changes manually.

3. How do you add a special character?
   - **A.** From the Home ribbon
   - **B.** By selecting the correct font from the fonts list in the Home ribbon
   - **C.** By searching for the special character in the Navigation pane
   - **D.** From in the Symbol window

4. How do you apply a format from one selected block of text to another block?
   - **A.** By clicking the Format Painter icon in the Home ribbon and selecting the other block
   - **B.** Seeing what style the block of text has in the Home ribbon or Styles text
   - **C.** By searching for the special character in the Navigation pane
   - **D.** From the Symbol window

5. How do you apply the formatting from one selected block of text to multiple blocks of text in your document?
   - **A.** See what style is applied to the text, and then apply the style to other types of text.
   - **B.** Scroll through the document manually, select the text, and apply the style that looks like the right one from in the Home ribbon.
   - **C.** Double-click Format Painter in the Home ribbon, and then select each block of text to apply the formatting.
   - **D.** Select each block of text and then apply font and paragraph changes by clicking the appropriate icons in the Home ribbon.

6. How many columns can you add in a document within the Columns drop-down menu?

   A. One

   B. Two

   C. As many as you want

   D. Three

7. What happens when you click the Increase Indent icon in the Home ribbon?

   A. The Paragraph dialog box opens so that you can set the indent.

   B. The first line of the paragraph is moved to the right by a half-inch.

   C. Word highlights the ruler below the ribbon so that you can set the indent.

   D. The paragraph is right-indented.

8. What happens when you add a page break?

   A. A new page opens, and your cursor appears at the top of the page so that you can start typing.

   B. You're still on the same page where the break is located, so you can't see the new page that opened after this one.

   C. A new document opens.

   D. The Page Setup dialog box opens.

9. How do you put a break in one column so that you can continue working in the next column?

   A. In the Layout ribbon, click Columns and then add a column by clicking One in the drop-down menu.

   B. In the Insert ribbon, click Page Break.

   C. In the Layout ribbon, click Breaks and then click Column in the drop-down menu.

   D. Press the Tab key to create a new column and start typing in it.

10. What is a section?

   A. A page

   B. An area in the document that contains its own formatting

   C. It's related to a header and footer.

   D. It's a feature that lets you create an odd or even page.

Chapter 3

Managing Tables and Lists

MICROSOFT EXAM OBJECTIVES COVERED IN THIS CHAPTER:

✓ **Manage tables and lists**

- ▪ Create tables
    - ▪ Convert text to tables
    - ▪ Convert tables to text
    - ▪ Create tables by specifying rows and columns
- ▪ Modify tables
    - ▪ Sort table data
    - ▪ Configure cell margins and spacing
    - ▪ Merge and split cells
    - ▪ Resize tables, rows, and columns
    - ▪ Split tables
    - ▪ Configure a repeating row header
- ▪ Create and modify lists
    - ▪ Format paragraphs as numbered and bulleted lists
    - ▪ Change bullet characters and number formats
    - ▪ Define custom bullet characters and number formats
    - ▪ Increase and decrease list levels
    - ▪ Restart and continue list numbering
    - ▪ Set starting number values

Tables and lists are great ways to present information in your document in a way that's easy for readers to digest. In this chapter, I start by showing you how to create tables. This includes changing existing text to tables, switching tables to text, and creating a table from scratch.

Next, I talk about how to modify tables after you've created them so that they look the way you want them to appear. You'll learn how to sort table data, manipulate the sizes of *cells* and tables, split cells and tables, and create a row header at the top of your table so that the header in your table appears on every page where the table resides.

Then I will show you how to create and format text lists. Word allows you to create bulleted and numbered lists easily, and you'll learn how to add and modify them. Finally, you'll learn how to change number values and *list levels* so that you can manage changes in your lists more easily.

Creating Tables

Word makes it easy for you to create a table. Here's how:

1. Place the cursor within the page where you want to add a table.
2. Click the Insert menu option.
3. Click the Table icon.
4. Move your mouse pointer over the grid in the drop-down menu. Cells in the grid light up as you move the pointer so that you can see the size of the table in terms of *rows* and *columns*.
5. When the table is the size you want, click the highlighted cell, as shown in Figure 3.1.

Et voilà—the table appears on the page with the number of rows and columns you selected in the grid.

FIGURE 3.1   The selected table cells

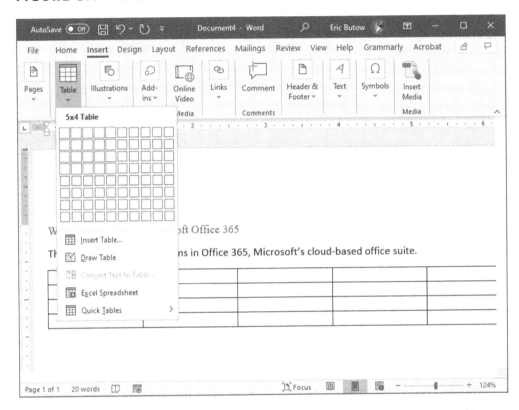

Create Tables Quick!

Your boss comes to you first thing in the morning and tells you to put together a document for a sales meeting with a big client in two hours. Word has you covered. Here's what to do to add some nice-looking tables to your document in a jiffy:

1.   Place your cursor where you want to add the table on the page.

2.   Click the Insert menu option.

3.   In the Insert ribbon, click the Table icon.

4.   In the drop-down menu, move the mouse pointer over Quick Tables.

5.   In the side menu containing built-in tables, as shown here, scroll up and down the list of built-in table styles.

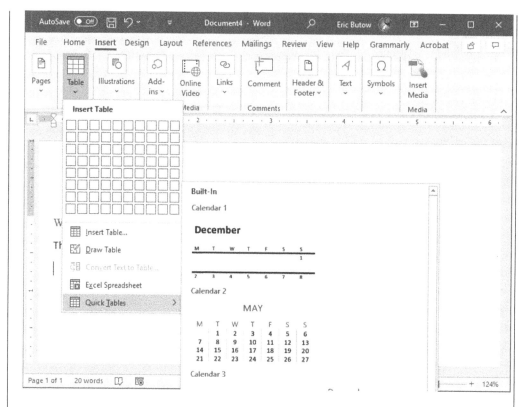

6. When you find a table that you like, click the style in the list. The table appears within your document so that you can start changing the text, add rows and columns, and make any other changes that you need to shine in front of that client (and your boss).

Converting Text to Tables

If you decide that some text in your document would be better presented as a table, Word has tools that make it easy to convert that text into a table when you follow these steps:

1. Select the text in the document.
2. Click the Insert menu option.
3. In the Insert ribbon, click the Table icon.
4. Click the Convert Cell To Table icon in the drop-down menu.
5. In the Convert Text To Table dialog box, shown in Figure 3.2, select the number of rows and columns that you want in the table in the Table Size section.

FIGURE 3.2   Convert Text To Table dialog box

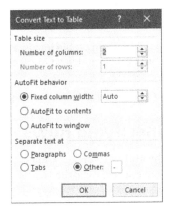

6. In the AutoFit Behavior section, you can set the specific width of a column or have Word do it by clicking one of the AutoFit options.

7. In the Separate Text At section, you can decide how to put each group of text in each table cell.

8. When you finish, click OK.

Now your text is in the table, though you may have to do some more tweaking to get it to appear the way you want it to.

Switching Tables to Text

As you work on a table, you may think that what's in a table may read better either in a paragraph of text or in a list. Or the amount of text may be so small that a table simply isn't needed. Whenever you want to change a table into text, start by clicking a cell in your table and then follow these steps:

1. Click the Layout menu option to the right of the Table Design option.

2. In the Layout ribbon, click the Select icon.

3. Click Select Table in the drop-down menu. Now all cells are gray, which means that Word has selected your entire table.

4. Click the Convert To Text icon in the Data section in the ribbon.

5. In the Convert Table To Text dialog box, choose if you want to separate text in each cell with paragraph marks, tabs (the default option), commas, or another character.

6. When you're done, click OK.

All your table text in the default paragraph style is selected in place of the table.

 If there are nested tables (one table inside another table cell), the Convert Nested Tables check box is active so that you can convert those nested tables as well.

Creating Tables by Specifying Rows and Columns

The Insert Table grid gives you the ability to create a maximum table size of only 10 columns and 8 rows. If you need more control over the size of your columns when you create a table, follow these steps:

1. Place the cursor on the page where you want to insert the table.
2. Click the Insert menu option (if you haven't done so already).
3. Click the Table icon.
4. Click Insert Table in the drop-down menu, as shown in Figure 3.3.

FIGURE 3.3   Insert Table menu option

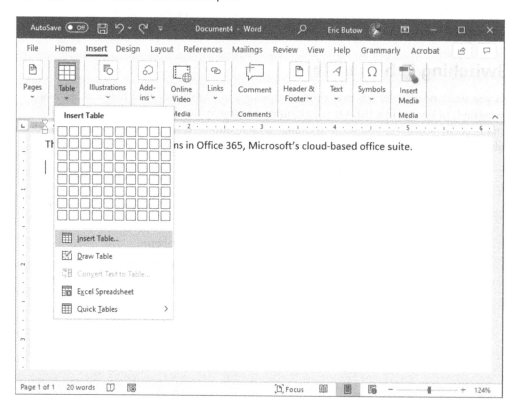

5. In the Insert Table dialog box (Figure 3.4), specify the number of columns and rows that you want in the Number Of Columns and Number Of Rows boxes, respectively. The default is five columns and two rows.

FIGURE 3.4   Insert Table dialog box

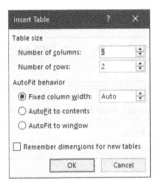

Now you can change the size of the columns in the AutoFit Behavior area. The default fixed column width is Auto, which means that Word takes care of it automatically. Here's what you can do to adjust the column and table widths:

- Click the up and down arrows to the right of the Fixed Column Width box to change the width of the box in tenths of an inch. The minimum width that you can set is 0.3 inches.
- Click AutoFit To Contents to have Word adjust the column width automatically.
- Click AutoFit To Window to have Word adjust the table width automatically.

You can save the settings for the next time you create a table by clicking the Remember Dimensions For New Tables check box. Once you're done, place your new table on the page by clicking OK.

EXERCISE 3.1

Creating a Table

1. Open a new document.

2. Type three words on five lines in the page.

3. Select all the text.

4. Convert the text to a table.

5. Press Enter.

6. Create a new table with three rows and two columns.

7. Type text into each table cell.

8. Click the Layout menu option to the right of the Table Design option.

9. In the Data section in the ribbon, click Convert To Text.

10. In the Convert Table To Text dialog box, keep Tabs as what you use to separate text and click OK.

11. Place the cursor below the selected text.

12. Insert a new table with 5 columns and 15 rows, and AutoFit the table to the window.

13. Click OK and enjoy your new table.

Modifying Tables

Word gives you a lot of power to modify your tables as you see fit. As in Microsoft Excel, you can sort text and/or numbers in a table. You can also take advantage of more tools to change the look of your table cells, rows, columns, and even the entire table.

You can also merge cells in your table. If you already have merged cells, or you have a cell that you think is too big, you can *split* it into two or more cells. And you can even split the entire table.

If your table is long, then it will likely appear on more than one page. To ensure that your readers know what they're looking at on each page, you can create a header row and tell Word to show that header row on every page in your table.

Sorting Table Data

A common *sorting* method for a table is to sort text in alphabetical order. Word also gives you the ability to sort by number and date. What is more, you can sort in multiple columns.

For example, you can sort the text in the first column alphabetically. After Word sorts all the text in the first column, it can sort the numbers in the second column.

After you create a table, click the table cell and then click the Layout menu option to the right of the Table Design option. In the Layout ribbon, click the Sort icon in the Data section, as shown in Figure 3.5.

In the Sort dialog box (see Figure 3.6), you can sort by three different columns. If the column has a header, then select the column name by clicking the Sort By box and then selecting the name in the drop-down list.

FIGURE 3.5 Sort icon

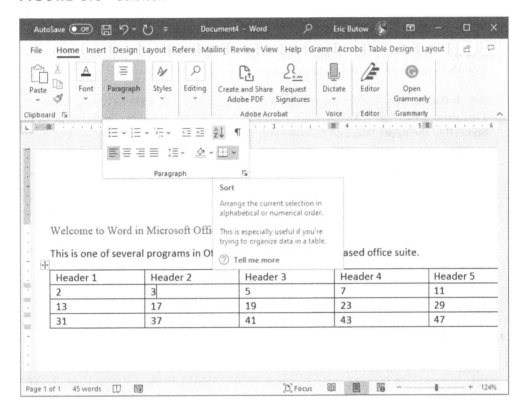

FIGURE 3.6 Sort dialog box

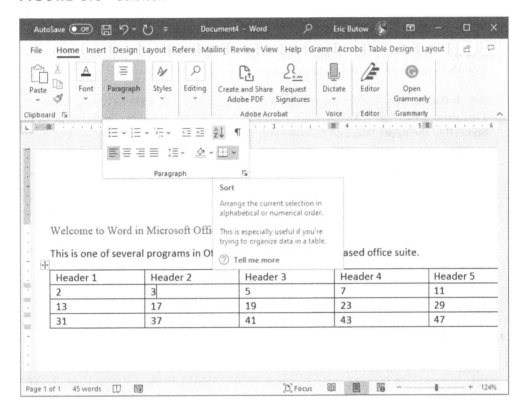

The Sort dialog box is almost a table itself, as it contains three setting columns and four setting rows. The first row allows you to set the basic parameters of your search in each of the three columns as follows:

Sort By   If there are no columns, you see the column numbers starting with Column 1 on the left side of the table and incrementing from left to right.

Search Parameters   Select the type of column for which you want to search in the Type drop-down list: Text (Default), Number, or Date. Word figures out the type of the first cell in the upper left, and it shows you the two types in the Type box.

In the Using box, sort by paragraphs, headings, or fields in a cell. When you click the box, the column type will determine what cell search types you see in the drop-down list.

Sort Order   Sorting in Ascending order is the default; that is, letters from A to Z. Click Descending in any of the three sort areas to sort from Z to A. If you sort by number, Word sorts by the first number in the text. For example, if you have the numbers 10 and 5 in a column, Word will list 10 first because 1 comes before 5. You can change this by sorting by number in the Type drop-down list.

The following two Then By rows allow you to sort by additional columns after Word sorts through the first column. For example, after you sort by name in the first column, you can sort by a number in the second column.

The Header Row button is selected by default at the bottom of the dialog box. If you don't want to use the header row as part of the sort, click the No Header Row button.

Click the Options button to open the Sort Options dialog box and to change other sort settings, such as making the sort text case sensitive.

When you're done, click OK. The table rows are reordered except for the header row, as shown in the example in Figure 3.7.

Configuring Cell Margins and Spacing

It's easy to configure margins and spacing around text in one or more table cells. All you have to do is click a cell and then change the column width either by using your mouse or by setting the height and width with the table's Layout ribbon.

FIGURE 3.7   The reordered table rows

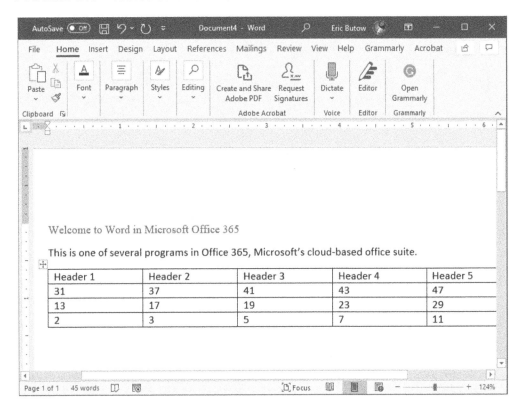

Use Your Mouse

To configure your cell width by clicking and dragging your mouse pointer, move the pointer on the right side of the column boundary you want to move until it becomes a resize pointer, which looks like a double-headed arrow, as shown in Figure 3.8.

Now drag the boundary until the column is the width you want and then release the mouse button.

If you want to get a precise measurement as you click and drag with your mouse, turn on the Word ruler (if it's not open already) by clicking the View menu option and then clicking the Ruler check box in the Show section in the ribbon.

FIGURE 3.8 Double-headed arrow icon

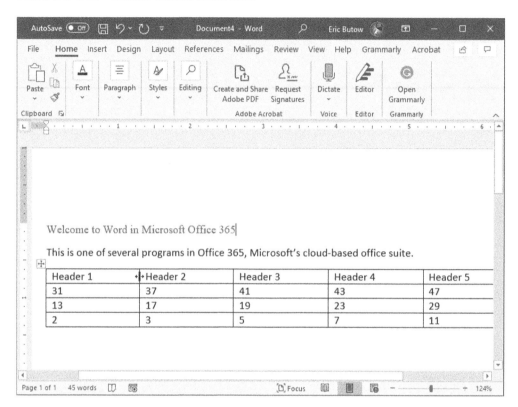

Once you see the ruler above your document (and just below the ribbon), click a cell in your table that you want to resize. The ruler shows trapezoid-shaped markers at the bottom edge of the ruler. These markers tell you where the cell begins and ends.

Move the cell border by clicking and dragging on the marker. When you hold down the Alt key as you click and drag, you see the exact width of the cell in inches, and the width changes as you move the marker to the left and right.

Set to a Specific Width

To change the width to a specific measurement, click a cell in the column that you want to resize. Click the Layout menu option to the right of the Table Design option.

The Cell Size section in the ribbon includes settings for the cell height and width in inches, and you can change the width by clicking in the Width box and typing the width in hundredths of an inch. Click the up or down arrow to the right of the box to increase or decrease, respectively, the width in increments by one-tenth of an inch.

Add or Change the Space Inside the Table

To add space inside your table, you can adjust cell margins or cell spacing. The difference? Cell margins are inside the table cell, and cell spacing is between cells. Here's how to add or change both cell margins and spacing:

1. Click a cell in the table.
2. Click the Layout menu option to the right of the Table Design option.
3. In the Layout ribbon, click the Cell Margins icon in the Alignment section.
4. The Table Options dialog box appears, as shown in Figure 3.9.

FIGURE 3.9 Table Options dialog box

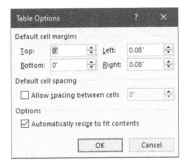

5. The Default Cell Margins area contains four boxes so that you can use to adjust the Top, Bottom, Left, and Right margins. Click the up or down arrow to the right of each box to increase or decrease, respectively, the margin by one-hundredth of an inch.
6. In the Default Cell Spacing area, click the Allow Spacing Between Cells check box, and then enter the measurement you want in the box. The default measurement is 0.01 inches.
7. Click OK.

 The settings that you choose are available only in the active table. Any new table that you create will use that table's default settings.

Merging and Splitting Cells

There may be times when you need to *merge* multiple cells into one larger one. You may also find that when you have a cell with a lot of text, it's easier to read when you split that cell into two or more cells. Word makes it easy to do both tasks.

Merge Cells

You can combine two or more table cells located in the same row or column into a single cell. For example, you can merge several cells horizontally to create a heading row that spans several columns at the top of your table. Here's how:

1. Select the cells that you want to merge.

2. Click the Layout menu option to the right of the Table Design option.

3. In the Layout ribbon, click the Merge Cells icon in the Merge section, as shown in Figure 3.10.

FIGURE 3.10   Merge Cells menu option

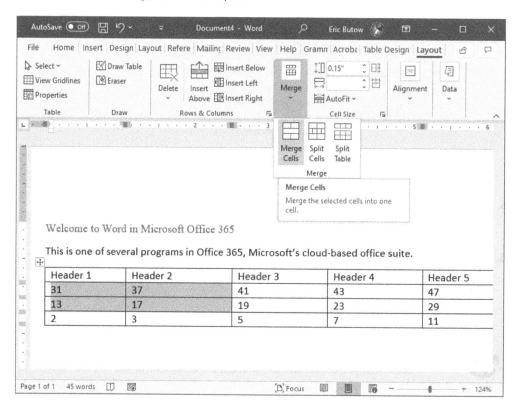

If there is text in several cells that you merged, you see several lines of text in the merged cell.

Split Cells

You can split one cell into multiple rows or columns by following these steps:

1. Click the cell, or select multiple cells, that you want to split in your table.

2. Click the Layout menu option to the right of the Table Design option.

3. In the Layout ribbon, click the Split Cells icon.

4. In the Split Cells dialog box, shown in Figure 3.11, type the number of columns and/or rows into which you want to split the cell.

FIGURE 3.11   Split Cells dialog box

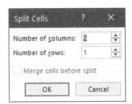

5. Click OK.

If you specify more rows and cells than there is text in the merged cell, then a lot of split cells won't have text in them.

Resizing Tables, Rows, and Columns

As you create a table, you may find that you want to resize one or more rows or columns. You may also need to resize the entire table.

Change Row Height

Configure the row height by moving your mouse pointer on the right side of the column boundary that you want to move until it becomes a resize pointer, which looks like a double-headed arrow with the arrows pointing up and down.

If you want to get a precise measurement as you click and drag with your mouse, click a cell in your table that you want to resize. The ruler on the left side of the Word window shows black boxes in the ruler that tell you where the cell begins and ends.

Move the cell border by clicking and dragging on the marker. When you hold down the Alt key as you click and drag, you see the exact width of the cell in inches, and the width changes as you move the marker up and down.

You can also set a specific height for all rows in a table. Here's how to do that:

1. Click a cell in the row that you want to change.

2. Click the Layout menu option to the right of the Table Design option.

3.   In the Cell Size section, click the Height box. Word highlights the existing cell height, as shown in Figure 3.12.

FIGURE 3.12   Table Row Height box

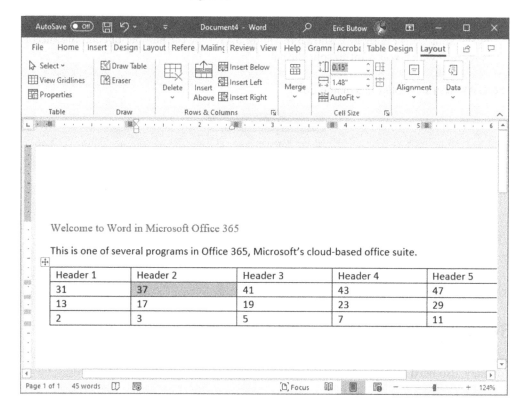

4.   Type the cell height in the box. You can specify the height in hundredths of an inch if you want.

5.   Press the Tab key.

The height for all rows in your table changes in your document. You can change the exact height by following the previous steps.

Click the up or down arrow to the right of the box to increase or decrease, respectively, the height in increments of one-tenth of an inch.

Resize a Column or Table Automatically with AutoFit

If you don't want to bother with resizing a column and/or table so that everything fits just right, let Word do it. Here's how:

1. Select a cell in the column you want to resize.
2. Click the Layout menu option to the right of the Table Design option.
3. In the Layout ribbon, click the AutoFit icon in the Cell Size section.
4. Click one of the following three sections, as shown in Figure 3.13:

FIGURE 3.13   AutoFit drop-down list

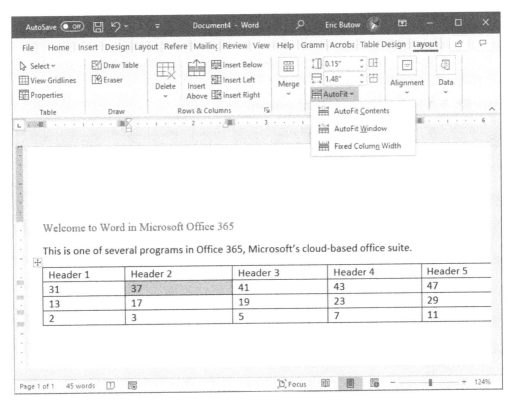

- Adjust the column width to the widest column by clicking AutoFit Contents.
- Adjust the table width to the full width of the page (minus the margins, of course) by clicking AutoFit Window.
- Keep Word from adjusting the column size as you type text by clicking Fixed Column Width.

Turn Off AutoFit

If you don't want AutoFit to set width in a column to fit the size of the text, here's how to turn it off:

1. Select a cell in the column that you want to resize.
2. Click the Layout menu option to the right of the Table Design option.
3. In the Layout ribbon, click the AutoFit icon in the Cell Size section.
4. Click Fixed Column Width in the drop-down menu.

Resize an Entire Table Manually

Word automatically creates a table so that it fits the entire width of the page. To resize, start by moving the cursor to the lower-right corner of the table. A white box appears at the lower right of the table.

Place the cursor on the box until it becomes a double-headed arrow (see Figure 3.14).

FIGURE 3.14   Double-headed arrow cursor

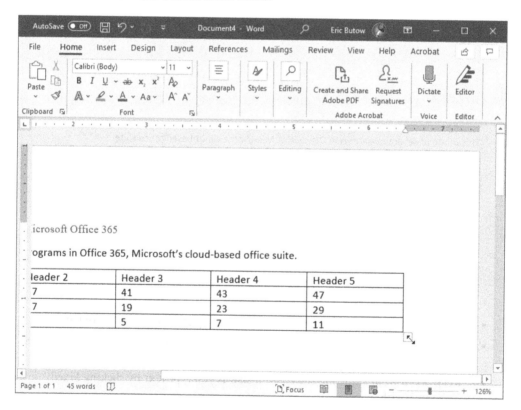

Now you can click and drag the box and watch the size of the table (and the contents in it) change. If you have text below the table, that text will move down as you stretch the table vertically.

Make Multiple Columns or Rows the Same Size

You may want to make more than one column or row the same size. For example, if you resize one column but you want that column and two columns to the left to be the same size, then you can make all three columns the same size in the space of the total width of those three columns.

Start by selecting the columns or rows that you want to make the same size. Figure 3.15 shows three selected columns. If you want to select noncontiguous rows or columns, hold down the Ctrl key as you select each row or column.

FIGURE 3.15   Selected columns

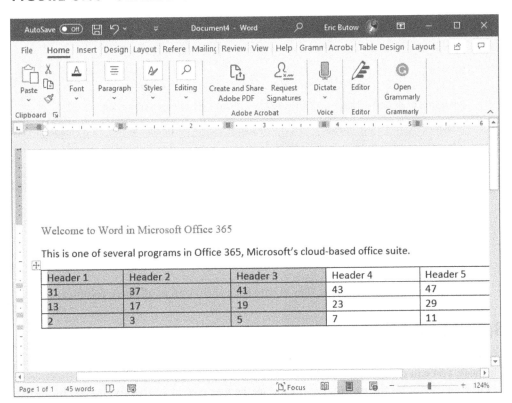

Next, click the Layout menu option to the right of the Table Design option. In the Layout ribbon in this example, click the Distribute Columns icon in the Cell Size section, as shown in Figure 3.16.

FIGURE 3.16   Distribute Columns icon

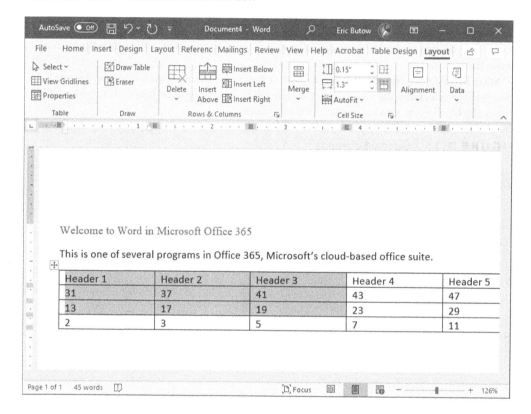

The columns change size so that they evenly span the width of all three columns.

Splitting Tables

Once you have a table in Word, you might decide to *split* that table into two or more tables. This way, you can create smaller tables or add text in between two tables.

Put your cursor on the row that you want as the first row of your second table. In the table shown in Figure 3.17, it's on the third row.

FIGURE 3.17   Cursor on third row

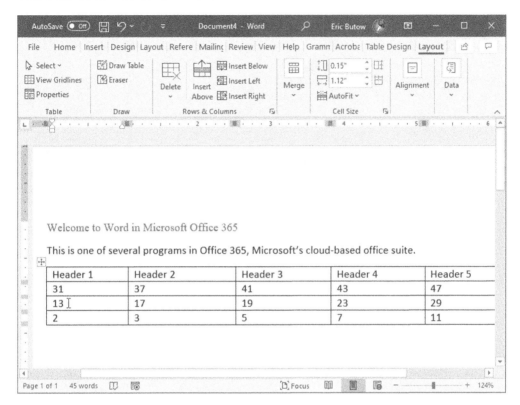

Now click the Layout menu option to the right of the Table Design option. In the Layout ribbon, click the Split Table icon in the Merge section (see Figure 3.18).

The row on which you placed the cursor is now the first row of the new table that appears below the other table. All rows underneath that first row appear underneath that first row.

FIGURE 3.18   Split Table icon

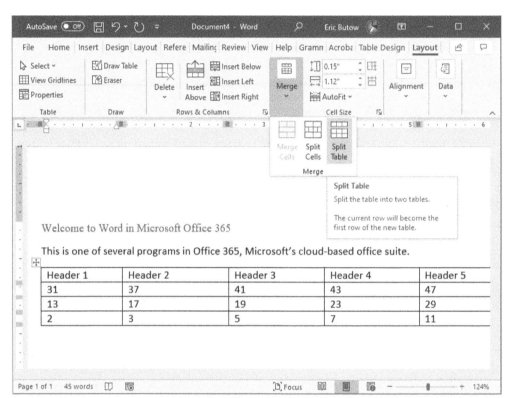

Configuring a Repeating Row Header

When you work with a table that is longer than the height of the page, cells that don't fit on that page appear on subsequent pages. You can set up the table so that the table header row or rows appear on each page automatically.

If your table has a header row, you can set up your table so that the header row appears at the top of each page, making your table easier to read. You can do this in one of two ways.

One way is to place the cursor somewhere in the header row of your table. Next, click the Layout menu option to the right of the Table Design option. In the Layout ribbon, click the Repeat Header Rows icon in the Data section (see Figure 3.19).

FIGURE 3.19   Repeat Header Rows icon

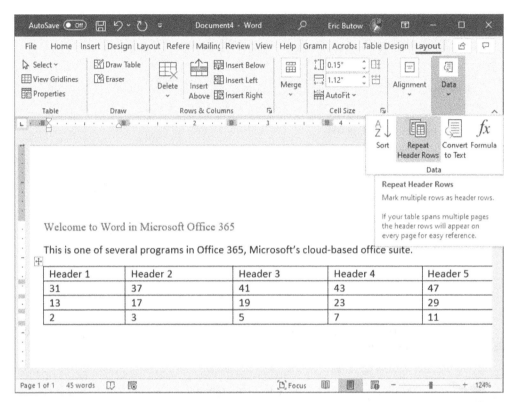

The other way is to right-click any cell in the header row of your table. In the context menu, click Table Properties. In the Table Properties dialog box, click the Row tab and then click the Repeat As Header Row At The Top Of Each Page check box, as shown in Figure 3.20.

FIGURE 3.20   Repeat At Header Row

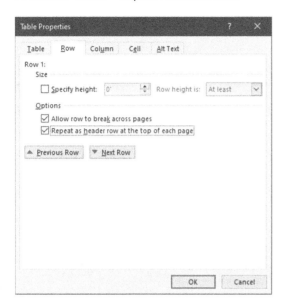

Click OK. No matter what method you choose, the header row will now appear on each page where your table is located.

As you work with headers, keep the following in mind:

- Repeated table headers are visible only in Print Layout view or when you print the document.

- If you change a table header on the first page, the header changes on all other pages as well. You can modify the table header only on the first page—the header rows on subsequent pages are locked.

- Although Word automatically repeats table headers on new pages that result from automatic page breaks, it does not repeat a header if you insert a manual page break in a table.

EXERCISE 3.2

Modifying a Table

1. Open a new document.

2. Add a new table with four columns and seven rows.

3. Populate the table with numbers.

4. Sort each column in ascending order.

5. Resize all the rows in the table.

6. Resize two of the columns in the table.

7. Split one of the merged cells.

8. Resize the columns with AutoFit.

9. Split the table into two tables.

Creating and Formatting Lists

Lists are an effective way of presenting information that readers can digest easily, as demonstrated in this book. Word includes many powerful tools to create lists easily and then format them so that they look the way you want them to appear.

Word provides two different types of lists. Each entry in a numbered list starts with a number, but you can also change the numbers to appear as letters. In a *bulleted list*, each entry starts with a special character, which is a black circle by default. You can change the special character to another special character, a symbol, or even a picture.

Structuring Paragraphs as Numbered and Bulleted Lists

An entry in a list, whether it's a few words or a few sentences, is treated as a paragraph. Word makes it easy to change a paragraph to a numbered list or a bulleted list.

Create a List

You don't need to do anything special to create a numbered or bulleted list.

Start a numbered list by typing 1, a period (.), a space, and then your text. When you finish typing your text, press Enter. Word formats the first entry in your list and places you on the next line in the numbered list with the number 2.

Create a bulleted list by typing an asterisk (*), a space, and then your text. When you're done typing, press Enter. The asterisk changes to a black circle and places you on the next line with another black circle to the left so that you can continue working on your list.

You can also start a numbered or bulleted list from within the Home ribbon. If you don't see it, click the Home menu option. In the ribbon, click the Bullets icon or the Numbered icon in the Paragraph section, as shown in Figure 3.21.

FIGURE 3.21   Bullets and Numbering icons

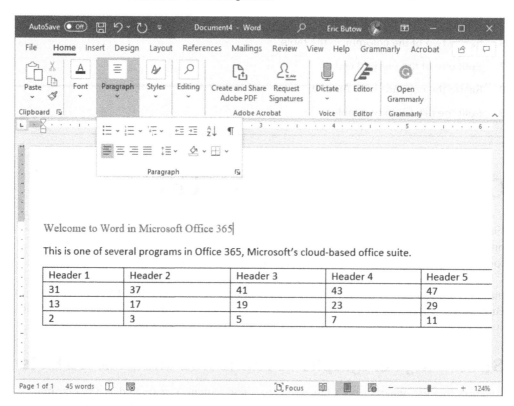

Now you see the number 1 or a bullet circle to the left of your cursor, and you can start typing your list. When you reach the last item in your list, press Enter twice to switch the bullets or numbering off.

Create a List from Existing Text

Using the Home ribbon, you can easily create a list from text you've already written. Start by selecting the text on the page, and then click the Bullets or Numbering icon in the Paragraph section. Each paragraph in the text appears as a separate number or bullet in the list.

You can continue the list by clicking the last item in the list and then pressing Enter. If the list is fine as is, click outside the selection.

Changing Bullet Characters and Number Formatting

You can change the format of the bullets or the numbers in a list by selecting from several different common *bullet characters* or *numbering* systems.

Bullets

Click one entry in your bulleted list. In the Home ribbon, click the down arrow to the right of the Bullets icon. The bullet style tiles appear in the drop-down list, as shown in Figure 3.22.

FIGURE 3.22   Bullet style tiles

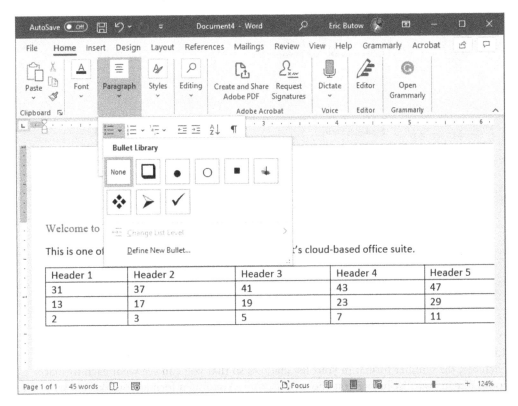

You can select a style in the Recently Used Bullets, Bullet Library, and Document Bullets sections. As you move the mouse pointer over each tile, all bullets in your list change so that you can see what the bullets look like in your list before you choose one. Once you find a bullet you like, click the tile. Or, if you don't want a bullet character in your list, click None.

Numbering

Click anywhere in your numbered list. In the Home ribbon, click the down arrow to the right of the Numbering icon. The number style tiles appear in the drop-down list (see Figure 3.23).

FIGURE 3.23   Number style tiles

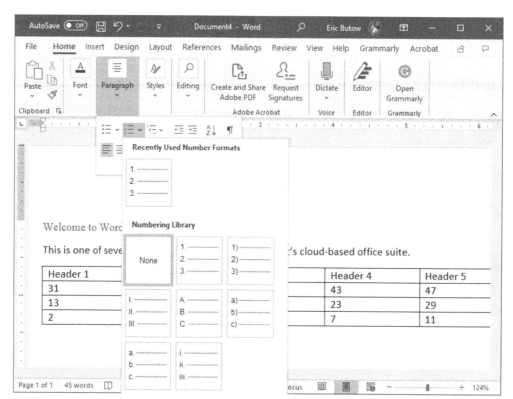

You can select a numbering style in the Recently Used Number Formats, Numbering Library, and Document Number Formats sections. As you move the mouse pointer over each tile, the number format in your list changes so that you can see what each format looks like in your list before you choose one. Once you find a format you like, click the tile. If you don't want numbers in your list, click None.

Defining Custom Bullet Characters and Number Formatting

The common bullet characters or number formatting may not be to your liking. No worries; Word has a number (ahem) of other formats from which you may choose.

Bullets

You may need custom bullet characters or symbols to represent what you do better. For example, if your company uses a triangle in its logo, you can change your bullet characters to triangle symbols.

Here's how to create a new bulleted list with a symbol:

1. Place the cursor where you want to add the bulleted list in your document.

2. Click the Home menu option if you're not there already.

3. In the Home ribbon, click the down arrow to the right of the Bullets icon in the Paragraph section.

4. Click Define New Bullet in the drop-down menu.

5. In the Define New Bullet dialog box, as shown in Figure 3.24, click Symbol.

FIGURE 3.24   Define New Bullet dialog box

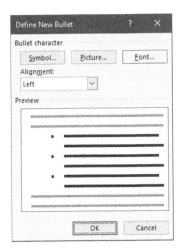

6. In the Symbol dialog box, scan the list of symbols and then click the symbol you want to use.

7. Click OK.

8. In the Define New Bullet dialog box, click OK.

The first bulleted list entry with your new symbol appears on the screen. The symbol also appears in the Recently Used Bullets and Bullets Library sections in the Bullets drop-down menu.

Numbering

Here's how to access all the numbering formats in the Define New Number format dialog box:

1. Place the cursor where you want to add the numbered list in your document.

2. Click the Home menu option if you're not there already.

3. In the Home ribbon, click the down arrow to the right of the Numbering icon in the Paragraph section.

4. Click Define New Number Format in the drop-down menu.

5. In the Define New Number Format dialog box, as shown in Figure 3.25, change the style by clicking the down arrow next to the Number Style box.

FIGURE 3.25 Define New Number Format dialog box

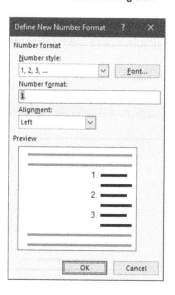

6. Select from one of the numbered styles, text styles, or other chronological format such as 1st, 2nd, and 3rd.

7. Click the Font button to change the numbering font, color, and other styles.

8. Click OK to close the Font dialog box.

9. If desired, add other text after the number, such as parenthetical text, in the Number Format text box.

10. Change the number alignment by clicking the Alignment box and then selecting Left, Centered, or Right in the drop-down list. You can see the results of the alignment change in the Preview box.

11. Click OK.

The numbered list in your document now displays its new numbering format. The new format also appears as an icon in the Recently Used Number Formats and Numbering Library sections in the Numbering drop-down menu.

Increasing and Decreasing List Levels

You can change list levels for both bulleted and numbered lists by indenting an entry in your list. As you change list levels, the bullet or number format changes to match the built-in level styles for each format.

View the format of each list level and apply a new list level by clicking the list entry to which you want to apply the new level.

Next, click the Home menu option if you haven't already. Depending on the type of list, click the down arrow to the right of the Bullets or Numbering icon in the Home ribbon.

In the drop-down menu, move the mouse pointer over Change List Level. The submenu appears, as shown in Figure 3.26.

FIGURE 3.26   Change List Level menu

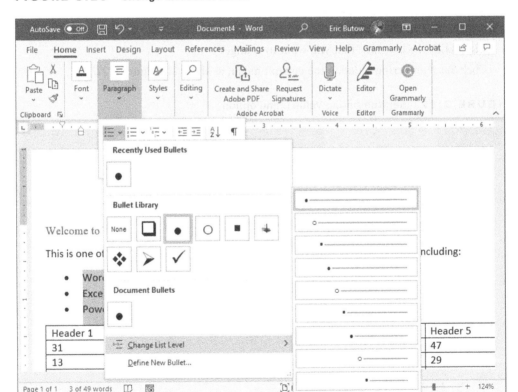

The list shows nine levels, starting with the first level at the top. Each level shows you the bullet character and indent spacing used for that level. Apply a level to your item by clicking the level in the list. If you're changing a list entry with a lower level, click a higher level in the list. Your entry appears with the applied list level. All other entries in the list are unaffected.

When you want to change the list level for multiple entries, or for the entire list, select the entries in the list and then follow the steps in this section.

> If you have a custom bullet style, you will see the same bullet no matter the list level.

Restarting and Continuing List Numbering

As you work with numbered lists, you may find that Word can get confused about starting a new list or continuing a previous one. It may be tempting to change numbers in a list manually, but that will only cause more confusion (and headaches) when you work with a list further along in your document.

So, here's how to change numbering values in Word the right way:

1. Right-click the list entry that you want to change.

2. Click Set Numbering Value in the context menu, as shown in Figure 3.27.

FIGURE 3.27 Set Numbering Value menu option

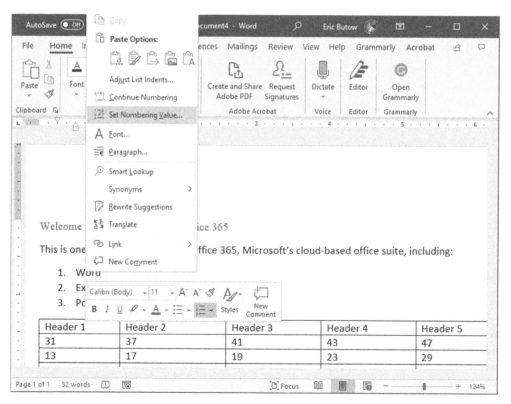

3.   In the Set Numbering Value dialog box (see Figure 3.28), type the new value in the Set Value To text box.

FIGURE 3.28   Set Numbering Value dialog box

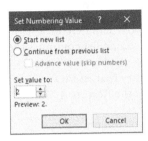

The list entry shows the new number you gave it. Entries that follow your newly renumbered one will continue from that new number in sequential order.

Changing number values is especially useful when you have two lists (or more) separated by other text with different formats. If you want one list to continue the numbering of the previous list, all you have to do is right-click the first entry in the numbered list that you want to renumber, and then click Continue Numbering in the context menu, as shown in Figure 3.29.

FIGURE 3.29   Continue Numbering option

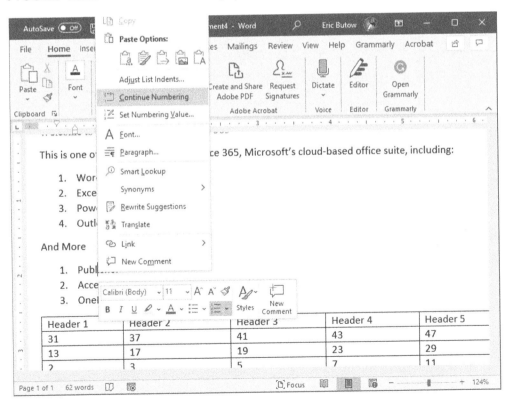

Your list has the number that follows the last number in the previous number list. Word also renumbers subsequent entries in the list so that they continue in sequential order.

Setting Starting Number Values

If you need to restart one entry in your numbered list with the numbered one, or if you broke up one list into two and the second list continues the numbering from the previous list, you can reset the starting value number in a list entry.

Start by right-clicking the list entry that you want to change to 1. In the context menu that appears (see Figure 3.30), click the Restart At 1 menu option.

FIGURE 3.30   Restart At 1 menu option

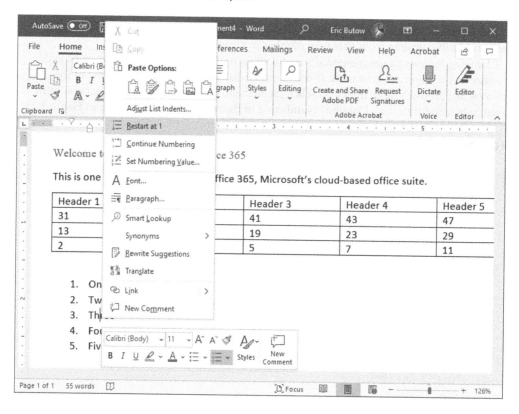

The entry appears with the number 1, and all list entries under that new entry number 1 continue with the numbers 2, 3, and so on.

EXERCISE 3.3

Formatting Your List

1. Open a blank document.

2. Create one bulleted list with four items.

3. Press Enter three times, and then create one numbered list with four items.

4. Click anywhere in the bulleted list and change the bullet style to a check mark.

5. Click anywhere in the bulleted list and change the number format to A, B, C.

6. Click the second item in the bulleted list and then change the list level to Level 2.

7. Click the last item in the numbered list and then change the list level to Level 3.

8. Create a new numbered list after the numbered list with at least one blank line between the two numbered lists.

9. Click the first entry in the second numbered list and continue the line numbering from the previous list.

Summary

This chapter started by showing you how to create a table from selected text. Then you saw how to reverse the process and convert a table into text. You also learned how to use Word table tools to create a table from scratch.

After you created a table, you learned how to modify tables. I discussed how to sort data in a table. Next, you learned how to modify the look and feel of your tables, including changing the cell margins; spacing, merging, and splitting cells; and resizing parts of your table. I discussed when you would need to split a table in two and how to do that. And you learned how to create a repeating row header in case your table is longer than one page and you want the header to appear at the top of each page.

Next I discussed how to create and format text lists, and I started with converting paragraphs into numbered and bulleted lists. You learned how to change and define bullet characters and format numbered lists. After that, I discussed how to increase and decrease list levels in a list.

Finally, you learned several important things about managing numbered lists, including how to restart and continue list numbering properly as well as how to set starting number values.

Key Terms

bullet characters

bulleted list

cells

columns

header row

list levels

merge

number formatting

numbering

Rows

Sorting

Split

Tables

Exam Essentials

Understand how to convert text to tables, and vice versa. Know how to use the Table option in the Insert menu to convert text to tables, or to switch tables back to text.

You must understand structuring paragraphs as numbered and bulleted lists; changing bullet characters and number formatting; defining custom bullet characters and number formatting; increasing and decreasing list levels; restarting and continuing list numbering; and setting starting number values.

Know how to specify rows and columns. Understand how to add a specific number of rows and columns in a table.

Understand how to modify a table. Know how to sort data in a table; change margins and spacing in a cell; merge and split cells and tables; and resize elements of a table, including rows, columns, and the entire table. You also need to know how to configure a repeating row header.

Know how to create numbered and bulleted lists. Understand the difference between bulleted lists and numbered lists, and how to create each one.

Understand how to format numbered and bulleted lists. Know how to use formatting tools to change the look and feel of bulleted lists and numbered lists.

Be able to change list levels. Know how to increase and decrease the levels in a bulleted list and a numbered list.

Know how to manage list numbering. Know how to change the numbering in a list to ensure each number in the list continues sequentially. You need to understand how to set values in a new numbered list so that it does not continue numbering from the previous list.

Review Questions

1. How do you create a table with built-in styles?
   A. Click the Table icon in the Insert ribbon.
   B. Open the Styles panel.
   C. Click the Insert ribbon, click Table, and then move the mouse pointer over Quick Tables in the drop-down menu.
   D. Click the Columns icon in the Layout menu.

2. How do you create a table with three columns and seven rows?
   A. Click the Table option in the Insert ribbon to open a dialog box.
   B. Click the Table option in the Insert ribbon and move the mouse pointer over the grid.
   C. Click the Table option and then click Draw Table.
   D. Click the Table option in the Insert ribbon and then click Insert Table.

3. In what order is a sort from the letters Z to A?
   A. Ascending
   B. Alphabetical
   C. Descending
   D. Backward

4. How do you see the exact measurement of a table row or column when you resize it using the mouse?
   A. Holding down the Alt key as you drag
   B. Holding down the Ctrl key as you drag
   C. Looking at the ruler above the document
   D. Holding down Ctrl+Shift as you drag

5. How do you resize a table or columns to fit the size of your content?
   A. Quick Tables
   B. Orientation
   C. Size
   D. AutoFit

6. What menu options appear when you click inside a table?
   A. Table Design and Layout
   B. Shape Layout

    C. Format and Table Design

    D. Chart Design

7. What types of bullets can you add to a list?

    A. Symbols and fonts

    B. Symbols, fonts, and pictures

    C. Special characters

    D. Asterisks

8. What search parameter types can you use for sorting table contents?

    A. Text and numbers

    B. Special characters

    C. Text, numbers, and dates

    D. Text and symbols

9. How do you create a bulleted list as you type text?

    A. Press the period (.) key.

    B. Press the plus (+) key.

    C. Press the asterisk (*) key.

    D. Press the caret (^) key.

10. Why shouldn't you change the numbers in a list manually?

    A. Because Word will stop running

    B. Because Word will convert the numbered list to text

    C. Because your document will close without saving

    D. Because Word will lose track of what you've done and get confused

Chapter

4

Building References

MICROSOFT EXAM OBJECTIVES COVERED IN THIS CHAPTER:

✓ **Create and manage references**

  ✓ **Create and manage reference elements**

    ▪ Insert footnotes and endnotes

    ▪ Modify footnote and endnote properties

    ▪ Create and modify bibliography citation sources

    ▪ Insert citations for bibliographies

  ✓ **Create and manage reference tables**

    ▪ Insert tables of contents

    ▪ Customize tables of contents

    ▪ Insert bibliographies

When you first learned about writing *references* in school, you may have realized that it would help you later in your studies when you wrote a lot of papers. Now that you're into your professional career, you may be surprised by how much you need to find references for your documents and credit their source properly so that you don't get into trouble with your legal department (and your boss).

Word includes all of the tools that you need to add and manage reference elements. In this chapter, I will talk about adding those elements, including footnotes, endnotes, citations, and bibliographies. You also don't have to worry about formatting your references correctly, because Word comes with styles for 12 different writing style manuals.

I also discuss adding a *table of contents (TOC)* to a document so that readers can jump to different locations in your document easily.

Creating and Managing Referencing Elements

Three types of reference elements that you can add into a Word document are as follows:

Footnotes: Notes of references, explanations, or comments placed at the bottom of a page.

Endnotes: Like footnotes, with the key difference being that all of the endnotes are placed at the end of the document.

Citations: References to entries in a bibliography. Later in this chapter, you'll learn more about what a bibliography is and how to add one.

These references not only help give your readers complete information, but also place supplemental information out of the way so that readers can refer to it at their leisure.

Inserting Footnotes and Endnotes

Word makes it easy to add one or more footnotes at the bottom of the page where you insert the footnotes.

Add Footnote

Here's how to add a footnote on a page:

1. Place the cursor where you want to add the footnote.
2. Click the References menu option.
3. In the ribbon, click Insert Footnote in the Footnotes section (see Figure 4.1).

FIGURE 4.1   Insert Footnote option

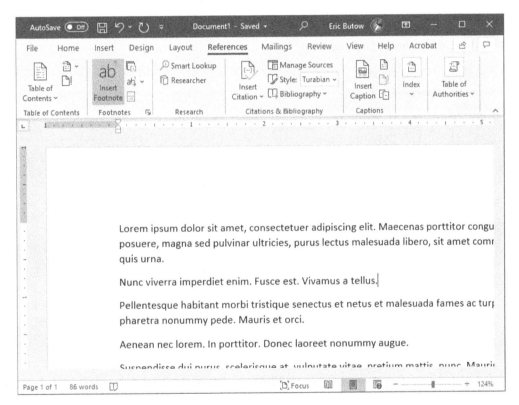

The footnote number appears at the insertion point in superscript format. The footnote itself appears in the page footer with a line above it to set it off from the rest of the text. The cursor is blinking within the footnote so that you can enter the footnote text.

When you're done, click the cursor anywhere else in the document to continue editing your document. If you need to edit the footnote again, all you need to do is place the cursor within the footnote text.

As you add and edit text, the footnote stays on the page until the text that includes the footnotes moves to a different page. The footnote moves with it.

Place Endnote

Adding endnotes is as easy as adding footnotes. Just follow these steps:

1. Place the cursor where you want to add the endnote.

2. Click the References menu option.

3. In the ribbon, click the Insert Endnote icon in the Footnotes section, as shown in Figure 4.2.

FIGURE 4.2   Insert Endnote icon

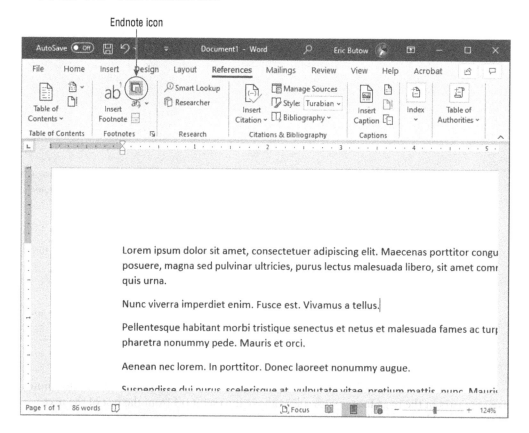

Word places your cursor within the endnote at the end of the document so that you can type it.

Endnotes are within the text, not in the footer. Word inserts a line above it to set it off from the rest of the text. The cursor is blinking within the end so that you can type it.

When you finish typing it, you must go back to the page where you inserted the endnote. The endnote number is in superscript style, just as in a footnote.

Now you can click the cursor anywhere else in the document to finish editing.

How do you delete a footnote or endnote? Select the superscript number in the text that's connected to the footnote or endnote, and then press Delete on your keyboard. The footnote or endnote disappears.

Modifying Footnote and Endnote Properties

There is no style for footnotes and endnotes. Word simply uses its default 10-point Calibri font.

If you want to change the font, double-click anywhere in the footnote text. In the menu that appears above the text, as shown in Figure 4.3, select the font, size, and more. When you change the size, the superscript number size changes, too.

FIGURE 4.3   Pop-up menu for changing the footnote style

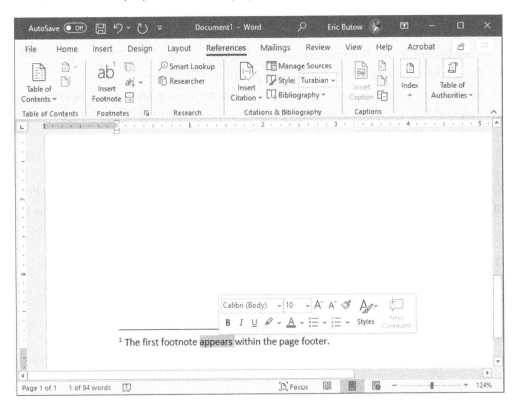

Creating and Modifying Bibliography Citation Sources

A *bibliography* is what the Merriam-Webster online dictionary defines as "the history, identification, or description of writings or publications." Those writings and publications can be books, websites, films, and other types of media.

You can cite these works by adding them as sources to your document, and Word supports 16 different specific source types. Once you create a source, Word makes it easy for you to insert a citation in one or several locations in your document.

Create a Source

Before you cite a source, you must add it to your Word document. Here's how:

1. Place the cursor where you want to add the citation in the document.
2. Click the References menu option.
3. In the Citations & Bibliography section in the ribbon, click the down arrow to the right of Turabian to change the style guide.
4. Select the style to use for your citation in the drop-down list, as shown in Figure 4.4.

   Turabian is the default because it's widely used for academic papers, but Chicago (for Chicago Manual of Style) is the guide used commonly for book publishing and so it's comprehensive. You may need to check with your boss to find out what style your company uses, if any.

5. Click Insert Citation in the Citations & Bibliography section.
6. Click Add New Source in the drop-down menu.
7. In the Create Source dialog box, shown in Figure 4.5, click Book in the Type Of Source drop-down box to view all the types of sources that you can add in the list.
8. Click a source in the list.

   The information that you can add in the fields depends on the style type and what type of source you add. For this example, I used the default, Book.

9. Type the author name by using the suggested format near the bottom of the dialog box.
10. After you add all the information, you can view the fields to add to the bibliography by clicking the Show All Bibliography Fields check box. A book reference has many fields, including the state and country, edition number, and number of pages in the book.
11. Word fills in the tag name with the first few characters of the author name, but you can change this by clicking the Tag Name box and typing the new name.
12. When you finish, click OK.

The citation appears in parentheses at the insertion point. You'll learn how to add a citation that references your source later in this chapter.

FIGURE 4.4   Writing styles list

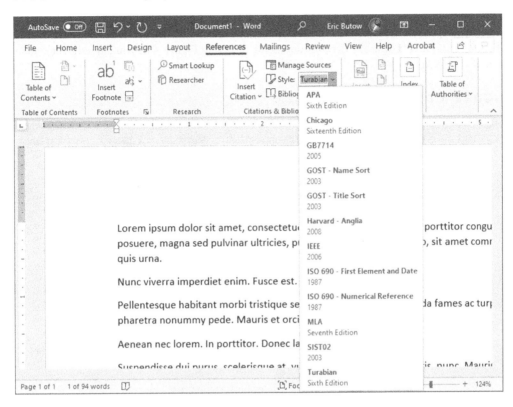

FIGURE 4.5   Create Source dialog box

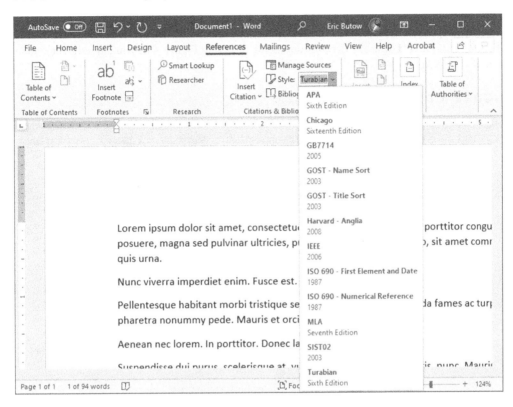

Modify a Source

If you ever need to change source information, such as to change spelling or add more information, click anywhere within the citation and then click the down arrow to the right of the citation text. Using the drop-down menu shown in Figure 4.6, you can edit the citation or the source.

FIGURE 4.6 Citation drop-down menu

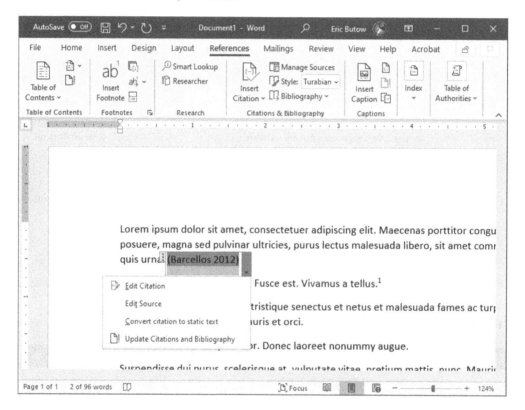

Edit Citation

Click Edit Citation for a quick edit. In the Edit Citation dialog box, add the page that you're referencing by typing it in the Pages box.

If you want to hide the author, year, and/or title of the work you're referencing, click the appropriate check box.

When you're done, click OK. The document reflects the changes that you made.

Edit Source

Click Edit Source in the menu. The Edit Source dialog box appears so that you can edit and add citation information as you learned to do when you created a citation. When you're done, click OK. The document reflects the changes you made.

Inserting Citations for Bibliographies

When you click Insert Citation in the ribbon, the citation appears in the drop-down list (see Figure 4.7) so that you can easily add it to other locations in your document.

FIGURE 4.7   Added citation in drop-down list

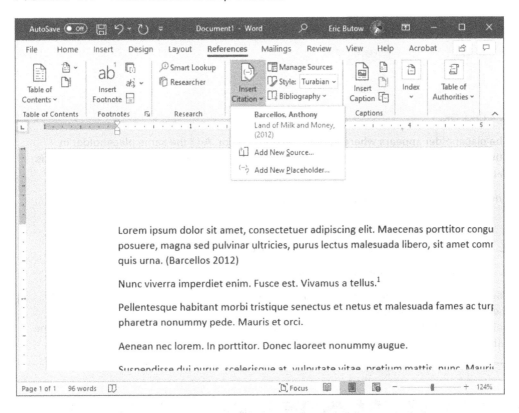

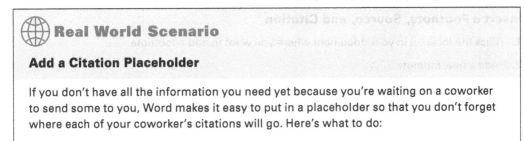

Add a Citation Placeholder

If you don't have all the information you need yet because you're waiting on a coworker to send some to you, Word makes it easy to put in a placeholder so that you don't forget where each of your coworker's citations will go. Here's what to do:

1. Place your cursor where you want to add the placeholder on the page.

2. Click the References menu option.

3. In the References ribbon, click the Insert Citation icon.

4. In the drop-down menu, click Add New Placeholder.

5. In the Placeholder Name dialog box, press Backspace on your keyboard to delete the default name in the name box and then type the new one.

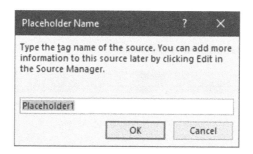

6. Click OK.

The placeholder appears where you placed your cursor. Add the same placeholder in other location(s) in your text by adding it as you would a citation; the placeholder name is in the Insert Citation drop-down list.

When you have the source information, here's what to do next:

1. Click the placeholder name.

2. Click the down arrow to the right of the placeholder name.

3. In the drop-down menu, click Edit Source.

You can add the new source information as you would any other source. After you add the new source, the information appears within the placeholder instead of the place-holder name. Word also updates any other citations that have the same placeholder name with the new citation.

EXERCISE 4.1

Insert a Footnote, Source, and Citation

1. Click the location in your document where you want to add a footnote.

2. Add a new footnote.

3. Click another location on the same page in your document where you want to add the second footnote.

4. Add the second footnote.

5. Change the font in both footnotes to Times New Roman.

6. Create a source for one of your favorite books that includes the author, title, and publication year.

7. Place your cursor on another page in your document where you want to add a citation to a source.

8. Insert the citation.

9. Add the publication year to the citation.

Working with Referencing Tables

You can add two different types of reference sources in your document, which Microsoft calls reference tables:

A *table of contents (TOC)*: This gives your readers an easy way to find information in your document. Word scans your TOC for text with a Heading style, and then adds it into the correct location within your TOC.

A *bibliography*: This usually appears as an appendix at the end of a document so that people who want to see the works you referenced can get all the information concisely.

Word makes it easy to add a TOC and a bibliography from the References menu ribbon.

Inserting Tables of Contents

A TOC usually appears on the first page(s) of a document. So, place the cursor at the beginning of your document, and then follow these steps to add a TOC:

1. Click the References menu option.

2. In the Table of Contents section in the ribbon, click Table Of Contents.

3. In the drop-down menu, shown in Figure 4.8, click one of the two built-in automatic table styles that automatically creates a TOC based on styles in your document. Alternatively, you can click Manual Table to add a TOC that you can edit independently of the content. For this example, I used Automatic Table 1.

Level 1 is flush left, Level 2 is indented once, Level 3 is indented twice, and so on, up to Level 9. The automatic table styles add levels based on the Heading style number—that is, Heading 1 through Heading 9.

Contents appear with the Automatic Table 1 style format at the insertion point in the document.

FIGURE 4.8   TOC styles menu

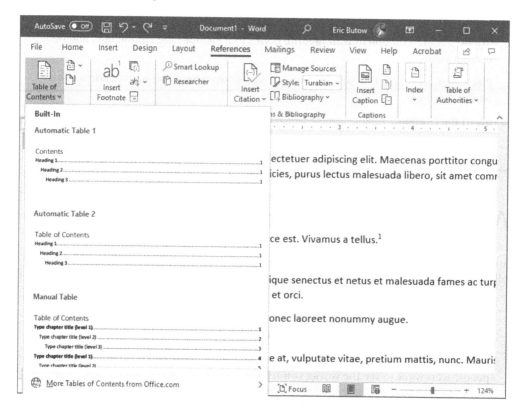

 In the Table Of Contents drop-down list, click More Tables Of Contents From Office.com to check whether Microsoft has added any new styles lately.

Customizing Tables of Contents

When you add a TOC, it reflects the contents of the document. Word doesn't update the TOC automatically after you make changes elsewhere in your document. You can customize your TOC in one of two ways.

Start by clicking anywhere in the TOC. A box appears around your TOC and two buttons appear at the top of the box. A button with a page icon is on the left and a button that says Update Table is on the right.

Change Style or Remove TOC

When you click the down arrow to the right of the page icon, the Built-In drop-down menu appears (see Figure 4.9).

In the Built-In drop-down menu, select a new built-in style or remove the TOC.

FIGURE 4.9   TOC styles in the Built-In menu

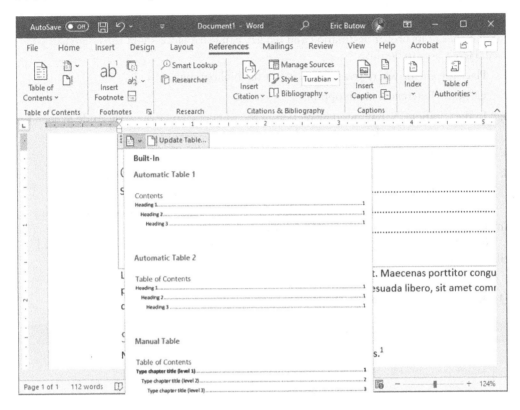

In the drop-down menu, you can select a new built-in style, and after you click the style tile, your TOC reflects the new style.

When you select Remove Table Of Contents from the menu, the TOC disappears.

Update Table

After you click Update Table, the Update Table Of Contents dialog box allows you to choose to update only the page numbers by default. Do this if headings are still at the same level but on different pages. When you click OK in the dialog box, Word updates the page numbers in the TOC.

Click the Update Entire Table button if you have new heading text, if some heading text has new levels, and/or you deleted some heading text. After you click OK, Word updates the entire TOC, including page numbers.

Change the Styles in the TOC

Word adds TOC styles for each level automatically when you add the TOC. You can access these styles by pressing Alt+Ctrl+Shift+S to open the Styles list. The styles are listed TOC 1 through TOC 9, where the number is the TOC level. Even if you delete the TOC, the styles remain in case you add another TOC in your document.

Adding Bibliographies

You know how to add a citation, but now you need to add the bibliography so that the citation goes to its proper destination and readers can learn more about the references you used. Here's how to do this:

1. Place the cursor where you want to insert the bibliography.

2. Click the References menu option.

3. In the Citations & Bibliography section in the ribbon, change the style guide in the same way you did when you created a citation.

4. Click Bibliography.

5. Select the built-in bibliography style that you want from the drop-down menu, as shown in Figure 4.10.

Click Insert Bibliography at the bottom of the menu to add your bibliography without any heading text that is included in the built-in styles.

No matter what kind of bibliography you insert, Word allows you to edit the inserted bibliography as you see fit.

FIGURE 4.10 Bibliography styles

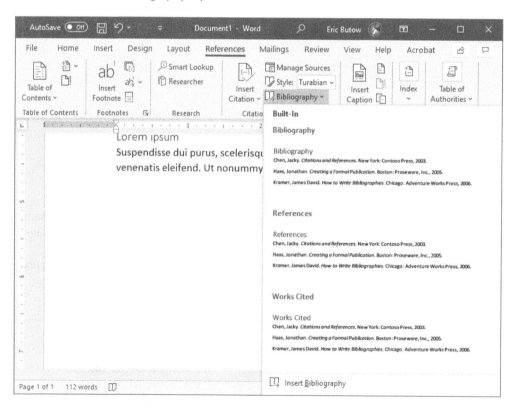

EXERCISE 4.2

Adding a TOC and Bibliography

1. Place your cursor at the beginning of your document.

2. Add a TOC with your preferred style.

3. Change the TOC 1 style to Times New Roman bold.

4. Add some more text to your document that includes at least one line with a heading style.

5. Update the TOC.

6. Go to the last page of your document and place the cursor at the end of the page.

7. Add a bibliography with the Chicago writing style and the Bibliography format.

Summary

This chapter started with a discussion about adding and modifying footnotes and endnotes. I followed up by discussing how to add and change citation sources and then insert them for your bibliography of references.

Next, I discussed how to add two types of reference tables. The table of contents (TOC) usually appears at the beginning of the document and contains a list of text with heading styles so that readers can go to a section in your document quickly.

I concluded by talking about adding a bibliography of your sources with the correct style prescribed by a writing style guide that you can select from the References menu ribbon.

Key Terms

bibliography

citations

endnotes

footnotes

references

table of contents (TOC)

Exam Essentials

Understand how to add footnotes and endnotes.   Footnotes, which appear at the bottom of the page, are great ways to give readers more information about text in your document without that additional information getting in the way. If you have too many footnotes in a page or in a document, consider putting those notes at the end of your chapter by using endnotes. Word gives you the tools you need to add and modify both footnotes and endnotes.

Know how to create and modify bibliography sources.   Before you create a bibliography, you need to understand how to use Word tools to create sources you'll cite throughout your document. Then you need to know how to modify the source format to give readers the information you think they should see in each citation.

Understand how to add a citation for a bibliography.   Know how to select from an existing citation easily so that you can add the same citation in several different locations in your document.

Be able to add and modify a table of contents.   Understand how to add and customize a table of contents (TOC) to make it easy for readers to find the sections of text that they want to read.

Understand how to create a bibliography.   Know how to create a bibliography at the end of your document with the correct writing style format so that you properly document references that you used to support the text in your document.

Review Questions

1. What menu option do you click to add a footnote or endnote?

   A. Insert

   B. Design

   C. References

   D. Home

2. How do you change the style of a footnote or endnote?

   A. Select a style in the Home ribbon.

   B. Select the footnote text, and then change the properties in the pop-up menu.

   C. Click the Design layout option to change the properties in the ribbon.

   D. Click the layout option to change the indents, spacing, and other styles.

3. Why do you set a writing style before creating a citation?

   A. Because you need to know what a writing style is

   B. Because you can't add a citation otherwise

   C. Because the style affects the format of the citation

   D. You don't have to because the default Turabian style is good enough.

4. How do you add a page number to an existing citation?

   A. Click the citation, click the down arrow to the right of the citation, and then click Edit Citation.

   B. Type the number after the author name within the parentheses.

   C. Click Manage Sources in the References ribbon.

   D. Click the Insert menu option, and then click Page Number in the Insert ribbon.

5. How do you add a placeholder for a citation that you plan to add later?

   A. Click the Insert menu option, and then click Bookmark in the ribbon.

   B. Click the References menu option, and then click Manage Sources in the ribbon.

   C. In the References ribbon, click Mark Citation.

   D. In the References ribbon, click Insert Citation and then click Add New Placeholder.

6. What is a TOC level?

   A. A means of determining how text with certain heading styles should appear in your TOC

   B. How many times each entry in the TOC is indented

   C. How Word keeps track of all the different TOC elements

   D. How Word determines the TOC layouts from which you can choose

7. How do you change a style in a TOC?

   A. Click the References menu option, and then click Update Table in the ribbon.

   B. Change the TOC in the Styles pane.

   C. Click the TOC in the document.

   D. Click the Design menu option, and then change the theme in the ribbon.

8. Why do you need to update a TOC?

   A. You don't, because Word updates it automatically as you type.

   B. Because it's a good idea to keep your TOC up to date

   C. Because Word doesn't update the TOC automatically with new page numbers and headers

   D. You don't, because Word automatically updates the TOC when you save the document.

9. Why do you need to change the writing style before you add a bibliography?

   A. You don't, because the default Turabian style is the only one used for bibliographies.

   B. Because no writing style is applied before you write a bibliography

   C. Because Word formats any bibliography you add with the correct writing style formats

   D. You don't, because the default bibliography options already contain the correct writing style.

10. What are the three types of bibliography templates from which you can choose?

    A. Turabian, Chicago, APA

    B. APA, MLA, Chicago

    C. Last Name, Date, Title of Work

    D. Bibliography, References, Works Cited

Chapter

5

Adding and Formatting Graphic Elements

MICROSOFT EXAM OBJECTIVES COVERED IN THIS CHAPTER:

✓ **Insert and format graphic elements**

- Insert illustrations and text boxes
    - Insert shapes
    - Insert pictures
    - Insert 3D models
    - Insert SmartArt graphics
    - Insert screenshots and screen clippings
    - Insert text boxes
- Format illustrations and text boxes
    - Apply artistic effects
    - Add picture effects and picture styles
    - Remove picture backgrounds
    - Format graphic elements
    - Format SmartArt graphics
    - Format 3D models
- Add text to graphic elements
    - Add and modify text in text boxes
    - Add and modify text in shapes
    - Add and modify SmartArt graphic content
- Modify graphic elements
    - Position objects
    - Wrap text around objects
    - Add alternative text to objects for accessibility

Word has taken plenty of features from desktop publishing software, and today you can use Word not only to type text, but to add graphical elements to make a document more engaging for your readers as well.

This chapter starts by showing you how to add shapes using the built-in Word shape editor. Word also allows you to insert pictures and 3D models, either from your own computer or from stock libraries installed with Word. What's more, you can add screenshots on your computer and place screen clippings, which are a portion of your screen, into your document.

Word also contains its own custom diagrams, called SmartArt, so that you can add things like organizational charts and process charts easily.

If you need to add text in an area outside the main area of text, such as in a sidebar, you can add text boxes and modify how the text appears within the text box.

I also talk about formatting your graphics and text boxes, adding text to graphic elements, and positioning those images so that they look good on the page. Finally, you learn how to add alternative, or Alt, text to illustrations and photos so that people who cannot see them can read a description.

Inserting Illustrations and Text Boxes

Word makes it easy to choose and insert shapes, pictures, 3D models, SmartArt graphics, screenshots, screen clippings, and even text boxes all from one location: the Insert menu ribbon. (If the Word window isn't very wide, you may need to click Illustrations in the Ribbon to view a drop-down ribbon that contains many of the icons discussed in this section.)

Adding Shapes

Word contains many built-in *shapes* that you can add to your document, from lines to callouts like the speech balloons you find in graphic novels and comic strips. When you add a shape, you place the item on the page and then size the shape to your needs.

Add a shape by following these steps:

1. Click the Insert menu option.
2. In the Insert ribbon, click Shapes in the Illustrations section.
3. Click a shape icon in the drop-down list (see Figure 5.1). The mouse pointer changes from an arrow to a cross.

FIGURE 5.1   The shapes drop-down list

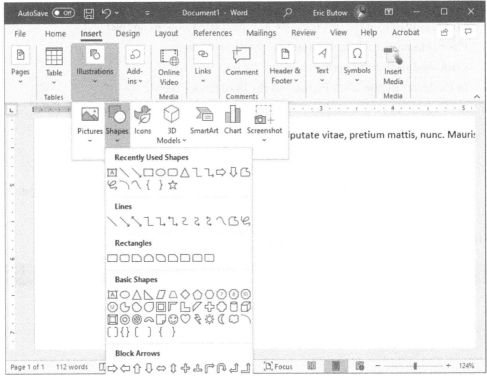

4. Move the pointer to the location in your document where you want to add the shape.

5. Hold down the mouse button, and then drag the shape to the size you want.

6. When you're done, release the mouse button. The shape appears in front of the text in the document.

You'll learn how to wrap text around your image later in this chapter.

 You can also create a separate area for drawing within your document by clicking New Drawing Canvas at the bottom of the drop-down list. A new drawing area appears in the canvas box where your cursor is located so that you can select shapes in the Shape Format ribbon and then draw those shapes within the box.

Including Pictures

You can add *pictures* stored on your computer, stock images that were installed with Word, or pictures available on the Office.com website. Here's how to do this:

1. Place your cursor where you want to insert the image.
2. Click the Insert menu option.
3. In the Insert ribbon, click Pictures in the Illustrations section.
4. In the drop-down menu, shown in Figure 5.2, click one of the following options:

   This Device: Click this to browse for and select a photo from your computer.

   Stock Images: Click this to view and open a stock image on your computer.

   Online Pictures: Click this to view and open an image from Office.com.

   For this example, I'll open a stock image. By default, the Stock Images tab is open in the photos dialog box.

FIGURE 5.2   Pictures drop-down menu

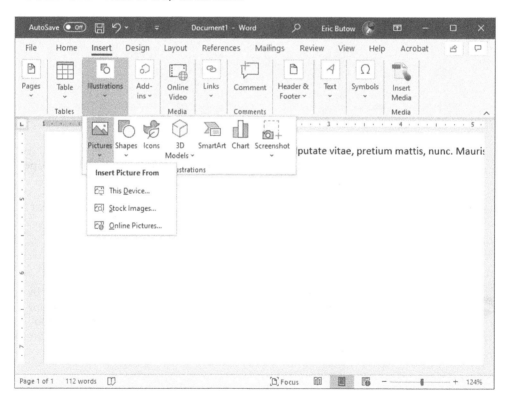

5. Click one of the other tabs to open icons, cut out photos of people, or choose from stickers. I'll keep the default Stock Images.

6. Under the Search box, click one of the category tiles, shown in Figure 5.3, to view photos within that category. You can view more categories by clicking the right arrow at the right side of the category tiles row.

FIGURE 5.3   Category tiles

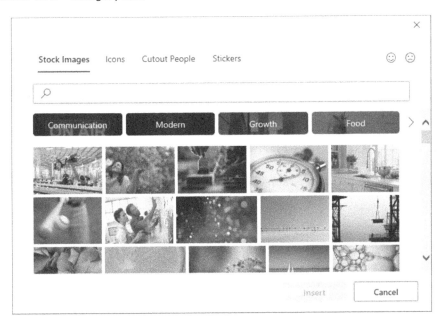

7. Scroll up and down in the list of thumbnail images until you find the one that you want, and then click the image.

8. Click Insert.

The image appears in the document, and text moves underneath the image. You'll learn how to move the image and change the text wrapping style later in this chapter.

Inserting 3D Models

You can insert *3D models* into a document and then change the orientation. Follow these steps:

1. Place your cursor where you want to insert the 3D model.

2. Click the Insert menu option.

3. In the Insert ribbon, click 3D Models in the Illustrations section.

4. You can search for 3D models on your computer or stock 3D models that were installed with Word. For this example, I'll click Stock 3D Models.

5. In the Online 3D Models dialog box (see Figure 5.4), scroll up and down the list of categories and then click the category tile you want.

FIGURE 5.4   3D model category list

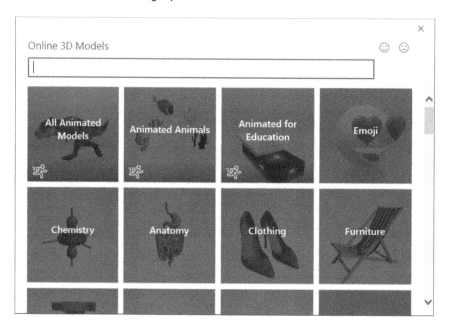

6. Click the 3D model you want and then click Insert.

The model appears in the document in front of the rest of the text. You'll learn how to modify the location and position of the 3D model, as well as change the text wrapping style, later in this chapter.

Adding SmartArt Graphics

SmartArt graphics are built-in art types for conveying specific kinds of information, such as a flow chart to show a process or a decision tree to show a hierarchy. Follow these steps to add a SmartArt graphic:

1. Place your cursor where you want to insert your SmartArt graphic.

2. Click the Insert menu option.

3. In the Insert ribbon, click SmartArt in the Illustrations section.

4. In the Choose A SmartArt Graphic dialog box, shown in Figure 5.5, select a category from the list on the left side of the dialog box.

FIGURE 5.5   SmartArt categories

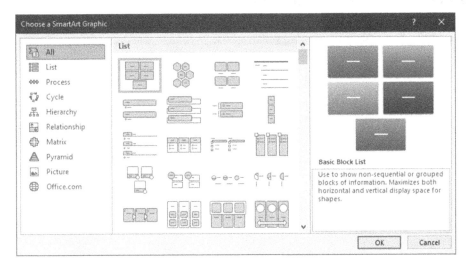

The default is All, which shows all the SmartArt graphics from which you can choose. The list of SmartArt graphic type icons in the center of the dialog box depends on the category you chose. For this example, I chose Hierarchy.

5. Click the graphic type that you want to insert. A description of the graphic type appears at the right side of the dialog box.

6. Click OK.

The graphic appears in the document, and text moves underneath the image.

You'll learn how to set up a graphic to look the way you want, as well as change the text wrapping style, later in this chapter.

Placing Screenshots and Screen Clippings

You can take a photo of another window and add it directly into your document from within Word. You can also clip a portion of your screen within Word and add it to your document automatically.

Screenshot

Add a *screenshot* to your document by following these steps:

1. Place your cursor where you want to insert the screenshot.

2. Click the Insert menu option.

3. In the Insert ribbon, click Screenshot in the Illustrations section. If there are any windows open, Word scans your computer and places thumbnail images of the windows within the drop-down list, as shown in Figure 5.6.

FIGURE 5.6 Screenshots drop-down list

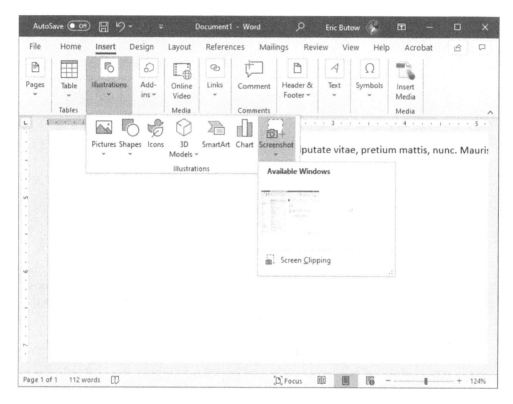

The currently open Word window is one of the windows that Word finds. When you click the window in the list, Word places the screenshot at the insertion point in your document.

Screen Clipping

Here's how to add a *screen clipping*, where you can clip the entire screen or a portion of it:

1. Click Screen Clipping in the drop-down list. Word automatically opens the last window that you had open prior to using Word. If you didn't have a window open, you see the desktop. The screen has a transparent white overlay, and the mouse pointer changes to a cross, which means that Word is ready for you to capture the screen.

2. Move the cursor to the location where you want to start capturing the screen.

3. Hold down the mouse button and drag until you've captured your selection (see Figure 5.7).

4. Release the mouse button.

Capture area

The clipped image appears under the insertion point in your document and shows Alt text—alternative descriptive text that Word thinks is close to what's in the image, intended for people who can't see the image. You'll learn how to change the Alt text and modify the image later in this chapter.

Inserting Text Boxes

If you want to have an area outside of the text of your document with its own formatting, such as a sidebar, Word allows you to create a separate area of text outside the main area in your document. Then you can place *text boxes* to the side of the text or even over the text. Here's how to add a text box:

1. Place your cursor where you want to insert the text box.

2. Click the Insert menu option.

3. In the Insert ribbon, click Text Box in the Text section. (If the Word window isn't very wide, you may need to click the Text icon in the ribbon to view the Text Box icon in the drop-down ribbon.)

4. In the drop-down list, scroll up and down to view the different text box styles in each thumbnail-sized icon (see Figure 5.8).

FIGURE 5.8   Text box styles

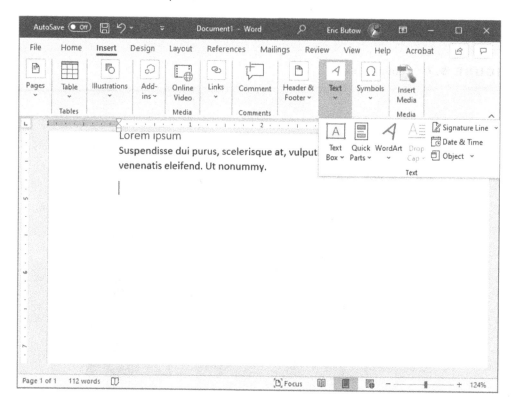

The text box appears at a location near the insertion point, depending on the box you selected, and the style name appears underneath the icon.

You can also view more text boxes, if any, on Office.com by moving the mouse pointer over More Text Boxes From Office.com and then clicking a text box style on the side menu.

You'll learn how to format a text box in the next section.

Draw your own text box by clicking Draw Text Box at the bottom of the drop-down list. When you do, the mouse pointer changes to a cross and you can add a text box on the page by holding down the mouse pointer and dragging the box until it's the size that you want.

After you release the mouse button, the text box appears on the page with a white background and in front of any text. The cursor blinks in the text box so that you can start typing text in the Word default font.

EXERCISE 5.1

Inserting Shapes and Graphics

1. Go to the page where you want to add a shape or create a new page.

2. Add a pentagon on the page.

3. Go to another page in your document or add a new page.

4. Place your cursor where you want to add a picture.

5. Add a stock image of your choice on the screen.

6. Under the picture, add a 3D model of your choice.

7. Go to another page in your document or add a new page.

8. Place your cursor where you want to add a SmartArt graphic.

9. Add a SmartArt pyramid image of your choice on the screen.

10. Under the SmartArt image, add a new text box and add text within it.

Formatting Illustrations and Text Boxes

After you add an illustration and/or a text box, Word gives you plenty of tools to format them to make them look the way you want and then place them where you want on the page.

Applying Artistic Effects

Word contains 22 *artistic effects* that you can apply to a photo in your document, from making the photo look as if it was drawn with a marker to applying a glow effect. Apply an artistic effect as follows:

1. Click the image.

2. Click the Picture Format menu option.

3. Click Artistic Effects in the Adjust area.

4. Select from the effects by clicking on the effect tile in the drop-down menu (see Figure 5.9). When you place the mouse pointer over the tile for a couple of seconds, the description of the effect appears in a pop-up box.

FIGURE 5.9 The effects tiles

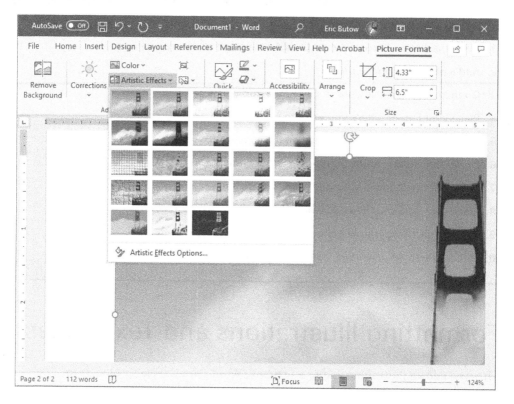

5. Click the tile you want, and Word will apply the effect to your photo.

Since the effects tiles in the drop-down menu can be small, applying an effect can show you what it looks like. You can always remove the effect once you've seen it by pressing Ctrl+Z.

 You can apply only one artistic effect at a time to a picture. So, applying a different artistic effect removes the previously applied artistic effect.

Adding Picture Effects and Picture Styles

Word also allows you to set effects from within the Picture Format ribbon. However, if you don't need to have fine-tuned effects on your picture, Word has prebuilt styles for you that you can apply to the selected picture by clicking the appropriate tile in the ribbon.

Add a Picture Effect

Here's how to choose and add a *picture effect*:

1. Click the picture.

2. Click the Picture Format menu option.

3. Click Picture Effects in the Picture Styles section.

4. In the drop-down menu, move the mouse pointer to one of the seven effects that you want to add. I selected Shadow in this example.

5. In the side menu, move the mouse pointer over the tile that contains the shadow style. The style is applied to the picture in your document so that you can see what it looks like (see Figure 5.10).

FIGURE 5.10   Offset: Center shadow style applied to the picture

6. When you find an effect that you like, click the tile in the menu.

If you want to change the effect, click Options at the bottom of the menu. For example, in Shadow, click Shadow Options. The Format Picture pane appears on the right side of the Word window so that you can make more detailed changes, such as the color of the shadow.

Apply a Picture Style

Apply a *picture style* from the ribbon by following these steps:

1. Click the image.
2. Click the Picture Format menu option.
3. Move the mouse pointer over the style thumbnail icon in the Picture Styles section, as shown in Figure 5.11. (If the Word window isn't very wide, you may need to click Quick Styles in the ribbon to view a drop-down ribbon with the style icons.)

FIGURE 5.11   Picture Styles section

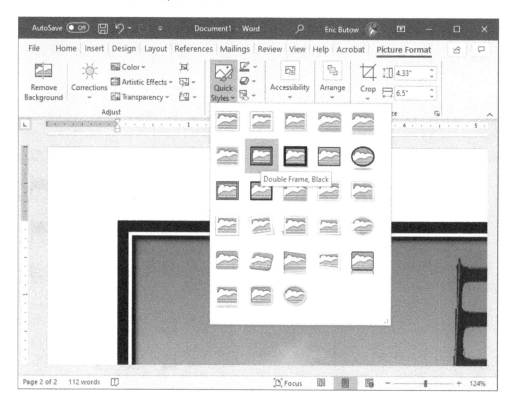

As you move the pointer over every style icon, the picture in your document changes to reflect the style.

4. Apply the style by clicking the icon.

If you don't like any of the styles, move the icon away from the row of styles and the picture reverts to its default state.

Removing Picture Backgrounds

If you want the background of an image to have the background color of the page, here's what to do:

1. Click the image.
2. Click the Picture Format menu option.
3. Click Remove Background at the left side of the ribbon.

   The default background area has the color that Word uses to mark it for removal, whereas the foreground retains its natural coloring (see Figure 5.12).

FIGURE 5.12   Removed background

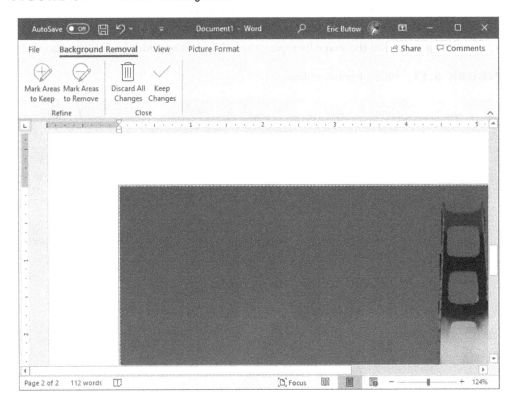

If parts of the picture that you want to keep are magenta (marked for removal), select Mark Areas To Keep and use the free-form drawing pencil to mark the areas on the picture that you want to keep.

To remove more parts of the picture, select Mark Areas To Remove and use the drawing pencil to draw the boundaries of photo areas that you want to remove.

When you're done, select Keep Changes or Discard All Changes.

Formatting Graphic Elements

How you format graphic elements is different depending on the type of graphic you're editing. This section looks at formatting options that you can use aside from the ones detailed previously. In the case of SmartArt, you'll learn more about that in the next section.

Shapes

After you create a shape, the Shape Format menu ribbon appears (see Figure 5.13) so that you can make a variety of changes to the shape, including the following:

- Editing points in the shape by clicking Edit Shape in the Insert Shapes section
- Changing shape styles, including the shape fill, outline, and effects, in the Shape Style section
- Changing the size of the shape by typing the height and/or width in the Size section

FIGURE 5.13   Shape Format ribbon

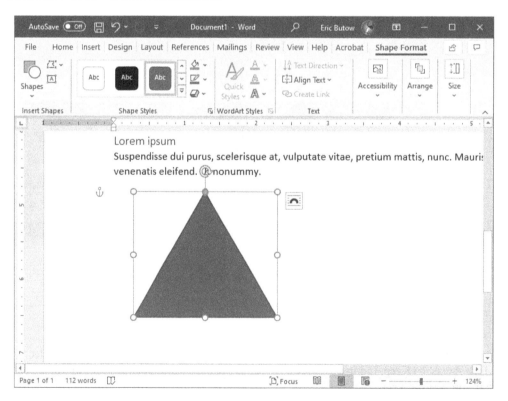

Pictures

In addition to removing picture backgrounds, applying styles, and applying effects, you can format the picture by clicking the Picture Format menu option. In the Picture Format ribbon, shown in Figure 5.14, you can format the picture in various ways:

- Setting corrections (such as brightness and contrast), color, and transparency, setting picture file compression to save disk space, and resetting the picture to its original state in the Adjust section

- Changing the picture border, as well as applying a picture layout style, such as formatting the picture with rounded corners and text underneath, in the Picture Styles section

- Changing the size of the picture by typing the height and/or width in the Size section

FIGURE 5.14   Picture Format ribbon

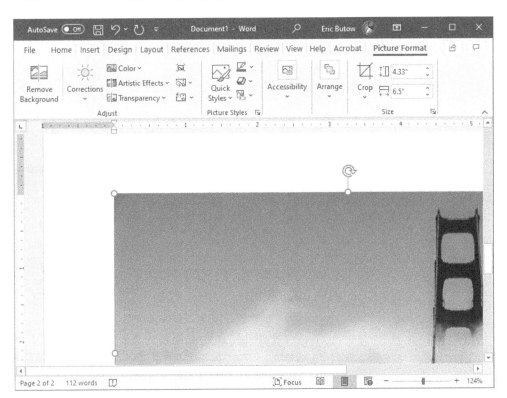

Screenshots and Screen Clippings

When you add a screenshot or a screen clipping, the Picture Format menu ribbon appears (see Figure 5.15) so that you can make a variety of changes to the shape, including the following:

- Editing points in the shape by clicking Edit Shape in the Insert Shapes section

- Setting shape styles, including the shape fill, outline, and effects, in the Shape Style section

- Changing the size of the shape by typing the height and/or width in the Size section

FIGURE 5.15 Picture Format ribbon

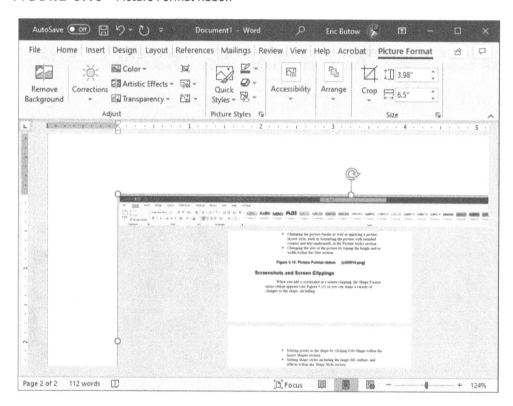

Setting Up SmartArt Graphics

After you add SmartArt, the Type Your Text Here box appears to the left of the image. You can type the text that will appear in the image by clicking [Text] in each bullet line and replacing that template text with your own.

Click the SmartArt Design menu option so that you can make any changes you want in the ribbon. The type of SmartArt you added determines the options that appear in the ribbon.

For example, I created an organizational chart, shown in Figure 5.16, and in the ribbon I can change the following:

- The layout of the chart in the Create Graphic section

- The layout type in the Layouts section

- The chart box colors and styles in the SmartArt Styles section

FIGURE 5.16   Designing an organizational chart using SmartArt

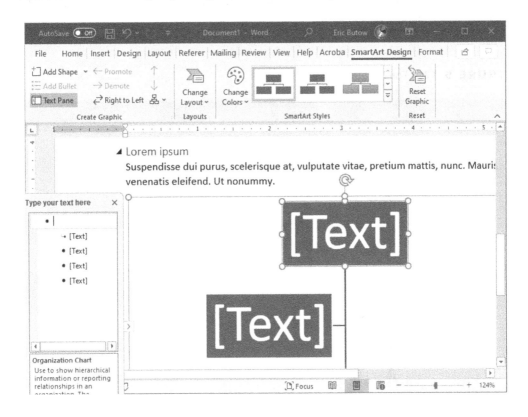

Remove all graphic style changes you made and return the graphic to its original style by clicking the Reset Graphic icon.

When you finish making any changes to your SmartArt graphic, click on the page outside the graphic to deselect it.

Once you stop editing your SmartArt graphic and deselect it, you won't be able to remove any previous changes that you made to the graphic.

Working with 3D Models

You can change the size of a 3D model by clicking the model, clicking one of the circular handles on the perimeter of the selection box, holding down the mouse button, and then dragging. When the model is the size you want, release the mouse button.

Rotate the 3D model 360 degrees in any direction by clicking and holding down the Rotate icon in the middle of the model graphic (see Figure 5.17), and then dragging the mouse pointer to see how the model moves. When the model looks the way you want on the page, release the mouse button.

FIGURE 5.17   The Rotate icon

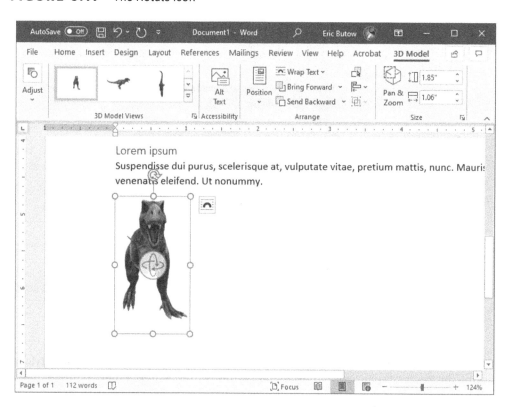

You can change the size of a shape, picture, SmartArt, screenshot, or screen clipping image by clicking the image, moving the mouse pointer over one of the circular handles on the perimeter of the image, holding down the mouse button, and dragging the image. When the image is the size you want, release the mouse button.

EXERCISE 5.2

Formatting Pictures and Graphics

1. Place the cursor in your document where you want to add a picture.

2. Add a stock image of your choice.

3. Select the picture, and then apply the Glow Edges artistic effect.

4. Add another stock image picture in another location in your document.

5. Remove the picture background.

6. Place the cursor in another location in your document.

7. Add a SmartArt pyramid graphic.

8. Switch the layout to an inverted pyramid and apply the Polished style.

9. Add a new 3D model of your choice below the SmartArt graphic.

10. Rotate the model until it looks the way that you want.

Adding and Organizing Text

Word makes it easy to add text, not only in text boxes, but also to your shapes and Smart-Art graphics. What's more, you can format the text to your liking with built-in text styles and alignment options.

Formatting Text in Text Boxes

You can format text in a text box just as you would in the rest of your document. Just click the Home menu option and change the font, paragraph, and styles as you see fit.

You can also format the text in other ways. Select the text that you want to format. Now you can change the text as follows in the Shape Format ribbon.

Apply WordArt Styles

In the WordArt Styles section, you can click one of the three built-in text effect icons (see Figure 5.18):

- Click Text Fill (the letter A on top of a black line) to change the text color in the drop-down menu.

- Click Text Outline (an outlined letter A on top of a black line) to add an outline, including color and outline line width, in the drop-down menu.

- Click Text Effects (a blue outlined letter A) to view and add other effects to the text. In the drop-down menu, move the mouse pointer over one of the effects to see how each effect appears in your photo. You can choose from Shadow, Reflection, Glow, Bevel, 3-D Rotation, or Transform.

FIGURE 5.18   Text effects options in the WordArt Styles section

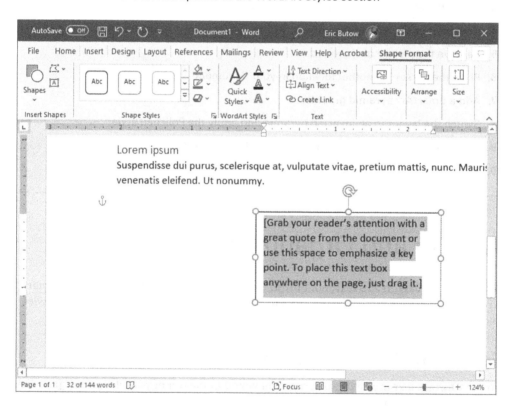

Change Text Appearance

In the Text section, shown in Figure 5.19, you can do three things:

- Click Text Direction to rotate the text 90 degrees or 270 degrees.
- Click Text Alignment to align the text vertically with the top, middle, or bottom of the shape. The default is Middle.
- Click Create Link to link the text to a second text box. When you type so much text in the shape that the shape can't hold any more, the overflow text appears in the second text box.

FIGURE 5.19 Text appearance options in the Text section

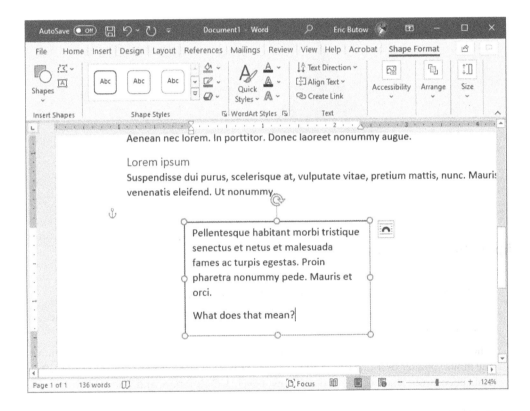

Adding Text in Shapes

When you need to add text in a shape, Word has you covered. Start by right-clicking anywhere in your shape and then clicking Add Text in the context menu.

The cursor appears in the center of the shape so that you can type your text. If you want to format it, select the text that you want to format. Now you can change the style of the text in two sections in the Shape Format ribbon: the WordArt Styles section and the Text section (see Figure 5.20).

FIGURE 5.20   Shape Format ribbon

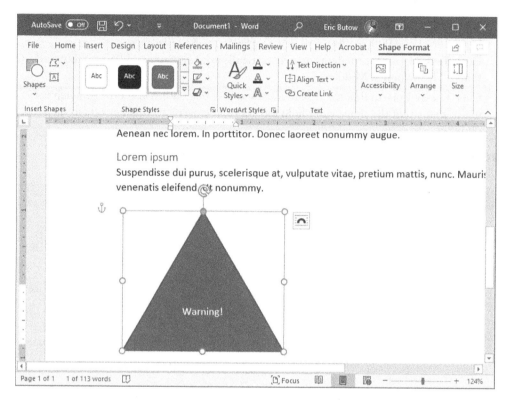

Apply WordArt Styles

In the WordArt Styles section, you can click one of three built-in text effects:

- Click Text Fill to change the text color in the drop-down menu.
- Click Text Outline to add an outline, including color and outline line width, in the drop-down menu.
- Click Text Effects to view and add other effects to the text. In the drop-down menu, move the mouse pointer over one of the effects to see how each effect appears in your photo. You can choose from Shadow, Reflection, Glow, Bevel, 3-D Rotation, and Transform.

Change Text Appearance

In the Text section, you can change the text appearance in one of three ways:

- Click Text Direction to rotate the text 90 degrees or 270 degrees.
- Click Text Alignment to align the text vertically with the top, middle, or bottom of the shape. The default is Middle.
- Click Create Link to link the text to a second text box. When you type so much text in the shape that the shape can't hold any more, the overflow text appears in the second text box.

> You can also select the text and use the standard Font, Paragraph, and Styles tools on the Home tab to format your text. You can also right-click your text and change styles in the context menu.

Changing SmartArt Graphic Content

SmartArt graphics include text placeholders automatically. For example, when you create an organizational chart, Word puts text placeholders in each box so that you can fill in those boxes with the appropriate person.

All you have to do is click [Text] in one of the boxes (see Figure 5.21) and then enter your text.

The Type Your Text Here box appears to the left of the graphic. As you enter text in the box, the text appears in the outline in the box. You can add more text by clicking [Text] in each box or by clicking [Text] in each bullet in the outline and typing the text to replace the [Text] placeholder.

FIGURE 5.21   Text in an organizational chart

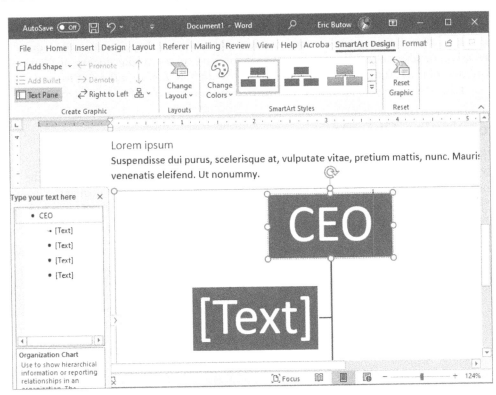

EXERCISE 5.3

Adding Text to Shapes and Graphics

1. Place your cursor on a page where you want to add a shape or create a new page.

2. Add a new shape of your choice.

3. Add text to your shape.

4. Add a new text box underneath the shape.

5. Type text in the text box.

6. Align the text to the top of the text box.

7. Under the text box, add a SmartArt graphic of your choice.

8. Add as much text as you can fit in each entry in the graphic.

Modifying Graphic Elements

Fortunately, Word makes it easy to change where you can put a shape, picture, 3D model, screenshot, or screen clipping (or even all five if you have room) in your document. You can move your objects around on a page and then tell Word how you want the text to move around the image. You can even instruct Word to put text in front of or behind the image.

Positioning Objects

When you add a new shape or image, the image appears in front of the rest of the text on the page, if any. Now you can move the shape or image in your document by moving the mouse pointer over the image, holding down the mouse button, and then moving the image.

If you need to position your shape or image at just the right location, Word gives you three options for moving a shape or image, depending on what you need.

Small Increments   If you only need to move your shape or image in small increments to get the position just right, click the picture. Next, hold down the Ctrl key and then click one of the arrow keys to move the image.

Move Several Objects   You can move several images or shapes by grouping them together. Start by selecting the first object, and then hold down the Ctrl key. Next, select the other images and/or shapes you want to group.

Now right-click on one of the selected shapes and/or images, move the mouse pointer over Group in the context menu, and then click Group in the side menu. Now you can move all the images and/or shapes around at once.

You can ungroup them by right-clicking one of the images and/or shapes, moving the mouse pointer over Group in the context menu, and then clicking Ungroup in the side menu.

Size and Position   You can specify exact measurements for the size and position of an image, shape, or group by right-clicking the object and then clicking Size and Position in the menu. In the Layout dialog box, you can change size, position, and text wrapping options, which you will learn about in the next section.

Wrapping Text Around Objects

If you want to push text around an image or shape, select the object and then click the Layout Options button to the upper right of the shape. (It looks like an upside-down U.) The Layout Options menu appears and displays icons with the various text wrap options, as shown in Figure 5.22.

FIGURE 5.22   Layout Options menu

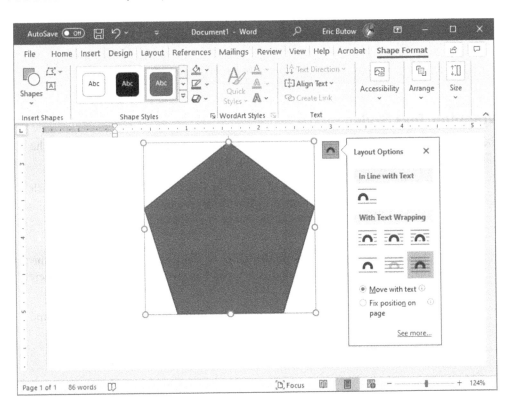

However, this menu doesn't give you as much control as you may need. You can view and change more options by clicking the See More link at the bottom of the menu.

The Layout dialog box appears. If the Text Wrapping tab isn't selected, click it to display the text wrapping options, as shown in Figure 5.23.

FIGURE 5.23   Text Wrapping tab in Layout dialog box

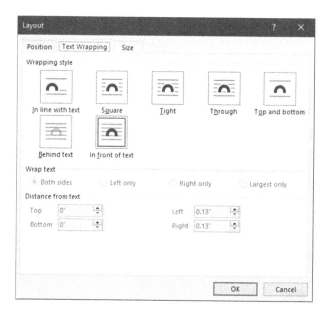

Wrapping Text Styles

The current wrapping text style icon is already selected for you. You can click one of the following seven icons to change the text wrapping style:

In Line With Text   This style places the image or shape in a paragraph just as with any line of text. The picture or shape moves with the paragraph when you add or remove text. As with text, you can cut the image or shape and paste it on another line of text.

Square   This style wraps text around the image or shape in a square pattern. If the image or shape tapers, such as a triangle, then you have white text around the tapered parts of the image or shape.

Tight   The text wraps at the same distance between the edge of the image or shape and the text.

Through   This style allows you to customize the areas in which the text wraps around the visible image, but not any space (either white or a solid color) that surrounds the image. Note that this option does not work with vector images.

Through acts much like Tight, except that you can change the wrap points so that text can fill in the spaces between elements in an image. If the image or shape doesn't have any spaces, then text wrapping works just like Tight.

Top And Bottom   The text wraps on the top and bottom of the image or shape and doesn't put any text along the left or right sides of the photo no matter how wide the image or shape is.

Behind Text   Word places the image or shape behind the text and doesn't wrap the text around it. Note that selecting this option means that you must be more precise when selecting the image or shape with your cursor, because otherwise Word will think you're trying to select the text.

In Front Of Text   Word places the picture or shape on top of the text and doesn't wrap the text. Some of your text may be hidden behind the image or shape, which means some of it may be blocked, depending on the transparency of the image.

These options control whether text wraps around an image on both sides, left, right, or wherever the largest distance between the image and the margin.

Specific Wrapping

The Square, Tight, and Through wrapping styles allow you to add specific distance measurements between text and your image or shape. When you click one of these styles, the Wrap Text and Distance From The Text settings become active.

Both Sides   Wraps text around both sides of the image or shape

Left   Wraps text around only the left side of the image or shape and leaves the space to the right of the image or shape blank

Right   Wraps text around only the right side of the image or shape and leaves the space to the left of the image or shape blank

Largest Only   Wraps text on the side of the image or shape that has the larger distance from the margin. For example, if the distance between the left margin and the image is one inch, and the distance between the image and right margin is 3 inches, Word wraps the text around the right side of the image.

Distance From The Text   You can enter the specific distance between the text and the image or shape in inches. You can independently set distances for the top, bottom, left, and right margins. Also, you can specify the distance in hundredths of an inch if you want to be that precise.

🌐 **Real World Scenario**

Placing Your Graphics for Easy Reading

Your boss has come to you and asked you to put together a document for the sales team. The document is all about the neat new company widget that was just announced, so the boss wants a lot of graphics.

There is a limit to the number of graphics that you should add to a document so as not to overwhelm the reader. A reader's eyes follow a pattern as they look across a page: from the upper-left corner to the lower-right corner, and then to the lower-left corner.

So, if you want to get the attention of your customers (and please your boss), position your graphics in one or more of those locations in your document and then set text wrap settings accordingly. When readers visually scan those graphics, they will likely pick up on some of the text you have in your document, too.

Adding Alt Text to Objects

Alt text, or alternative text, tells anyone who views your document in Word what the image, shape, or SmartArt graphic is when the reader moves their mouse pointer over it. If the reader can't see your document, then Word will use text-to-speech in Windows to read your Alt text to the reader audibly.

Here's how to add Alt text:

1. Click the shape, picture, or SmartArt graphic. If you clicked a SmartArt graphic, skip to step 3.

2. In the Shape Format or Picture Format ribbon, click the Alt Text icon. (If your Word window isn't very wide, you may need to click the Accessibility icon and then click Alt Text.)

3. In the Alt Text pane on the right side of the Word window (see Figure 5.24), type one or two sentences in the text box to describe the object and its context.

   Some images, especially stock images, already have this information in the text box, but you can change it.

4. Click the Mark As Decorative check box if your image, shape, or SmartArt graphic adds visual interest but isn't informative, such as a line.

5. When you're done, close the pane.

FIGURE 5.24   Alt Text pane

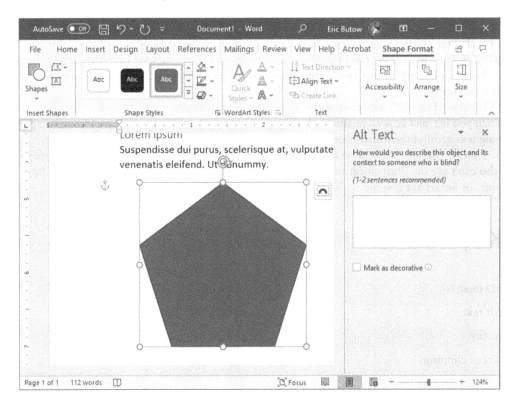

Positioning Graphics and Adding Alt Text

1. Place your cursor on a page where you want to add a shape or create a new page.

2. Add a new shape of your choice.

3. Position the shape so that it's on the left side of the page.

4. Wrap text so that it goes around the right of your shape.

5. Add Alt text that describes your shape.

Summary

This chapter started with a discussion about all the ways you can add illustrations to a Word document. You learned how to add pictures, shapes, SmartArt graphics, screenshots, and screen clippings. Then you learned how to add text boxes to have different areas of text in a document.

I followed up with a discussion about how to format illustrations as well as text boxes. Then you learned how to position illustrations and text boxes on a page, including wrapping text around the illustration or text box the way you want.

Finally, you learned how to add Alt text to any type of illustration to ensure that people who can't see the illustration will know what that picture, shape, screenshot, screen clipping, or SmartArt graphic is about.

Key Terms

3D models	screenshots
Alt text	shapes
pictures	text box
screen clippings	wrap text

Exam Essentials

Understand how to add different types of graphics.   Word allows you to add a variety of graphics and photos to your document, including shapes, 3D models, and Word SmartArt graphics. You need to know how to add these graphics as well as pictures, screenshots of open windows, and clip portions of your screen to your document.

Know how to add and format text boxes.   Understand how to add a text box that is separate from other text on a page, modify a text box, and format text in a text box.

Understand how to position graphics and wrap text around them.   Know how to position your graphic on the page and set options for wrapping text around the graphic, moving the text in front of the graphic or moving the graphic in front of the text.

Be able to add Alt text.   Understand why Alt text is important for your readers and know how to add Alt text to a graphic or picture.

Review Questions

1. How do you add a rectangle?
   A. Click the Design menu option, and then select a new theme in the Design ribbon.
   B. Click the Insert menu, and then click SmartArt in the Insert ribbon.
   C. Click the Insert menu option, and then click Shapes in the Insert ribbon.
   D. Select the rectangle style from the Home ribbon.

2. How do you add an organizational chart to your document using the Insert menu ribbon?
   A. Click Shapes.
   B. Click SmartArt.
   C. Click Chart.
   D. Click Pictures.

3. Why should you add a text box?
   A. Because it's easier to read
   B. Because you need to add one before you can start typing text in your document
   C. You don't need to add one because you can add text directly on a page.
   D. To have text separate from the rest of the text in your document

4. How do you apply a specific picture style in the Picture Format ribbon?
   A. Click the Corrections icon.
   B. Click one of the picture styles tiles in the Picture Styles area.
   C. Click Picture Effects.
   D. Click Change Picture.

5. How do you clear style changes that you made to a SmartArt graphic?
   A. Use the SmartArt Design menu ribbon.
   B. Delete the SmartArt graphic.
   C. Click the Undo icon in the title bar.
   D. Use the Format menu ribbon.

6. How do you rotate a selected 3D model?
   A. Click one of the icons in the 3D Model Views section in the 3D Model menu ribbon.
   B. Click and drag the handles on the selection box around the model.
   C. Click and drag the icon in the middle of the model.
   D. Click the Position icon in the 3D Model menu ribbon.

7. If you have two text boxes in your document, how can you link them together?

    A. Click the Insert menu option, and then click Link in the ribbon.

    B. Use the Shape Format menu ribbon.

    C. Use the Layout ribbon.

    D. Click the Sort icon on the Home ribbon.

8. How do you add text to a shape?

    A. Use the Shape Format ribbon.

    B. Click the Layout Option icon next to the selected shape.

    C. Use the Insert ribbon.

    D. Right-click the shape.

9. How do you place a graphic so that it remains with the text above and below it when you wrap the text?

    A. Top and bottom

    B. Both sides

    C. In line with text

    D. Square

10. Why should you add Alt text to graphics and pictures?

    A. Because it's required for all graphics in a Word document

    B. To help people who can't see the graphic know what the graphic is about

    C. Because Word won't save your document until you do

    D. Because you want to be as informative as possible

Chapter

6

Working with Other Users on Your Document

MICROSOFT EXAM OBJECTIVES COVERED IN THIS CHAPTER:

✓ **Manage document collaboration**

- Add and manage comments

    - Add comments

    - Review and reply to comments

    - Resolve comments

    - Delete comments

- Manage change tracking

    - Track Changes

    - Review tracked changes

    - Accept and reject tracked changes

    - Lock and unlock change tracking

Word is built for sharing documents with others, which is vital whether you work with several people in one office or people in more than one location. Microsoft includes a tool in Word that allows you to add *comments*, which appear within boxes in the right margin of the page. This approach ensures that the comments don't clutter or obscure the page text. You can also reply to comments within a comments box. If you are the person who sends a document for review and are responsible for managing all of the comments, Word also includes tools for resolving comments and deleting them as well.

If other people will be adding information directly in the document, Word has a nifty *Track Changes* feature that allows you to view all additions and deletions that other reviewers made. You can also decide what level of changes you want to view on the page.

All reviewers can accept and/or reject tracked changes. And, if you don't want people either to turn Track Changes off or accept or reject changes, you can lock Track Changes before you send the document for review.

Adding Comments

It's easy to add a comment about something in your document within the text itself. However, if you use comments in the text, you can clutter up your pages with a lot of comments, even if they are in a different style that sets comment text apart from the rest. Comments in text can also add to your page count, which may throw off reviewers who expect the document to be a set number of pages long.

What to do? Use the Review menu option to add a new comment in a new, right margin that Word creates automatically. These comments appear in a box and point to the place in the text where you added the comment.

Inserting Comments

Here's how to insert a comment into a document:

1. Select the text on which you want to comment.
2. Click the Review menu option.
3. In the Review menu ribbon, click New Comment in the Comments section.

Word shows your comment in a box in a margin appended to the right side of the page (see Figure 6.1).

FIGURE 6.1 A new comment

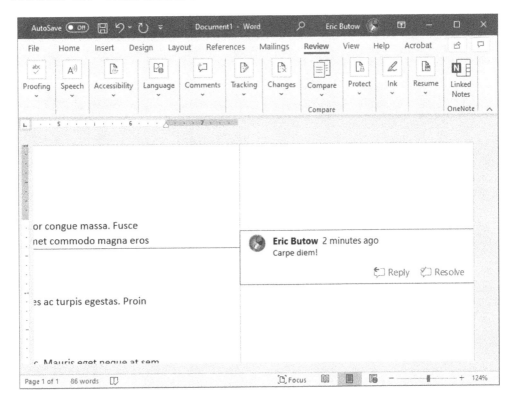

The outline color represents the default color of the primary reviewer. (That's you.) As you type the comment, you can press Enter to break up sections of your comment for easier reading. Word assigns different colors to different commenters automatically.

When you're done, click in the document again. The comment appears in the margin.

 At the top of the comment box, Word displays your Microsoft 365 username, your avatar, and how long ago you wrote the comment. An avatar is an icon that you created for yourself when you created a Microsoft 365 account. If you don't have one, then Word shows a placeholder avatar.

Reviewing and Replying to Comments

You can review comments by scrolling through the document, but you can also use the Review menu ribbon to go to the next comment. Start by clicking the Review menu option. In the Review menu ribbon, click Next in the Comments section to see the next comment (see Figure 6.2).

FIGURE 6.2   The next comment

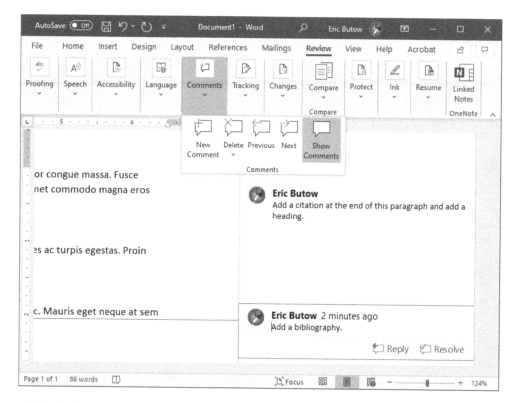

Word takes you to the page that contains the next comment in the document. Go to the previous comment in the document by clicking Previous in the ribbon.

If you see a comment from someone else (or even yourself) and you want to reply, click Reply in the comment box and then enter your reply. When you're finished, click in the document. You see the reply indented underneath the first comment.

Resolving Comments

When you decide that a comment is resolved but you want to keep the comment in the document for your notes or to let reviewers know the comment is resolved, click Resolve in the lower-right corner of the comment box.

The comment text is gray. When you place the cursor in the document, only the commenter name and the first few words in the comment (about 40 characters) appear in the margin, but the comment isn't deleted, as shown in Figure 6.3.

FIGURE 6.3   Resolved comment

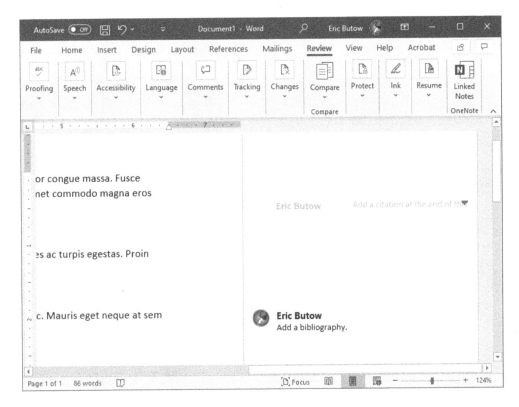

Click the grayed-out comment to view it. You can reopen the comment by clicking Reopen in the lower-right corner of the comment box.

Deleting Comments

Here's how to delete one or more comments when you decide that you no longer need them:

1. Click in the comment box.
2. Click the Review menu option, if necessary.
3. In the Review menu ribbon, click the Delete icon in the Comments section (see Figure 6.4).

Word deletes the comment and any replies within that comment.

FIGURE 6.4   Deleting a comment

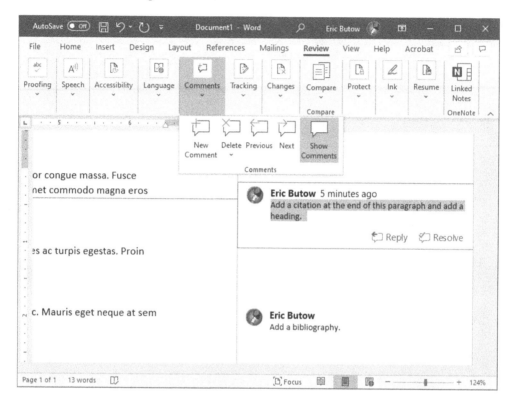

You can delete all comments in the document, even without selecting a comment, by clicking the down arrow underneath the Delete icon in the ribbon. In the drop-down menu, click Delete All Comments. All comments in the document disappear, and so does the appended margin on the right side of the page.

EXERCISE 6.1

Inserting, Replying to, and Deleting a Comment

1. Place your cursor where you want to add a comment in your document.

2. Write a new comment.

3. Reply to your comment.

4. Resolve the comment.

5. Restore the comment you resolved.

6. Delete the comment.

Tracking Your Changes

The Track Changes feature is vital when you review changes made by other reviewers. You can see what changes were made, when they were made, and by whom. When you have Track Changes on, Word alerts you to changes in the text with vertical *change lines* that reflect the reviewer color assigned by Word.

By default, Track Changes only shows change lines, not any other formatting in the text such as strikethrough text for deletions, which Word calls *markup*. You will learn how to display different markup levels later in this chapter.

Turning On Track Changes

Word does not turn on Track Changes automatically when you open a new document, so you have to turn the feature on. Start by clicking the Review menu option. In the Review menu ribbon, click the Track Changes icon in the Tracking section, as shown in Figure 6.5.

FIGURE 6.5   Track Changes icon

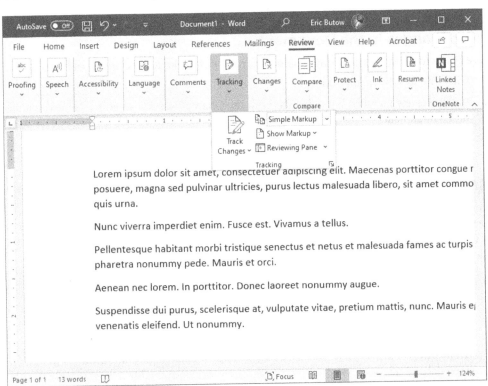

Now the Track Changes icon in the ribbon has a gray background, which means that Track Changes is on. You can turn off Track Changes by following the same steps you took to turn on the feature.

When Track Changes is off, Word stops marking changes. However, the changes in your document remain until you accept or reject them, which you'll learn about later in this chapter.

If you can't turn on Track Changes, you might need to turn off the document protection feature. In the Protect section in the Review ribbon, click Restrict Editing, and then click Stop Protection in the Restrict Editing panel on the right side of the Word window. You may also need to type the document password to gain access.

Reviewing Tracked Changes

You can review tracked changes by just scrolling through the document, but that can be cumbersome for long documents. Word makes it easy for you to go to the next or previous change in your document in the Review menu ribbon.

View Changes in the Document

Here's how to view changes in the document from within the Review menu ribbon:

1. Click the Review menu option.

2. In the Review menu ribbon, click Next in the Changes section to go to the next change in the document.

3. Click Previous in the Changes section to go to the previous change in the document (see Figure 6.6).

Modify Change Markup Settings

You can also review tracked changes by setting how Word displays changes in the document from within the Review menu ribbon.

In the Tracking section in the ribbon, click the down arrow to the right of Simple Markup (see Figure 6.7).

Next, click one of the four options in the drop-down menu:

Simple Markup: This is the default selection. You see only change lines. All added and deleted text still appears in the document, but without any formatting such as strikethrough text.

All Markup: This is where you see all the change formatting. In addition to change bars, deleted text is marked with strikethrough format and additions are marked with an underline. The text also sports the colors of various reviewers who made changes.

No Markup: This option shows any added text (or doesn't show any deleted text) but does not show any other markup formatting, including change bars.

Original: This means you see the document without any changes that have been made to it.

FIGURE 6.6   Previous and Next options

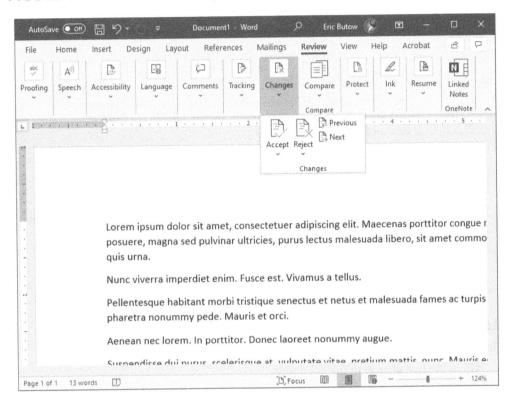

Accepting and Rejecting Tracked Changes

Word gives you the power to accept one change, several changes, or all changes in the document. The same is true for rejecting changes made by other reviewers.

If you can't see any changes in the text before you accept or reject changes, change the markup setting to All Markup, as described in the previous section.

FIGURE 6.7   Markup drop-down menu

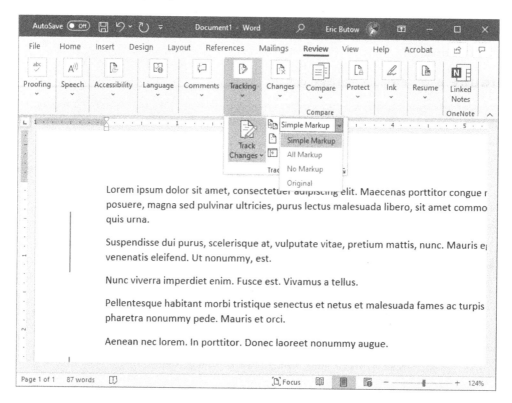

Accept Tracked Changes

Here's how to accept one, several, or all changes:

1. Go to the first change in the document.

2. Click the Review menu option.

3. In the Review menu ribbon, click the down arrow under the Accept icon in the Changes section (see Figure 6.8).

4. In the drop-down menu, click one of the following options:

    ■   Accept the change by clicking Accept This Change.

    ■   Accept the change and move to the next one by clicking Accept And Move To Next.

    ■   Accept all changes in the document, but keep Track Changes on, by clicking Accept All Changes.

    ■   Accept all changes and turn off Track Changes by clicking Accept All Changes And Stop Tracking.

FIGURE 6.8   Accept menu

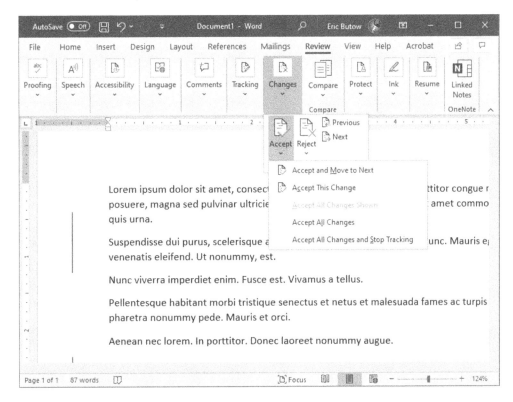

Now you can go to the previous change by clicking Previous in the ribbon or go to the next change by clicking Next.

Reject Tracked Changes

Here's how to reject one, several, or all changes in your document:

1. Go to the change in the document that you want to reject.

2. Click the Review menu option.

3. In the Review menu ribbon, click the down arrow under the Reject icon in the Changes section (see Figure 6.9).

4. In the drop-down menu, click one of the following options:

   - Reject the change by clicking Reject Change. Word removes all the changes.

   - Reject the change and move to the next one by clicking Reject And Move To Next.

   - Reject all changes in the document, but keep Track Changes on, by clicking Reject All Changes.

   - Reject all changes and turn off Track Changes by clicking Reject All Changes And Stop Tracking.

FIGURE 6.9   Reject menu

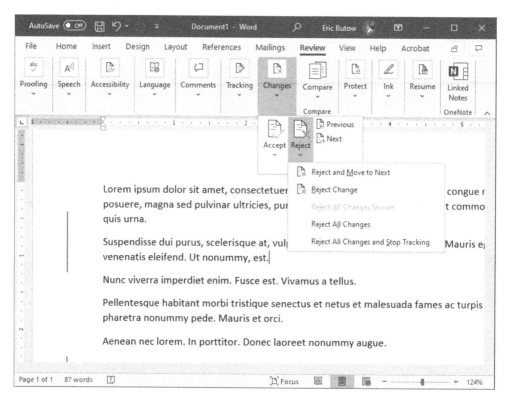

Now you can go to the previous change by clicking Previous in the ribbon or go to the next change by clicking Next.

Locking and Unlocking Change Tracking

If you want to lock Track Changes so that you don't turn the feature off until you have to, or you want your reviewers to know Track Changes should stay on, here's how to do it:

1. Click the Review menu option.

2. In the Review menu ribbon, click the Track Changes text underneath the Track Changes icon in the Tracking section.

3. In the drop-down menu shown in Figure 6.10, click Lock Tracking.

   The Lock Tracking dialog box appears so that you can add a password to keep anyone but yourself from accepting changes, rejecting changes, and turning Track Changes off.

4. Lock changes without adding a password by moving ahead to step 7. Otherwise, continue to step 5.

5. Type your password in the Enter Password (Optional) box.

6. Type the password again in the Reenter To Confirm box.

7. Click OK.

FIGURE 6.10   Track Changes drop-down menu

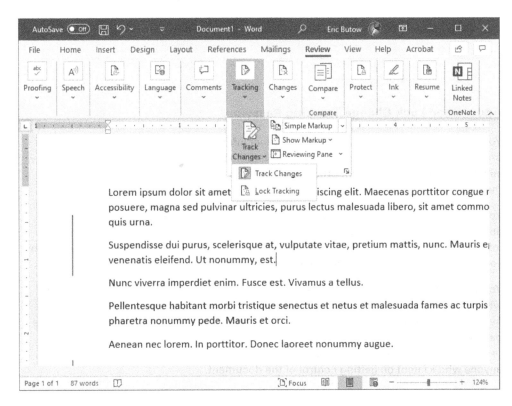

Now the Track Changes icon in the ribbon is disabled, so people can't turn off Track Changes.

You can unlock Track Changes by following steps 1 through 3. If you have no password, then Word unlocks Track Changes.

If you have a password, the Unlock Password dialog box appears (see Figure 6.11). Type the password in the Password box and then click OK.

Once you unlock Track Changes, the ribbon shows that Track Changes is on. You can turn off Track Changes by clicking the Track Changes icon, or by accepting or rejecting all changes and turning off Track Changes, as you learned to do earlier in this chapter.

FIGURE 6.11   Unlock Password dialog box

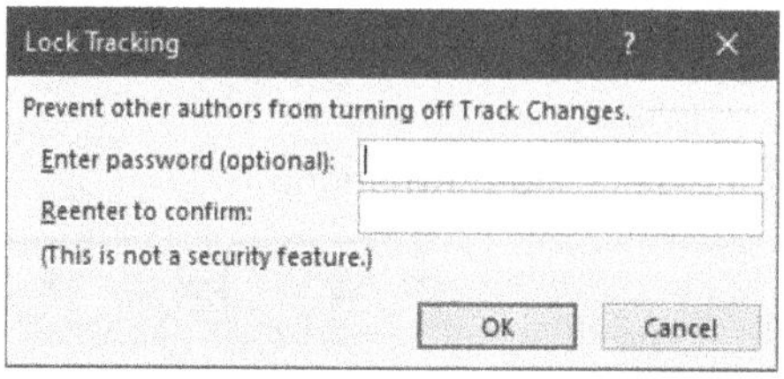

> **Real World Scenario**
>
> ## Add a Good Lock Change Tracking Password
>
> You're responsible for creating the new product information booklet for the company's brand-new product. This document will be distributed at trade shows around the country, so different people at different offices will need to review the document and comment on it.
>
> You don't know who else in each office will review the document besides the sales and marketing teams. You also don't know most of the people on those teams. The information from the product management team doesn't have all its photos ready yet, so you just need to share the text in a Word document.
>
> You've decided to lock Track Changes to give you control, but anyone can just turn it off when they feel like it. That could add a lot of confusion to the editing process. So, you need to add a password when you lock Track Changes, but be mindful: you need to use a password that you know but one that others can't guess easily. Using the product name or a simple numeric code like 12345 will make it likely that the lock will be bypassed by anyone who's intent on getting control of the document.

EXERCISE 6.2

Track Changes

1. Turn Track Changes on.

2. View All Markup.

3. Add new text and edit existing text in your document so that you can see how Word shows additions and deletions.

4. Accept all changes.

5. Turn off Track Changes.

Summary

This chapter started by showing you how to add comments to a document. Once you learned about adding comments, I discussed how to add a reply to a comment and how to resolve a comment but keep the comment in the document for future reference by you and/ or your reviewers.

You also learned how to use the Review menu ribbon to move between comments in your document, as well as how to delete one or all comments within a document.

Next, I discussed how to turn Track Changes on and off so that you can see which reviewer made changes in which text. You also learned how to change the Track Changes view settings to view certain elements of Track Changes markup text and change lines. Then you learned how to move through all of the changes and accept and reject one or all changes.

I wrapped up the chapter with a discussion about locking Track Changes so that no other users can accept or reject changes or turn off Track Changes.

Key Terms

change lines   markup

comments   track changes

Exam Essentials

Understand how to add and manage comments.   Know how to add a comment to a document, reply to a comment, resolve a comment, restore a comment if the issue is not resolved after all, and delete one or all comments in a document.

Know how to turn on and use Track Changes.   Understand how to turn Track Changes on and off, how to view different types of markup in the document, and how to accept and reject changes.

Be able to lock and unlock Track Changes.   Know why you need to lock Track Changes when you share documents, how to add a password when locking Track Changes, and how to unlock Track Changes.

Review Questions

1. How can you tell who wrote a comment?
   A. The color of the change bar
   B. The color of the box around the comment
   C. The Review menu ribbon tells you who wrote it.
   D. The person's name appears at the top of the comment box.

2. How do you respond directly to a comment?
   A. Click Resolve in the comment box.
   B. Click Reply in the comment box.
   C. Write another comment.
   D. Click the Reject icon in the Review menu ribbon.

3. How do you know a comment is resolved?
   A. The comment no longer appears in the document.
   B. The Show Comments icon in the Review menu ribbon is no longer selected.
   C. The comment is grayed out in the right margin.
   D. Track Changes turns off.

4. How do you restore a resolved comment?
   A. Click the Accept icon in the Review menu ribbon.
   B. Click the comment and then click Reopen.
   C. Create a new comment so that you can repeat your question and/or ask the person who commented to insert their comment again.
   D. Show All Markup.

5. How do you delete all comments in a document?
   A. Click in the comment, and then click the Resolve icon.
   B. Click the Delete icon in the Review menu ribbon.
   C. Click the Reject icon in the Review menu ribbon, and then click Reject All Changes in the menu.
   D. Click the Delete icon in the Review menu ribbon, and then click Delete All Comments in the menu.

6. What menu option do you need to click to open Track Changes?
   A. Review
   B. View
   C. Home
   D. Insert

7. How do you see markup formatting within your document?

   A. Turn on Track Changes.

   B. Select All Markup in the Review menu ribbon.

   C. Click Show Markup in the Review menu ribbon.

   D. Click Accept in the Review menu ribbon.

8. How do you reject every change in your document and keep Track Changes on?

   A. Click Reject in the Review menu ribbon, and then click Reject And Move To Next in the drop-down menu.

   B. Click the Reject icon in the Review menu ribbon.

   C. Click Reject in the Review menu ribbon, and then click Reject All Changes in the drop-down menu.

   D. Show No Markup.

9. How do you accept a change and then move to the preceding change to review it?

   A. Click the Accept icon in the Review menu ribbon.

   B. Click Previous in the Review menu ribbon, and then click the Accept icon.

   C. Click the down arrow under the Accept icon, and then click Accept And Move To Next.

   D. Click the Accept icon, and then click the Previous icon.

10. Why should you add a password when you lock Track Changes?

   A. To keep others from unlocking Track Changes

   B. Because you don't trust other people with whom you share your documents

   C. Because Word requires it

   D. To keep people from turning Track Changes on

Excel
Exam MO-200

PART
II

Chapter

7

Managing Worksheets and Workbooks

MICROSOFT EXAM OBJECTIVES COVERED IN THIS CHAPTER:

✓ **Manage worksheets and workbooks**

- Import data into workbooks
    - Import data from .txt files
    - Import data from .csv files
- Navigate within workbooks
    - Search for data within a workbook
    - Navigate to named cells, ranges, or workbook elements
    - Insert and remove hyperlinks
- Format worksheets and workbooks
    - Modify page setup
    - Adjust row height and column width
    - Customize headers and footers
- Customize options and views
    - Customize the Quick Access toolbar
    - Display and modify workbook content in different views
    - Freeze worksheet rows and columns
    - Change window views
    - Modify basic workbook properties
    - Display formulas
- Configure content for collaboration
    - Set a print area
    - Save workbooks in alternative file formats
    - Configure print settings
    - Inspect workbooks for issues

Welcome to this book, designed to help you study for and pass the MO-200 Microsoft Excel (Excel and Excel 2019) exam and become a certified Microsoft Office Specialist: Excel Associate. If you're all settled in, it's time to get this show on the road.

In this chapter, I'll start by showing you how to import data in other formats into Excel spreadsheets, which Excel calls *worksheets*, as well as collections of spreadsheets that Excel calls a *workbook*. Next, I'll show you how to navigate within a workbook and get comfortable with the Excel interface.

When you feel good about creating an Excel spreadsheet, I'll show you how to format that spreadsheet so that it looks the way you want. You'll also learn how to change the way information is presented to make Excel work better for you.

Finally, I'll show you how to get your spreadsheets ready to share in print and online. You'll also learn how to *inspect* your workbooks so that you can find and remove hidden properties as well as fix any issues with accessibility and compatibility.

I'll have an exercise at the end of every section in this chapter so that you can practice doing different tasks. Then, at the end of this chapter, you'll find a set of Review Questions that mimic the test questions you'll see on the MO-200 exam.

Importing Data into Workbooks

If you need to import existing data into a workbook, you should first check to see if the file is in a format that Excel likes. The most common formats are the native Excel, text, and *comma-delimited value (CSV)* formats.

The native Excel format has the .xls filename extension that dates all the way back to MS-DOS days, so you can obviously open those files. However, if you open an older XLS file, you may experience some issues with formatting.

It is more likely that you will receive files in text format with the .txt file extension and in comma-separated values (CSV) format with the .csv file extension. These two formats are what Microsoft focuses on in the MO-200 exam.

Text and CSV formats use a *delimiter*, which is a character that separates blocks of text, like between numbers. A text file will use a tab character to separate those blocks. A CSV file uses commas to separate each block of text.

After you open a text file, Excel does not change the format of the file. The file remains with the .txt or .csv extension as you save updates to it.

Excel allows you to import and export up to 1,048,576 rows and 16,384 columns of text from or to a TXT or CSV file.

Bringing in Data from TXT Files

When you receive a text file from someone else, check the file to ensure that it has a delimiter character. (If you don't see any, then you must decide whether to add the delimiter character or just return the text file to the sender and tell that person to fix the file.)

Once you are satisfied that the text file is ready for Excel, open the text file as follows:

1. Click the File menu option.

2. Click the Open menu option on the left side of the screen.

3. Click Browse.

4. In the Open dialog box, click All Excel Files in the lower-right area of the box.

5. Select Text Files from the drop-down list.

6. Navigate to the location that created the text file.

7. Click the text filename.

8. Click Open.

The Text Import Wizard dialog box opens (see Figure 7.1) and shows you what the text file looks like in step 1 of the wizard. Click the Next button to see what the text will look like in an Excel worksheet, and then click Next again to see the data format Excel assigns to each column.

FIGURE 7.1   Text Import Wizard dialog box

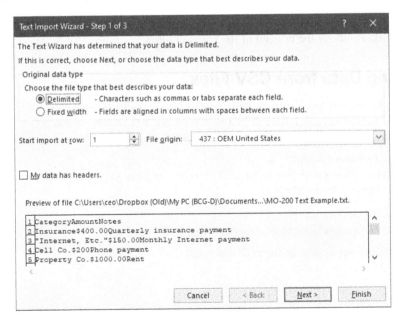

Though you can make changes in each of these steps, you don't need to know how to do that for the MO-200 exam. So, click the Finish button to view the imported spreadsheet.

A Cautionary Note About Formatting in a Text File

You see a yellow bar above the worksheet that cautions you about possible data loss if you save the worksheet in text format. Click Save As to save the file in another format (preferably Excel) or click Don't Show Again to hide this bar when you import other text files during the time you have Excel open. If you want to hide the bar but have it display the bar again if you import other text files, click the X icon at the right side of the bar.

Import a Text File into an Existing Worksheet

If you have text in another file that you want to place into a new worksheet within a workbook, here's how to do it:

1. Click the Data menu option.
2. If you see the Need To Import Data pop-up box, click Got It in the box.
3. In the Get & Transform Data section in the Data ribbon, as seen in Figure 7.2, click the From Text/CSV icon.
4. In the Import Data dialog box, navigate to the folder that contains the file.
5. Select the filename in the list.
6. Click Import.

The preview dialog box opens and shows you how the text will appear in the file. Click Load to import the data into a new worksheet with the name Sheet1, as you can see in the list of spreadsheet tabs at the bottom of the Excel window.

Importing Data from CSV Files

A CSV file is formatted specifically to be imported into spreadsheet software, and Excel knows CSV formatting cold. Each cell in a row is on one line of text separated by a comma with no spaces before or after the comma. For example:

Title,Column 1,Column 2
Excel considers each line in a CSV file to be one row, so you may have a
CSV file that looks like this:

Date,Payee,Amount,Notes
10/1,InsuranceCo,$400.00,Quarterly insurance payment

A comma does not appear at the end of a line.

FIGURE 7.2 Get & Transform section

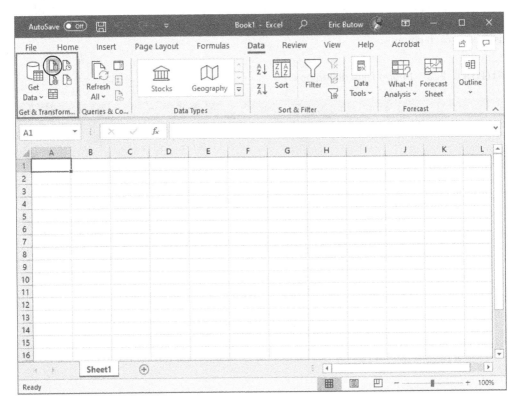

 What do you do when you have text that includes a comma in it? Put the text into quotes, and then add a comma outside the quote to start a new cell. For example, use **"One, Two",3,5** to add three separate cells in the row.

Add a CSV format file by following these steps:

1. Click the File menu option.

2. Click the Open menu option on the left side of the screen.

3. Click Browse.

4. In the Open dialog box, click All Excel Files in the lower-right area of the box.

5. Select Text Files from the drop-down list.

6. Navigate to the location that created the text file.

7. Click the text filename.

8. Click Open.

The Text Import Wizard dialog box opens (see Figure 7.3) and shows you what the text file looks like in step 1 of the wizard. Click the Next button to see what the text will look like in an Excel worksheet, and then click Next again to see the data format that Excel assigns to each column.

FIGURE 7.3 Import Data dialog box

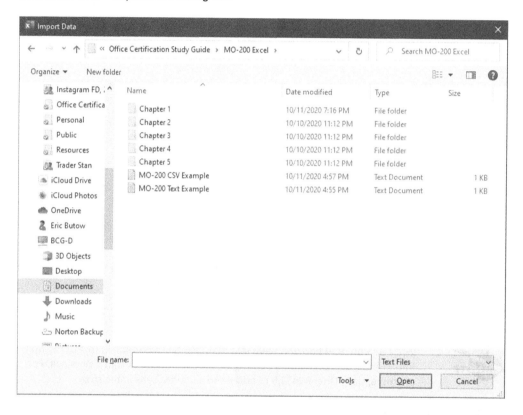

Insert a CSV File into a New Worksheet

You can also add a CSV file into a new worksheet within a workbook, much as you did with a text file, as follows:

1. Click the Data menu option.

2. If you see the Need To Import Data pop-up box, click Got It in the box.

3. In the Get & Transform Data section in the Data ribbon (see Figure 7.2), click the From Text/CSV icon.

4. In the Import Data dialog box (see Figure 7.3), navigate to the folder that contains the CSV file.

5. Click the filename in the list.

6. Click Import.

The preview dialog box appears, as shown in Figure 7.4, and it shows you how the text will appear in the file. Click Load to import the data into a new worksheet with the name Sheet1, as you can see in the list of spreadsheet tabs at the bottom of the Excel window.

FIGURE 7.4 Preview dialog box

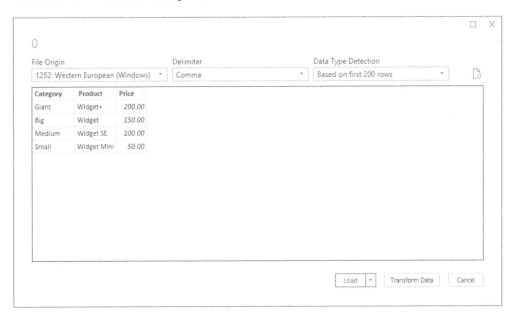

EXERCISE 7.1

Importing Text and CSV Format Files

1. Open a new workbook in Excel.

2. Import a text file into the workbook.

3. Import a CSV file into the workbook.

4. Save the workbook by pressing Ctrl+S.

Navigating Within Workbooks

After you populate a workbook, it can seem daunting to try to find the data within it. Excel has tools that make it easy.

Click the Search box in the Excel title bar, and then type the text that you want to find.

Searching for Data Within a Workbook

You can search for data on any worksheet in a workbook by following these steps:

1. Click the Home menu option, if necessary.

2. In the Editing section in the Home ribbon, click the Find & Select icon.

3. Select Find from the drop-down menu.

The Find And Replace dialog box appears so that you can search for information or replace one or more search terms, including specific formatting, with new text and/or formatting. If you want to replace text, select the Replace tab.

 You can also open the Find And Replace dialog box by pressing Ctrl+F. If you want to open the dialog box with the Replace tab active, press Ctrl+H.

Now you can replace text by typing the text you want to replace in the Find What text box, and then typing the replacement text in the Replace With text box.

Before you find and/or replace text, you may need to specify more information about what you want to find and/or replace. For example, you may want to change not only text in a cell, but also change the font and alignment of that text.

Open all find and replace options by clicking Options in the dialog box. The Find And Replace dialog box expands (see Figure 7.5) so that you can click one of the buttons or boxes to change information, as follows:

FIGURE 7.5   Find And Replace dialog box

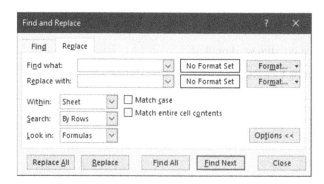

No Format Set   Informs you that no formatting has been applied to the text that you want to find and/or replace. If you change the format, the text in this button changes to Preview so that you can see how the text looks in the worksheet.

Format   Click the button to open the Find Format dialog box and change the format in one of six areas: Number, Alignment, Font, Border, Fill, and Protection. You will learn more about formatting cells later in this chapter.

Match Case   Find text that has the same case as what you typed in the Find box, such as a capitalized first letter in a word.

Match Entire Cell Contents   Find text that appears exactly like what you have typed in the Find box.

Within   The default selection in the Within box is Sheet, which searches for the text in the currently open worksheet. Click Sheet to select from the worksheet or the entire workbook in the drop-down list.

Search   The default selection in the Search box is By Rows, which searches for all instances of the search text in all rows. If you want to search for all instances of the text in all columns, click By Rows and then click By Columns in the drop-down list.

Look In   The Look In box has Formulas selected by default, which means that Excel will look for the search term in a specific type of text within the worksheet. If you have the Find tab open, then you can choose from Formulas, Values, Notes, or Comments in the drop-down list. If you have the Replace tab open, you can only select Formulas.

When you're ready to search for the text that you typed in the Find What text box, click the Find Next button to go to the next instance of the text in the open worksheet. If you search in the entire workbook, Excel searches for the text in the open worksheet first, and then it proceeds to search for all other instances of the text in subsequent worksheets.

If you click Find All, a dialog box appears that lists every instance of the text that Excel found in the worksheet or in the entire workbook. Click the instance in the list to open the cell in the corresponding worksheet.

Click Replace to replace only the next instance of the text with your replacement. If you want to replace any other text that meets your criteria, click the Replace button again to go to the next instance and replace that.

Replace all instances of the text and/or formatting in the Find text box by clicking the Replace All button. When Excel completes its search, a dialog box appears in the middle of the screen and tells you how many changes it made. Close the dialog box by clicking OK.

Important Search Tips

Unlike Microsoft Word, Excel allows you to add *wildcard* characters in the Find What box. Here's how:

- Add the question mark (?) to find a single character, such as **th?n** to find the words than, then, and thin.

- Add the asterisk (*) to find all characters that appear before or after a character, or between two characters. For example, type **d*r** to find dollar, divisor, and door.

- Add a tilde (~) before a question mark, asterisk, or another tilde to find cells that include a question mark, asterisk, or a tilde. For example, if you search for **Comment~?**, Excel shows all cells that have the text *Comment?*.

Navigating to Named Cells, Ranges, or Workbook Elements

Excel allows you to define names for a specific cell or for a *range* of cells, such as a block of income for a specific month. Here's how:

1. Select several cells by clicking and holding on one cell, then dragging the mouse pointer until all cells in the worksheet are highlighted, and then releasing the mouse button.

2. Click the Formulas menu option.

3. In the Defined Names section in the Formulas ribbon, as shown in Figure 7.6, click Define Name. (If the Excel window width is small, click the Define Name icon in the ribbon and then select Define Name from the drop-down menu.)

4. In the New Name dialog box, press Backspace and then type the new name in the Name box.

5. Click OK.

Now that you named a cell, go to another location in your worksheet or another worksheet in the workbook. You can find that named range by following these steps:

1. Click the Home menu option, if necessary.

2. Click Find And Select in the Editing section in the Home ribbon. (If the Excel window width is small, click the Editing icon in the ribbon and then click the Find And Select icon.)

3. From the drop-down menu, select Go To.

4. In the Go To dialog box, shown in Figure 7.7, click the name of the named range.

5. Click OK.

Excel highlights the named range within its worksheet.

 A faster way to open the Go To dialog box is to press Ctrl+G.

FIGURE 7.6   The Define Name menu option

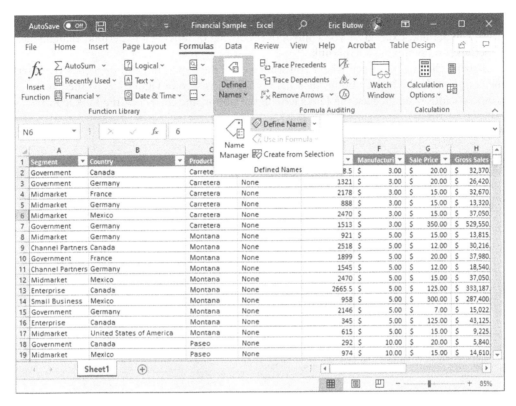

FIGURE 7.7   Go To dialog box

Inserting and Removing Hyperlinks

You can install as many *hyperlinks* as you want within the text of your workbook. After you insert a hyperlink, Excel gives you control over copying or moving a hyperlink, changing a hyperlink, and removing a hyperlink.

Start by clicking in the cell where you want to add the hyperlink, and then click the Insert menu option. In the Insert ribbon, click the Link icon, as seen in Figure 7.8. (If the Excel window width is small, click the Links icon in the ribbon and then click the Link icon.)

FIGURE 7.8   The Link icon

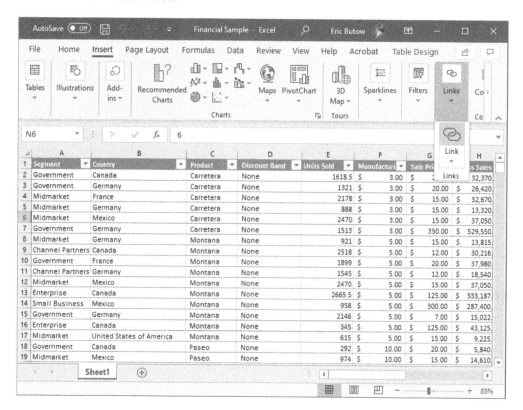

The Insert Hyperlink dialog box appears (see Figure 7.9) so that you can add your hyperlink.

You can add a hyperlink within the same worksheet, to another worksheet in your workbook, to another file or web page, or to an email address.

You can also open the Insert Hyperlink dialog box by pressing Ctrl+K.

FIGURE 7.9   The Insert Hyperlink dialog box

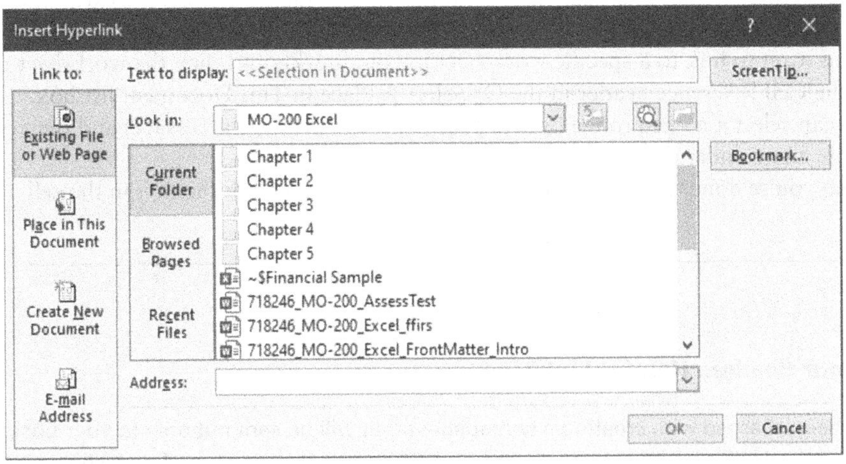

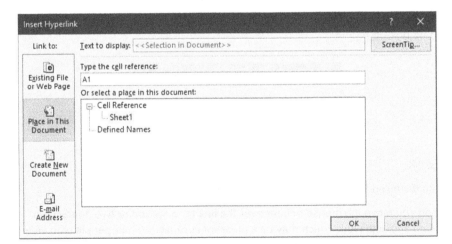

Within a Workbook

Adding a hyperlink to another location in a worksheet or workbook is useful when you need to move between cells quickly, and especially if you have long worksheets, many worksheets in a workbook, or both.

Start by clicking the cell and then opening the Insert Hyperlink dialog box. In the Link To box on the left side of the dialog box, click Place In This Document, as shown in Figure 7.10.

FIGURE 7.10   The Place In This Document menu option

In the Type The Cell Reference text box, you can type the cell that you want to link to by typing the column letter and then the row number. For example, typing **C24** will link to the cell in column C, row 24.

If you want to link to a specific worksheet in your workbook, click the worksheet name under the Cell Reference header in the Or Select A Place In This Document list box.

You can select a named range by scrolling down in the list (if necessary) and then clicking the range name under the Defined Names header.

When you're done, click OK and the hyperlink appears within the text in the cell.

 **Real World Scenario**

Give Your Readers Helpful Link Tips

You've been charged with creating a spreadsheet that will be sent not only to your boss, but also to senior leadership. You know that your workbook will have several worksheets, and you want to add links in cells that take people to different cells in the same worksheet and different worksheets. But how do you tell people what a link is all about when the link is in a cell that has a number in it?

ScreenTips to the rescue. When you add a *ScreenTip* to a link, a pop-up box appears when the user moves the mouse pointer over the link. Here's how to add a ScreenTip to a link:

1. Click the cell where you want to add the link.

2. Open the Insert Hyperlink dialog box, as you learned to do earlier in this section.

3. Click ScreenTip to the right of the Text To Display text box.

4. In the Set Hyperlink ScreenTip dialog box, type the text that you want to appear in the pop-up box.

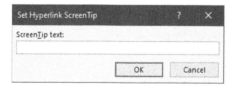

5. Click OK.

6. Close the Insert Hyperlink dialog box by clicking OK.

Now when you move the mouse pointer over the link for a second or two, the Screen Tip appears above the link, which may be a pleasant surprise to other people who view your workbook.

Link to an Existing File

You can add a hyperlink to another file, such as a Word file, that is important to your readers. When you link to another file, the appropriate program, such as Word, opens to view the linked file. Here's how to link to an existing file:

1. Click the cell where you want to add the hyperlink.

2. Click the Insert menu option.

3. In the Link section in the Insert ribbon, click the Link icon that you saw in Figure 7.8. (If the Excel window width is small, click the Links icon in the ribbon and then click the Link icon.)

4. In the Link To box on the left side of the dialog box, click Existing File Or Web Page, if necessary.

5. Click Current Folder (if necessary) or Recent Files to view the contents in the default Excel folder or all files that you have opened recently, respectively (see Figure 7.11).

6. Navigate to the folder that contains the file in the list, if necessary.

7. Click the file and then click OK.

FIGURE 7.11 A list of recently opened files

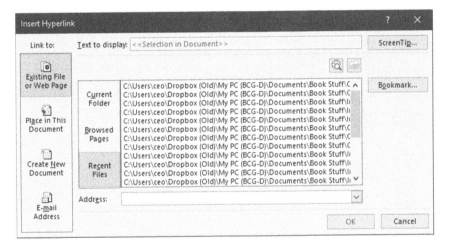

Link to a Web Page

You can add a hyperlink to a web page either on the web or on your network. That web page can be the home page, in which case you only need to type the URL of the site. If you need to link to a specific web page, you must type the full URL, including the web page name. You can also view recently browsed pages and select the page from the list.

When you link to a website, the default web browser opens and displays the page (or an error if the link is incorrect). Here's how to link to a web page:

1. Click the cell where you want to add the hyperlink.

2. Click the Insert menu option.

3. In the Link section in the Insert ribbon, click the Link icon that you saw in Figure 7.8. (If the Excel window width is small, click the Links icon in the ribbon and then click the Link icon.)

4. In the Link To box on the left side of the dialog box, click Existing File Or Web Page, if necessary.

5. Click Browsed Pages to view a list of all the web pages (see Figure 7.12).

6. Scroll up and down the list (if necessary), click the web page that you want to open, and then proceed to step 8.

7. If you don't see the web page that you want in the list, type the full URL in the Address box. That is, type **http://** or **https://** before the website and any specific web pages.

8. Click OK.

FIGURE 7.12   Browsed Pages list

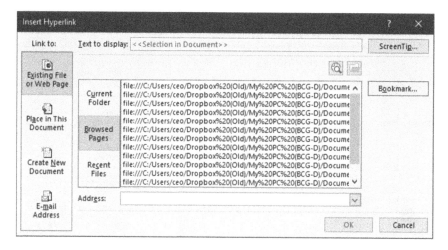

The link appears in the cell, and you can click the link to see if it opens the web page.

To an Email Address

Excel allows you to open a new email message so that you can send a message to that email address. You can also add a subject to the message. When you click the link, the default email program opens a new message window so that you can begin typing your message to the recipient.

Link to an email address by following these steps:

1. Click the cell where you want to add the hyperlink.
2. Click the Insert menu option.
3. In the Link section in the Insert ribbon, click the Link icon that you saw in Figure 7.8. (If the Excel window width is small, click the Links icon in the ribbon and then click the Link icon.)
4. In the Link To box on the left side of the Insert Hyperlink dialog box (see Figure 7.13), click E-mail Address.
5. Type the email address in the E-mail Address text box.
6. Add a subject for your message in the Subject text box.
7. Click OK.

FIGURE 7.13   E-mail Address menu option

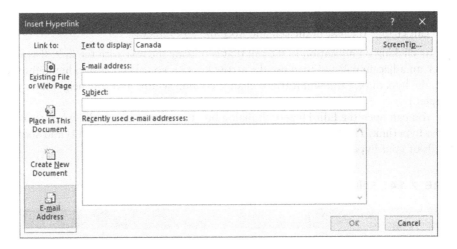

 If you type an email address in a cell, Excel adds a link to that email address automatically.

Copy and Move a Hyperlink

Once you create a hyperlink, you can copy it or move it to another cell. Here's how to do this:

1. Click the cell with the link that you want to move.
2. Click the Home menu option, if necessary.
3. Copy the cell with the link by clicking the Copy icon in the Clipboard section in the Home ribbon, and then proceed to step 5.

4. Move the cell with the link by clicking the Cut icon in the Clipboard section in the Home ribbon.

5. Click the cell in the workbook where you want to paste the text with the link.

6. Click the Paste icon in the Clipboard section in the Home ribbon.

As in Word, you can copy the linked text within a cell by pressing Ctrl+C, cut the linked text from a cell by pressing Ctrl+X, and paste the text into a new cell by pressing Ctrl+V.

Change a Hyperlink

Excel allows you to change a hyperlink in a cell in one of three ways:

- You can change the destination of the link.

- You can change how the link appears in the cell.

- You can change the text in the cell and keep the link intact.

Start by clicking on a location in the cell that is outside the text with the link. If you can't, then click an adjacent cell and then use the arrow keys on your keyboard to highlight the cell with the hyperlink. (You will learn to change column widths and row height later in this chapter.)

Now you can open the Edit Hyperlink dialog box the same way you did when you inserted a hyperlink. The Edit Hyperlink dialog box appears (see Figure 7.14) and shows you the details of your hyperlink.

FIGURE 7.14   Edit Hyperlink dialog box

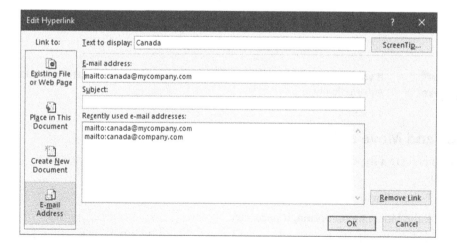

For example, if you link to an email address, then the E-mail Address option is selected in the Link To box, and you can see the email address and subject (if there is one) so that you can update that information quickly.

If you need to change the linked text that appears in the hyperlink, you can do so in the Text To Display box at the top of the dialog box.

When you finish making your changes, click OK. If you changed the link destination or email address, you may want to click the link to make sure that it works the way you expect.

You can change an existing hyperlink in your workbook by changing its destination, its appearance, or the text or graphic that is used to represent it.

Delete a Hyperlink

If you need to delete hyperlinked text in a cell, all you have to do is right-click the cell that has the link. In the context menu, as seen in Figure 7.15, click Remove Hyperlink. The link disappears from the text.

FIGURE 7.15   The Remove Hyperlink option in the context menu

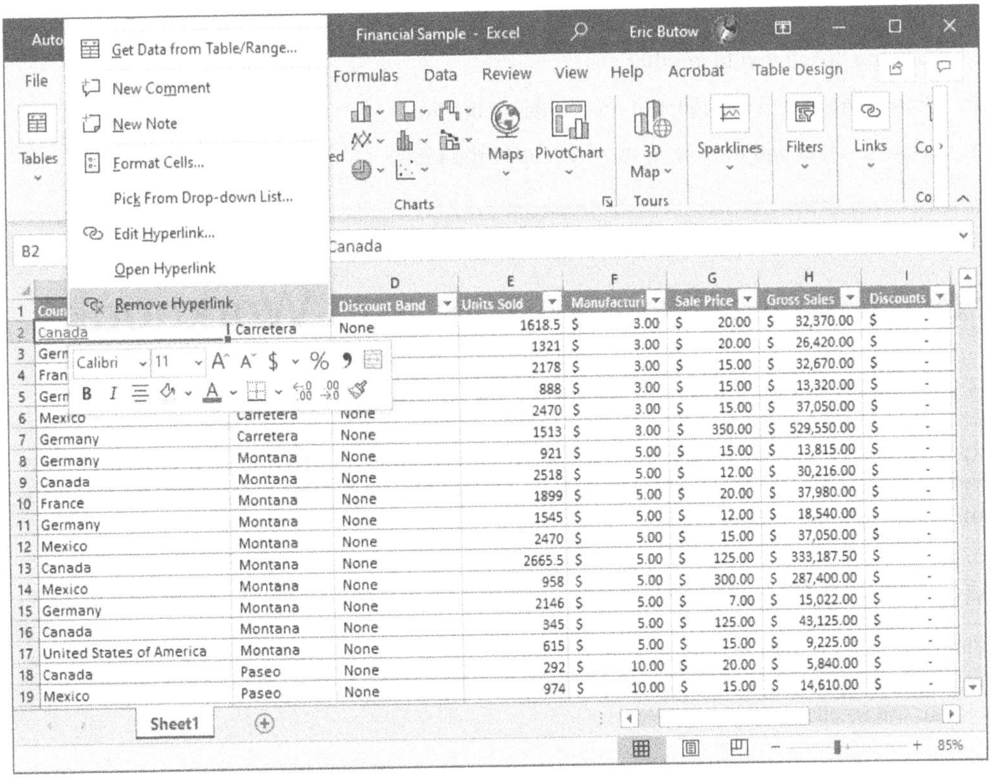

You can also delete the text in the cell as well as the link by right-clicking on the cell and then clicking Clear Contents in the context menu.

EXERCISE 7.2

Navigating in a Workbook

1. Open a new workbook.

2. Type text in 20 rows and 3 columns in the worksheet.

3. Select the 10 bottom rows and name the range.

4. Go to the top of the spreadsheet.

5. Search for the named range.

6. Click the first cell in the range.

7. Add text to the cell.

8. Link the text in the cell to a web page.

9. Copy the linked text to another cell.

10. Change the text in the cell, but don't change the link.

11. Delete the text and the link in the first cell in the table.

Formatting Worksheets and Workbooks

As you work with Excel, you may want to format how worksheets in a workbook appear, perhaps because you want it to look that way, people with whom you share the workbook expect it to look a certain way, or both. Excel allows you to modify the page settings, adjust the height of rows and the width of columns, and add headers and footers to pages, much as you would in a Word document.

Modifying Page Settings

When you need to modify page settings, begin by clicking the Page Layout menu option. The Page Setup section in the Page Layout ribbon (see Figure 7.16) shows you all the tools that you can use to change the page settings.

FIGURE 7.16   Page Setup section options

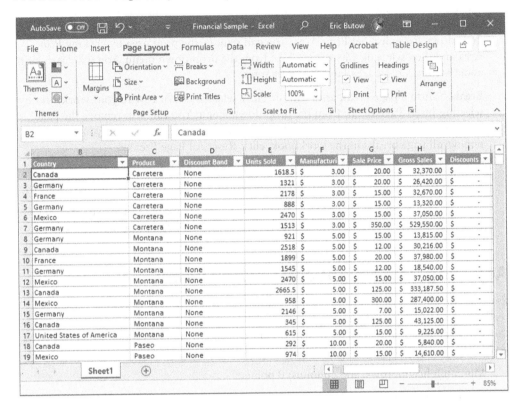

All of these icons appear in the ribbon no matter whether your window width is 800 pixels, as seen in Figure 7.16, or larger. Click one of the following options to make changes:

Margins   Change the margins for each printed page within a worksheet in the drop-down menu. The default is Normal, but you can select from Wide and Narrow margins. If none of the default options work for you, click Custom Margins at the bottom of the menu and then set your own margins in the Page Setup dialog box.

Orientation   Change between Portrait and Landscape orientation in the drop-down menu. The default is Portrait.

Size   Set the paper size in the drop-down menu. The default is Letter, which is 8.5 inches wide by 11 inches high. If none of the paper sizes meet your needs, click More Page Sizes at the bottom of the menu and then set your own paper size in the Page Setup dialog box.

Print Area   If you want to print a range of cells within a worksheet, select the cells by clicking and holding one cell in the range and then dragging until Excel selects all the cells. When you're done, release the mouse button and then click Print Area. From the drop-down list, select Set Print Area. You can remove the print area by clicking Print Area and then selecting Clear Print Area from the drop-down menu. You will learn more about setting a print area later in this chapter.

Breaks   Add a page break after the currently selected cell or row in your worksheet by selecting Insert Page Break from the drop-down menu. You can also remove the page break after the currently selected cell by clicking Remove Page Break. If you want to remove all page breaks in the workbook, click Reset All Page Breaks.

Background   Add a background image to your worksheet. You can add an image from a file on your computer, from the web using a Bing search, or from a OneDrive folder.

Print Titles   Opens the Page Setup dialog box so that you can tell Excel to print the same rows at the top and/or same columns at the left side of your printed worksheet.

Adjusting Row Height and Column Width

Excel has default row heights and column widths, but you may have to change those for readability. For example, you may need to extend the column width so that you can see all of the text in a cell within that column. The minimum, default, and maximum heights for rows and columns are as follows:

Minimum height, rows, and columns: 0 points

Default row height: 15 points

Default column width: 8.43 points

Maximum row height: 409 points

Maximum column width: 255 points

There are 72 points in an inch, or 2.54 centimeters.

Set Column to Specific Width

Here's how to change the column width:

1. Select a cell in the column.
2. Click the Home menu option, if necessary.

3. In the Cells section in the Home ribbon, click the Format icon. If your Excel window width is smaller, as shown in Figure 7.17, click the Cells icon and then click the Format icon.

4. Select Column Width from the drop-down menu, as shown in Figure 7.17.

5. In the Column Width dialog box, press the Backspace key to delete the highlighted measurement.

6. Type the new width in points.

7. Click OK.

FIGURE 7.17 Column Width option

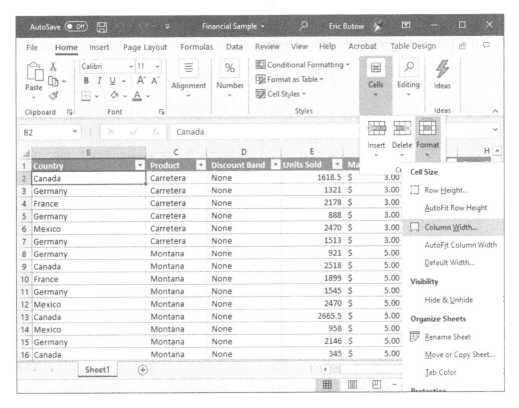

 You can also open the Column Width dialog box by right-clicking the column letter in the heading above the worksheet and then selecting Column Width from the context menu.

Change the Column Width to Fit the Contents Automatically with AutoFit

Excel has a built-in AutoFit feature that allows you to fit the width of the contents automatically. AutoFit a column by following these steps:

1. Select a cell in the column.

2. Click the Home menu option, if necessary.

3. In the Cells section in the Home ribbon, click the Format icon. If your Excel window width is smaller, as shown in Figure 7.18, click the Cells icon and then click the Format icon.

4. Select AutoFit Column Width from the drop-down menu, as shown in Figure 7.18.

FIGURE 7.18   AutoFit Column Width option

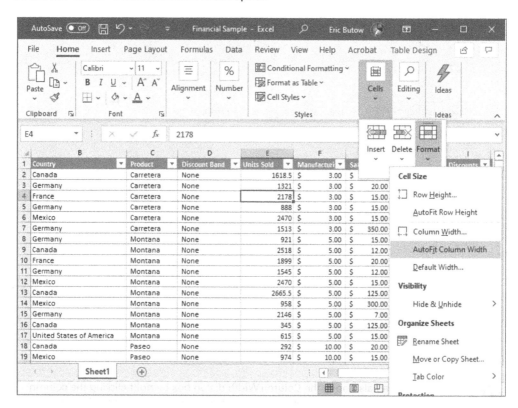

The column width changes to accommodate the text in the cell with the longest width.

Match the Column Width to Another Column

If you want more than one column to have the same width, here's how to do that:

1. Click a cell within the column that has your preferred width.
2. Click the Home menu option, if necessary.
3. In the Clipboard section in the Home ribbon, click Copy.
4. Click a cell in the column to which you want to apply the width.
5. In the Clipboard section in the Home ribbon, click the down arrow under the Paste icon.
6. Click the Keep Source Column Widths icon in the drop-down menu, as shown in Figure 7.19.

FIGURE 7.19 Keep Source Column Widths icon

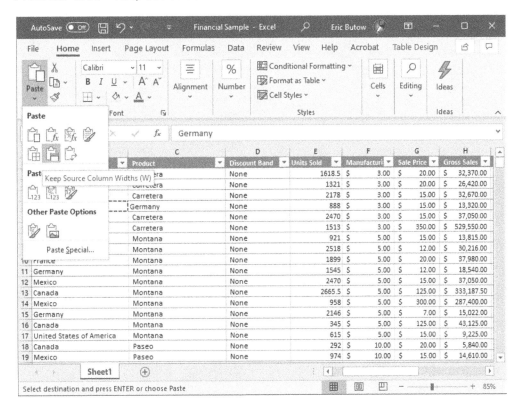

When you move the mouse pointer over the icon, the column width changes automatically so that you can preview the width of the column before you click the icon. If you move the mouse pointer away from the icon, the column reverts to its previous width.

Change the Default Width for All Columns on a Worksheet

If all you need is one width for all columns within a worksheet, change the default width by following these steps:

1. Click the Home menu option, if necessary.

2. In the Cells section in the Home ribbon, click Format. If the width of your Excel window is smaller, click the Cells icon and then click Format.

3. Select Default Width from the drop-down menu, as shown in Figure 7.20.

4. In the Standard Width dialog box, press Backspace to delete the width in the Standard Column Width text box.

5. Type the new width in points.

6. Click OK.

FIGURE 7.20 Default Width option

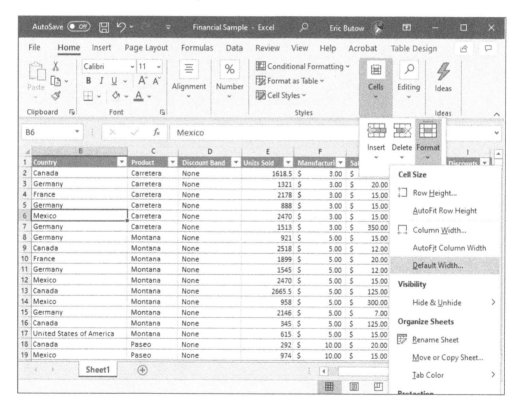

Excel resizes all columns in the worksheet to the width you specified.

Change the Width of Columns by Using the Mouse

When you want to change the width of a column by using the mouse, move the mouse pointer to the right border of the column heading above the worksheet. The cursor changes to a double-headed arrow, as shown in Figure 7.21.

FIGURE 7.21   The resize mouse pointer between two column headings

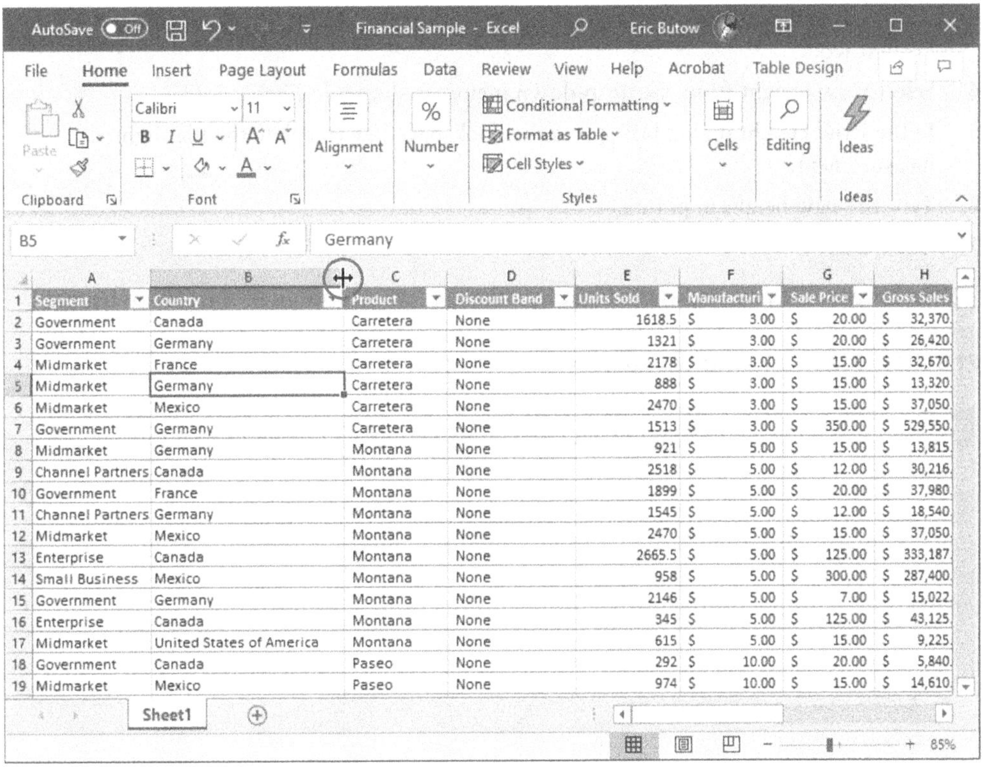

Now you can click, hold, and drag the boundary of the column heading to the left or right. As you drag, the width of the column to the left of the pointer changes, and a pop-up box above the pointer shows you the exact width of the column. When the column is the size that you want, release the mouse button.

> **NOTE** You can automatically fit a column to the width of the text inside it by moving the mouse pointer to the border on the right side of the column header and then double-clicking on the border.

Set a Row to a Specific Height

When you want to set a row to a specific height, the process for doing so is much the same as setting a column to a specific width, as follows:

1. Select a cell in the row.

2. Click the Home menu option, if necessary.

3. In the Cells section in the Home ribbon, click the Format icon. If your Excel window width is smaller, as shown in Figure 7.22, click the Cells icon and then click the Format icon.

4. Select Row Height from the drop-down menu, as shown in Figure 7.22.

5. In the Row Height dialog box, press the Backspace key to delete the highlighted measurement.

6. Type the new height in points.

7. Click OK.

Excel resizes the row and vertically aligns the text at the bottom of the cells in the row.

FIGURE 7.22 Row Height option

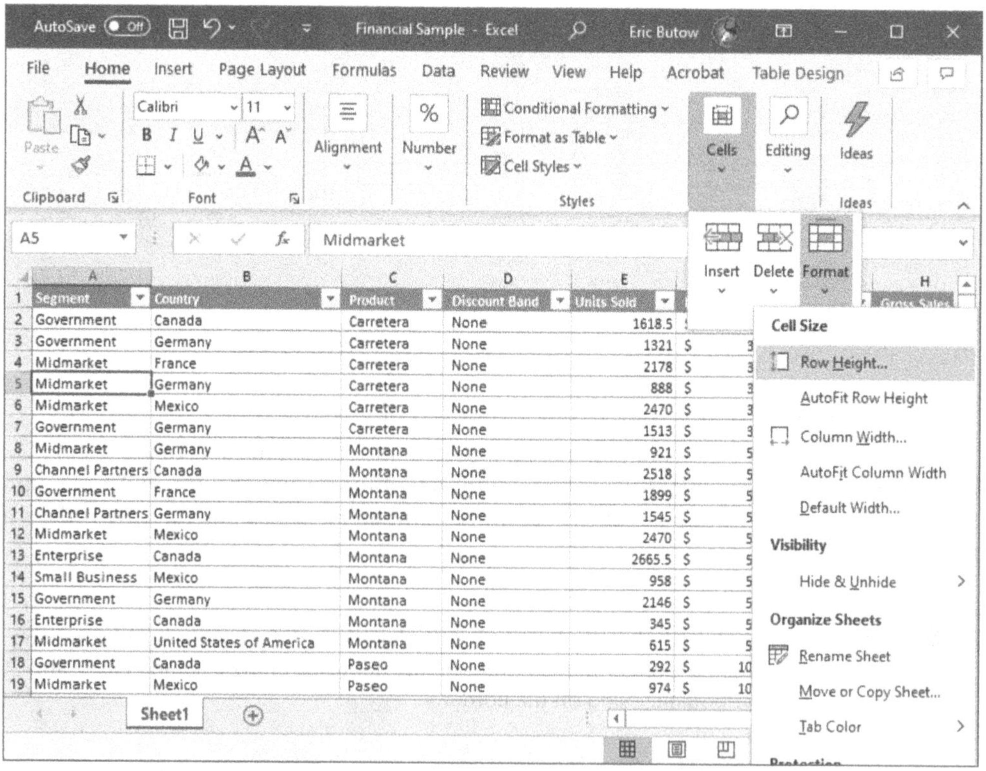

You can also open the Column Width dialog box by right-clicking the row number to the left of the worksheet and then selecting Row Height from the context menu.

Change the Row Height to Fit the Contents with AutoFit

As with columns, the built-in AutoFit feature allows you to fit the height of rows automatically to match the largest height in a row. Here's how to do this:

1. Select a cell in the row.
2. Click the Home menu option, if necessary.
3. In the Cells section in the Home ribbon, click the Format icon. If your Excel window width is smaller, as shown in Figure 7.23, click the Cells icon and then click the Format icon.
4. Select AutoFit Row Height from the drop-down menu, as shown in Figure 7.23.

The row height changes to accommodate the text in the cell with the largest height.

FIGURE 7.23   AutoFit Row Height option

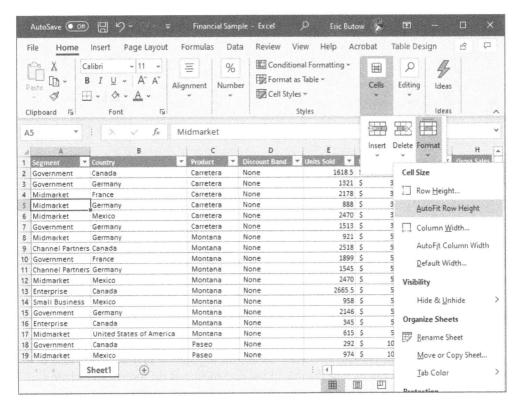

Change the Height of Rows by Using the Mouse

You can change the height of a row more quickly by using the mouse. Start by moving the mouse pointer to the bottom border of the row heading to the left of the worksheet. The cursor changes to a double-headed arrow, as shown in Figure 7.24.

FIGURE 7.24   The resize mouse pointer between two row headings

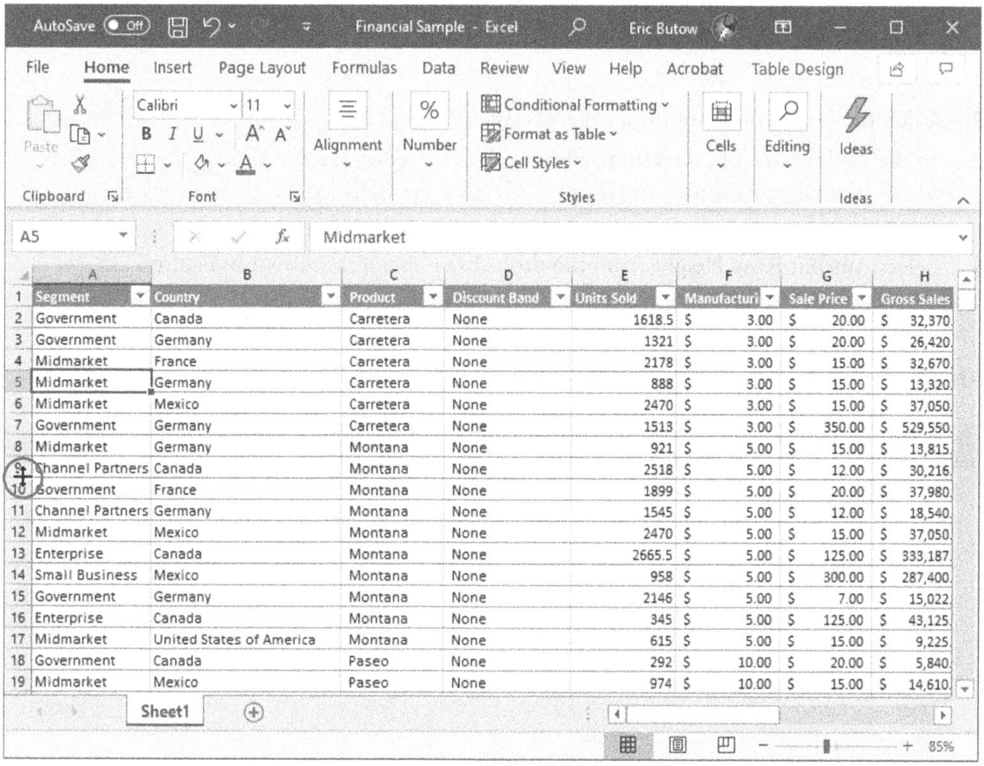

Now you can click, hold, and drag the boundary of the row heading up and down. As you drag, the height of the row above the pointer changes, and a pop-up box above the pointer shows you the exact height of the row. When the row is the size that you want, release the mouse button.

Customizing Headers and Footers

As with a Word document, you can add headers and footers into an Excel spreadsheet that will make it easier for users who view your documents in paper or PDF format to read it. For example, a header can include the title of the document and the footer can include a page number. Excel also makes it easy to customize headers and footers.

Add a Header or Footer

Add a header and footer into a worksheet by clicking the Insert menu option. In the Text section in the Insert menu ribbon, click the Header & Footer icon in the Text section (see Figure 7.25).

FIGURE 7.25   Header & Footer icon

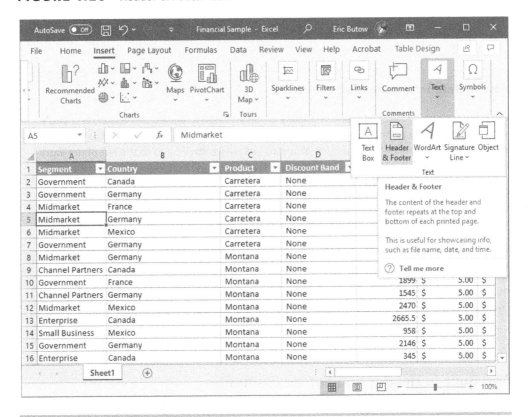

If your Excel window has a small width, and you don't see the Text section, here's what to do:

1. Click the right arrow button at the right side of the ribbon to view the rest of the ribbon icons.
2. Click the Text icon.
3. Click the Header & Footer icon.

The worksheet appears in Page Layout view with the cursor blinking within the middle section of the header. The cursor is in the center position so that the text will be centered on the page.

Click the left section of the header to place the cursor so that it is left-aligned in that section. Click the right section of the header to place the cursor right-aligned in that header. The text in all three sections in the header are vertically aligned at the top.

The Header & Footer ribbon appears automatically so that you can add a footer by clicking the Go To Footer icon in the Navigation section. The footer section appears at the bottom of the spreadsheet page with the cursor blinking in the center section of the footer.

Like the Header section, the footer is divided into three sections, but the text in all three sections is vertically aligned at the bottom. You can return to the header by clicking the Go To Header icon in the ribbon.

How to Hide the Header and Footer

The Page Layout view appears automatically when you add a header and footer, and you'll notice that the page is laid out in the default paper size, which is Letter (8.5 inches by 11 inches), as well as the default margins. You also see rulers above and to the left of the worksheet as you would in a Word document.

If you want to return the worksheet view to the default Normal view, click anywhere inside the worksheet (but not in the header or footer). Click the View menu option, and then click Normal in the Workbook Views section in the View ribbon.

Note that when you return to Normal view, gray page separator dashes appear in the worksheet.

You can view the header again by clicking the Page Layout View icon in the View ribbon. Then you can edit the header or footer by clicking the appropriate section.

Add Built-In Header and Footer Elements

Excel contains a number (ahem) of features for adding header and footer elements so that you don't have to update them automatically, such as with a page number.

After you add a header or footer and you have clicked within a section, the Header & Footer ribbon appears. You can add built-in elements from the Header & Footer and the Header & Footer Elements sections.

Header & Footer Section

In the Header & Footer section in the ribbon, click the Header icon to view a list of built-in header elements that you can add (see Figure 7.26).

FIGURE 7.26 Header element drop-down list

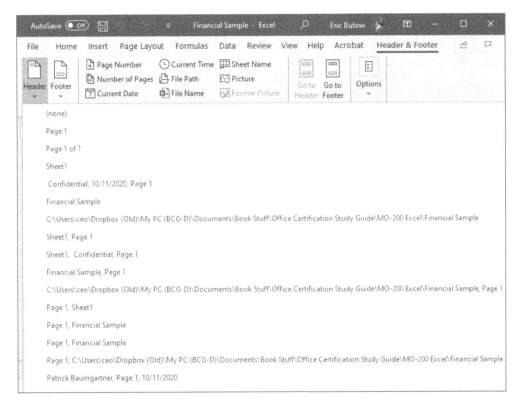

Some entries in the list have two or three options. An entry with two elements will place them in the header sections specified within the built-in entry. For example, the page number appears in the center section and the worksheet name appears in the right section.

After you select a header element from the drop-down list, Excel adds the header automatically and places the cursor back in the worksheet so that you can resume your work.

If you click within a footer, you can add a built-in footer element by clicking the Footer icon and then selecting a built-in footer element from the drop-down list. Once you do, Excel adds the footer and places the cursor in the worksheet.

Header & Footer Elements

The Header & Footer Elements section contains nine elements, as shown in Figure 7.27.

 If you don't see the Header & Footer ribbon, click the Header & Footer menu option.

FIGURE 7.27   Header & Footer Elements section

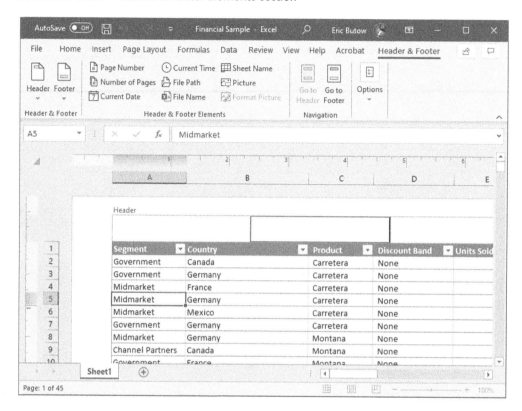

When you click one of the buttons (except for Format Picture, which is only active after you add a picture), its field name appears within brackets and preceded by an ampersand (&), such as &[Date]. Some fields are preceded by text, such as Page &[Page].

After you add the element and click outside the header or footer, the element appears properly. Click one of the icons in the ribbon to add the element.

Page Number   Adds the current page number in the worksheet

Number Of Pages   Displays the number of pages in the worksheet that contain data

Current Date   Displays the current date. Excel does not update the date until you click the date in the header or footer and then click in the worksheet again.

Current Time   Displays the current time. Excel updates the time when you click the time in the header or footer and then click in the worksheet.

Add the workbook folder path and file name   Add a page break after the currently selected cell or row in your worksheet by selecting Insert Page Break from the drop-down menu. You can also remove the page break after the currently selected cell by clicking Remove Page Break. If you want to remove all page breaks in the workbook, click Reset All Page Breaks.

Add the workbook file name   Add a background image to your worksheet. You can add an image from a file on your computer, from the web using a Bing search, or from a OneDrive folder.

Add the worksheet name   Opens the Page Setup dialog box so that you can tell Excel to print the same rows at the top and/or the same columns at the left side of your printed worksheet

Picture   Opens the Insert Pictures dialog box so that you can insert a picture from a file on your computer or network, from a Bing Image Search, or from your default One-Drive folder. If the picture is larger than the header or footer, the picture appears on the page within the left and right margins.

Format Picture   Opens the Format Picture dialog box so that you can change the size and orientation, crop the picture, change the color, brightness, and contrast settings, and add alternative (Alt) text

Delete a Header and Footer

If you need to delete the element, double-click the element name to select it, and then press Delete on the keyboard. The header and footer remain in the document, and the page separator dashes appear in the worksheet.

You can delete the header and footer from the entire workbook by following these steps:

1. Click the Page Layout menu option.
2. In the Page Setup section in the Page Layout ribbon, click Print Titles.
3. In the Page Setup dialog box, as shown in Figure 7.28, click the Header/Footer tab.
4. Click the header and/or footer name in the Header or Footer box, respectively.
5. Click (none) in the list. (You may need to scroll up and down in the list to find it.)
6. Click OK.

Even when you remove a header and/or footer, the header and footer place-holder remains in the document if you want to add a header or footer later.

You can view the header and footer again by clicking the View menu option, clicking the Page Layout icon in the Workbook Views section, and then clicking Add Header or Add Footer at the top and bottom of the page, respectively.

FIGURE 7.28   Page Setup dialog box

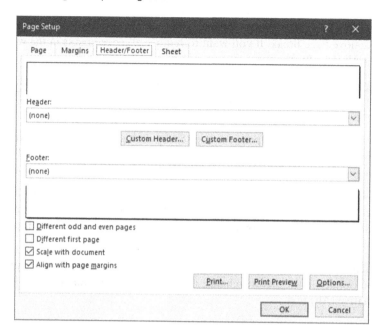

EXERCISE 7.3

Formatting a Workbook

1. Open a new workbook.

2. Change the column A width to 40 points.

3. Increase the height of row 1 as you see fit by using the mouse.

4. Add a header with the current date.

5. Add a footer with the page number.

6. Return to the normal workbook view and continue working in your worksheet.

Customizing Options and Views

Excel offers you plenty of ways to change the options that you can access as you work in a workbook, as well as what you see in ribbons and toolbars so that you can get your work done more quickly.

You can customize the Quick Access Toolbar, create and modify custom views, and freeze rows and columns in a worksheet so that they don't move as you navigate within a worksheet.

Customizing the Quick Access Toolbar

Excel includes a toolbar for accessing tools and commands quickly without having to click the menu option and then find the option in the ribbon. Microsoft naturally calls this the Quick Access Toolbar, and you can add features from a ribbon to the toolbar.

The toolbar itself appears at the left side of the Excel window title bar, but you can move the toolbar below the ribbon instead. By default, there are only four commands that you can access in the toolbar:

- You can turn the AutoSave feature off and on; the default setting is off.

- Save

- Undo

- Redo

As you use the Quick Access Toolbar, keep the following in mind:

- You can only add commands and tools to the toolbar, not other things that you may want to add quickly, such as cell styles.

- The toolbar only appears on one line. If there are more icons in the toolbar than it can hold, then you will see a right arrow at the right side of the toolbar that you can click to view more icons.

- The button sizes in the toolbar are fixed.

Add a Command to the Quick Access Toolbar

You can add a command to the toolbar in one of two ways. The first is to add the command from a ribbon. The other is to add a command from the Customize Quick Access Toolbar menu.

Add from the Ribbon

Whenever you're in a ribbon and you see an option that you want to add to the Quick Access Toolbar, here's what to do:

1. Click the menu option to open its associated ribbon.

2. In the ribbon, right-click the word or icon associated with the command that you want to add to the toolbar.

3. Select Add To Quick Access Toolbar from the drop-down menu (see Figure 7.29).

   You see the new icon at the right side of the toolbar, as you can also see in Figure 7.29.

FIGURE 7.29   The new icon in the Quick Access Toolbar

	A	B	C	D	E	F	
1	Segment	Country	Product	Discount Band	Units Sold	Manufactur	Sal
2	Government	Canada	Carretera	None	1618.5	$ 3.00	$
3	Government	Germany	Carretera	None	1321	$ 3.00	$
4	Midmarket	France	Carretera	None	2178	$ 3.00	$
5	Midmarket	Germany	Carretera	None	888	$ 3.00	$
6	Midmarket	Mexico	Carretera	None	2470	$ 3.00	$
7	Government	Germany	Carretera	None	1513	$ 3.00	$
8	Midmarket	Germany	Montana	None	921	$ 5.00	$
9	Channel Partners	Canada	Montana	None	2518	$ 5.00	$
10	Government	France	Montana	None	1899	$ 5.00	$
11	Channel Partners	Germany	Montana	None	1545	$ 5.00	$
12	Midmarket	Mexico	Montana	None	2470	$ 5.00	$
13	Enterprise	Canada	Montana	None	2665.5	$ 5.00	$
14	Small Business	Mexico	Montana	None	958	$ 5.00	$
15	Government	Germany	Montana	None	2146	$ 5.00	$
16	Enterprise	Canada	Montana	None	345	$ 5.00	$

Add from the Customize Quick Access Toolbar Menu

You can also add a command from the Customize Quick Access Toolbar drop-down menu. Start by clicking the down arrow at the right side of the Quick Access Toolbar in the Excel window title bar. If you haven't added any icons to the toolbar, you will see the icon to the right of the Redo icon.

Next, click one of the options without a check mark to the left of the command name in the drop-down menu, as you can see in Figure 7.30. (You will learn how to remove options from the toolbar later in this chapter.)

If you want to see a list of all commands and add them to the Quick Access Toolbar, select More Commands from the drop-down menu to open the Excel Options dialog box. Using this dialog box to add commands is (mostly) beyond the scope of this book, but you can explore this dialog box at your leisure.

FIGURE 7.30   Customize Quick Access Toolbar drop-down menu

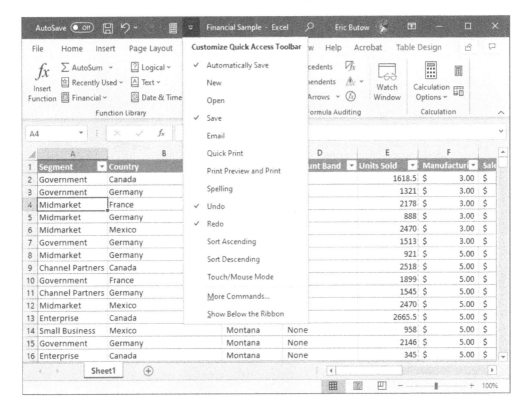

Remove a Command from the Quick Access Toolbar

There are two ways that you can remove a command from the Quick Access Toolbar:

- Right-click the command in the toolbar, and then select Remove From Quick Access Toolbar from the drop-down menu.

- Click the down arrow at the right side of the Quick Access Toolbar, and then click a command that has a check mark next to it.

In both cases, the icon disappears from the toolbar and you can go back to work.

Move the Quick Access Toolbar

By default, the Quick Access Toolbar appears within the Excel window title bar. You can move the toolbar below the ribbon, where it will stay even if you close Excel and reopen it.

All you need to do to move the Quick Access Toolbar is click the down arrow at the right side of the toolbar and then click Show Below The Ribbon. The toolbar appears under the ribbon (see Figure 7.31).

FIGURE 7.31   The Quick Access Toolbar below the ribbon

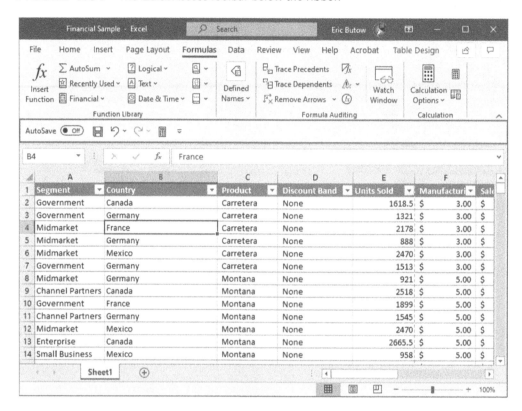

If you want to move the toolbar back, click the down arrow at the right side of the toolbar and then select Show Above The Ribbon from the drop-down menu.

Reset the Quick Access Toolbar to the Default Settings

Follow these steps if you need to reset the Quick Access Toolbar to its default settings:

1. Click the down arrow at the right side of the Quick Access Toolbar.
2. Select More Commands from the drop-down menu.
3. Click Reset in the Excel Options dialog box, as shown in Figure 7.32.
4. Select Reset Only Quick Access Toolbar from the drop-down menu.
5. Click Yes in the Reset Customizations dialog box.
6. Click OK.

All of the commands that you added in the toolbar disappear, and you see only the four default options.

FIGURE 7.32   Reset button in Excel Options dialog box

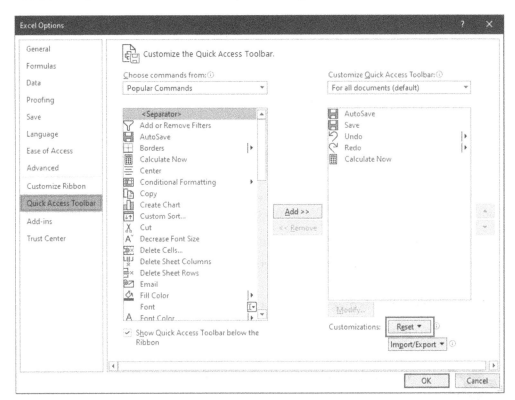

Displaying and Modifying Workbook Content in Different Views

Excel allows you to change the view on the document so that you can zoom in and zoom out within a worksheet, but Excel only has five built-in magnification levels, from 25 percent to 200 percent, as well as the ability to fit the worksheet to the window.

What's more, you can set your own custom view type. Here's how:

1. Click the View menu option.

2. In the Zoom section in the View ribbon, click the Zoom icon.

3. In the Zoom dialog box, as shown in Figure 7.33, select the custom view or type it in the Custom box. The default custom setting is 100 percent.

4. Click OK.

FIGURE 7.33   Zoom dialog box

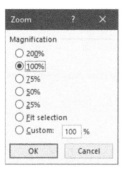

When you view your document, Excel allows you to create a custom view to make workbook content appear the way you prefer. You can save three different types of views:

Display settings: Used to hide rows, columns, and filter settings

Print settings: Used to set margins, headers, footers, and other worksheet and page settings

A specific print area: Settings applied to a particular print area

You can also create multiple views, each with a different name.

When you add a custom view, keep the following in mind:

- You can only add a custom view to a worksheet that you added within that one worksheet. If you create a different worksheet in the same workbook or a new one, you need to create new custom views for that worksheet.

- If any worksheet in the workbook contains an Excel table, which you will learn about in Chapter 9, "Working with Tables and Table Data," then Custom Views is disabled.

Create a Custom View

Here's how to create a custom view in a worksheet:

1.   Click the View menu option.

2.   In the Workbook Views section in the View ribbon, click the Custom Views icon (see Figure 7.34).

3.   In the Custom Views dialog box, click Add.

4.   In the Add View dialog box, as shown in Figure 7.35, type the name for the view in the Name box.

FIGURE 7.34 Custom Views icon

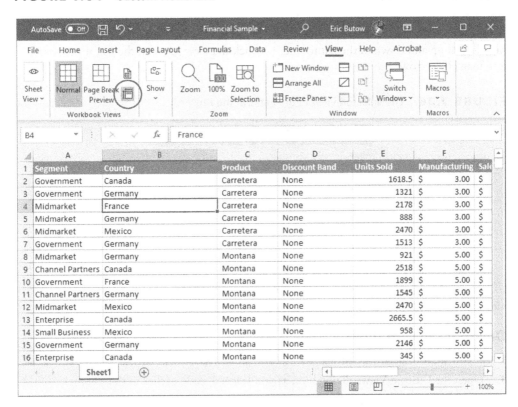

5. The two view settings are selected by default so that you will view print settings as well as hidden row, column, and filter settings. Turn one or both views off by clicking the appropriate check box.

6. Click OK.

FIGURE 7.35 Add View dialog box

Apply a Custom View

When you want to show a view, open the Custom Views dialog box again. You see the view highlighted in the list, as seen in Figure 7.36. (If you have more views than the window can hold, scroll up and down in the list to find it.) Click the view name in the list, if necessary, and then click Show.

FIGURE 7.36   The selected view in the list is at the top.

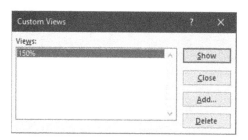

You see the changes in your view. For example, if your custom view is 150 percent, the view of your worksheet changes to 150 percent of the default magnification.

Delete a Custom View

When you want to delete a custom view, follow these steps:

1. Open the Custom Views dialog box, as you learned to do earlier in this chapter.
2. In the Custom Views dialog box, click the view that you want to delete in the list.
3. Click Delete.
4. Click Yes in the dialog box.

The view disappears from the list. Close the dialog box by clicking Close.

Freezing Worksheet Rows and Columns

You can freeze a row or column in a worksheet so that a row and/or column remains visible on the worksheet even as you scroll through it. This feature is especially useful if you have header rows or columns to which you will need to refer as you scroll through a worksheet that doesn't fit in the Excel window.

Freeze the First Column

If you only want to freeze the first column in the worksheet (that is, column A), follow these steps:

1. Click the View menu option.
2. In the Window section, click Freeze Panes.
3. Select Freeze First Column from the drop-down menu, as shown in Figure 7.37.

FIGURE 7.37   Freeze Panes drop-down menu

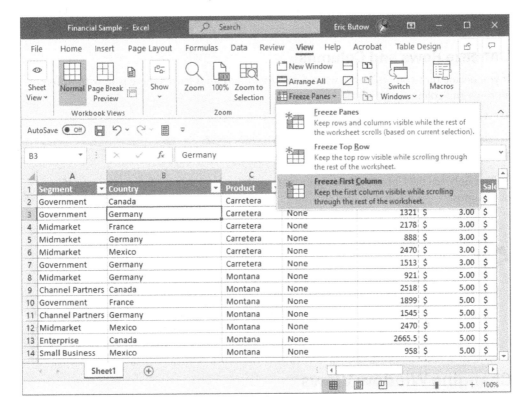

A darker line appears at the right edge of column A, which shows you that the column is frozen.

Freeze the First Row

If you want to freeze only the first row in the worksheet (that is, row 1), follow these steps:

1. Click the View menu option.
2. In the Window section in the View ribbon, click Freeze Panes.
3. Select Freeze Top Row from the drop-down menu in Figure 7.37.

A darker line appears at the right edge of row 1, which shows you that the row is frozen.

Freeze Any Column or Row

You can select one or more columns or rows to freeze. However, you need to select the cell below the row(s) and to the right of the column(s) that you want to freeze. After you do that, follow these steps:

1. Click the View menu option.
2. In the Window section, click Freeze Panes.
3. Select Freeze Panes from the drop-down menu in Figure 7.37.

The line above the selected cell and the line to the left of the selected cell are darker. This means that all rows above the darker line and all columns to the left of the darker line are frozen.

Unfreeze Rows and Columns

If you decide that you no longer want a row and/or column frozen, here is how to unfreeze all rows and columns:

1. Click the View menu option.

2. In the Window section in the View ribbon, click Freeze Panes.

3. Select Unfreeze Panes from the drop-down menu.

You only see the Unfreeze Panes option if you have one or more frozen rows and/or columns.

There are two issues that you will encounter when freezing panes:

- You cannot unfreeze panes by clicking Undo. You must unfreeze panes using the Unfreeze Panes option in the View ribbon.

- You cannot view frozen panes in Page Layout View. If you try to switch to Page Layout View, a dialog box warns you that all cells will be unfrozen. Click OK to unfreeze all panes and view your work in Page Layout view.

Changing Window Views

By default, Excel shows the worksheet in what it calls Normal view, which shows the worksheet. When you need to view the worksheet before you print it to your printer or to a PDF file, you can view where the page breaks are on each page in the Page Break Preview view, as well as how the worksheet will appear on each page in the Page Layout view.

Page Break Preview

View all the page breaks in your worksheet by first clicking the View menu option. Then, in the View ribbon, click the Page Break Preview icon in the Workbook Views section. The worksheet appears with page breaks, as shown in Figure 7.38.

Pages are bordered by a solid blue line. Page breaks are denoted by a dashed blue line. As you scroll up and down the pages, you see gray page numbers in the background, but Excel does not print these page numbers.

Page Layout View

If you need to see how a worksheet appears on printed pages, as well as add a header and/or footer, you need to view your worksheet in Page Layout view.

FIGURE 7.38   Page Break Preview view

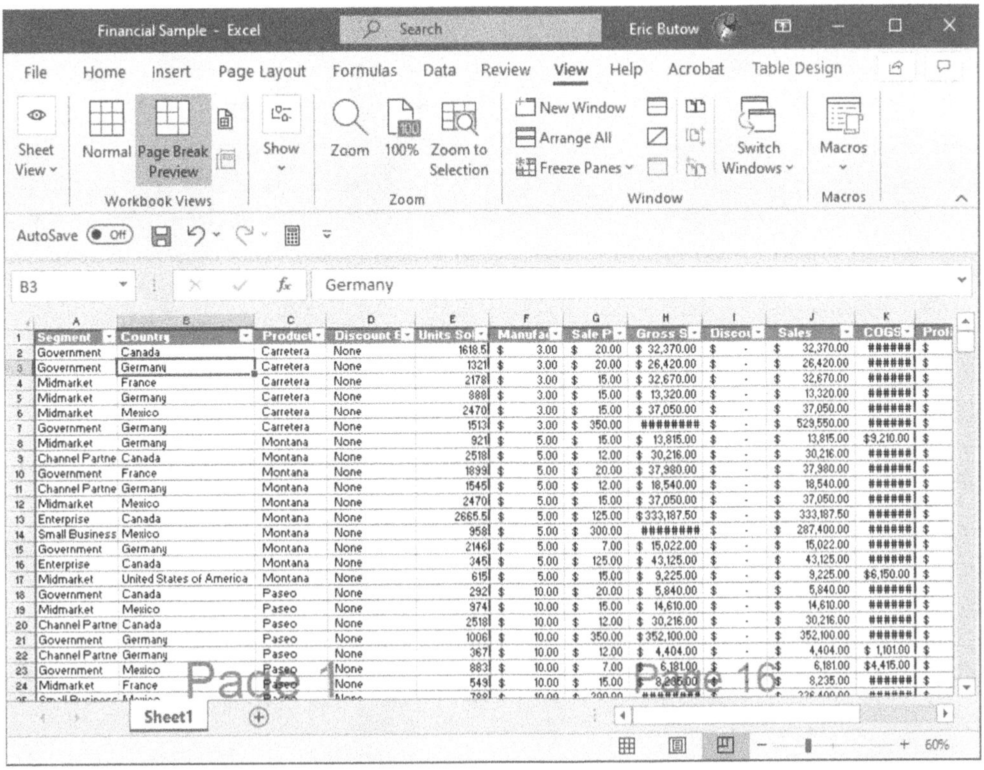

Start by clicking the View menu option. In the View ribbon, click the Page Layout View icon. You see the worksheet contained within graphic representations of pages along with a ruler above and to the left of each page (see Figure 7.39).

Click Add Header at the top of the page and click Add Footer at the bottom of the page to add a header and footer, respectively.

Normal View

If you're viewing the worksheet in Page Break Preview view or Page Layout view, you can return to Normal view by first clicking the View menu option. Then, in the View ribbon, click the Normal icon in the Workbook Views section.

> If you're in Page Break Preview view or in Page Layout view and then go back to Normal view, Excel displays page breaks in your worksheet as dashed gray lines. If you want to turn off these page breaks, you must close the worksheet and then reopen it.

FIGURE 7.39 Page Layout view

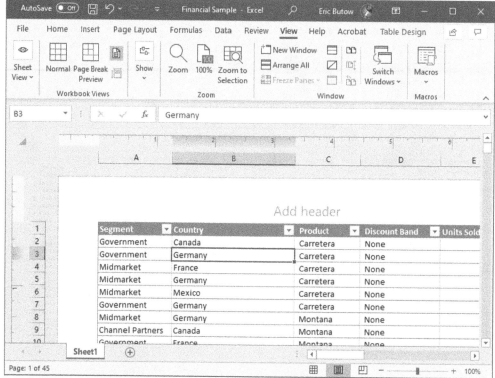

Modifying Basic Workbook Properties

Excel constantly keeps track of basic properties about your workbook, including the size of the workbook file, who last edited it, and when the workbook was last saved.

If you need to see these properties and add some of your own, click the File menu option. In the menu on the left side of the File screen, click Info. Now you see the Info screen, which is shown in Figure 7.40.

The Properties section appears at the right side of the screen. Scroll up and down in the Info screen to view more properties. Excel doesn't show all properties by default, but you can reveal the hidden properties by clicking the Show All Properties link at the bottom of the Properties section.

You can also add properties, including a workbook title, a tag (which is Microsoft's term for a keyword), and a category. For example, click Add A Title in the Properties section to type the workbook title in the box.

FIGURE 7.40   Info screen

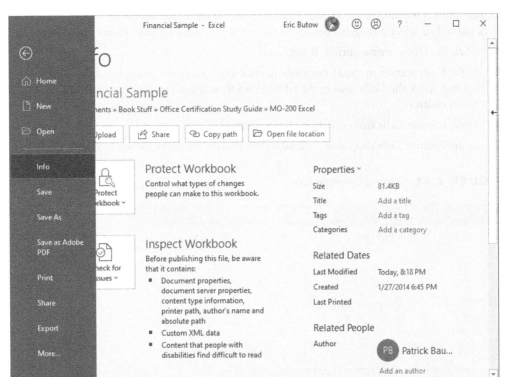

Displaying Formulas

Excel gives you ways to display and hide *formulas*, as well as their results, from within a workbook. You can also protect the worksheet to keep your views from being changed by anyone with whom you share your workbook.

Switch Between Displaying Formulas and Their Results

By default, Excel shows the results of a formula within the worksheet but only shows the formula in the Formula Bar above the worksheet.

You can display the formula by pressing Ctrl+`. The grave (`) accent is on the key with the tilde (~) on most keyboards. You can hide the formula again by pressing Ctrl+`.

When you show the formula in the worksheet, the width of the column changes to accommodate as much of the formula as possible. When you show the result again, Excel returns the column width to where it was before you displayed the formula.

Hide a Formula in the Formula Bar

You can hide a formula in the Formula Bar, but only if the worksheet is protected. After you click the cell or select a range of cells with formulas you want to hide, follow these steps:

1. Click the Home menu option, if necessary.
2. In the Cells section in the Home ribbon, click Format. (If the Excel window width is small, click the Cells icon in the ribbon and then select Format from the drop-down menu.)
3. Select Format Cells from the drop-down menu.
4. In the Format Cells drop-down menu, select Protect Sheet, as shown in Figure 7.41.

FIGURE 7.41   Protect Sheet option

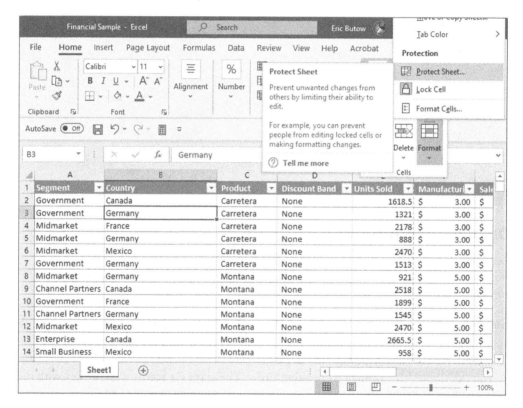

5. Click the Hidden check box.
6. Click OK.
7. Click the Review menu option.

8. In the Protect section in the Review ribbon, click Protect Sheet (see Figure 7.42). (If the Excel window width is small, click the Protect icon in the ribbon and then select Protect Sheet from the drop-down menu.)

FIGURE 7.42 Protect Sheet dialog box

9. In the Protect Sheet dialog box, leave all the check boxes selected. You can add a password in the Password To Unprotect Sheet text box if you plan to share the workbook with anyone else. Otherwise, click OK.

The formula no longer appears in the Formula Bar.

When you hide a formula in the Formula Bar, there is no way to edit the formula until you unprotect the worksheet. You can unprotect the sheet by clicking the Review menu option and then clicking Unprotect Sheet in the Protect section in the Review ribbon.

EXERCISE 7.4

Changing Workbook Properties and Views

1. Open a new or existing workbook.

2. Move the Quick Access Toolbar under the ribbon.

3. Create a custom view of 50 percent magnification.

4. Freeze the first column and row in the worksheet, or the first worksheet in the workbook.

5. View how the worksheet page breaks will appear.

6. Add a title to the workbook.

7. Click a cell in a worksheet that has a formula.

8. Hide the formula in the Formula Bar.

Configuring Content for Collaboration

Excel makes it easy to share workbooks with other people, such as people in the finance, sales, and marketing departments who need to see financial forecasts for the next quarter. Before you do that, you must determine what information you want to share.

You can set a print area within a worksheet, save your workbook in a different format, configure your print settings before you print a document to share on paper or electronically, and inspect your workbook so that you can hide information that you want to keep hidden.

Setting a Print Area

If you print a specific area of rows and columns often, such as a summary of the company's profit and loss for the current quarter, Excel allows you to define a print area within a worksheet.

After you select the cells that you want in the print area within the worksheet, set the print area as follows:

1. Click the Page Layout menu option.

2. In the Page Setup section in the Page Layout ribbon, click Print Area.

3. Click Set Print Area, as shown in Figure 7.43.

4. Click outside the selected area in the worksheet to view the print area, which has a dark gray border around the cell or group of cells in the print area.

Excel saves the print area after you save the workbook.

FIGURE 7.43 Set Print Area option

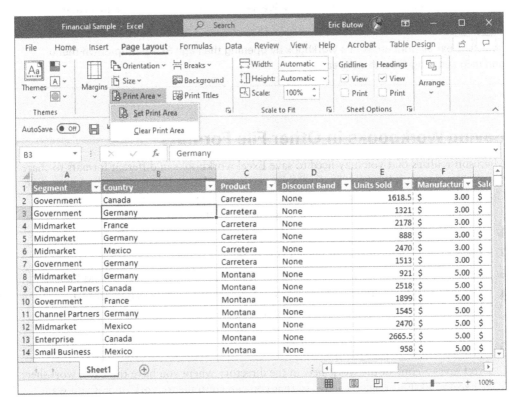

Configuring Print Areas

If you set a single cell as a print area, a dialog box opens and asks you to confirm that this is what you want. Click OK to proceed.

After you set a print area, you can add cells to a print area by selecting one or more cells outside the print area. After you open the View menu ribbon, click Print Area, and then select Add To Print Area from the drop-down menu. The added print area appears with a darker gray line around the cell(s).

You can also set multiple print areas. Each print area prints as a separate page. After you select the first cell or group of cells, hold down the Ctrl key and then select each subsequent cell or group of cells in the worksheet. When you're done, set the print area. Each print area prints as a separate page.

How do you view all of the page areas? Click the View menu option. In the Workbook Views section in the View ribbon, click Page Break Preview. You see all of the print areas in different sections on the screen.

You can clear all print areas in a workbook by opening the Page Setup drop-down menu and then selecting Clear Print Area.

Saving Workbooks in Other File Formats

Microsoft realizes that you may need to save Excel workbooks in different formats to share them with other people who may have older versions of Excel, other spreadsheet apps (like Google Sheets), or no spreadsheet program at all. Rest easy—Excel has you covered.

Here's how to save a workbook in a different file format:

1. Click the File menu option.
2. Click Save As in the menu on the left side of the File screen.
3. On the right side of the Save As screen, click the Excel Workbook (*.xlsx) box.
4. Select one of the file formats from the list shown in Figure 7.44. These formats come from a variety of categories, including older versions of Excel, CSV, HTML, XML, PDF, and text.
5. Click Save.

Excel saves a copy of the worksheet in the directory where you have the Excel worksheet. Your Excel worksheet remains active so that you can continue to work on it if you want.

After you save to some file formats such as delimited text, you may see a yellow warning bar above the worksheet warning you that you may have some data loss. This bar also displays buttons that you can click to hide the bar in the future or to save the Excel file in a different format.

Configuring Print Settings

Before you print to either a printed page or to PDF format, you can view the print preview settings and make changes in Excel.

Excel easily detects the default printer that you're using in Windows and lets you change the printer settings so that your document appears on paper the way you want.

Start by clicking the File menu option, and then click Print in the menu on the left side of the File screen. Now you see the Print screen, and the print preview area appears on the right side so that you have a good idea of what the worksheet will look like on the printed page.

FIGURE 7.44   A partial list of file formats

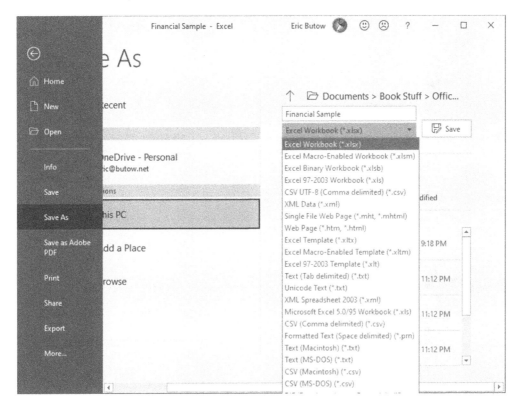

Between the menu area on the left and the print preview area, the Settings menu you see depends on the printer you have.

In my case, I can change the printer to another one that I have installed in Windows, as shown in Figure 7.45. I can also change different settings for the selected printer, including how many pages to print, the page orientation, and whether I should print on one or both sides of the paper.

Inspecting Workbooks for Issues

Before you share a workbook with other people, such as in an email attachment, you should take advantage of the Document Inspector in Excel to find information that you may not realize is saved with your workbook. For example, Excel saves author information, and you may not want to share that information when you share the workbook with someone outside your company.

FIGURE 7.45   Print screen

> Before you inspect your workbook and perhaps remove some information, you may want to save a copy of your workbook and remove the information from that copy. Excel may not be able to restore data when you click Undo in the Quick Access Toolbar, or press Ctrl+Z, so it's better to be safe than sorry.

Start by clicking the File menu option. Click Info in the menu bar on the left side of the File screen. Now that you're in the Info screen, click the Check For Issues button. From the drop-down list, select Inspect Document.

Now you see the Document Inspector dialog box, as shown in Figure 7.46. Scroll up and down the list of content that Windows will inspect.

By default, the following check boxes next to the content category names are selected:

- Comments
- Document Properties And Personal Information
- Data Model
- Content Add-Ins

FIGURE 7.46   Document Inspector dialog box

- Task Pane Add-Ins
- PivotTables, PivotCharts, Cube Formulas, Slicers, and Timelines
- Embedded Documents
- Macros, Forms, And ActiveX Controls
- Links To Other Files
- Real Time Data Functions
- Excel Surveys
- Defined Scenarios
- Active Filters
- Custom Worksheet Properties
- Hidden Names
- Ink
- Long External References
- Custom XML Data
- Headers And Footers

- Hidden Rows And Columns

- Hidden Worksheets

- Invisible Content (which is content that has been formatted as such but that does not include objects covered by other objects)

These check boxes mean that the Document Inspector will check content in all those areas. Select Ink, the only clear check box, if you want to check whether someone has written in the workbook with a stylus, such as the Microsoft Surface Pen.

When you decide what you want Excel to check out, click Inspect. When Excel finishes its inspection, you can review all the results in the dialog box.

The results show all content categories that look good by displaying a green check mark to the left of the category name. If Excel finds something that you should check out, you see a red exclamation point to the left of the category. Under the category name, Excel lists everything it found. Remove the offenders from your workbook by clicking the Remove All button to the right of the category name.

You can reinspect the workbook by clicking Reinspect as often as you want, until you see that all of the categories are okay. When you're done, click the Close button to return to the Info screen.

When you remove hidden rows, columns, or even worksheets that contain data, you may find that calculations and formulas no longer give you the results you want. . .or fail entirely. If you are not sure what will happen if you remove hidden data in a workbook, unhide the affected cells and inspect them before Excel does.

EXERCISE 7.5

Changing Print Settings and Inspecting a Workbook

1. Open a new workbook, and then add text in two columns and five rows.

2. Save the workbook.

3. Select all cells in the first three rows.

4. Set a print area in the selected cells.

5. Select all cells in the fourth row and then add those cells to the print area.

6. Save a copy of the workbook as a CSV file.

7. Inspect the worksheet and remove all problems found.

Summary

This chapter started by showing you how to import data stored in TXT and CSV files into Excel. Aside from Excel-formatted files, you will most likely receive other files from text and CSV-formatted files because those formats are ubiquitous.

Next, I discussed how to navigate within a workbook. You can search for data; navigate to named cells, ranges, and other workbook elements; and insert and remove hyperlinked text within a cell.

Then, you learned how to format worksheets and workbooks to look the way that you want. You learned how to modify the page setup, adjust row width and column height, and customize headers and footers.

You then went further by learning how to customize Excel and its options so that features in the Excel window look the way you want. Those customization features include customizing the Quick Access Toolbar, displaying and modifying the look of workbook content, freezing worksheet rows and columns, changing window views, modifying basic workbook properties, and displaying formulas.

Finally, you learned how to configure your content for collaboration. You learned how to set a print area in a worksheet and workbook, save a workbook in a different file format, configure your print settings, and inspect workbooks for issues, including hidden content that you don't want to share.

Key Terms

AutoFit	hyperlinks
comma-delimited value	range
delimiter	wildcard
footer	workbook
formulas	worksheet
header	

Exam Essentials

Understand how to import TXT and CSV files into a worksheet. Know how to import files in both TXT and CSV formats into a worksheet using the built-in file import tools.

Know how to search for data in a workbook.   Understand how to search for data by using the Find And Replace feature in Excel to find search terms in a worksheet or all the sheets in a workbook, and then replace your search term(s) with other terms and/or formatting.

Understand how to navigate to different elements in a workbook.   Know how to go to different elements using the Go To feature to go to a specific cell, range of cells, or another worksheet in your workbook.

Know how to insert and remove hyperlinks.   Understand how to insert a hyperlink within a cell and remove a hyperlink if you want.

Understand how to format worksheets and workbooks.   Know how to use Excel formatting tools to format worksheets and workbooks, including how to modify the page setup, adjust row height and column width in a worksheet, and customize headers and footers.

Be able to set and change Excel options and spreadsheet views.   Know how to change options and views, including how to customize the Quick Access Toolbar, display content in different views, modify workbook content in different views, change window views, freeze worksheet rows and columns, modify basic workbook properties, as well as display and hide formulas.

Know how to set a print area and configure print settings.   Understand how to set a print area within a worksheet and configure your print settings, including changing the printer, the worksheet(s) to print, and the page orientation.

Understand how to save workbooks in other file formats.   Know the file formats to which Excel can save a workbook, how to select the format you want, and how to save the workbook in your preferred format.

Be able to inspect workbooks for issues.   Know how to inspect a workbook before you share it, including how to look for hidden information contained in the Excel file that you may not want to share, how to check for accessibility issues, and how to check for compatibility issues.

Review Questions

1. What kinds of characters can be a delimiter? (Choose all that apply.)

   A. Tab

   B. Semicolon

   C. Comma

   D. Period

2. How do you search for a cell that has the question mark in the text?

   A. Search for the question mark character.

   B. Type a tilde before the question mark.

   C. Add two question mark characters in a row.

   D. Type the grave accent mark before the question mark.

3. How do you make a column fit to the text that takes up the most width in a cell within that column?

   A. Use the mouse to drag the right edge of the column until it's the size of the text.

   B. Double-click at the right edge of the cell.

   C. Double-click at the right edge of the column in the header.

   D. Triple-click at the right edge of the column in the header.

4. What can you add to the Quick Access Toolbar? (Choose all that apply.)

   A. Styles

   B. Tools

   C. Views

   D. Commands

5. What formats can Excel save to? (Choose all that apply.)

   A. PDF

   B. Text

   C. Word

   D. Web page

6. Where can you place the Quick Access Toolbar? (Choose all that apply.)

   A. Under the ribbon

   B. In the ribbon

   C. In the menu bar

   D. In the title bar

7. How do you provide additional information for a link within a cell?

    A. Type the description in the cell after the link.

    B. Add a Screen Tip.

    C. Type the description in a cell adjacent to the link.

    D. Right-click the link to view more information.

8. In what view do you add a header or footer?

    A. Custom Views

    B. Page Break view

    C. Page Layout view

    D. Normal view

9. How do you hide a formula in the Formula Bar?

    A. By right-clicking the Formula Bar and then clicking Hide

    B. By using the Home menu ribbon

    C. By protecting the worksheet

    D. By using the View menu ribbon

10. What menu ribbon do you use to set a print area?

    A. View

    B. Home

    C. Data

    D. Page Layout

Chapter

8

Using Data Cells and Ranges

MICROSOFT EXAM OBJECTIVES COVERED IN THIS CHAPTER:

✓ **Manage data cells and ranges**

- Manipulate data in worksheets
  - Paste data by using special paste options
  - Fill cells by using Auto Fill
  - Insert and delete multiple columns or rows
  - Insert and delete cells
- Format cells and ranges
  - Merge and unmerge cells
  - Modify cell alignment, orientation, and indentation
  - Format cells by using Format Painter
  - Wrap text within cells
  - Apply number formats
  - Apply cell formats from the Format Cells dialog box
  - Apply cell styles
  - Clear cell formatting
- Define and reference named ranges
  - Define a named range
  - Name a table
- Summarize data visually
  - Insert Sparklines
  - Apply built-in conditional formatting
  - Remove conditional formatting

After you add data into a worksheet, you probably need to make changes to make the text and numbers work the way you want. Manipulating data can be repetitive—not to mention boring—but you have Excel tools at your disposal to make your job faster and easier.

Those tools include a wide variety of paste options, Auto Fill (to add sequential data like numbers and dates), the ability to insert and delete multiple rows and columns, as well as the ability to insert and delete cells.

Once you have the data the way you want it, you may want to format cells the way you want. Excel gives you the tools that you need to merge (and unmerge) cells, modify how data appears in a cell, use Format Painter (which you may know from Word), wrap text in a cell, apply cell and number formats, and apply cell styles. If you need to remove a style from text, Excel has you covered there, too.

A nice time-saving feature when you're searching for data or want to add data in a group of cells to a formula is the ability to name a range of cells. You can also name a table, and this chapter offers a sneak peek at using tables (you will learn more in Chapter 9, "Working with Tables and Table Data").

Finally, you will learn how to summarize data visually using the Sparklines feature to add visual data about a specific group of cells. You'll also learn how to apply conditional formatting, such as when you need to highlight a group of cells to make an important point to your readers.

Manipulating Data in Worksheets

Microsoft knows that copying and pasting data, inserting data, and filling in data is a core component of all its Microsoft 365 programs. Without this functionality, Microsoft 365 would not exist, let alone be the standard suite of office applications for businesses.

Excel, like its sibling programs in Microsoft 365, has copying and pasting data down cold. You can also use other tools, such as Auto Fill to speed up data entry, as well as tools that help with inserting and deleting cells, rows, and columns more quickly.

Pasting Data by Using Special Paste Options

In Chapter 7, "Managing Worksheets and Workbooks," you learned about some basic data paste options. Excel contains a slew of paste options so that the pasted text looks the way you want.

After you open a workbook, or you have created a new one and entered some data, select a cell to copy by clicking the cell. Click the Home menu option (if necessary), and then click Copy in the Clipboard section in the ribbon—or you can press Ctrl+C.

Next, click the cell where you want to paste the data. Now view your paste options by clicking the down arrow under the Paste icon in the Clipboard section. The drop-down menu is divided into three sections, as shown in Figure 8.1.

FIGURE 8.1   The Paste drop-down menu

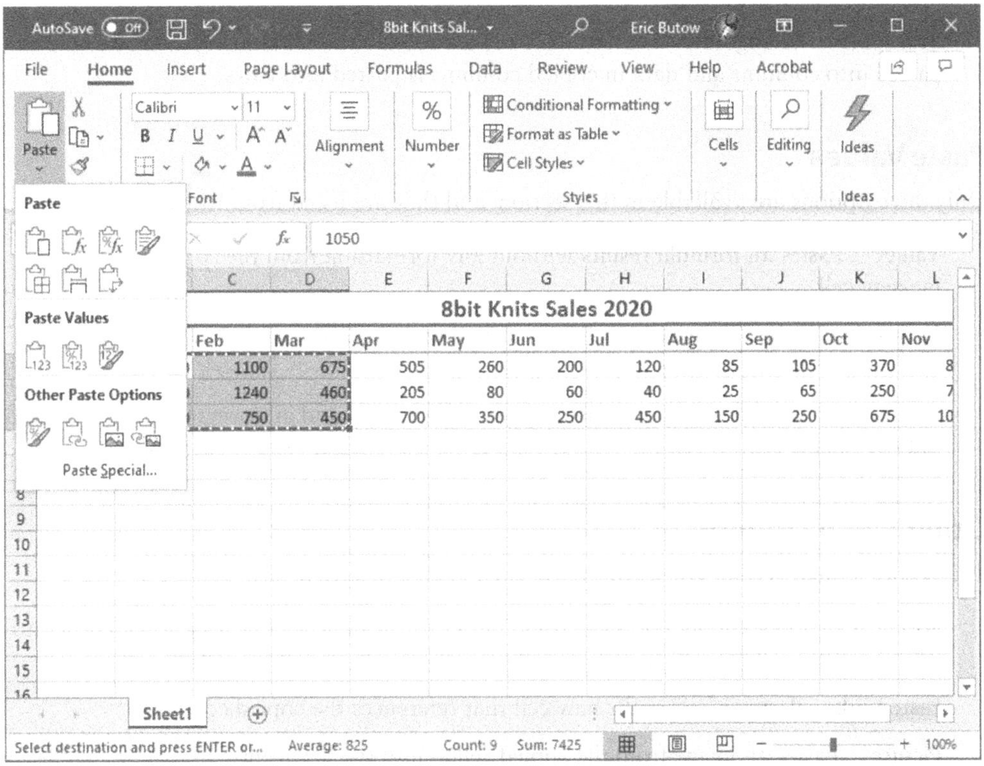

Paste

The seven icons in this section are listed from left to right, top to bottom:

Paste   Pastes all data in the copied cell, including formulas and formatting, into the new cell

Formulas   Pastes the formulas without any formatting from the copied cell into the new cell

Formulas & Number Formatting   Pastes only the formulas and number formatting from the copied cell into the new cell

Keep Source Formatting   Pastes all text formatting from the copied cell into the new cell

No Borders   If the copied cell has a cell border, then Excel does not paste the cell border into the new cell.

Keep Source Column Widths   Excel resizes the column width in the new cell to match the width of the copied cell.

Transpose   Changes the orientation of copied cells so that data in copied rows is pasted into columns and data in copied columns is pasted into rows

Paste Values

Only three options are available in this section, and they are listed from left to right:

Values   Pastes all formula results without any formatting from the copied cell into the new cell

Values & Number Formatting   Pastes formula results with number formatting from the copied cell into the new cell

Values & Source Formatting   Pastes all formula results and all formatting in the copied cell to the new cell

Other Paste Options

This section contains four icons, which are listed from left to right:

Formatting   Pastes only the formatting, but none of the data, from the copied cell(s) to the new cell(s)

Paste Link   Pastes a link in the new cell that references the copied cell

Picture   Pastes an image from the copied cell(s) into the new cell(s)

Linked Picture   Pastes an image from the copied cell(s) along with a link to the original cell(s) into the new cell(s). When you make changes to the image in the original cell(s), Excel updates the new cell(s) with the new image automatically.

Paste Special

If you don't see the paste option you want, the Paste Special link appears at the bottom of the drop-down menu, as you saw in Figure 8.1. After you click the link, the Paste Special dialog box appears (see Figure 8.2).

FIGURE 8.2   Paste Special dialog box

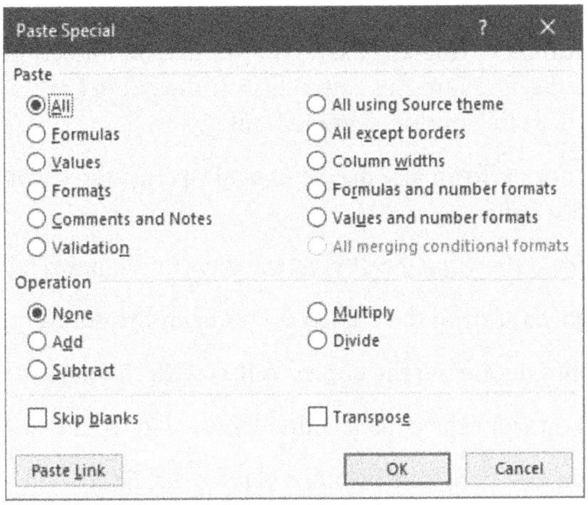

Click one of the following options in the dialog box. Note that you can only click one option in the Paste section and only one option in the Operation section. You can also click one or both check boxes below the Operation section.

All   Pastes all contents and formatting from the copied cell(s) into the new cell(s)

Formulas   Pastes only the formulas from the copied cell(s) into the new cell(s)

Values   Pastes only the values, not the formulas, of the copied cell(s) into the new cell(s)

Formats   Pastes only the formatting in the copied cell(s) into the new cell(s)

Comments And Notes   Pastes only comments and notes with the copied cell(s) into the new cell(s)

Validation   Pastes data validation rules in the copied cell(s) into the new cell(s). *Validation* controls what users can enter in a cell, such as five numbers for a ZIP code.

All Using Source Theme   Pastes all cell contents that have document theme formatting from copied cell(s) into new cell(s)

All Except Borders   Pastes all cell contents and formatting, but not cell borders, from copied cell(s) into new cell(s)

Column Widths   Excel resizes the column width in the new cell(s) to match the width of the copied cell(s)

Formulas And Number Formats   Pastes only formulas and number formatting from the copied cell(s) into the new cell(s)

Values And Number Formats   Pastes only values and number formatting from the copied cell(s) into the new cell(s)

All Merging Conditional Formats   Pastes all of the data and conditional formatting options in the copied cell(s) into the new cell(s). If the copied cell(s) does not have any conditional formatting, this option is grayed out.

None   Excel will not perform any mathematical operations when it pastes copied data into one or more new cells.

Add   Adds data from the copied cell(s) to the data in the new cell(s)

Subtract   Subtracts data from the copied cell(s) from the data in the new cell(s)

Multiply   Multiplies data from the copied cell(s) with the data in the new cell(s)

Divide   Divides data from the copied cell(s) by the data in the new cell(s)

Skip Blanks   When you copy one or more blank cells, Excel will not put a value in the corresponding new cell(s)

Transpose   Changes the orientation of copied cells so that data in copied rows is pasted into columns and data in copied columns is pasted into rows

If you click Paste Link, the dialog box closes, and you create a link to the copied cell(s) within the new cell(s). If you don't want to add a link, click OK. The pasted cell(s) reflect the options you selected in the dialog box.

Filling Cells by Using Auto Filling

As you enter data in a worksheet, you may find yourself wondering why you have to keep entering the same data over and over, or why you have to type in a sequence of numbers or even dates. The Excel Auto Fill feature makes it easy to fill cells with the same data or a data sequence.

Start by adding data into a cell. You can add the following types of data:

- The same number or a series of numbers, such as 10, 20, and so forth
- The abbreviated or full day of the week, such as Mon or Monday
- The abbreviated or full month of the year, such as Jan or January
- The date in mm/dd format, such as 10/15

If you're repeating only one number in other cells, type the number in the first cell. If you're adding a series of numbers, type the first two numbers into the first two cells in a row or column.

If you want to add a series of the same number or letter, or if your data is a month name (like January) or date (like 10/15), type the first number, month name, or date into the first cell in the row or column.

Next, move the mouse pointer to the green dot in the lower-right corner of the selected cell. The pointer changes to a plus sign. Click and hold the left mouse button, and then drag over the cells that you want to fill. As you drag, a small pop-up box appears above the pointer that tells you what value will be filled in the cell (see Figure 8.3).

FIGURE 8.3   Pop-up box shows what value you will fill.

	A	B	C	D	E	F	G	H	I	J	K	L
1							8bit Knits Sales 2020					
2		Jan	Feb	Mar	Apr	May	Jun	Jul	Aug	Sep	Oct	Nov
3	Hats	1050	1100	675	505	260	200	120	85	105	370	8
4	Scarves	1200	1240	460	205	80	60	40	25	65	250	7
5	Toys	500	750	450	700	350	250	450	150	250	675	10
6												
7												
8												
9		Jan										
10			Feb									
11												
12												
13												
14												
15												

Drag outside selection to extend series or fill; drag inside to clear

When you drag over all the cells that you want to fill, release the mouse button. Excel fills the cells with the months, dates, or number sequence.

If you fill more rows than there are 7 days in a week or 12 months in a year, then Excel starts over after the day or month sequence finishes. For example, Excel starts over again on Monday in the seventh empty column or row that you fill.

Inserting and Deleting Multiple Columns or Rows

As you work with data, you may need to insert multiple columns or rows, such as when you need to add a new expense with a particular month. You may also need to delete a row or column, such as when you don't want to include a column to identify a type of product. Excel allows you to insert multiple columns and rows at once to save you time and effort.

Insert Multiple Columns

Follow these steps to insert multiple columns into a worksheet:

1. Click the column header where you want to insert columns. The column can contain text in its cells.
2. Click, hold, and drag to the left or right to select the number of columns that you want to insert. For example, if you select column C and then drag to column D, you will insert two columns.
3. When you select the number of columns to insert, release the mouse button.
4. Right-click one of the selected columns.
5. Click Insert in the pop-up menu.

The number of inserted columns with blank cells is highlighted in the worksheet. If you selected columns that had populated cells, those columns move to the column immediately to the right of the inserted columns (see Figure 8.4).

Insert Multiple Rows

Here's how to insert multiple rows into a worksheet:

1. Click the row header where you want to insert rows. The row can contain text in its cells.
2. Click, hold, and drag up or down to select the number of rows that you want to insert. For example, if you select row 5 and then drag to row 10, you will insert six rows.
3. When you select the number of rows to insert, release the mouse button.
4. Right-click one of the selected rows.
5. Select Insert from the pop-up menu.

The number of inserted rows is highlighted in the worksheet. If you selected rows that had populated cells, those rows move to the row immediately below the inserted rows (see Figure 8.5).

FIGURE 8.4   Inserted columns

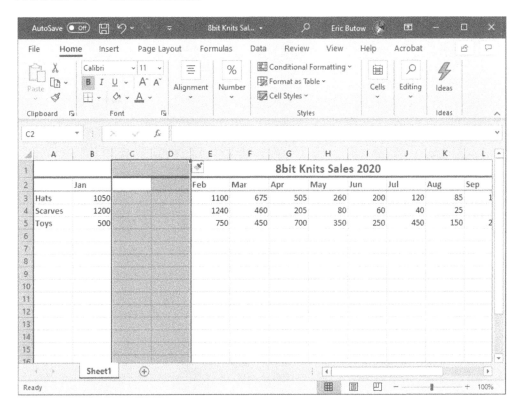

Deleting Multiple Rows and Columns

You can delete rows and columns much as you did when you inserted them. Here's how:

1. Click the row or column header where you want to delete rows or columns.
2. Click, hold, and drag left and right for columns, or up and down for rows, to select the number of columns or rows that you want to insert. For example, if you select row 5 and then drag to row 10, you will delete six rows.
3. After you have selected the rows or columns, release the mouse button.
4. Right-click one of the selected rows.
5. Select Delete from the pop-up menu.

The selected cells disappear. Any columns to the right of the deleted columns move left, and any rows below the selected rows move up.

FIGURE 8.5 Inserted rows

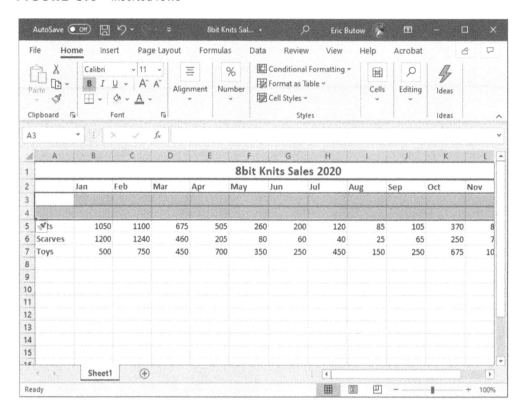

Adding and Removing Cells

Adding and removing cells is a part of life when you edit a worksheet. Deleting data in a cell is as easy as clicking the cell and then pressing Delete on your keyboard. You can delete data in all cells within a row or column by clicking the row or column header and then pressing Delete.

You can also delete a column or row as well as all of the data within it by following the instructions in one of the following two sections.

Add and Remove a Column

Insert a column by clicking the column header above the column. In the Home ribbon, click the Insert icon in the Cells section. (If your Excel window width is small, click the Cells icon and then click the Insert icon.) Then select the Insert Sheet Columns option from the drop-down menu, as shown in Figure 8.6.

FIGURE 8.6 Insert Sheet Columns menu option

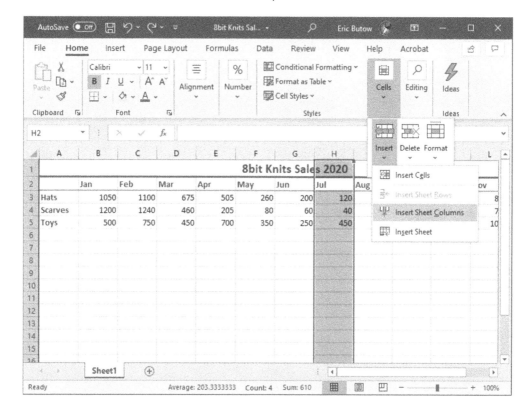

All columns to the right of the selected column move one column to the right.

You can delete a selected column by clicking the Delete icon in the Cells section in the ribbon, and then selecting the Delete Sheet Columns option from the drop-down menu. All columns to the right of the deleted column move to the left.

Insert and Delete a Row

Insert a row by clicking the row header to the left of the row. In the Home ribbon, click the Insert icon in the Cells section. (If your Excel window width is small, click the Cells icon and then click the Insert icon.) Then select the Insert Sheet Rows option from the drop-down menu, as shown in Figure 8.7.

All rows below the selected row move one row down.

You can delete a selected row by clicking the Delete icon in the Cells section in the ribbon and then selecting the Delete Sheet Rows option from the drop-down menu. All rows below the deleted row move up.

FIGURE 8.7   Insert Sheet Rows menu option

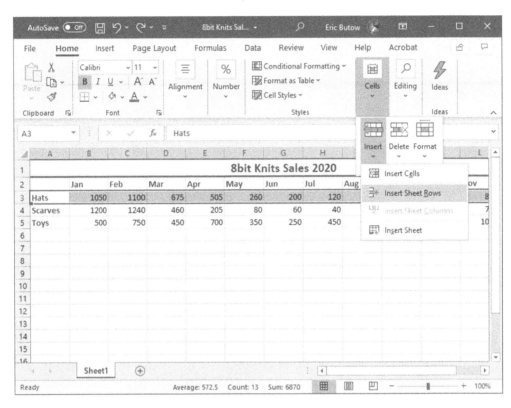

When you select a row or column that has formatting, such as bold text, applied to it, Excel applies that formatting to the new row or column that you insert.

EXERCISE 8.1

Manipulating Data

1. Open an existing workbook or create a new workbook and add data in four columns and four rows.

2. Copy one cell and paste it to a blank cell.

3. Insert a new column.

4. Auto Fill all 12 months of the calendar.

5. Insert two rows within the third row of the worksheet.

6. Delete the second column from the worksheet.

Formatting Cells and Ranges

Another common editing task is formatting cells or a group of cells, which Excel calls a *range*. Excel includes tools for merging and unmerging cells and modifying cells to look the way you want. Use Format Painter to format text in cells quickly, just as with text in Word; wrap text around images in your worksheet; format numbered lists; and apply styles to cells—a task that, you guessed it, is similar to Word's.

Merging and Unmerging Cells

It's easy to merge multiple cells into one. A common example is making a title row. You type the title into row 1, column 1 in the worksheet. Then you select several contiguous cells within the same row and click Merge & Center in the Home ribbon. The title appears centered across all the columns that you selected.

Start by clicking the cells you want to merge in a row, and then click the Home menu option (if necessary). In the Alignment section in the Home ribbon, click the down arrow to the right of Merge & Center. (If your Excel window width is small, click the Alignment icon and then click the down arrow to the right of Merge & Center.)

Now you can select from one of three merge options in the drop-down menu, as shown in Figure 8.8:

Merge & Center   Merges all the selected cells in the merge area and centers the text contained in the upper-left cell within the merged area. If you merge multiple rows, Excel vertically aligns the text at the bottom of the merged cells.

Merge Across   Merges all the selected cells in the row(s) but keeps the text in the upper-left cell aligned left. If you merge cells in multiple rows, Excel merges each row separately.

Merge Cells   Merges all selected cells in the merge area and keeps the text in the upper-left cell aligned left within the merged area.

When you need to unmerge cells, click the merged cell and then click the down arrow to the right of Merge & Center in the Home ribbon. Then select Unmerge Cells from the drop-down menu, as you saw in Figure 8.8.

What You Can and Can't Do When Merging

If you try to merge cells when more than one cell in the merge area has text in them, a dialog box appears that reminds you that only text in the upper-left cell within the merge area is intact in the merged cell. When you click OK, you see the text from the upper-left cell in the merged cell. Excel deletes all the text in the other cells.

You also cannot split an unmerged cell into smaller cells. If you need smaller cells, reduce the width of the column in which the cell resides.

FIGURE 8.8 Merge options in the drop-down menu

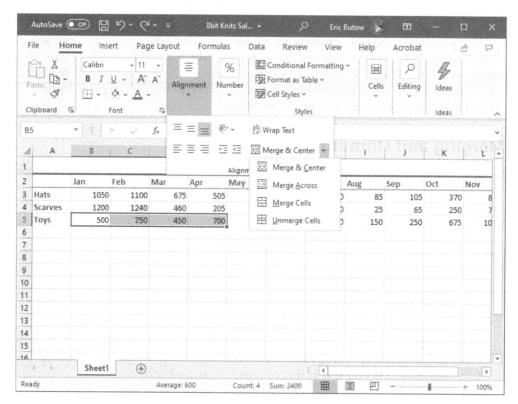

Modifying Cell Alignment, Orientation, and Indentation

When you have the data in a worksheet the way you want, you can change how the cell looks when other people read it. Excel gives you the power to change the cell alignment and orientation, and to align the cell differently so that it stands out from the rest of the text and/ or numbers.

Align a Column or Row

When you need to align data in rows or columns to appear a certain way, such as numbers in a column right-aligned in every cell, here's how to do that:

1. Select the cell(s), column(s), and/or row(s) that you want to align. You can align data in a single cell if you want.

2. Click the Home menu option, if necessary.

3. In the Alignment section in the Home ribbon, click the Align Left, Center, or Align Right icon, as shown in Figure 8.9. (If your Excel window width is small, click the Alignment icon and then click the down arrow to the right of Merge & Center.)

FIGURE 8.9   Align Left, Align Center, and Align Right icons

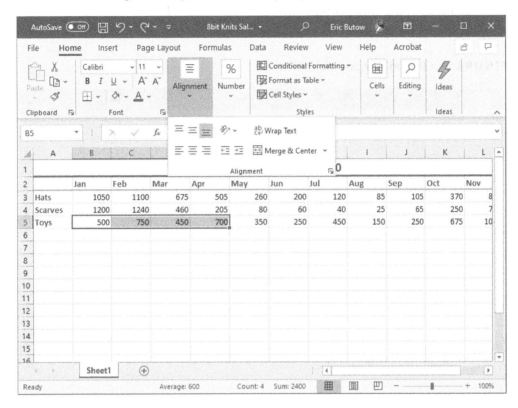

The default alignment for cells is Align Left. If you want to align the cells vertically, click the Top Align, Middle Align, or Bottom Align icon. The default vertical alignment in all cells is Bottom Align.

 If you want to select all cells in a worksheet quickly, click a blank cell and then press Ctrl+A.

Change the Orientation of Text in a Cell

You may want to change the orientation of data in a cell, a range of cells, a row, or a column by changing the text rotation. For example, you may want to rotate text in the first row 90 degrees. Change the orientation by following these steps:

1. Select the cell, range, row(s), or column(s).
2. Click the Home menu option, if necessary.

3. In the Alignment section in the Home ribbon, click the Orientation icon. (If your Excel window width is small, click the Alignment icon and then click the Orientation icon.)

4. Select one of the options in the menu shown in Figure 8.10.

FIGURE 8.10   Orientation drop-down menu

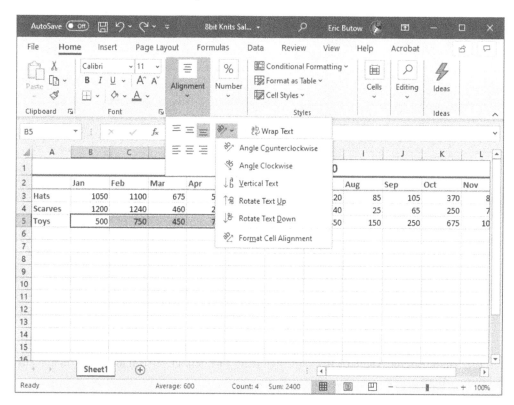

You can select from one of the following options:

Angle Counterclockwise: Rotates the text 45 degrees

Angle Clockwise: Rotates the text –45 degrees

Vertical Text: Makes the text vertical but does not rotate the text so that each letter appears on a separate line of text

Rotate Text Up: Rotates the text 90 degrees (counterclockwise)

Rotate Text Down: Rotates the text –90 degrees (clockwise)

Rotate Text to a Precise Angle

If you need to rotate text to a specific angle instead of the built-in angles that Excel provides, open the Orientation drop-down menu and then click Format Cell Alignment.

In the Format Cells dialog box (see Figure 8.11), the Alignment tab is selected by default.

FIGURE 8.11   Format Cells dialog box

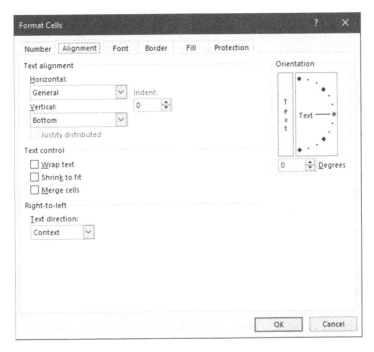

On the right side of the dialog box, type the number of degrees in the Degrees box in either positive or negative numbers. The preview area above the box shows you how the text will look. You can also increase or decrease the degrees by one degree by clicking the up and down arrows, respectively, to the right of the Degrees box.

You will learn more about the Format Cells dialog box later in this chapter.

Formatting Cells by Using Format Painter

All Microsoft 365 programs include the Format Painter feature, which is a quick and easy way to apply formatting from selected data in a cell to data in another cell. Follow this process to get started:

1. Select the text or click text in a paragraph that has the formatting you want to copy.

2. Click the Home menu option if it's not selected already.

3. In the Home ribbon, click the Format Painter icon in the Clipboard section, as shown in Figure 8.12.

FIGURE 8.12 Format Painter icon

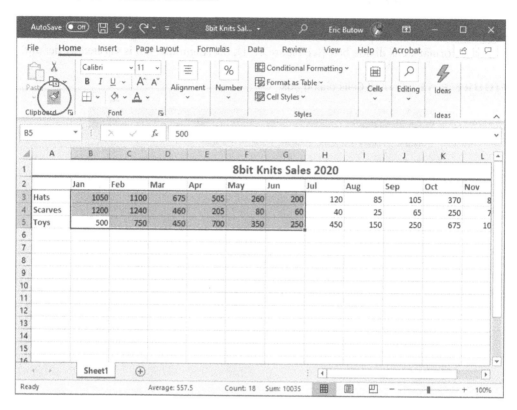

The mouse pointer changes to the standard Excel plus icon combined with a paintbrush. Now you can select text in another cell. The text in the cell that you selected now shows the format you copied.

This process works only once, but you can change the format of multiple blocks of text. After you select the text with the formatting that you want to copy, double-click the Format Painter icon in the Home toolbar and then select the cells. When you're done, press the Esc key.

Wrapping Text Within Cells

After you change the width of a column, the text within the selected column stays on the screen. If you want the text to stay within the column width, you can wrap the text. You can also add line breaks within text so that you have better control of where the text wraps in a cell.

Wrap Text

When you want to wrap text, start by selecting the cell(s), range, row(s), or column(s). Next, click the Home menu option, if necessary. In the Home menu ribbon, click Wrap Text in the Alignment section, as shown in Figure 8.13. (If your Excel window width is small, click the Alignment icon and then click Wrap Text.)

FIGURE 8.13   Wrap Text option

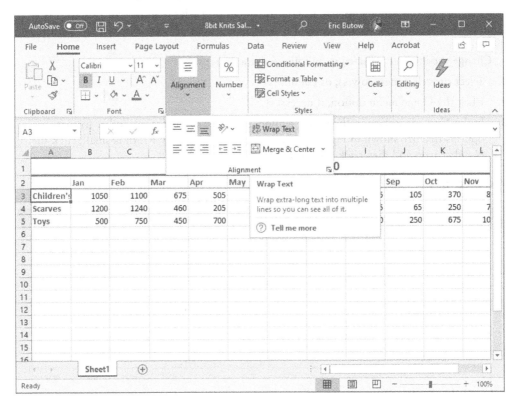

Excel automatically wraps the text within the width of the column(s). Change how the wrapped text appears in the cell(s) by changing the width of each affected column.

Add a Line Break

When you need a line break within text in a cell, start by double-clicking the cell. The text cursor appears within the text. Now click on the location within the text where you want to add the line break, and then press Alt+Enter.

The text after the line break appears on a new line and may appear in front of text in the cell underneath the cell you're editing. Click outside the cell to view the text with your line break. Excel automatically increases the height of the cell and the entire row to accommodate the text on multiple lines.

Wrapping text and line breaks do not work with numbers or formulas in a cell. When you reduce the width of a column so that a number cannot fit within the cell width, Excel places pound or hash (#) marks in the cell instead.

Using Number Formatting

You may need to change the format of your numbers for easier reading. For example, if your numbers denote currency, you may want to add the appropriate currency symbol in front of the number.

Change the number formatting by following these steps:

1. Select the cell, range, row(s), or column(s).

2. Click the Home menu option, if necessary.

3. In the Number section in the Home ribbon, click one of the three number format options that are shown in Figure 8.14. (If your Excel window width is small, click the Number icon and then click one of the number format icons.)

FIGURE 8.14   Number format options

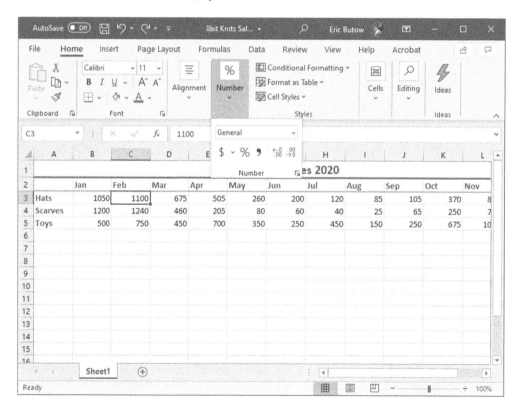

You can click the Accounting Number Format icon (which is a $ symbol), the Percent Style icon (%) to add a percentage with the number, or the Comma Style icon (which looks like a large comma) to apply a comma within a number larger than 999. If you apply a number format to an empty cell, then you won't see the formatting until you type a number into it.

> If you need to view all number formats, click the down arrow next to the General button in the Number section. You can view more number formats in the Format Cells dialog box, which has the Number tab open by default. You will learn more about the Format Cells dialog box in the next section.

Applying Cell Formatting from the Format Cells Dialog Box

The Format Cells dialog box contains all the format styles that you can apply to data within cells. Open the dialog box by clicking the Home menu option (if necessary), and then clicking Format in the Cells section. (If your Excel window width is small, click the Cells icon and then click Format.)

Now select the Format Cells option at the bottom of the drop-down menu, which is shown in Figure 8.15.

The Format Cells dialog box appears (see Figure 8.16) with the Number tab active by default.

You can select from one of the following tabs to view all formatting options and change them as you see fit:

Number   Allows you to set 11 different specific number formats to one or more cells, from Number to a custom format. The default selection is General, which means that there is no specific number format.

Alignment   Allows you to change the text alignment, control, direction, and/or orientation in one or more cells

Font   Shows the current font and font style assigned to the cell. The default is 11-point Calibri. You can change the font, the font style, and the font size; apply effects; and apply a color.

Border   Allows you to add a border on one or more sides of a cell or a range

Fill   Displays the current background of the cell or range. The default is No Color, but you can select a fill color, set a pattern, and add a fill effect.

Protection   Allows you to lock and/or hide a cell or a range in the worksheet

FIGURE 8.15   Format Cells option

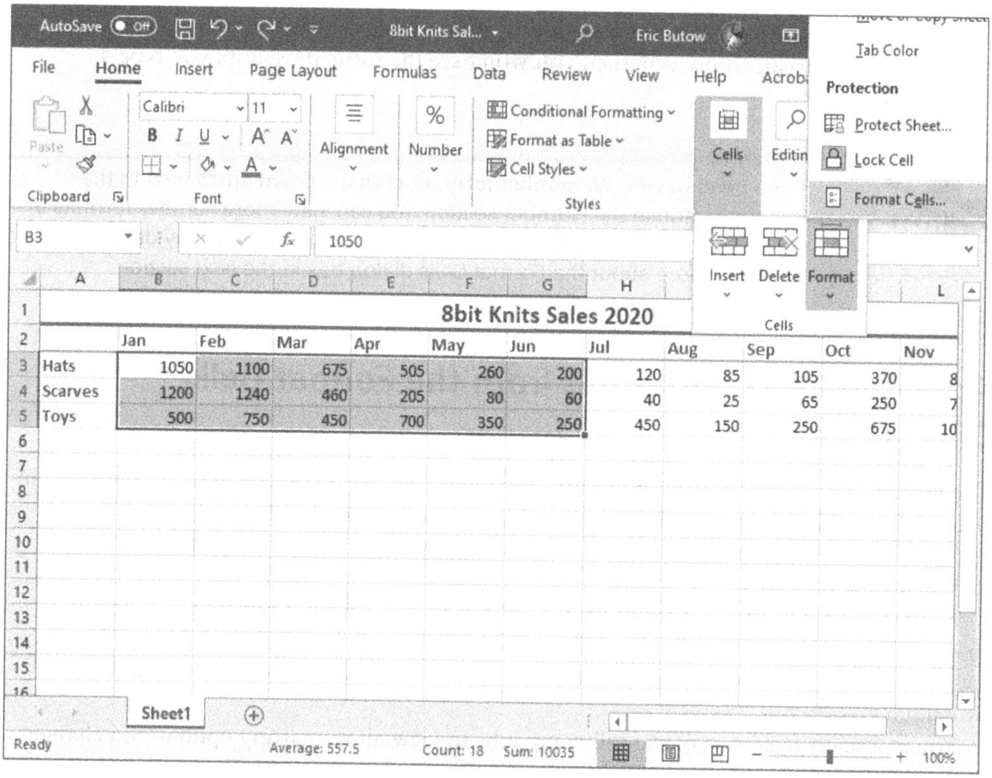

Working with Cell Styles

You can apply styles to a cell within the Home menu ribbon without having to open the Format Cells dialog box. You can also apply prebuilt styles or add your own. A *style* is a set of format settings that you can apply so that you don't have to apply each format setting one at a time.

Apply a Cell Style

Start by selecting the cell or the range of cells, and then click the Home menu option, if necessary. In the Styles section in the Home menu ribbon, click the Cell Styles icon in the Styles section. The Cell Styles drop-down list appears below the icon (see Figure 8.17).

FIGURE 8.16   Format Cells dialog box

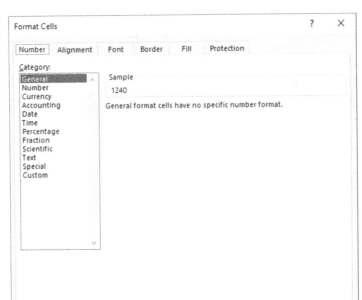

A selected style has a white border around the style tile, and the default style is Normal. You can apply a prebuilt style by clicking one of the style tiles in one of the following list sections:

- Good, Bad, and Neutral

- Data and Model

- Titles and Headings

- Themed Cell Styles

- Number Format

After you apply the style, Excel applies the style formats to the cell(s). If you apply a style to a blank cell, the cell may show some of the style formatting, such as a color in the cell background.

FIGURE 8.17 Cell Styles drop-down list

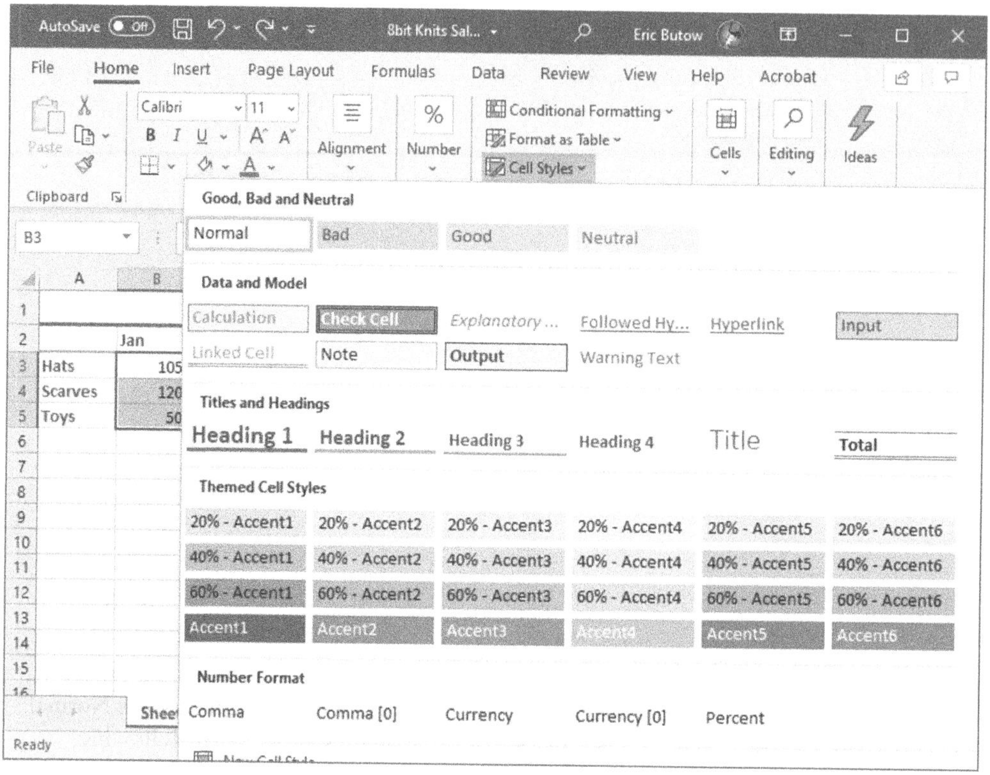

Remove a Cell Style from Data

If you decide that you don't want a style applied to a cell or range anymore and want to revert to the default format, select the cell or range. Next, open the Cell Styles drop-down list as you did in the previous section, and click Normal in the Good, Bad, and Neutral section.

Clearing Cell Formatting

If you need to clear formatting from a cell, Excel gives you several options. For example, you may have text in a cell as a hyperlink and you want to remove the hyperlink but keep the rest of the cell formatting intact.

Here's how to clear one or more formats from a cell or range of cells:

1. Select the cell, range, row(s), or column(s).

2. Click the Home menu option, if necessary.

3. In the Editing section in the Home ribbon, click Clear. (If your Excel window width is small, click the Editing icon and then click Clear.)

Now you can select from one of the six options in the Clear drop-down list, shown in Figure 8.18:

Clear All: Clears all contents, including formats and comments from the cell(s)

Clear Formats: Clears all formats from the cell(s) but leaves the contents and leaves intact any comments and/or notes attached to the cell(s)

Clear Contents: Clears all contents in the cell(s) but leaves the formatting and any attached comments and/or notes intact

Clear Comments and Notes: Clears all comments and/or notes attached to the cell(s) but leaves contents and formatting intact

Clear Hyperlinks: Clears all hyperlinks from the cell(s) but keeps the formatting. That is, the text in the cell(s) is still blue and underlined but has no functioning link

Remove Hyperlinks: Clears all hyperlinks and formatting from the cell(s)

FIGURE 8.18   Clear drop-down list

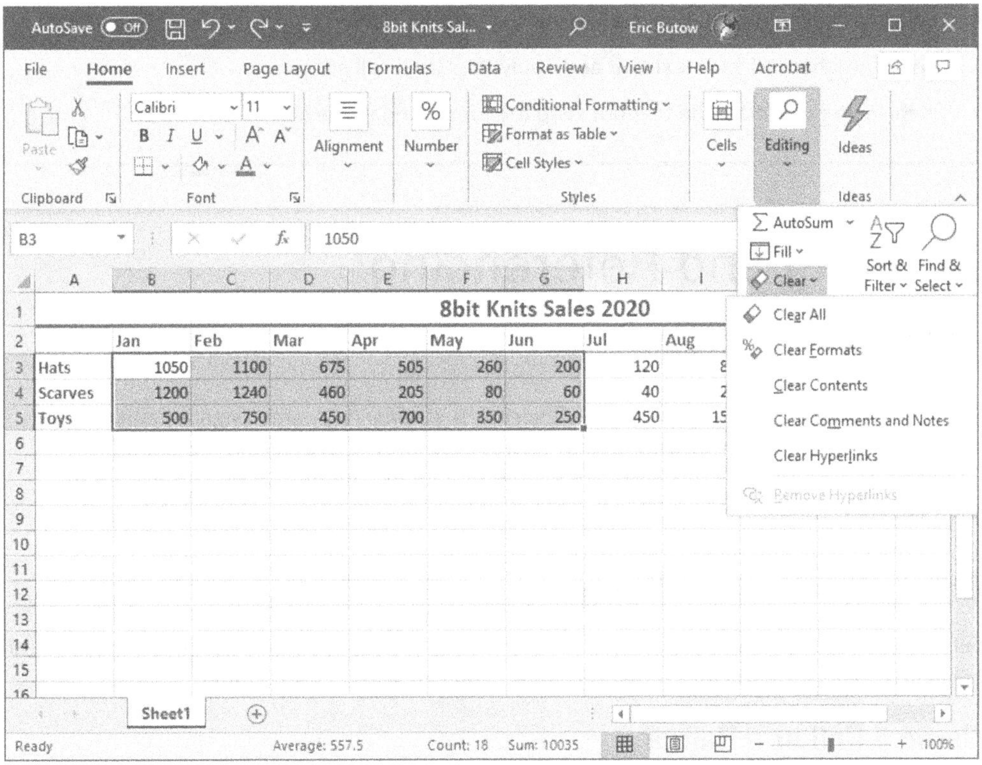

If you click Clear All or Clear Contents, the cell no longer contains a value. Any formula that refers to that cleared cell returns a value of 0.

EXERCISE 8.2

Formatting Cells and Ranges

1. Open an existing workbook.

2. Create a new row at the top of the worksheet.

3. Select all the cells in the new row that span the width of the rest of the worksheet and then merge and center those cells.

4. Add new text in an empty cell and then rotate the text up.

5. Copy one style in a cell to another cell with Format Painter.

6. Select a cell and then add a separate line of text within that cell.

7. Select another cell and then change the cell color to blue.

8. Select another cell with text in it and apply the Good cell style.

9. In the same cell, clear the text but keep the formatting in the cell.

Defining and Referencing Named Ranges

When you select a group of cells, which Excel calls a *range*, you can assign a name to each range that you select. This feature makes it easier not only to find a range you want in a worksheet or workbook, but also to add a link to a named range within a formula in another cell.

Defining a Named Range

Before you can add a link to a range, you need to select and name a range. That range can be as small as one cell. After you name the range, you can add it to a formula.

Name a Cell or a Range

Here's how to attach a name to a cell or a range:

1. Select the cell or range in the worksheet.

2. Click the Formulas menu option.

3. In the Defined Name section in the Formulas ribbon, click Define Name. (If your Excel window width is small, click the Defined Names icon.)

4. Select Define Name from the drop-down list, as shown in Figure 8.19.

FIGURE 8.19 Define Name option

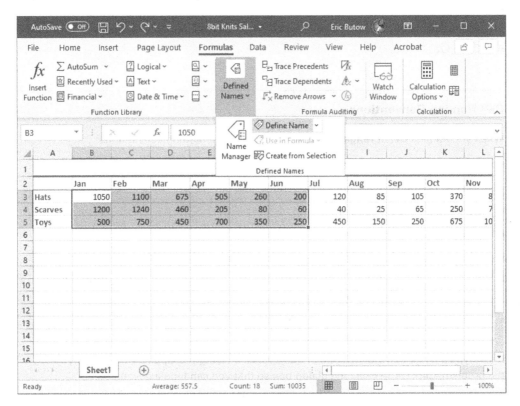

5. In the New Name dialog box, shown in Figure 8.20, type the name of the cell by pressing Backspace and then typing the new name in the Name text box. This name can be up to 255 characters long.

FIGURE 8.20 New Name dialog box

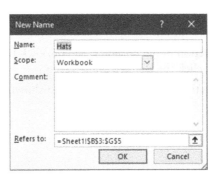

6. Click Workbook to select the scope of the range. Workbook is the default option, which means that any formula in the workbook can refer to the named cell. If you select the worksheet in the drop-down list, Excel applies the name only to the selected cells in that worksheet.

7. Add a comment up to 255 characters long in the Comment text box.

8. The Refers To box in the New Name dialog box reflects the cell location where you're adding the name, so leave this box as is.

9. Click OK.

Cell Naming Conventions

When you name a cell or range, you need to follow Excel naming conventions:

- The name must start with a letter or an underscore (_).

- You can use only letters, numbers, periods, and underscore characters.

- Names are not case sensitive.

- You cannot include spaces within a name.

- You can use the same name format as a cell reference, such as A1.

- Do not use the single letters C and R to name a range because Excel uses these letters for shortcuts to select a column and row, respectively.

- You cannot use an existing name in the workbook, even if the name you want to use is capitalized and the other one is not.

If you type a name that violates one of these rules, a dialog box appears that alerts you to the problem. Click OK to close the dialog box so that you can type a new name.

Define Names from a Selected Range

If you prefer to use a name based on text in one or more of the selected cells, you can create a name from the selection by following these steps:

1. Select the range in the worksheet.

2. Click the Formulas menu option.

3. In the Defined Name section in the Formulas ribbon, click Define Name. (If your Excel window width is small, click the Defined Names icon.)

4. Select Create From Selection from the drop-down list shown in Figure 8.21.

FIGURE 8.21 Create From Selection option

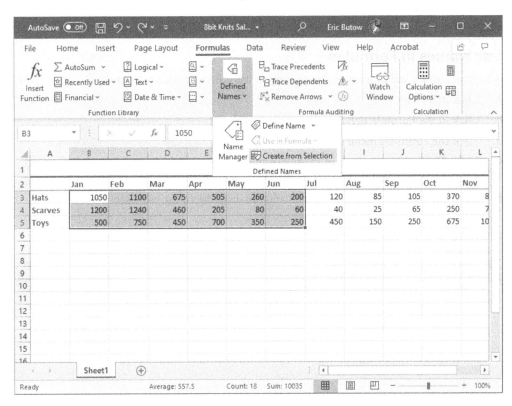

5. In the Create Names From Selection dialog box, shown in Figure 8.22, select one or more of the four Create Names From Values In check boxes: Top Row, Left Column, Bottom Row, or Right Column. (Excel may have one or more of these selected based on your selection.)

FIGURE 8.22 Create Names From Selection dialog box

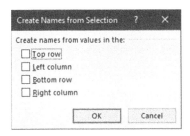

6. Click OK.

You may see a series of dialog boxes asking you to confirm that you want to change the names of different cells in the range. Click OK in each dialog box to complete the renaming process.

Use Names in Formulas

After you name a cell or a range, here's how to use a name within a formula:

1. Click in a blank cell.

2. Click in the Formula Bar.

3. Click the Formulas menu option.

4. In the Defined Names section in the Formulas ribbon, click Use In Formula. (If your Excel window width is small, click the Defined Names icon.)

5. Select the name of the cell or range from the drop-down list (see Figure 8.23).

FIGURE 8.23   Use In Formula drop-down menu

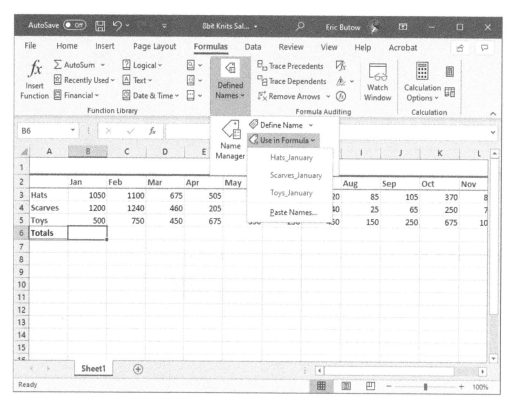

The cell name appears in the Formula Bar, and then you can continue to build the formula as you see fit.

Naming a Table

As in Word, you can add a separate table in an Excel worksheet. (You will learn more about creating tables in Chapter 9.) You can name a table in a worksheet, just as you can name a cell so that you can refer to it next time.

Start by clicking the table in the worksheet. Now follow these steps:

1. Click the Table Design menu option.

2. In the Properties section in the Table Design ribbon, click the table name in the Table Name Box, as shown in Figure 8.24. The default name is Table1, but you may see a different name.

FIGURE 8.24 Highlighted table name in the Table Name Box

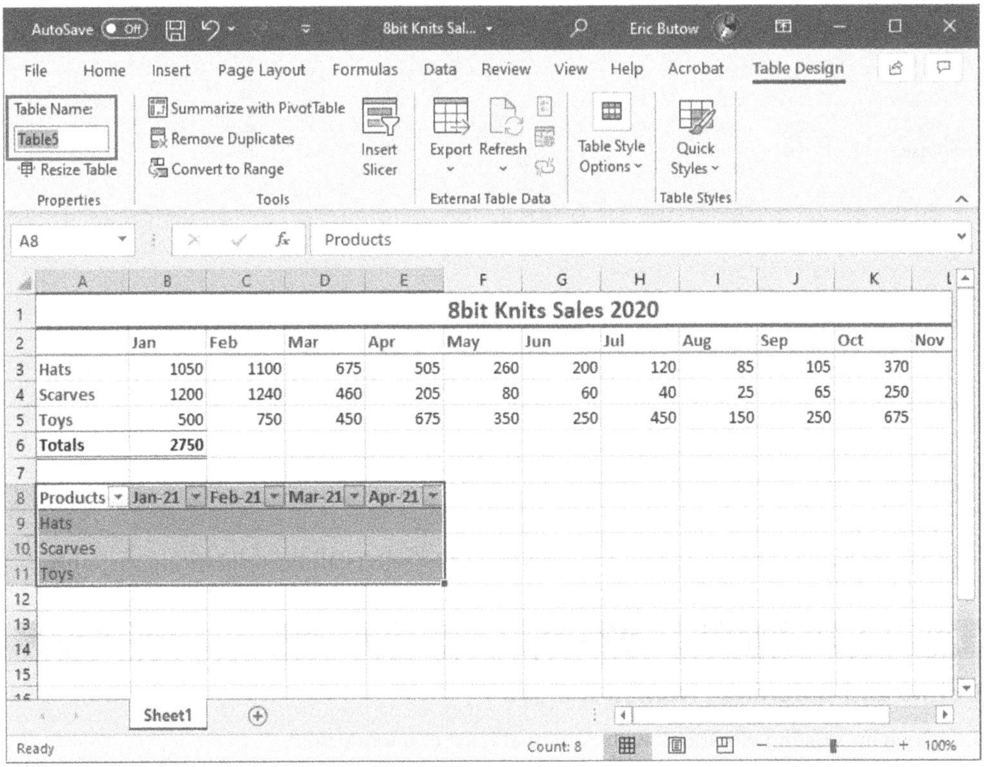

3. Press Backspace and then type the new name, as shown in Figure 8.24.

4. Press Enter.

When you want to go to the table quickly, click the down arrow in the Name Box, which is to the left of the Formula Bar. Then click the table name, as shown in Figure 8.25.

FIGURE 8.25 Highlighted table in the Name Box

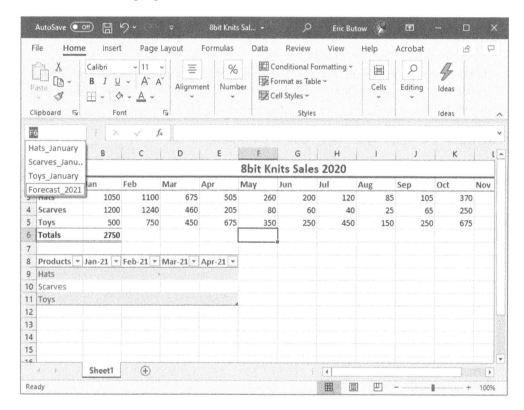

Excel moves to the table within the worksheet and selects all the cells within the table.

EXERCISE 8.3

Define and Reference Named Ranges

1. Open an existing workbook with data in at least one worksheet.

2. Create one bulleted list with four items.

3. Select a range of cells and name the range.

4. Select a second range of cells, and then name the range from cells in the top row.

5. Click an empty cell.

6. Add a formula that adds the two named ranges and view the result.

Summarizing Data Visually

Graphical charting has been an integral part of all spreadsheet programs since Lotus 1-2-3 introduced charting in 1983. Excel has taken visual representation of data down to small pieces of data that you can chart to show trends using *Sparklines*.

You can also point out data in a worksheet by using conditional formatting for some cells. As the name implies, you change the conditions of cells to show different visual cues in each cell.

Inserting Sparklines

A *Sparkline* is a tiny chart that appears in a cell and does not include any text data. So, a Sparkline is a great way to give a quick glance of a trend, such as product sales over a specific period. You can add three types of Sparkline charts: Line, Column, and Win/Loss.

After you add a Sparkline, you can format it to look the way you want. For example, you can change the color of a line chart to appear green to tell your audience that sales are growing.

Add a Sparkline

You add a Sparkline at the end of a row of data. For example, if you have monthly sales totals in row 6, and the last column of data is in column F, then place your cursor in cell G6.

Now add the Sparkline by following these steps:

1. Click the Insert menu option.

2. In the Sparklines section in the Insert ribbon, click the Line, Column, or Win/Loss icon, as shown in Figure 8.26. (If your Excel window width is small, click the Sparklines icon and then click one of the three icons.)

3. In the Create Sparklines dialog box, shown in Figure 8.27, type the data range of the cell, such as E1:E6, or select all the cells in the worksheet that you want to add to the data range. After you select all the cells, Excel populates the data range in the Data Range text box.

4. Click OK.

FIGURE 8.26 The three Sparkline icons

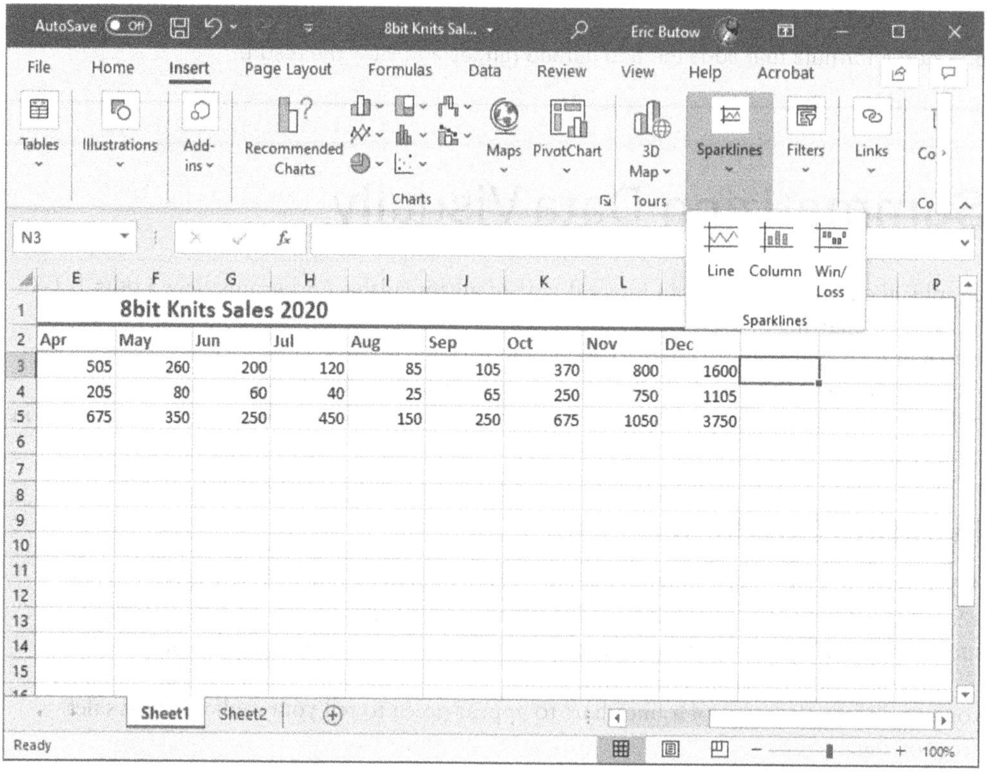

FIGURE 8.27 The selected cell range

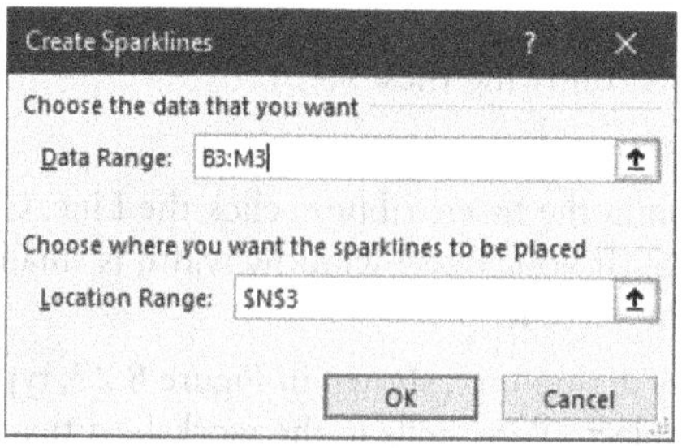

The small Sparkline chart appears in the cell to give readers a visual representation of the numbers in the row. For example, if you add a Line Sparkline chart, you see a line that curves up and down to reflect the ups and downs of numbers in each column within the row.

If you want to enlarge the Sparkline chart, increase the size of the row and the column that contains the chart.

Format a Sparkline Chart

After you add a Sparkline chart, the cell with the chart is highlighted and the Sparkline menu ribbon opens automatically (see Figure 8.28) so that you can format your chart the way you want.

FIGURE 8.28   Sparkline menu ribbon

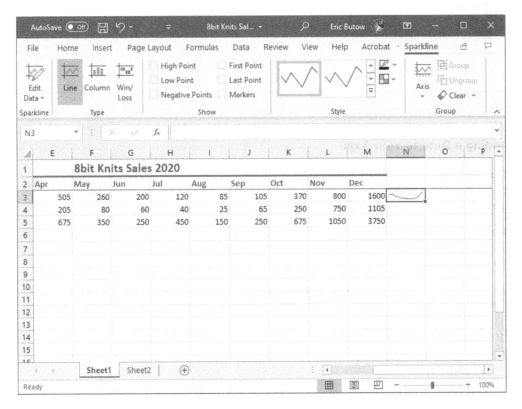

Now you can select functions in the following sections in the ribbon:

Sparkline   Click the Edit Data text below the Edit Data icon so that you can edit a group or single cell of data in a Sparkline chart, and change how empty or hidden cell settings appear in a Sparkline chart.

Type   Change the Sparkline chart type by clicking the Line, Column, or Win/Loss icon.

Show   Allows you to show different points within the Sparkline chart, such as where the high and low points are located.

Style   Change the colors of the Sparkline chart to one in a prebuilt style that you can choose, or change the colors to ones that you prefer.

Group   Show and change the horizontal and vertical axis settings, group and ungroup Sparkline charts, and clear a Sparkline chart from the cell.

You can't delete a Sparkline chart by clicking the cell and then pressing Delete. You must clear the Sparkline chart from the cell in the Group section in the ribbon.

Adding a Date to Your Axis

Your boss has told you that she likes your Sparklines because they give her a quick, at-a-glance data trend within a row. However, she noticed something troubling: in the cells, sales numbers for every month aren't available and she wants to know why.

After you explain that you haven't received any information for those months from the sales team, she wants to see that reflected in the Sparkline chart in part to remind her about the missing months.

But how do you change the Sparkline chart to show missing months within the chart? Follow these steps:

1. Click the Sparkline chart in the worksheet.

2. Change the chart type to Column. (This solution won't work if you select one of the other two types.)

3. In the Group area in the Sparkline menu ribbon, click the Axis icon.

4. Select Date Axis Type from the drop-down menu.

5. Select the cells that contain dates within the worksheet. For example, you may have the dates in the first row of the worksheet. The selected cells appear in the Sparkline Date Range dialog box.

6. Click OK in the dialog box.

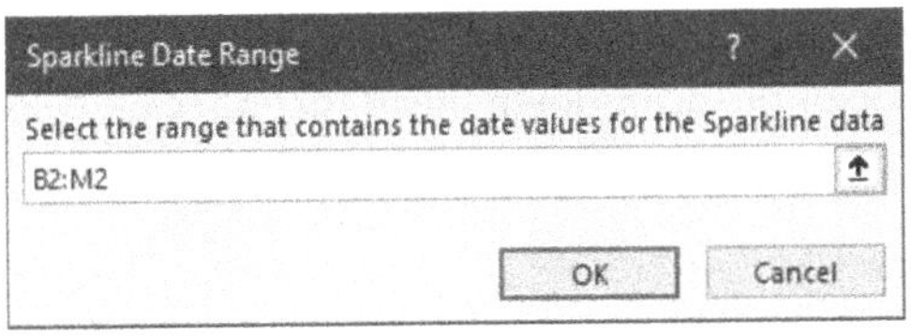

The Sparkline column chart shows bars in some columns and no bars in others. The areas with no bars show no data for those dates and gives a good visual representation to your boss about why she should call out the sales team for not giving you the data you need.

Applying Built-In Conditional Formatting

Excel lets you highlight cells in a range that you want readers to pay attention to. For example, when you get sales numbers from the sales department and plug those numbers into your spreadsheet, your conditional formatting for the sales totals for the month can change color depending on how much was made and how it compares to the target amount.

Start by selecting a range of cells. The *Quick Analysis* icon appears next to the lower-right corner of the selected range (see Figure 8.29).

FIGURE 8.29   Quick Analysis icon

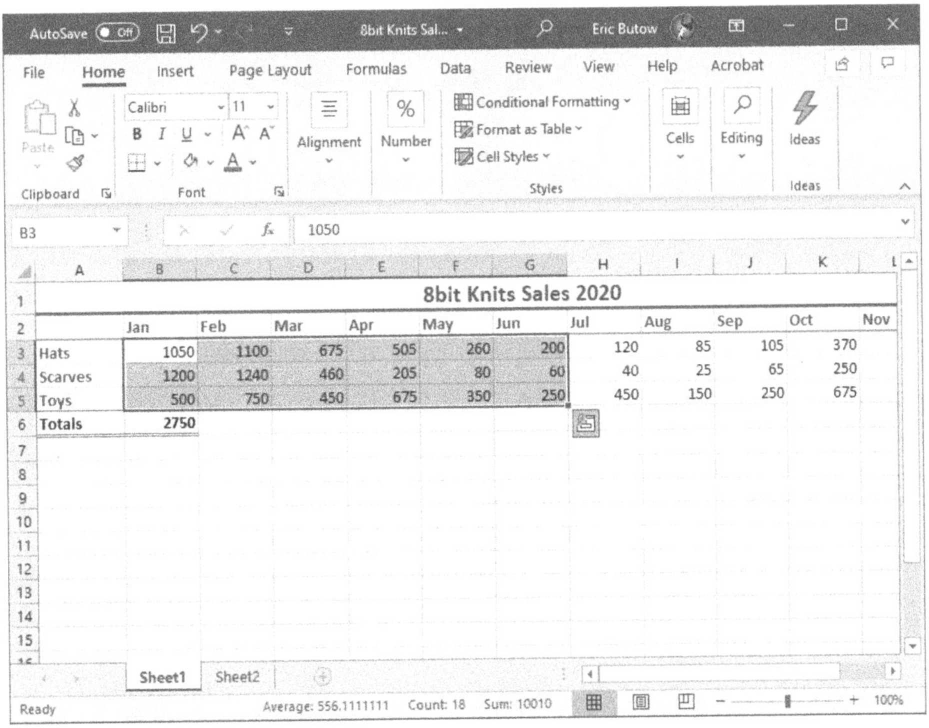

When you move the mouse pointer over the button, a pop-up box explains what the icon is about. Click the icon to open the drop-down menu that appears below the icon, as shown in Figure 8.30.

> After you select a cell or range, you can press Ctrl+Q to open the Quick Analysis drop-down menu.

FIGURE 8.30   Quick Analysis drop-down menu

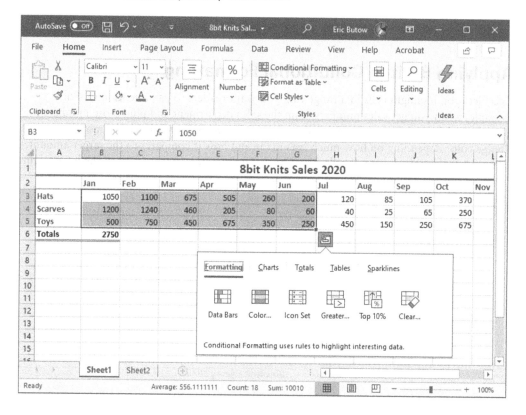

The Formatting tab is open by default, so you can select a formatting type by clicking the icon in the menu. When you move the mouse pointer over an icon, you see a preview of how the data will look in your selected cells once you click the icon.

The icons available in the pop-up box depend on the data you selected in the cells. For example, if you select cells with text, then you will see different formatting options than you would have if you had selected cells that contained only numbers, or cells with both numbers and text.

The example in Figure 8.30 has a range of numbers selected. Click on one of the following six format type icons:

Data Bars: Shows transparent data bars within each cell to show the amount in each cell compared to the largest value in the range

Color: Adds colors to cells in a manner that Excel thinks is relevant. For example, low numbers in the range will have red-colored cells and high numbers will have green-colored cells.

Icon Set: Adds up (green), down (red), and right (yellow) arrow icons to the left of every number to show relationships between numbers in the range (You may not agree with how Excel assigns an arrow to a cell.)

Greater: Opens the Greater Than dialog box so that you can assign a color to all cells with values that are over a certain number. For example, you can assign green to all cells with a value over 5,000.

Top 10%: Places the color in one or more cells that are within the top 10 percent of all values in the range

Clear: Clears all formatting from the range

When you click one of the icons, the drop-down menu disappears. You can open the Quick Analysis pop-up box again to view the drop-down menu and select an additional format style. For example, if you click Color and then click Icon Set, you will see the colors and the icons in all cells in the range.

If you don't see the preview in your cell or range when you move the mouse pointer over it, this means that you cannot use that format option in your cells.

For example, if you select cells with text, and there is no duplicate text in two or more cells within the range, then when you move the mouse pointer over the Duplicate icon, nothing happens because there is no duplicate text to show.

Removing Conditional Formatting

You can remove conditional formatting from an entire worksheet and within a selected range of cells. If you remove conditional formatting within a worksheet, you can clear all formats or all instances of only one format.

Clear Conditional Formatting on a Worksheet

Here's how to clear all conditional formatting throughout an entire worksheet:

1. Click the Home menu option if it's not selected already.

2. In the Styles section in the Home menu ribbon, click Conditional Formatting.

3. Move the mouse pointer over Clear Rules in the drop-down menu.

4. Click Clear Rules From Entire Sheet, as shown in Figure 8.31.

FIGURE 8.31   Clear Rules From Entire Sheet option

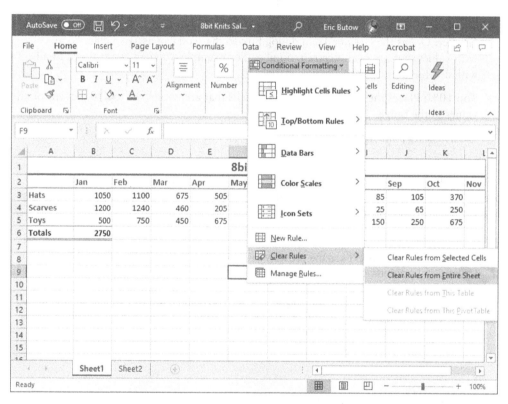

In a Range of Cells

If you want to remove conditional formatting only from a range of cells, follow these steps:

1. Select the range in the worksheet.

2. Click the Home menu option if it's not selected already.

3. In the Styles section in the Home menu ribbon, click Conditional Formatting.

4. Move the mouse pointer over Clear Rules in the drop-down menu.

5. Click Clear Rules From Selected Cells, as shown in Figure 8.32.

FIGURE 8.32 Clear Rules From Selected Cells option

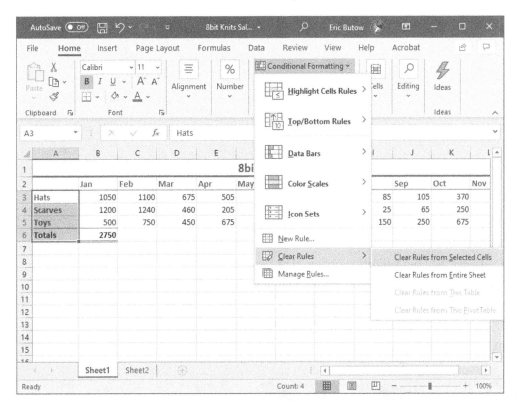

You can also open the Quick Analysis drop-down menu and click the Clear icon, as you learned earlier in this chapter.

Find and Remove the Same Conditional Formats Throughout a Worksheet

If you need to find all cells that have the same conditional formats throughout the worksheet, there is no easy way to do that. However, you can use the Find And Replace feature in Excel to find all instances of conditional formats in a row and then delete them. Here's how:

1. Click the cell that contains the conditional format that you want to remove.
2. Click the Home menu option if it's not selected already.
3. In the Editing section in the Home ribbon, click Find & Select. (If your Excel window width is small, click the Editing icon and then click Find & Select.)
4. Select Go To Special from the drop-down menu.
5. In the Go To Special dialog box, shown in Figure 8.33, click the Conditional Formats option.

FIGURE 8.33 Go To Special dialog box

6. Under the Data Validation option, click the Same button.

7. Click OK. Excel highlights all cells that have the conditional formatting in the row.

8. In the Styles section in the Home menu ribbon, click Conditional Formatting.

9. Move the mouse pointer over Clear Rules in the drop-down menu.

10. Click Clear Rules From Selected Cells, as you saw in Figure 8.32.

EXERCISE 8.4

Summarizing Data Visually

1. Open a new worksheet.

2. Add the months of the year within row 1.

3. Type numbers into all 12 columns within row 2 and row 3.

4. Add a Sparkline line chart in row 2.

5. Add a Sparkline column chart in row 3.

6. Apply color formatting to all the cells in row 2 and row 3.

7. Apply a data bar to all the cells in row 3.

8. Remove formatting within the first six columns in row 2.

Summary

This chapter started by showing you how to paste data using a variety of special paste options in Excel. Next, you learned how to fill in cells automatically using the Auto Fill feature. You also learned how to insert and delete multiple columns, rows, and cells.

After you saw how to add data into a worksheet, you learned how to format cells and a range of cells. I discussed how to merge and unmerge cells. Next, you learned how to modify cell alignment, orientation, and indentation. I showed you how to format cells using Format Painter and discussed how to wrap text within cells. Then you saw how to apply number formats, cell formats, and cell styles. And you learned how to clear one or more formats from one or more cells.

Next, I discussed how to define a named range, reference the named range in a formula, and name a table so that you can find it easily. Finally, you learned how to insert Sparkline charts, apply built-in conditional formatting to one or more cells, and remove conditional formatting.

Key Terms

Auto Fill	Sparklines
Format Painter	transpose
Quick Analysis	validation
range	wrap text

Exam Essentials

Understand how to paste and fill cells.   Know how to access data paste options and which option is right for your situation. You also need to understand how to use the Auto Fill feature to fill in repeating or sequential data in a range of cells.

Know how to insert and delete cells, rows, and columns.   Understand how to add and delete cells as a row and a column, as well as insert and delete multiple rows and columns.

Understand how to format cells and ranges of cells.   Know how to merge and unmerge cells; modify alignment, orientation, and indentation of data within a cell; format cells using Format Painter; wrap text within cells; apply number formats; apply cell formats and styles; and clear cell formatting.

Know how to define a named range.   Understand how to define a range of cells and refer to the named range in a formula.

Understand how to name a table.   Be able to name a table and move your cursor to the named table in a worksheet.

Be able to insert Sparklines.   Know how to add a Sparkline chart and change its format to summarize information in a row quickly.

Know how to apply and remove conditional formatting.   Understand how to add and apply conditional formatting to a range of cells, find cells with conditional formatting, and remove conditional formatting from a cell range.

Review Questions

1. What option do you use to paste formula formatting from one cell into a new cell?

   A. Paste Formulas

   B. Formulas And Number Formatting

   C. Paste

   D. Keep Source Formatting

2. What option do you use when you want to merge text but not affect the alignment?

   A. Merge Cells

   B. The Align Left icon in the Home ribbon

   C. Merge Across

   D. Merge & Center

3. What types of text can you use as the first character when you name a range? (Choose all that apply.)

   A. Numbers

   B. Letters

   C. Only the letters C or R

   D. Underscores

4. How do you select all cells in a worksheet quickly?

   A. Right-click a cell, and then click Select All in the context menu.

   B. Click the Find & Select icon in the Home menu ribbon, and then click Select All in the drop-down menu.

   C. Click the 100% icon in the View menu ribbon.

   D. Press Ctrl+A.

5. Where do you place a Sparkline chart?

   A. After the last column in a row

   B. Below the first column in a row

   C. Above the first column

   D. In the first row and column in a worksheet

6. What type of data can you use with Auto Fill? (Choose all that apply.)

   A. Dates

   B. Numbers

   C. Text

   D. Months of the year

7. What option do you use in the Orientation drop-down menu to give text a specific angle?

A. Angle Counterclockwise

B. Angle Clockwise

C. Format Cell Alignment

D. Rotate Text Up

8. What Quick Analysis formatting option do you use to show cell colors based on numeric criteria?

A. Top 10%

B. Color

C. Greater

D. Data Bars

9. How long can a named range be?

A. 127 characters

B. An unlimited length

C. 255 characters

D. Only as many characters as will fit in the text box

10. What types of currency number formats can you apply? (Choose all that apply.)

A. Accounting Number style

B. Fraction style

C. Percent style

D. Comma style

Chapter

9

Working with Tables and Table Data

MICROSOFT EXAM OBJECTIVES COVERED IN THIS CHAPTER:

✓ **Manage tables and table data**

- Create and format tables

  - Create Excel tables from cell ranges

  - Apply table styles

  - Convert tables to cell ranges

- Modify tables

  - Add or remove table rows and columns

  - Configure table style options

  - Insert and configure total rows

- Filter and sort table data

  - Filter records

  - Sort data by multiple columns

It may sound strange to talk about tables in an Excel spreadsheet. After all, isn't a worksheet just one giant table? Actually, a table in Excel is a specific object that contains a number of additional features that make your data easier to work with.

I start this chapter by showing you how to create a table and how the functionality in a table differs from data in a worksheet. After you create a style, you will learn how to apply a built-in table style. And if you have a table, you will learn how to convert a table back into a cell range.

Next, I will show you how to modify tables further. Excel allows you to add and remove table rows and columns easily. If you want to add a table style, you will learn how to configure them. And when you want to add total rows to a table, you will see how to insert and configure those.

Finally, you'll learn how to filter and sort data in your tables so that they look the way you want.

Creating and Formatting Tables

A table looks a lot like the cells in a worksheet, but an Excel table has plenty of built-in features that you can create more easily than you can within a worksheet.

These features include a header row, which appears by default at the top of the table. The *header row* in each column contains functionality to sort and filter data within the column. You can also add a formula in one column and apply that formula to other columns in your table.

Excel allows you to create tables from existing cell ranges, and vice versa. The Table Design menu ribbon also lets you format your table with different built-in or custom styles.

Creating Excel Tables from Cell Ranges

If you have existing cells in your worksheet and you decide that you want to put them into a table to take advantage of table functionality, here's how to create an Excel table from a range of cells:

1. Select the cell range.

2. Click the Home menu option, if necessary.

3. In the Styles section in the Home ribbon, click Format As Table.

4. Select one of the built-in formats from the drop-down menu, as shown in Figure 9.1.

FIGURE 9.1   Table styles in the Format As Table drop-down menu

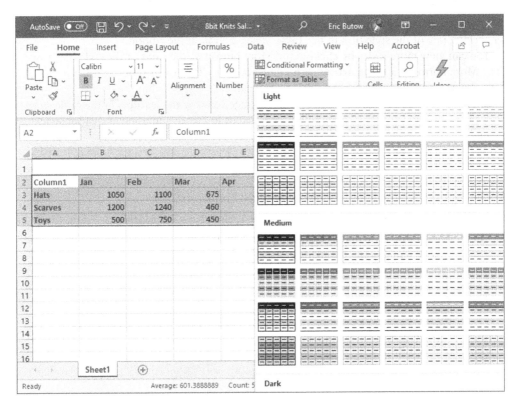

5. In the Format As Table dialog box (see Figure 9.2), select the My Table Has Headers check box if the cell range has no headers. Otherwise, proceed to step 6.

6. Leave the selected cells in the Where Is The Data box as it is and then click OK.

   The selected cells are still selected, but now they sport the style of your new table.

FIGURE 9.2   Format As Table dialog box

Applying Table Styles

After you create a table, the Table Design menu ribbon opens so that you can apply a style by clicking one of the style tiles in the Table Styles section in the ribbon.

You can view more styles by clicking the More button to the right of the style tiles row. (The More button is a down arrow with a line above it.) The list of styles appears in the drop-down menu you saw in Figure 9.1, so you can click a tile within the menu.

If none of the styles interests you, you can change some of the features in the table style or even create a style of your own. Follow these steps to create and apply a custom style to a table:

1. Click a cell in the table.

2. Click the Home menu option, if necessary.

3. In the Styles section in the Home ribbon, click Format As Table.

4. In the drop-down menu you saw in Figure 9.1, click New Table Style.

5. In the New Table Style dialog box, shown in Figure 9.3, press Backspace and then type the new style name in the Name box.

FIGURE 9.3 Highlighted default name in the New Table Style dialog box

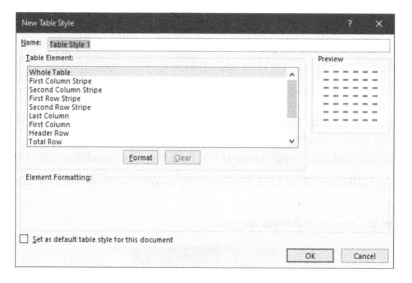

6. In the Table Element list, scroll up and down in the list to view all table elements, and then click an element. In this example, I selected Whole Table.

7. Click Format to open the Format Cells dialog box.

8. In the Format Cells dialog box, shown in Figure 9.4, you can change the font, border, and fill color and pattern by selecting the Font, Border, and Fill tabs, respectively.

FIGURE 9.4   Format Cells dialog box

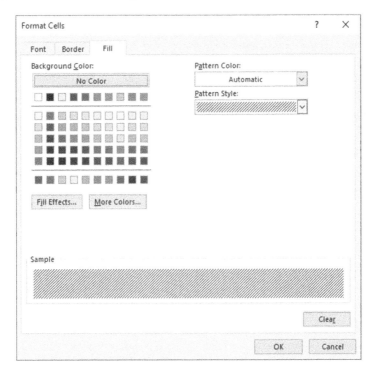

For this example, I selected the Fill tab, clicked the Thin Diagonal Strip pattern, and then clicked OK. The Preview area in the New Table Style dialog box shows all cells in the table with a gray background.

9. After you click OK, the table still looks the same in the worksheet. Now you have to repeat steps 1–3 and then select the custom table style from the drop-down menu in the Custom section.

You can only add a custom table style for all worksheets within one workbook. You cannot apply a custom table style in one workbook to another workbook.

Converting Tables to Cell Ranges

If you have a table and you think it would work better as a cell range in the worksheet instead, here's how to convert your table into a cell range:

1. Click a cell in the table.

2. Click the Table Design menu option.

3. In the Tools section in the Table Design ribbon, click Convert To Range, as shown in Figure 9.5.

FIGURE 9.5   Convert To Range menu option

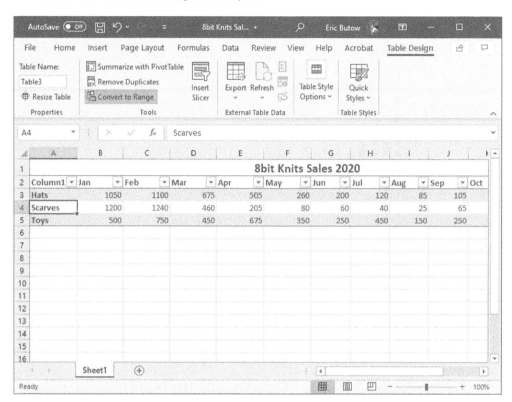

The table data appears in cells in the worksheet, but it keeps the same formatting. For example, if you have shading in the background of odd-numbered rows, the shading remains in those rows.

Remember that when you convert a table back into a cell, you no longer have all the features of a table, including the ability to quickly filter columns.

EXERCISE 9.1

Creating a Table

1. Open an existing workbook.

2. Convert a range of cells into a table.

3. Apply a blue background style of your choice.

4. Convert the table back into a cell range.

Modifying Tables

After you create a table, you may want to modify it to meet your needs. However, you modify cells in a table differently than you do with cells in a worksheet. As with tables in Word, you can add or remove table rows and columns, change prebuilt or custom table styles you already applied to a table, and add what Excel calls a *total row* so that you can total values in table columns quickly.

Adding or Remove Table Rows and Columns

As with cells in a worksheet, a common task of working in a table is to add and remove table rows and/or columns so that the table contains and presents its information the way you want.

Add Table Rows and Columns

Add row(s) and/or column(s) to your table by following these steps:

1. Click a cell in the table.
2. Click the Table Design menu option.
3. In the Properties section in the Table Design ribbon, click Resize Table, as shown in Figure 9.6.
4. You can either resize the table to include the existing table plus any other rows that you want to add, or you can type the cell number into the Resize Table dialog box, as shown in Figure 9.7.
5. Click OK in the dialog box.

The added cells appear below and/or to the right of your existing table. If your table has any formatting applied to it, then the new cells within your table also reflect that formatting.

If you don't select all the cells in your existing table along with the new cells that you want to add, a dialog box appears, stating that the range does not work because that range does not align with the existing table. Click OK to close the dialog box and select all the existing cells, as well as the new cells that you want to add.

Remove Table Rows and Columns

When you want to remove row(s) and/or column(s) from your table, follow these steps:

1. Select a cell within the table row or column you want to delete.
2. Click the Home menu option, if necessary.

3. In the Cells section in the Home ribbon, click the Delete icon as shown in Figure 9.8. (If your Excel window width is small, click the Cells icon and then click the Delete icon.)

4. Select Delete Table Rows or Delete Table Columns from the drop-down menu.

FIGURE 9.6   Resize Table option

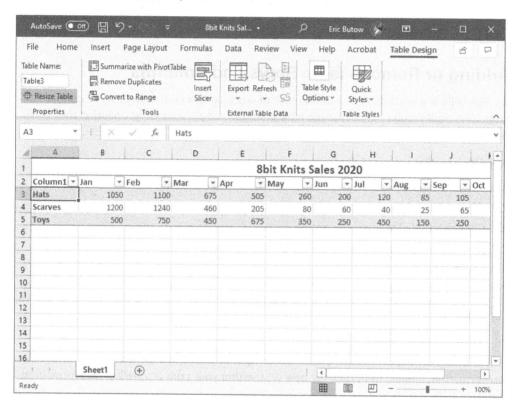

FIGURE 9.7   The reordered table rows

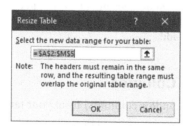

FIGURE 9.8   The Delete Table Rows and Delete Table Columns options

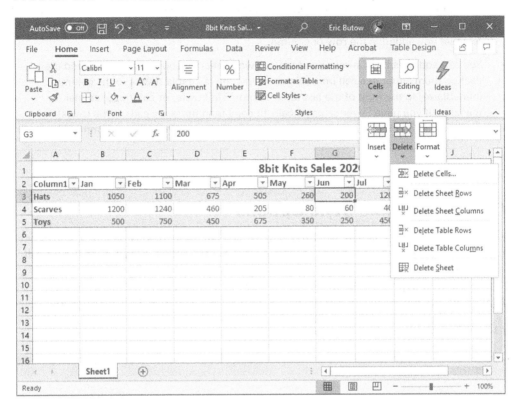

The row or column disappears from the table. If you need to get the row or column back, click the Undo icon in the Quick Access Toolbar on the left side of the Excel window title bar. You can also press Ctrl+Z.

Other Ways to Add and Remove Table Rows and Columns

Excel contains several other methods for removing rows and/or columns, depending on the circumstances:

- You can remove one or more duplicate columns by clicking in the table, clicking the Table Design menu option, and then clicking Remove Duplicates in the Tools section in the Table Design ribbon. In the Remove Columns dialog box, select the check box to the left of each column that you don't want to delete and then click OK. Excel promptly deletes the duplicated columns.

- Type in a cell within the column to the right of the last column in the table, or type in a cell within the row immediately below the last row of the table. After you finish typing and press Enter, Excel automatically adds a new row or column to the table with the text that you added in the row or column.

- You can add cells from another part of your worksheet by copying the cell(s) and then pasting them either in a cell immediately below the last table row or in the column immediately to the right of the last table column. The row(s) or column(s) appear in the table. If you have fewer selected cells to copy than there are cells in the row(s) or column(s), then Excel leaves the remaining cells in the new row(s) or column(s) blank.

Configuring Table Style Options

After you add a table, you may want to change how your table looks more quickly than having to create a new style, as you learned about earlier in this chapter. Start by clicking a cell in your table.

Next, click the Table Design menu option. The Table Style Options section, shown in Figure 9.9, contains seven check boxes that you can select to change how the table looks.

FIGURE 9.9   Table Style Options section check boxes

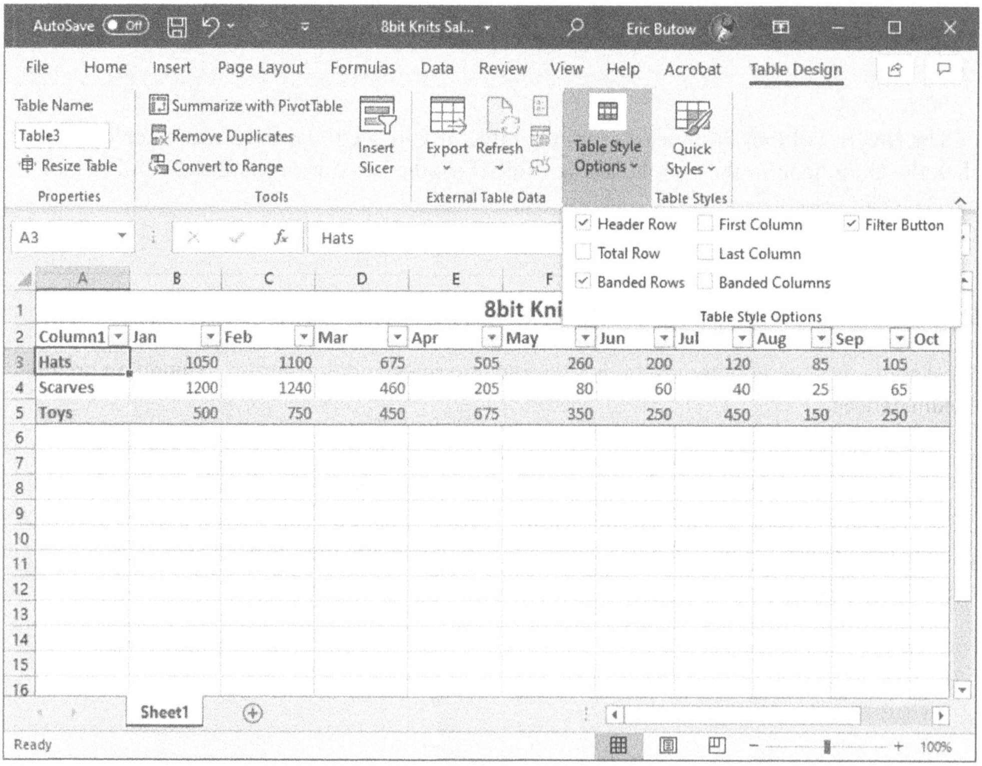

If your Excel window width is small, click the Table Style Options icon to view the drop-down list containing the seven check boxes.

Several of the check boxes are already checked to reflect the default Excel data style. You can click one of the following check boxes to turn the style off and on:

Header Row: Hide the header row.

Total Row: Add a total row, as you will learn about in the next section.

Banded Rows: Turn off shading in odd-numbered rows.

First Column: Apply the First Column style to the first column in the table.

Last Column: Apply the Last Column style to the last column in the table.

Banded Columns: Turn on shading in odd-numbered columns.

Filter Button: Hide the filter buttons within every column in the header row.

The style options that you choose apply to that table. Any new table that you create uses the default style options: Header Row, Banded Rows, and Filter Button.

Inserting and Configuring Total Rows

One big advantage of using a table instead of cells in a worksheet is when you have a lot of numbers and you need to total up those numbers. Instead of totaling numbers in each individual column, Excel lets you create a total row. Here's how:

1. Click a cell in the table.
2. Click the Table Design menu option.
3. In the Table Design ribbon, click the Total Row check box in the Table Style Options section, as shown in Figure 9.10. (If your Excel window width is small, click the Table Style Options icon to view the drop-down list containing the check box.)

The total row appears at the bottom of the table with the total of the numbers in the right column within the total row. However, numbers in your other columns are not totaled.

You can change that by clicking an empty cell within the total row, clicking the down arrow button to the right of the cell, and then selecting Sum from the drop-down menu (see Figure 9.11).

FIGURE 9.10   Total Row check box

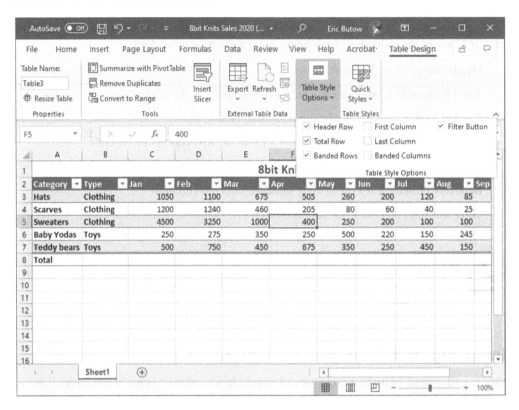

The total for all numbers in the column appears in the cell. If you want to display a different number instead of the total, you can select from one of the following options in the drop-down menu:

Average: The average of all numbers in the column

Count: The number of cells in the column, excluding the header row

Count Numbers: The number of cells that contains numbers within the column, excluding the header row

Max: The maximum number in the column

Min: The minimum number in the column

Sum: Totals all cells with numbers in the column

StdDev: The standard deviation of all numbers in the column

Var: The estimated variance based on all numbers in the column

FIGURE 9.11   Sum option in drop-down menu

	A	B	C	D	E	F	G	H	I	J
1					8bit Knits Sales 2020					
2	Column1	Jan	Feb	Mar	Apr	May	Jun	Jul	Aug	Sep	Oct
3	Hats	1050	1100	675	505	260	200	120	85	105
4	Scarves	1200	1240	460	205	80	60	40	25	65
5	Toys	500	750	450	675	350	250	450	150	250
6	Total									
7		None								
8		Average								
9		Count / Count Numbers								
10		Max / Min								
11		Sum								
12		StdDev / Var								
13		More Functions..								

If you want to view more functions, select More Functions from the bottom of the drop-down list. Then you can view all the functions and select one in the Insert Functions dialog box, but that is beyond the scope of the exam.

One drawback of the total row is that you can't select cells in multiple columns and sum them all at the same time. Instead, after you total your first column, click and hold the mouse button down on the green box (called the fill handle) at the bottom-right corner of the selected cells. Then drag the mouse pointer to the left or right until you fill the cells that you want in the total row. When you release the mouse button, all the cells that you selected sum all the numbers in their columns.

EXERCISE 9.2

Modifying a Table

1. Open a new workbook.

2. Create a worksheet with a header row, five rows, and six columns.

3. Fill the header row with the first six months of the year.

4. Add numbers in all the remaining rows and columns.

5. Add a new row anywhere in the table.

6. Add numbers to all the cells in each column within the row.

7. Convert the entire range to a table.

8. Resize two of the columns in the table.

9. Apply banded columns to the table.

10. Add a table row.

11. Apply a total row.

12. Total the numbers in the first column.

13. Apply the total from the first column in the total row to the other empty cells in the total row.

Filtering and Sorting Table Data

Tables make it easier to filter and sort data compared to entering information into a work-sheet. When you convert a cell range into a table, or you create a table from scratch, Excel automatically adds a header row with filter controls. Each filter control is a down arrow button at the right side of the selected cell within the header row. And, as when you enter data in a worksheet, Excel makes it easy to sort data in one or multiple columns.

Filtering Records

When you want to filter your table, start by clicking the down arrow to the right of the column within the header row. In the drop-down menu, shown in Figure 9.12, you see the data in all the cells within the column.

FIGURE 9.12   Filter drop-down menu

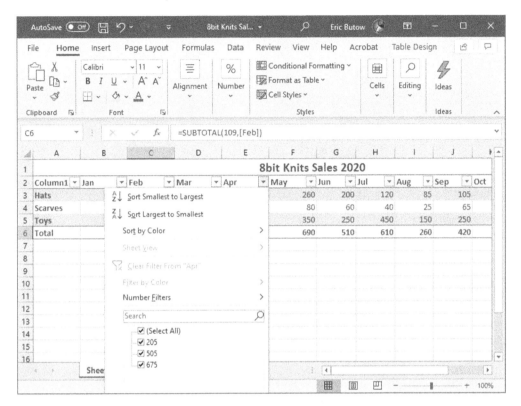

If you want to show only one or more cells within rows in your table, select the Select All check box to clear all the entries. Then you can click one or more check boxes to the left of the entry that you want to show in the table.

When you finish selecting the entry or entries, click OK. Excel filters the table so that it displays only the rows in the table that contain the cells you wanted to show within the column (see Figure 9.13).

The header row remains in the table, and if you have a total row, then the total row remains, too.

FIGURE 9.13   The filtered table shows one row that contains the cell.

Column1	Jan	Feb	Mar	Apr	May	Jun	Jul	Aug	Sep	Oct
			8bit Knits Sales 2020							
Hats	1050	1100	675	505	260	200	120	85	105	
Total	1050	1100	675	505	260	200	120	85	105	

Real World Scenario

Filter Your Numbers Even More

Your boss has told you that she wants to filter your numbers even more than usual to highlight strong sales as part of her presentation to a big customer that she wants to land. That is, she wants the table to reflect all sales numbers that are at or above 10,000 sold, which conveniently happens to be all of the sales numbers for your company's most popular products during the past two quarters.

Fortunately, Excel makes it easy for you to set a filter to show numbers that are greater than, equal to, or less than a certain level. Set a numeric filter by following these steps:

1. Click the Filter button in one of the column header rows.

2. Move the mouse pointer over Number Filters in the drop-down menu.

3. Click Greater Than Or Equal To.

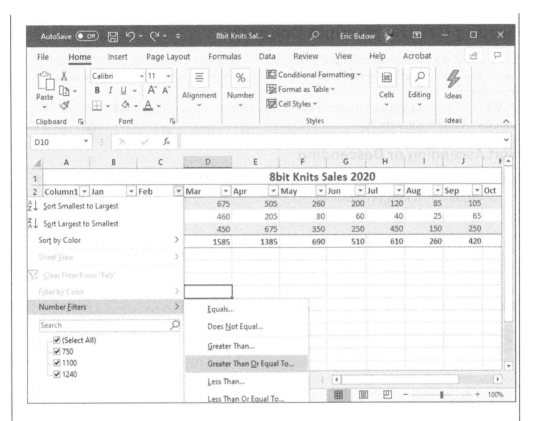

4. The cursor blinks in the top text box in the Custom AutoFilter dialog box so that you can type in the amount that you want to set.

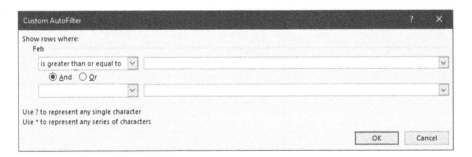

5. Click OK.

All of the rows that contain a number equal to or larger than 10,000 appear in the filtered table. You also see all the other columns within that row, so be careful; if one of the other columns in the row has a number lower than 10,000, that number will still show up in your table.

Sorting Data by Multiple Columns

Excel would not be a spreadsheet program if it could not sort data in one or multiple columns. You can sort cells in several columns within a table just as you do with cells in a worksheet.

What's more, you can sort using a built-in ascending or descending sort, or you can set your own custom sort criteria.

Sort Ascending or Descending

Sort cells in one or more columns in ascending or descending order by following these steps:

1. Select cells in at least two columns.
2. Click the Home menu option, if necessary.
3. In the Home ribbon, click the Sort & Filter in the Table Style Options section, as shown in Figure 9.14. (If your Excel window width is small, click the Editing icon and then click Sort & Filter.)

FIGURE 9.14   Sort & Filter drop-down menu

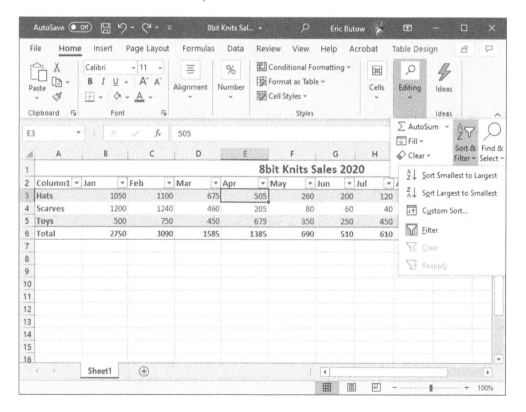

Now you can select from one of two built-in sort options in the drop-down menu:

Sort Smallest To Largest, or Sort A to Z: Sort the numbers in the column from smallest at the top to largest at the bottom if they're all numbers, or from A to Z if all the cells in the column have text.

Sort Largest To Smallest, or Sort Z to A: Sort the numbers in the column from largest at the top to smallest at the bottom if they're all numbers, or from Z to A if all the cells in the column have text.

When you sort from smallest to largest (or from A to Z), and vice versa, Excel sorts all the numbers or text within all the column(s).

If you have a total row in your table, Excel sorts that cell, too. When you sort columns in the table with a total row, the total row will appear in a different row than the bottom, which will completely mess up your table totals.

Create a Custom Sort

If you need more control over what you want to sort, here's how to do that:

1. Select cells in at least two columns.

2. Click the Home menu option, if necessary.

3. In the Home ribbon, click Sort & Filter in the Table Style Options section, as you saw in Figure 9.14. (If your Excel window width is small, click the Editing icon and then click Sort & Filter.)

4. Select Sort Custom from the drop-down menu, as you saw in Figure 9.14.

Excel selects all the cells in your table. In the Sort dialog box shown in Figure 9.15, you can sort in one of three ways:

- By column in the Column box. The default selection is the first column in the table.

- By what you sort in the Sort On box, including the default cell values, the cell color, the font color, or a conditional format.

- The sort order in the Order box. You can also create a custom list to sort in nonsequential order, such as clothes sizes.

Click one of the three drop-down boxes to change how you sort. What you select in one box will affect what you see in other boxes. For example, if you sort by a column of text, you see A To Z in the Order box. If you sort by number, then you see Smallest To Largest in the Order box.

When you're done setting your custom sort, click OK. Excel reorders the rows based on the sort order within the column you selected.

FIGURE 9.15 Sort dialog box

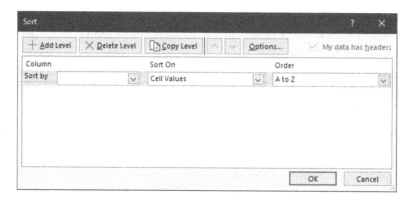

If you select an even number of cells within the column, Excel will sort by the type (letter or number), depending on whether the majority of cells have text or numbers. What happens if you have the same number of cells with text and the same amount with numbers? Excel sorts the cells by letter.

EXERCISE 9.3

Filtering and Sorting Your Table Data

1. Open a new workbook.

2. Create a new table that has four rows (excluding the header row) and five columns.

3. Enter numbers into the non-header cells within the table.

4. Filter two of the columns so that they appear largest to smallest.

5. Sort two different columns so that they appear smallest to largest.

Summary

This chapter started by showing you how to create a table from a cell range. Then you learned how to apply table styles. You also learned how to create a cell range from an existing table.

After you learned about creating a table and applying table styles, I discussed how to modify tables further by adding and removing multiple rows and columns. Next, you learned how to modify the table style options within the Table Design menu ribbon. You also saw how to create a total row to create totals quickly within columns that have numbers in their cells.

Finally, you learned how to filter columns using the built-in table filter tool, as well as how to sort one or more columns in a table.

Key Terms

filter

sort

tables

total rows

Exam Essentials

Understand how to create tables from cell ranges, and vice versa. Know how to convert a table from a cell range in the Home menu ribbon and how to change a table into a cell range in the Table Design menu ribbon.

Know how to add and apply table styles. Understand how to apply prebuilt and custom table styles to a table, as well as how to apply styles quickly in the Table Design menu ribbon.

Understand how to modify tables. Know how to add and remove rows and columns, as well as insert and configure total rows.

Know how to filter records. Understand how to use the built-in filter function in a table to filter a column in ascending or descending letter order, smallest to largest number, or largest to smallest number.

Be able to sort data by multiple columns. Know how to sort multiple columns in a table in ascending or descending letter order, smallest to largest number, or largest to smallest number.

Review Questions

1. When you convert a table into a cell range, what happens to the table formatting?

   A. The formatting disappears.

   B. A dialog box appears that asks you if you want to keep your formatting.

   C. The formatting remains.

   D. A dialog box appears that warns you that if you go ahead with the conversion, you will lose all formatting.

2. How do you quickly get back a deleted row or column in a table? (Select all that apply.)

   A. Click Insert in the Home menu ribbon to insert the row or column again.

   B. Press Ctrl+Z.

   C. Resize the table.

   D. Click Undo in the Quick Access Toolbar.

3. In what order is a sort from the letters Z to A?

   A. Ascending

   B. Alphabetical

   C. Descending

   D. Backward

4. What formats can you change in a table style? (Choose all that apply.)

   A. Font

   B. Alignment

   C. Border

   D. Fill color and pattern

5. What is the difference between Count and Count Numbers?

   A. They both count the number of cells in the column.

   B. They both tell you how many cells have numbers in them.

   C. The Count feature includes all blank cells in the column.

   D. The Count Numbers feature counts how many cells have numbers.

6. What are the three default styles applied to a table? (Choose all that apply.)

   A. Filter Button

   B. Banded Rows

   C. Banded Columns

   D. Header Row

7. What features appear in a table after you create one from a cell range? (Choose all that apply.)

    A. Header row

    B. Filter button

    C. Banded columns

    D. Total row

8. What is the required sort criterion for a custom sort?

    A. Header row

    B. Sort On

    C. Column

    D. Order

9. What column does a total row total by default?

    A. The first column

    B. The last column

    C. Excel only puts the total row in but doesn't total any columns.

    D. All of the columns

10. Where do you apply a table style after you create it?

    A. In the Home menu ribbon

    B. In the Insert menu ribbon

    C. In the Page Layout menu ribbon

    D. In the Table Design menu ribbon

Chapter

10

Performing Operations by Using Formulas and Functions

MICROSOFT EXAM OBJECTIVES COVERED IN THIS CHAPTER:

✓ **Perform operations by using formulas and functions**

- Insert references

    - Insert relative, absolute, and mixed references

    - Reference named ranges and named tables in formulas

- Calculate and transform datas

    - Perform calculations by using the AVERAGE(), MAX(), MIN(), and SUM() functions

    - Count cells by using the COUNT(), COUNTA(), and COUNTBLANK() functions

    - Perform conditional operations by using the IF() function

- Format and modify text

    - Format text by using RIGHT(), LEFT(), and MID() functions

    - Format text by using UPPER(), LOWER(), and LEN() functions

    - Format text by using the CONCAT() and TEXTJOIN() functions

When you type a formula in a cell, Excel makes it easy to refer to specific cells and ranges. You can add one of three types of references: relative, absolute, and mixed. As you'll see in this chapter, Excel also allows you to refer to a cell range and a table within a workbook.

Next, I will show you how to perform simple calculations and operations using built-in calculation commands that you type into the Formula Bar. These include calculating the average, minimum, maximum, and sum of a group of cells that contain numbers, counting cells in selected cells or a range, and performing conditional operations with the IF() function.

Finally, you'll learn how to format and modify text in a cell by using a variety of functions. This includes how to return one or more characters at the right, left, or midpoint area with a text string; change text in a cell to uppercase and lowercase; display the number of characters in a text string; and combine text in different strings into one string.

Inserting References

Excel labels each cell with the column letter and then the row number, such as A5. This identification system makes it easy for you to refer to a cell when you enter a formula in another cell. For example, when you're in cell D9 and you want to multiply the number in cell D9 by 3, all you need to type is =(D9*3) in the *Formula Bar*.

You can create three different types of references:

Relative   The default *relative cell reference* changes when you copy a formula from one cell into another cell. For example, if you type the formula =(D3*3) in cell D9 and then copy cell D9 to cell G9, Excel changes D3 in the formula to G3 because you are now in column G, as shown in the Formula Bar in Figure 10.1.

Absolute   The *absolute cell reference* contains a dollar sign to the left of the letter and number in the cell that you reference, such as A5. When you add an absolute cell reference in a formula, the formula refers to a fixed point in the worksheet. For example, if you type the formula =(D3*3) in cell D9 and then copy cell D9 to cell G9, cell G9 still calculates the formula using cell D3 (see the Formula Bar in Figure 10.2).

Mixed   A *mixed cell reference* contains a dollar sign to the left of the letter or number in the cell you reference, such as $A5. When you add a mixed cell reference in a formula, you specify that you want to refer to a value in a fixed column or row in a worksheet. For example, if you type the formula =($D3*3) in cell D9 and then copy cell D9 into cells D10 and D11, Excel multiplies the cells in cells D3, D4, and D5 and places those results in cells D9, D10, and D11, respectively (see Figure 10.3).

FIGURE 10.1   Relative cell reference

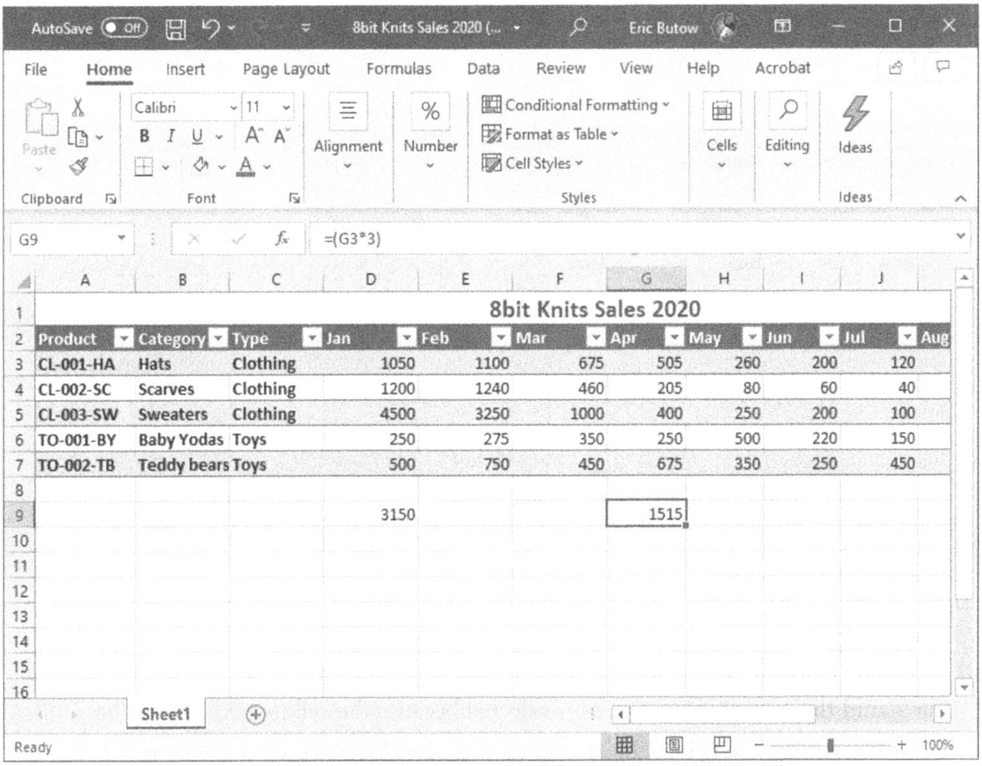

Inserting Relative, Absolute, and Mixed References

After you insert a reference into a formula, you may need to change the reference type from one type to another. Excel saves you some time by allowing you to change the reference type quickly. Here's how to do this:

1. Create a new workbook and add numbers to cells A1 through A4 in the worksheet.
2. In cell A6, type the formula =(A2*5) in the Formula Bar.

FIGURE 10.2   Absolute cell reference

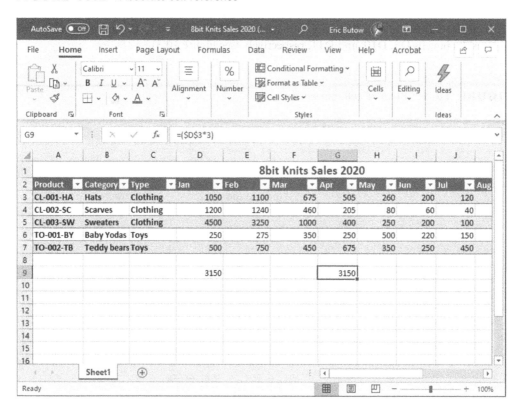

3. Press Enter.

4. In the Formula Bar, place the cursor to the left or right of A2 in the formula, or between the A and the 2. You know the cell is selected because the cell text A2 turns blue.

5. Press F4. The cell turns into the absolute reference A2, as shown in Figure 10.4.

6. Press F4 again. The cell turns into the mixed reference A$2.

7. Press F4 a third time. The cell turns into the mixed reference $A2.

8. Press F4 a final time to return the cell to its original relative reference A2.

9. Press Esc to exit the Formula Bar.

As you change each formula reference type in the Formula Bar, the new formula also appears in the cell.

FIGURE 10.3 Mixed cell reference

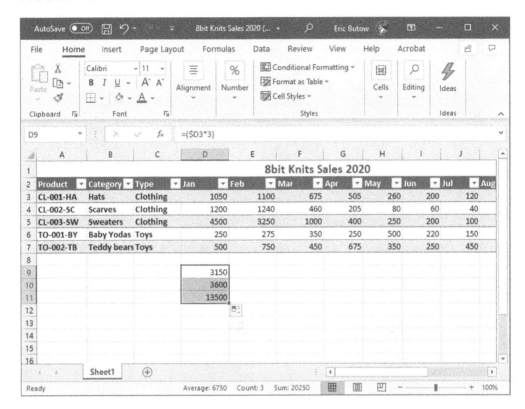

Referencing Named Ranges and Named Tables in Formulas

You don't need to use column names and numbers when you refer to cells in a formula. You can also refer to a named cell range or a named table within a formula. Here is an example that you can follow:

1. Open a workbook that has a cell range and a table with numeric values in a worksheet. If you don't have one, refer to previous chapters in this book to create a range and a table.

2. Click an empty cell below a column in the table.

3. In the Formula Bar, type **=SUM(** and then start typing the name of the table.

4. As you type, a list of potential matches appears in the drop-down list below the Formula Bar. Double-click the table name in the list.

FIGURE 10.4 Absolute reference in the Formula Bar

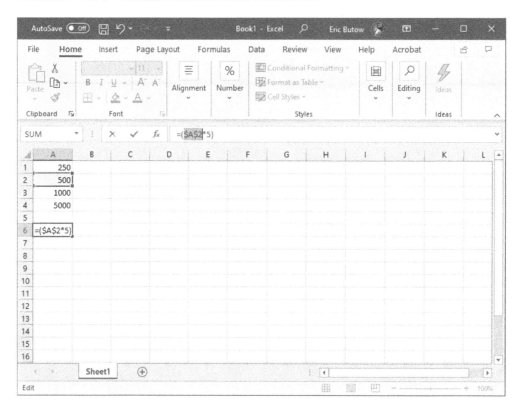

5. Now that the table name appears in the formula, start typing the name of the column in the table.

6. As you type, a list of potential matches appears in the drop-down list below the Formula Bar. Double-click the column name in the list.

7. Now that the column name appears in the formula, type) and then press Enter.

The total of all the numbers within the table appears in the cell, and Excel selects the cell directly below it. When you click the cell in the table, as shown in Figure 10.5, you see the formula in the Formula Bar.

If you need to check the name of the range or the table, click the down arrow at the right side of the Name Box, which appears to the left of the Formula Bar. Then click the name of the range or table. Excel highlights all the cells in the selected range or table. Now you can click the empty cell and add your formula using the range or table name.

FIGURE 10.5 The formula in the Formula Bar

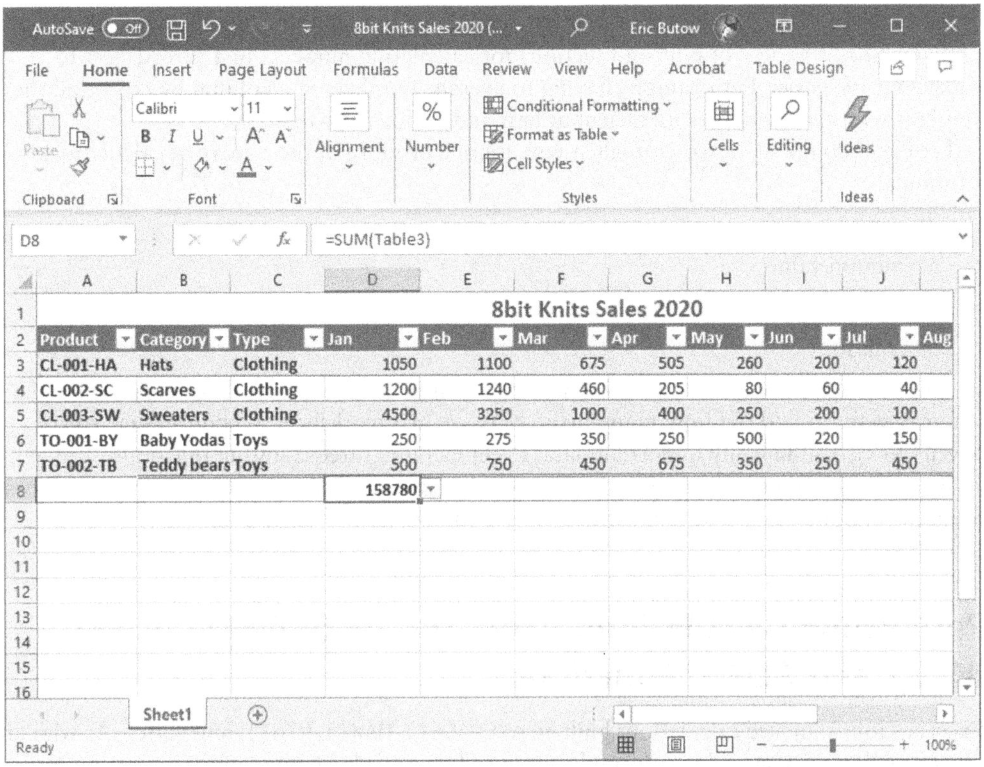

EXERCISE 10.1

Inserting References

1. Open a new worksheet.
2. Create a new table with four rows (with one header row) and four columns in the worksheet.
3. Label these columns Q1, Q2, Q3, and Q4.
4. Enter numbers in the cells within the table.
5. In cell A5, add a new formula that multiplies the amount in cell A2 by 4.
6. Move cell A5 to cell C5.
7. Change the formula in cell C5 to have an absolute reference to the cell.
8. Move cell C5 to cell B5.
9. Total the numbers in the name you have given to column D in the table.

Calculating and Transforming Datas

Excel includes a variety of built-in functions for calculating numbers in a spreadsheet to make your life easier. For example, having to average numbers in a column by typing all the numbers within a formula is inefficient at best and tedious at worst.

Let Excel do the work for you when you use one or more of the following calculations in a formula:

- Average
- Maximum value
- Minimum value
- Summation

You may also have times when you need to count instances in a worksheet. For example, you may want to find out how many blank cells are in a worksheet to confirm that you haven't missed adding any important data. Excel includes three counting functions.

If you need to go further and find out how many numeric values reach a certain threshold to meet a condition, such as where numbers are too hot or too cold, Excel includes the IF() function.

Performing Calculations Using the *AVERAGE()*, *MAX()*, *MIN()*, and *SUM()* Functions

Excel has four standard calculations built in: AVERAGE(), MAX(), MIN(), and SUM(). As with all other calculations you add to a formula, you need to precede any one of these arguments with the equal sign (=) in the Formula Bar.

AVERAGE()

The *average* is also known as the arithmetic mean, if you remember your middle school math. You can take the average of a group of cells in a worksheet, within a range, or within a table. You can also take an average of two numbers.

Average of Cells

In an empty cell, type **=AVERAGE** and then the cell range within the worksheet or table in parentheses. For example, if you type **=AVERAGE (D3:D7)** in the Formula Bar, as shown in the example in Figure 10.6, and then press Enter, the average of all five numbers in the column appears in the cell.

After you press Enter, Excel selects the cell directly below the cell with the average number. Click the cell with the average number to view the formula in the Formula Bar.

Average of Numbers

You can average as few as two or as many as 255 numbers by typing **=AVERAGE** and then entering up to 255 numbers within the parentheses. For example, if you

FIGURE 10.6   The average of all five numbers

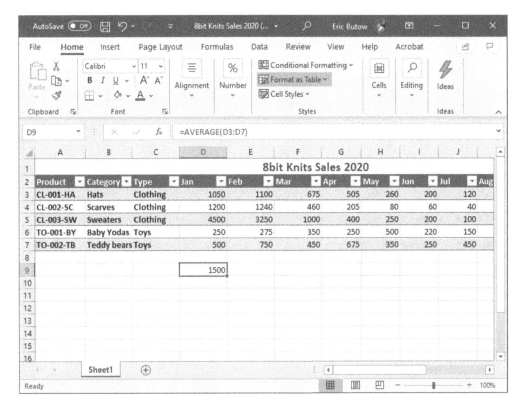

type **=AVERAGE(1,10,40,100,400)** in the Formula Bar (see Figure 10.7) and then press Enter, the average of all five numbers appears in the cell.

As you work with the AVERAGE() function, keep the following in mind:

- As you start typing **AVERAGE** in the Formula Bar, you see a drop-down list that shows functions that Excel thinks you want to add. If you would rather not finish typing the function, double-click AVERAGE in the list to add AVERAGE(to the Formula Bar.

- If you average cells within a range where a cell contains text, such as the text in a table header, then Excel does not include the information in those cells when it calculates the average.

- If one or more cells that you want to average contain errors, then the average will also return an error message.

- If you average cells within a range where a cell contains the number 0, then Excel includes that number in the average. However, if a cell in the range is empty, then Excel ignores that cell when it calculates the average.

FIGURE 10.7   Average of five numbers in the cell

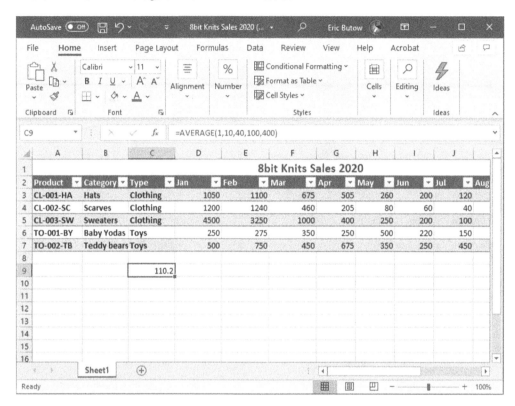

Real World Scenario

Use Averages for Different Criteria

Your boss has come to you with a request for the next company sales meeting. She wants you to show the average sales greater than $1,000 during the first quarter of the year. Then she wants to show the average sale for months that have brought in more than $1,000 but less than $4,000.

Excel gives you two functions for doing these tasks quickly: AVERAGEIF() and AVERAGEIFS(). The difference between the two? AVERAGEIF() finds averages that meet one criterion, and AVERAGEIFS() finds averages that meet every one of the multiple criteria you specify in the argument.

Here's how to use both of these functions to calculate what your boss wants to see:

1. Select the cell below the range or the table where you want to display the average for the first quarter.

2. Type **=AVERAGEIF(D3:F7, ">1000")** in the Formula Bar.

3. Press Enter to view the average in the cell, as shown in the following graphic.

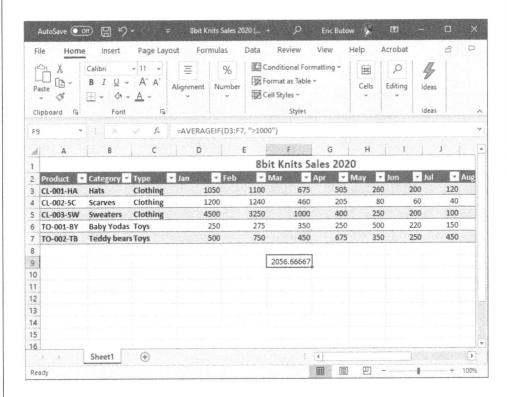

4. Select the cell below the range or the table where you want to display the average for the quarter.

5. Type **=AVERAGEIFS(M3:O7,M3:O7,">1000",M3:O7,"<4000")** in the Formula Bar.

6. Press Enter to view the average in the cell.

7. Click the cell again to view the formula in the cell, as shown in the following graphic:

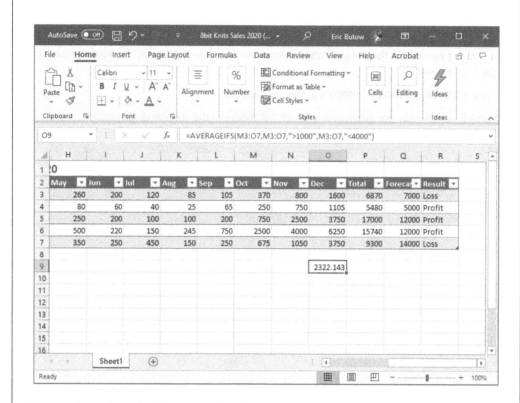

Note that if a selected cell is empty, then Excel treats the cell as including the number 0.

MAX()

If you need to find the largest number in a range of cells or cells within a table, the MAX() function is the tool you need. After you select a blank cell to add the formula, you can add the MAX() function in the Formula Bar in one of two ways:

- Type **=MAX(a,b,c . . .)**, where a, b, c, and so on are numbers of your choosing. You can add as many as 255 numbers. When you finish typing the formula, press Enter to see the result in the cell.

- Type **=MAX(** and then select a range of cells in the worksheet or the table. Excel automatically adds the cell range in your worksheet, so all you have to do is type) to close the formula and then press Enter. You can see the result in the cell shown in Figure 10.8.

FIGURE 10.8   The calculated MAX result in the cell and the formula in the Formula Bar

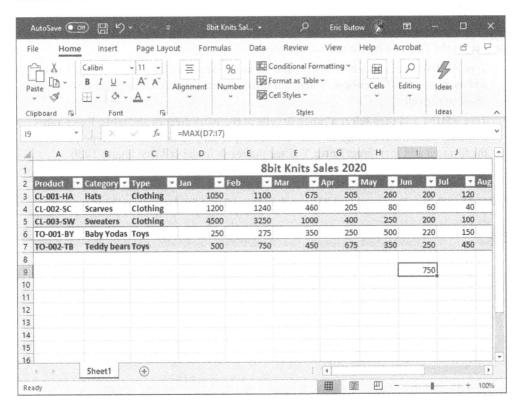

    Keep the following in mind when you work with the MAX() function:

- As you start typing **MAX** in the Formula Bar, you see a drop-down list that shows functions that Excel thinks you want to add to the formula. If you would rather not finish typing the function, double-click MAX in the list to add MAX(to the Formula Bar.

- If you calculate the maximum number of cells within a range where a cell contains text, such as the text in a table header, then Excel does not include the information in those cells when it calculates the maximum.

- If one or more cells that you selected contain errors, then the maximum calculation will also return an error message in the cell.

- If a cell in the range is empty, then Excel ignores that cell when it calculates the maximum.

MIN()

If you need to find the smallest number in a range of cells or cells within a table, use the MIN() function. After you select a blank cell to add the formula, you can add the MIN() function in the Formula Bar in one of two ways:

- Type =MIN(a,b,c . . .), where a, b, c, and so on are numbers of your choosing. You can add as many as 255 numbers. When you finish typing the formula, press Enter to see the result in the cell.

- Type =MIN(and then select a range of cells in the worksheet or the table. Excel automatically adds the cell range in your worksheet, so all you have to do is type) to close the formula and then press Enter. You see the result in the cell (see Figure 10.9).

FIGURE 10.9 The calculated MIN result in the cell and the formula in the Formula Bar

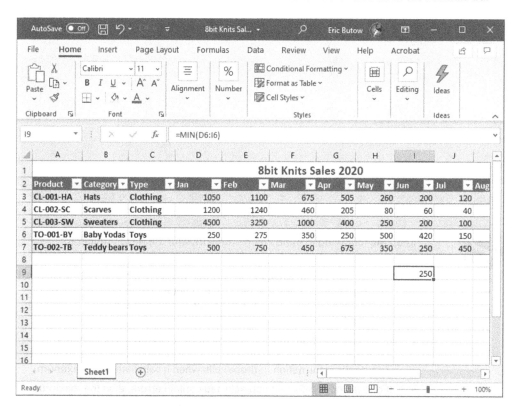

Keep the following in mind when you work with the MIN() function:

- As you start typing **MIN** in the Formula Bar, you see a drop-down list that shows functions that Excel thinks you want to add to the formula. If you would rather not finish typing the function, double-click MIN in the list to add MIN(to the Formula Bar.
- If you calculate the minimum number of cells within a range where a cell contains text, such as the text in a table header, then Excel does not include the information in those cells when it calculates the minimum.
- If one or more cells that you selected contain errors, then the minimum calculation will also return an error message in the cell.
- If a cell in the range is empty, then Excel ignores that cell when it calculates the minimum.

SUM()

When you need to summarize numbers or, more often, numbers in a range of cells, Excel makes this task easy with the SUM() function. After you select a blank cell to add the formula, you can add the SUM() function in the Formula Bar in one of three ways:

- Type =SUM(A1:A5), where you can replace A1:A5 with the starting and ending cells that you want to sum.
- You can sum multiple ranges of cells by typing commas between cell ranges, such as =SUM(A1:A5,D1:D5). When you finish typing the formula, press Enter to see the result in the cell.
- Type =SUM(and then select a range of cells in the worksheet or the table. Excel automatically adds the cell range in your worksheet, so all you have to do is type) to close the formula and then press Enter. You can see the result in the cell shown in Figure 10.10.

Counting Cells Using the *COUNT()*, *COUNTA()*, and *COUNTBLANK()* Functions

When you need to know how many cells in a worksheet or table have numbers, cells that are not empty, or cells that are empty, you don't have to go through a worksheet or table and count them yourself. You can use the three built-in counting functions.

FIGURE 10.10   The calculated SUM result in the cell and the formula in the Formula Bar

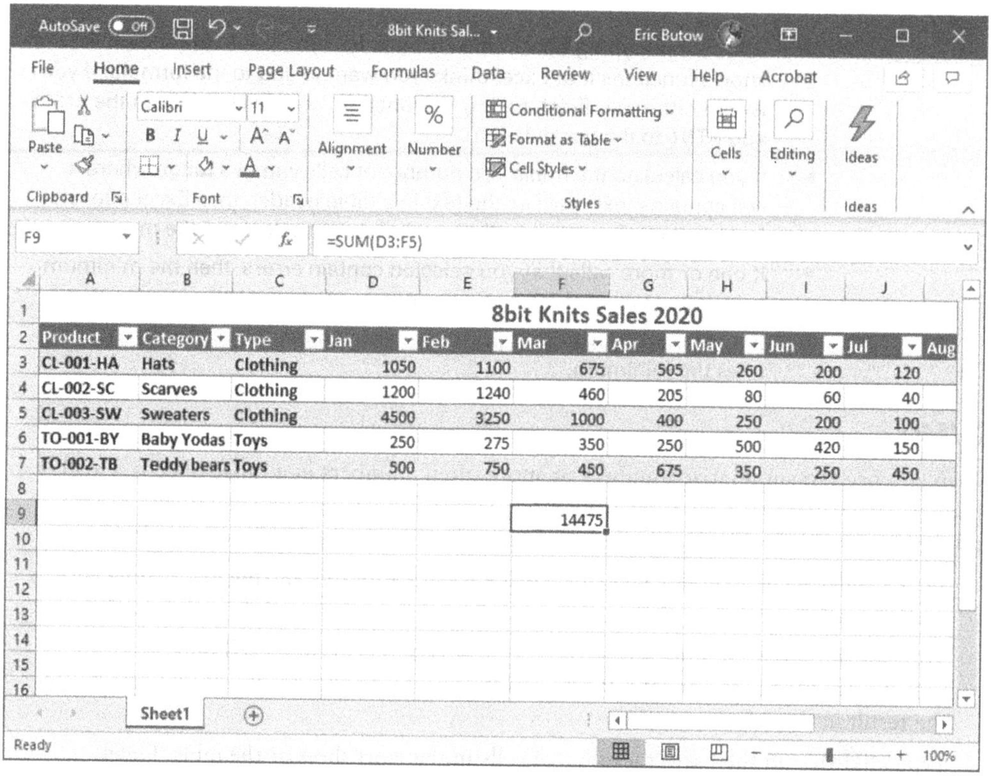

COUNT()

If you need to count how many cells in a range or cells within a table have numbers, use the COUNT() function. After you select a blank cell to add the formula, you can add the COUNT() function in the Formula Bar in one of three ways:

- Type =COUNT(a,b,c . . .), where a, b, c, and so on are numbers of your choosing. You can add as many as 255 numbers. When you finish typing the formula, press Enter to see the result in the cell.

- Type =COUNT(A1:A5), where you can replace A1:A5 with the starting and ending cells that you want to count.

- Type =COUNT(and then select a range of cells in the worksheet or the table. Excel automatically adds the cell range in your worksheet, so all you have to do is type) to close the formula and then press Enter. You can see the result in the cell shown in Figure 10.11.

FIGURE 10.11   The count result in the cell and the formula in the Formula Bar

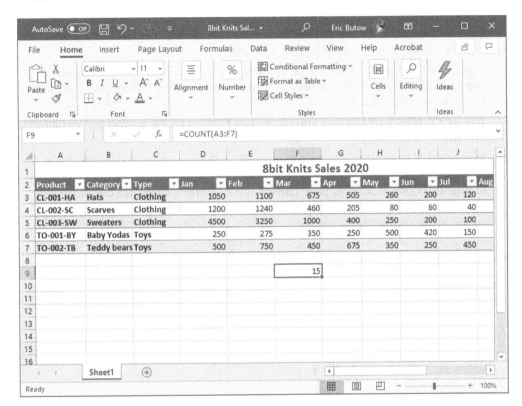

Keep the following in mind when you work with the COUNT() function:

- As you start typing **COUNT** in the Formula Bar, you see a drop-down list that shows functions that Excel thinks you want to add to the formula. If you would rather not finish typing the function, double-click COUNT in the list to add COUNT(to the Formula Bar. Then you can select or type the range, type), and then press Enter.

- Excel counts cells with numbers, dates, and even a text representation of numbers such as the number 5 in quotes ("5").

- If one or more cells that you selected contain errors, then the count will also return an error message in the cell.

- If a cell in the range is empty, then Excel ignores that cell during the count.

COUNTA()

You can use the COUNTA() function to count the number of cells that are not empty within a range in a worksheet or in a table. After you select a range, add the COUNTA() function in the Formula Bar using one of the following methods:

- Type =COUNTA(a,b,c ...), where a, b, c, and so on are numbers of your choosing. You can add as many as 255 numbers. When you finish typing the formula, press Enter to see the result in the cell.

- Type =COUNTA(E1:E5) where you can replace E1:E5 with the starting and ending cells that you want to count.

- Type =COUNT(and then select a range of cells in the worksheet or the table. Excel automatically adds the cell range in your worksheet, so all you have to do is type) to close the formula and then press Enter. You can see the result in the cell shown in Figure 10.12.

FIGURE 10.12   The COUNTA results in the cell and the formula in the Formula Bar

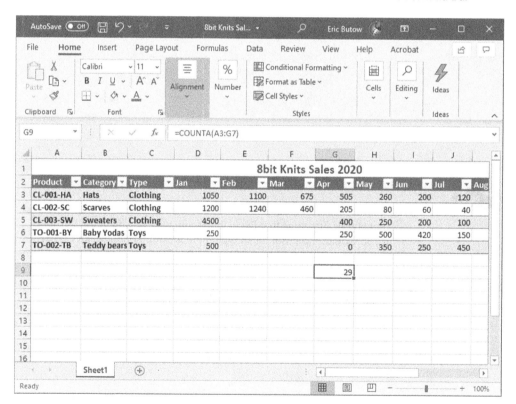

When you use the COUNTA() function, note the following:

- As you start typing **COUNTA** in the Formula Bar, you see a drop-down list that shows functions that Excel thinks you want to add to the formula. If you would rather not finish typing the function, double-click COUNTA in the list to add COUNTA(to the Formula Bar. Then you can select or type the range, type), and then press Enter.
- The COUNTA() function counts all cells with any type of information including cells that contain errors.
- If a cell in the range is empty, then Excel ignores that cell when it calculates the maximum.

COUNTBLANK()

The COUNTBLANK() function counts the number of empty cells within a selected range in a worksheet or table.

Once you select the range, add the COUNTBLANK() function in the Formula Bar by typing =COUNTBLANK(and then type the cell range, or you can select a range of cells in the worksheet or the table. Excel automatically adds the cell range in your worksheet, so all you have to do is type) to close the formula and then press Enter. You can see the result in the cell shown in Figure 10.13.

Keep the following in mind when you work with the COUNTBLANK() function:

- As you start typing **COUNTBLANK** in the Formula Bar, you see a drop-down list that shows functions that Excel thinks you want to add to the formula. If you would rather not finish typing the function, double-click COUNTBLANK in the list to add COUNTBLANK(to the Formula Bar. Then you can select or type the range, type), and then press Enter.
- If you type the number 0 in a cell, Excel considers that cell to be populated.

Perform Conditional Operations by Using the *IF()* Function

If you've ever taken a computer programming class or even used a spreadsheet program before, you know that the if-then operation is one of the basic operations that you can use to find out if text or a numerical value is true or false.

You can easily add an if-then condition to a cell in a worksheet or table by using the IF() function. There are two ways to compare values using the IF() function: by having Excel tell you if a cell contains text or a number or if a numeric value meets the condition.

FIGURE 10.13 The calculated COUNTBLANK result in the cell and formula in the Formula Bar

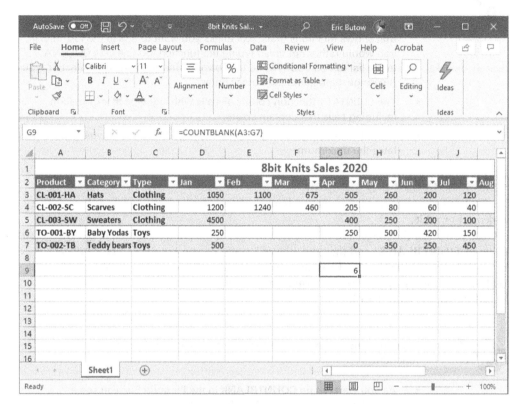

Show if a Cell Contains Text

Here's how to have Excel tell you if a cell contains the text you want to show:

1. Place the cursor in cell C9.

2. Type **=IF(C7="Clothing",true,false)** in the Formula Bar.

3. Press Enter.

   Excel shows FALSE within the cell, as shown in Figure 10.14.

The TRUE or FALSE result appears in all uppercase letters whether or not you capitalize some or all of the words "true" and "false" in the formula.

FIGURE 10.14 The FALSE result in the cell with the formula in the Formula Bar

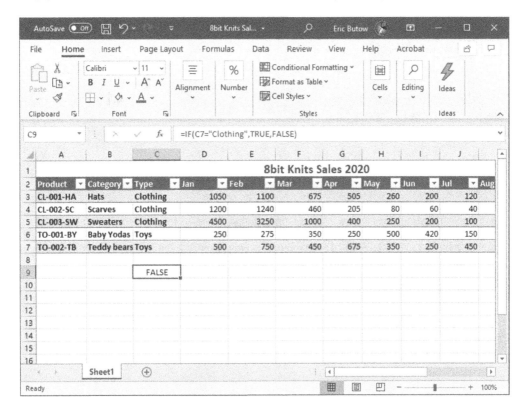

Show if the Numeric Value Meets the Condition

To show that a numeric value meets a certain condition, such as the value in one cell being smaller than another, follow these steps:

1. Click cell R3 in the table.

2. Type **=IF(P3<Q3,"Loss","Profit")** in the Formula Bar. In this formula, Loss is the condition if the comparison is true, and Profit is the condition if the comparison is false.

3. Press Enter.

In the table, Excel shows results not only in cell R3 but also within all cells within column R (see Figure 10.15).

Excel copied the formula into all cells, so now you can see if all of the totals in column O when compared with the forecast numbers in column P resulted in a loss or profit for the year.

FIGURE 10.15 The results of the formula in column R

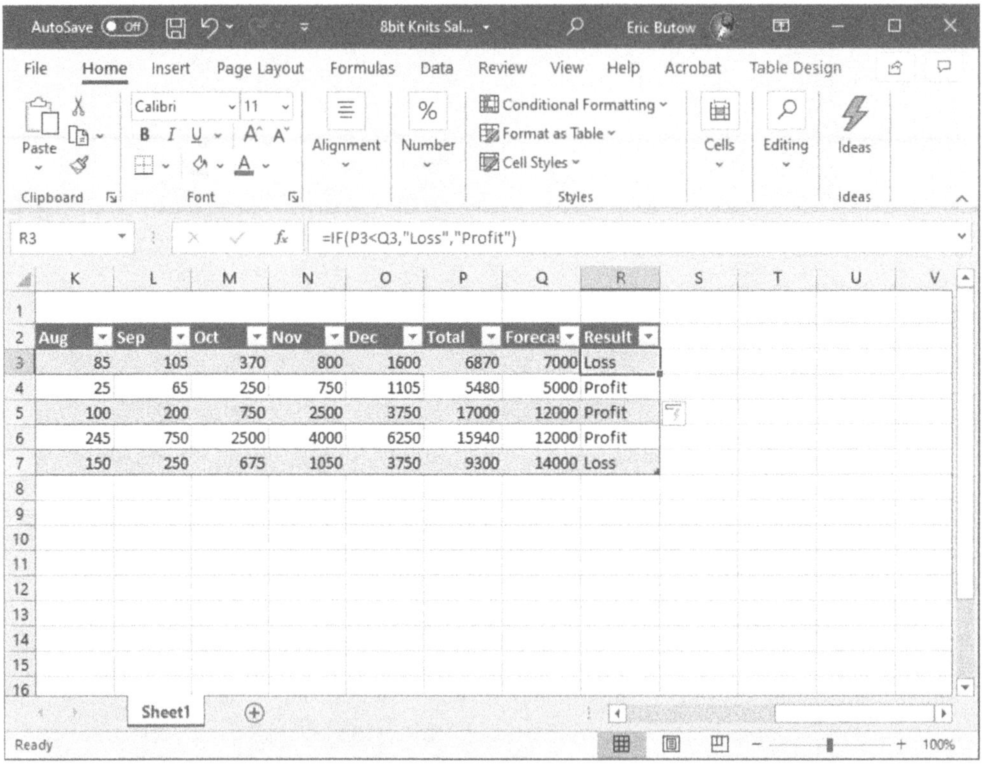

EXERCISE 10.2

Calculate and Transform Datas

1. Open a new document.
2. Add a new table with five columns and six rows.
3. Populate the table with numbers.
4. In column F, summarize all the numbers within each row.
5. In cell A7, view the maximum number of all the numbers in the column.
6. In cell B7, view the minimum number of all the numbers in the column.
7. In cell C7, count all the cells in the column.
8. In cell F7, have Excel report if cell F6 is greater than cell F1.

Formatting and Modifying Text

Lists are an effective way of presenting information that readers can digest easily, as demonstrated in this book. Excel includes many powerful tools to create lists easily and then format them so that they look the way you want them to appear.

Formatting Text Using the *RIGHT()*, *LEFT()*, and *MID()* Functions

When you need to extract specific characters from text to place it in another cell, such as only to show a prefix for a part name, you can do so by using the built-in RIGHT(), LEFT(), and MID() functions that you can add within a formula.

RIGHT()

The RIGHT() function shows the last characters in a string of text within a cell in a worksheet or table. Here's how to use the RIGHT() function in a cell:

1. Click cell A9 in the table.
2. Type **=RIGHT(A4,2)** in the Formula Bar. A4 is the cell and 2 is the number of characters to show in cell A9.
3. Press Enter.

    The last two letters in cell A4 appear in cell A9, as shown in Figure 10.16.

Keep the following in mind when you work with the RIGHT() function:

- As you start typing **RIGHT** in the Formula Bar, you see a drop-down list that shows functions that Excel thinks you want to add to the formula. If you would rather not finish typing the function, double-click RIGHT in the list to add RIGHT(to the Formula Bar. Then you can select or type the range, type), and then press Enter.
- Excel considers spaces as characters.
- If you don't add a number after the cell within the formula, such as RIGHT(A4), then Excel will return only the last character in cell A4.
- You can also add a string of characters instead of the cell within a formula, such as **RIGHT("Microsoft Excel",5)** to display the characters Excel in the cell where you added the formula.
- If you specify a number of characters in the formula greater than the number of characters within the cell, then the formula counts all the characters.
- Excel does not support the RIGHT() function in all languages, so if this function does not work, contact Microsoft to determine whether Excel supports this function for your language.

FIGURE 10.16 The last two letters in cell A4

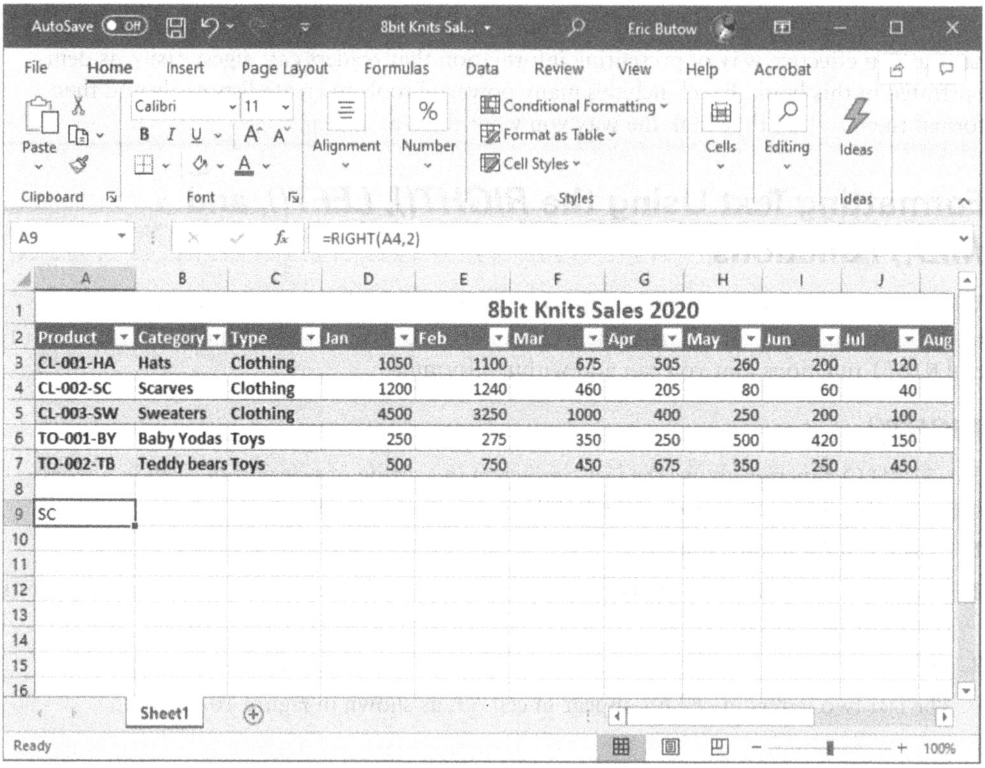

LEFT()

The LEFT() function shows the first characters in a string of text within a cell in a worksheet or table. Use the LEFT() function as demonstrated in the following example:

1. Click on cell A10 in the table.

2. Type **=LEFT(A6,2)** in the Formula Bar. A6 is the cell and 2 is the number of characters to show in cell A10.

3. Press Enter.

   The first two letters in cell A6 appear in cell A10 (see Figure 10.17).

FIGURE 10.17   The first two letters in cell A6

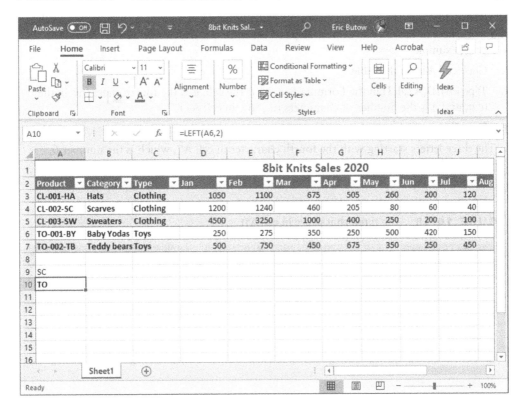

When you work with the LEFT() function, take note of the following:

- As you start typing **LEFT** in the Formula Bar, you see a drop-down list that shows the functions that Excel thinks you want to add to the formula. If you would rather not finish typing the function, double-click LEFT in the list to add LEFT(to the Formula Bar. Then you can select or type the range, type), and then press Enter.

- Excel considers spaces as characters.

- If you don't add a number after the cell within the formula, such as LEFT(A6), then Excel will return only the first character in cell A6.

- You can also add a string of characters instead of the cell within a formula, such as **LEFT("Microsoft Excel",5)** to display the characters Micro in the cell where you added the formula.

- If you specify a number of characters in the formula greater than the number of characters within the cell, then the formula counts all the characters.

- Excel does not support the LEFT() function in all languages, so if this function does not work, contact Microsoft to determine whether Excel supports this function for your language.

MID()

The MID() function shows a specific number of characters in a string of text within a cell in a worksheet or table. Follow these steps to use the MID() function, as shown in the following example:

1. Click cell A11 in the table.

2. Type **=MID(A7,4,3)** in the Formula Bar. A6 is the cell, 4 is the fourth character in the text, and 3 is the number of characters to show in cell A11.

3. Press Enter.

The three letters starting with the fourth character in cell A7, which is the number *0*, appear in cell A11 (see Figure 10.18).

FIGURE 10.18   The three characters in cell A11

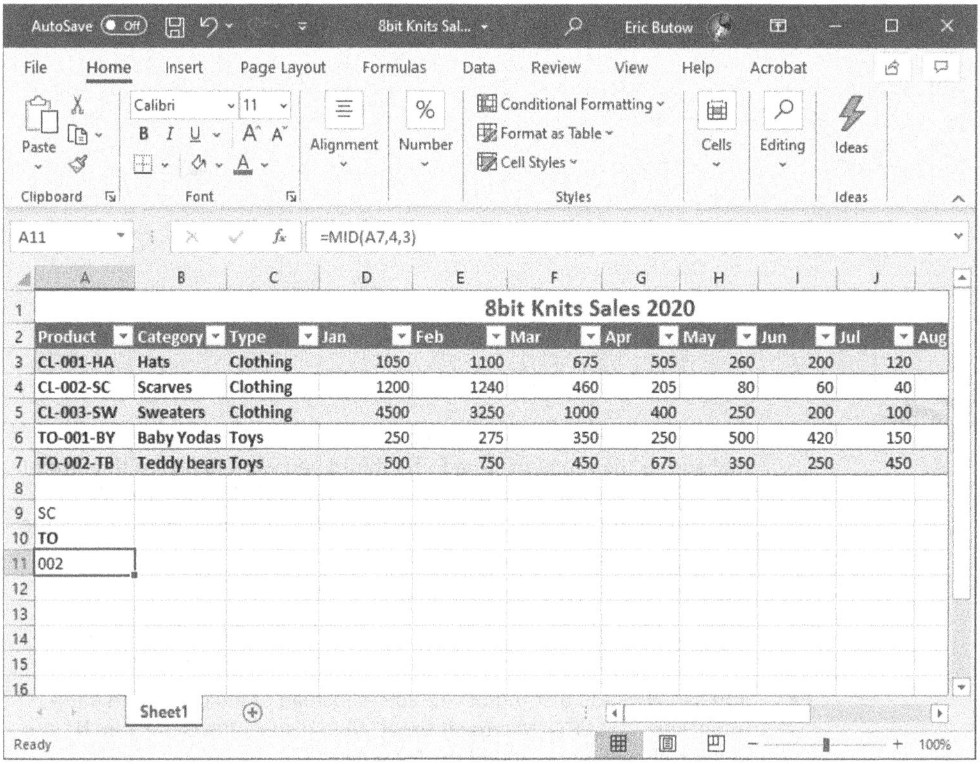

Here's more about what you need to be aware of when you work with the `MID()` function:

- As you start typing **MID** in the Formula Bar, you see a drop-down list that shows functions that Excel thinks you want to add to the formula. If you would rather not finish typing the function, double-click MID in the list to add `MID(` to the Formula Bar. Then you can select or type the range, type), and then press Enter.

- Excel considers spaces as characters.

- If you put the starting number in a location that is greater than the number of characters, then Excel simply returns no result. For example, the formula `MID(D4,15,5)` refers to cell D4 with only 11 characters in it, so the cell with the `MID()` formula shows nothing.

- If the number of characters that you want to show exceeds the number of characters, then Excel shows all the characters through the end of the text. For example, the formula `MID(D4,5,10)` refers to cell D4 with only 10 characters in it, so the cell with the `MID()` formula shows the last 6 characters of text.

- You can also add a string of characters instead of the cell within a formula, such as **MID ("Microsoft Excel",6,4)** to display the characters `soft` in the cell where you added the formula.

- If you specify a number of characters in the formula greater than the number of characters within the cell, then the formula counts all the characters.

- Excel does not support the `MID()` function in all languages, so if this function does not work, contact Microsoft to determine whether Excel supports this function for your language.

Formatting Text Using the *UPPER()*, *LOWER()*, and *LEN()* Functions

When you need to change the text in a cell to all uppercase or all lowercase letters, especially in multiple cells, then that task becomes tedious in no time. Excel has two built-in features for converting all text in cells within a worksheet or table to uppercase or lowercase.

UPPER()

The UPPER() function converts all text in one or more cells to uppercase. Follow these steps to use the UPPER() function:

1. Insert a new column to the left of column C.

2. Select cell C3.

3. Type =UPPER(B3) in the Formula Bar.

4. Press Enter.

Excel copies the formula into all cells in column C, so now all text in column B is uppercase in column C (see Figure 10.19).

FIGURE 10.19   All uppercase text in column C

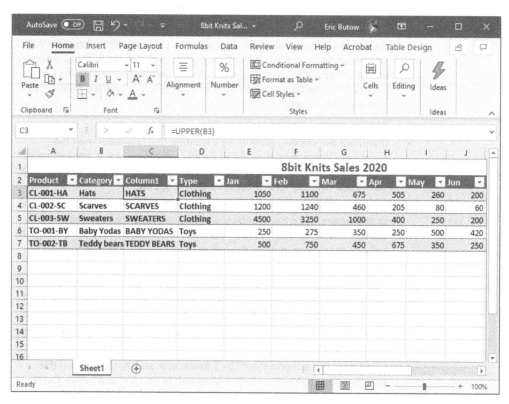

There are two things to know about using the UPPER() function:

- You can type a text string within the formula instead of a cell reference, such as **=UPPER("Excel")**, in the Formula Bar. If you add the formula within a table cell, then all cells in the column display EXCEL.

- If you have characters in your text that are numbers or special characters, Excel does not change them. For example, if you have the number 7, Excel does not change the 7 to &.

LOWER()

The LOWER() function converts all text in one or more cells to lowercase. Here's how to use the LOWER() function:

1. Insert a new column to the left of column C.

2. Select cell C3.

3. Type **=LOWER(B3)** in the Formula Bar.

4. Press Enter.

Excel copies the formula into all cells in column C, so now all text in column B is lowercase in column C (see Figure 10.20).

FIGURE 10.20   All lowercase text in column C

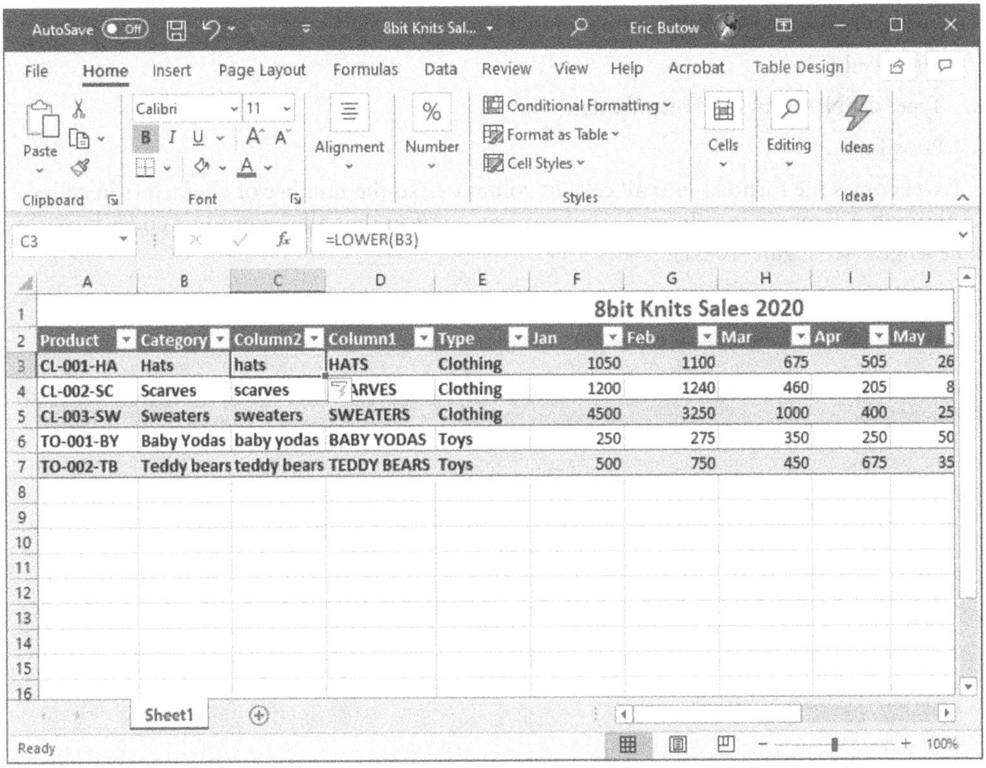

Product	Category	Column2	Column1	Type	Jan	Feb	Mar	Apr	May
CL-001-HA	Hats	hats	HATS	Clothing	1050	1100	675	505	26
CL-002-SC	Scarves	scarves	SCARVES	Clothing	1200	1240	460	205	8
CL-003-SW	Sweaters	sweaters	SWEATERS	Clothing	4500	3250	1000	400	25
TO-001-BY	Baby Yodas	baby yodas	BABY YODAS	Toys	250	275	350	250	50
TO-002-TB	Teddy bears	teddy bears	TEDDY BEARS	Toys	500	750	450	675	35

8bit Knits Sales 2020

Formula Bar: =LOWER(B3)

Here is some more information you should know about the LOWER() function:

- You can type a text string within the formula instead of a cell reference, such as **=LOWER("Excel")** in the Formula Bar. If you add the formula within a table cell, then all cells in the column display excel.

- If you have characters in your text that are numbers or special characters, Excel does not change them. For example, if you have the % symbol in the text, Excel does not change the % to 5.

LEN()

The LEN() function, which is short for length, tells you how many characters are in a text string within a cell. For example, you may need to have exactly 14 characters in a product code, and you want to find out which product code has too many or too few characters.

Add the LEN() function in a cell by following these steps:

1. Insert a new column to the left of column C.

2. Select cell C3.

3. Type **=LEN(A3)** in the Formula Bar.

4. Press Enter.

Excel copies the formula into all cells in column C, so the number of characters in cells A3 through A7 appear in column C, and you can confirm that all the product codes have the same length (see Figure 10.21).

FIGURE 10.21   Length in characters in column C

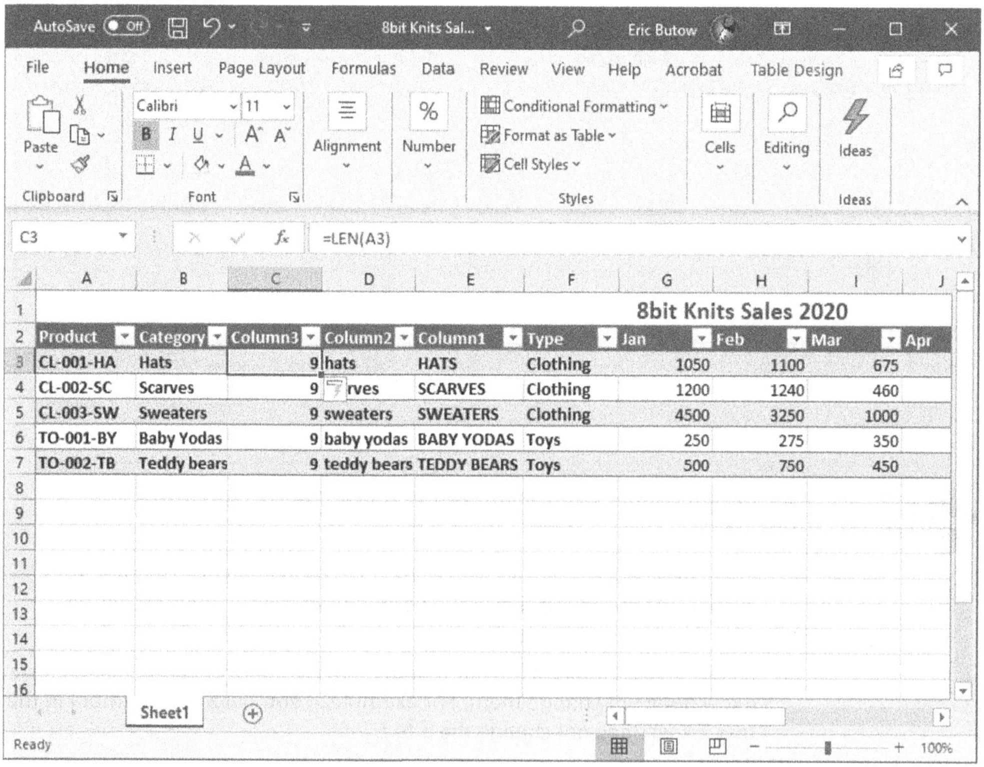

As with some other functions described in this chapter, Excel does not support the LEN() function in all languages, so if this function does not work, contact Microsoft to determine whether Excel supports this function for your language.

Formatting Text Using the *CONCAT()* and *TEXTJOIN()* Functions

When you need to join text from two or more cells and place the joined text into a new cell, Excel gives you two functions to do just that:

- CONCAT(), which replaces the CONCATENATE() function in earlier versions
- TEXTJOIN(), which is new in Excel 2019 and Excel for Microsoft Office 365

The Difference Between *CONCAT* and *TEXTJOIN*

Both the CONCAT() and TEXTJOIN() functions allow you to combine text. So, what's the difference?

- CONCAT() combines all text in two or more cells together with a delimiter such as a blank space. You simply add the range of cells you want to put together, and Excel shows you the combined text without any spaces in between.

- TEXTJOIN() gives you the option of adding a delimiter between each text string that you combine.

CONCAT()

Adding the CONCAT() function in the Formula Bar doesn't have as many arguments you need to add compared to TEXTJOIN(), but you don't get any options. Follow the steps in this example to see what I mean:

1. Click cell B9.
2. Type =CONCAT(B3:B4) in the Formula Bar.
3. Press Enter.

    You see the combined text from cells B3 and B4 in cell B9, as shown in Figure 10.22.

FIGURE 10.22 Combined text with CONCAT() function in the Formula Bar

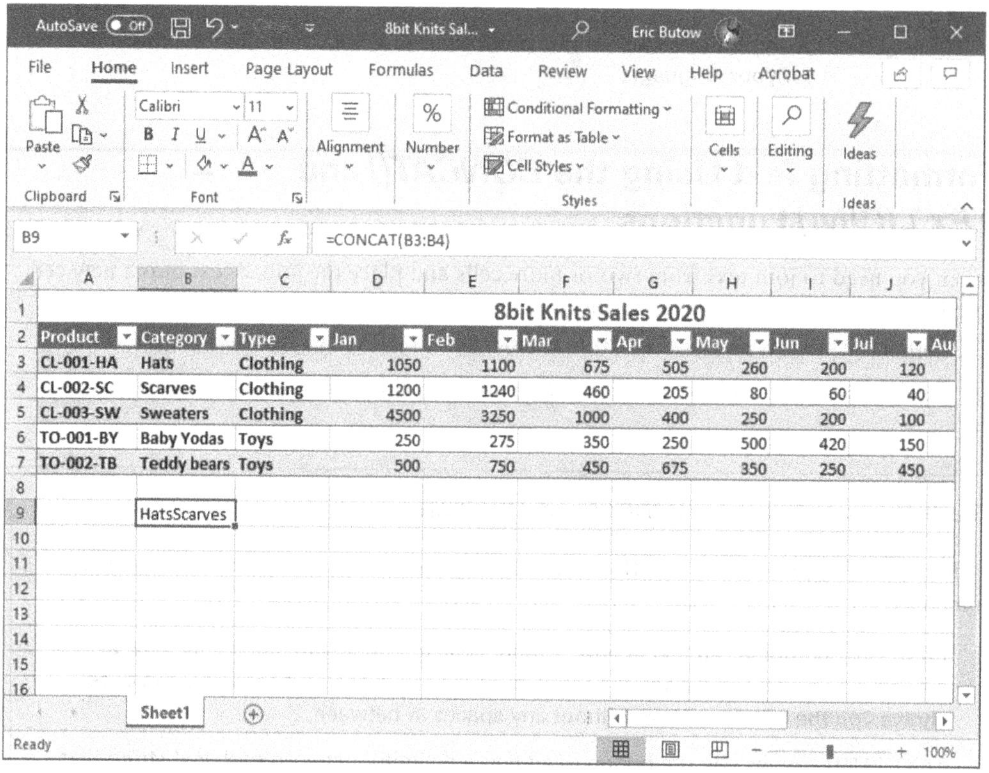

TEXTJOIN()

When you need to add spaces or another delimiter, such as a comma, between all the words in your combined text, the new TEXTJOIN() function is what you need. Here's how to use TEXTJOIN():

1. Click cell B10.

2. Type **=TEXTJOIN(" ",TRUE,B3:C5)** in the Formula Bar. The space between the quotes is a space, and the TRUE argument tells Excel to ignore any empty cells in the range.

3. Press Enter.

The combined text in the cell range appears in cell B10 (see Figure 10.23) with a space between each word.

FIGURE 10.23 The combined text with spaces between each text string

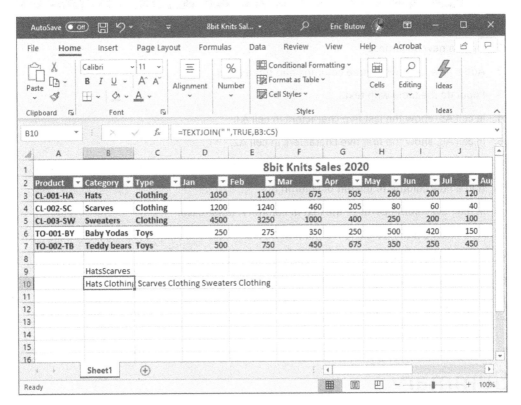

When you work with both the CONCAT() and TEXTJOIN() functions, keep the following in mind:

- You can type a text string within the formula instead of a cell reference, such as **=TEXTJOIN (" ",TRUE,"Microsoft","Excel")** or **=CONCAT("Micro","soft")** in the Formula Bar.

- With both the CONCAT() and TEXTJOIN() functions, the combined text string can be no longer than 32,767 characters. If the combined string is over that limit, then the cell with the CONCAT() or the TEXTJOIN() formula displays a #VALUE! error.

EXERCISE 10.3

Formatting and Modifying Text

1. Open a new document.

2. Add a new table with three columns and three rows.

3. Populate the table with text.

4. In cell A5, show the last five characters in cell A1.

5. In cell A6, show the first five characters in cell A2.

6. In cell A7, count five characters in the middle of the text starting with the third character.

7. Add a new column to the left of column B.

8. In the new column B, make the text in column A uppercase.

9. Add a new column to the left of column D.

10. In the new column D, make the text in column C lowercase.

11. In cell D5, get the length of cell D2.

12. In cell D6, join the text of cells D1 and D3 with a space delimiter.

Summary

This chapter started by showing you how to insert references in a worksheet or table, including relative, absolute, and mixed references. You also learned how to refer to named ranges and tables within a formula.

After you learned about references, you saw how to perform various calculations using built-in Excel functions, including the average, maximum, minimum, and sum functions. Then you learned how to count within cells using the three different counting functions in a formula. You also saw how to add the IF() function to perform conditional operations.

Next, I discussed how to format and modify text by using built-in functions to extract text from the right, left, and middle portions of a text string. You saw how to use functions to change text to all uppercase or all lowercase, as well as get the length of characters in a cell. Finally, you learned how to combine text in two or more cells together using the CONCAT() and TEXTJOIN() functions.

Key Terms

absolute	mixed
average	references
Formula Bar	relative
maximum	sum
minimum	

Exam Essentials

Understand how to add relative, absolute, and mixed references in a formula. Know the correct terminology for adding a cell to a formula that will give you relative and absolute results. You must also know how to refer to a named range or table in a worksheet.

Know how to calculate numbers in one or more cells. Understand how to find the average, maximum, and minimum values in a range of cells that contain numbers. You also need to know how to sum a group of selected cells that have numbers.

Understand how to count cells. Know how to count the cells in a selected range that have numbers, how many cells are not empty, and how many cells are empty.

Know how to perform conditional operations. Understand how to determine if a condition is true or false.

Understand how to extract text from another cell. Know how to use built-in functions to extract from the right, left, or middle of a string of text in one cell and place the extracted text in another cell.

Be able to change the case of text and find the length of text in a cell. Know how to change one or more cells to all uppercase letters or all lowercase letters. You also need to understand how to find the length of a text string in one cell and display the length in another cell.

Know how to join text in two or more cells. Understand how to use the CONCAT() and TEXTJOIN() functions to join text in two or more cells and know the difference between each function.

Review Questions

1. In a formula, how do you change the reference quickly?
   A. Change the cell reference manually.
   B. Click the Format icon in the Home ribbon, and then click Format Cells.
   C. Press F4.
   D. Right-click in the Formula Bar, and then click Format Cells.

2. What counting function do you use to view all cells in a selected range that have text?
   A. COUNT()
   B. COUNTA()
   C. COUNTALL()
   D. COUNTBLANK()

3. What does the function =RIGHT(A3,5) do?
   A. It shows the first five characters in cell A3.
   B. It shows the five rows to the right of cell A3.
   C. It shows the last five characters in cell A3.
   D. It shows the first three characters and last five characters of all cells with text in column A.

4. What are the three reference types? (Choose all that apply.)
   A. Mixed
   B. Name
   C. Relative
   D. Absolute

5. What happens when you try to calculate the average of a range of cells when one or more cells does not have a number in it?
   A. The function treats the empty cell as the number *0*.
   B. The result of the function is an error message.
   C. The function returns the number *0*.
   D. The function ignores the empty cells.

6. What happens when you show the first five characters of a text string that includes a space?
   A. Excel ignores the space.
   B. Excel shows a dialog box with an error message.
   C. An error message appears in the cell.
   D. Excel shows the space.

7. A2 is what type of cell reference in a formula?

   A. Absolute

   B. Relative

   C. None

   D. Mixed

8. What do you type first in a formula?

   A. The formula name

   B. The left parenthesis

   C. The equal sign

   D. A colon

9. What function do you use when you want to combine text in two cells and not have a space between the combined text?

   A. CONCAT()

   B. TEXTJOIN()

   C. SUM()

   D. COUNT()

10. What do you do when you want to summarize cells in multiple ranges?

   A. Type each SUM() formula for each range separated by a comma.

   B. Add all of the cells individually within the parentheses in the SUM() formula.

   C. Type each SUM() formula for each range separated by a plus (+) sign.

   D. Add a comma between each cell range within the parentheses in the formula.

Chapter

11

Managing Charts

MICROSOFT EXAM OBJECTIVES COVERED IN THIS CHAPTER:

✓ **Manage charts**

- ▪ Create charts
    - ▪ Create charts
    - ▪ Create chart sheets
- ▪ Modify charts
    - ▪ Add data series to charts
    - ▪ Switch between rows and columns in source data
    - ▪ Add and modify chart elements
- ▪ Format charts
    - ▪ Apply chart layouts
    - ▪ Apply chart styles
    - ▪ Add alternative text to charts for accessibility

A chart is an effective way to grasp data in a worksheet visually. You may remember how you had to create charts in math classes in school, where you learned the relationship between data and a graph. It should come as no surprise that Excel has charts built in since Excel deals a lot with math.

I start by showing you how to create charts, both in the same worksheet and in a separate worksheet in a workbook. Next, you'll learn how to modify charts by adding data series, switching between rows and columns, as well as adding and modifying various chart elements.

Finally, you'll learn how to format a chart by adding layouts, styles, and Alt text (short for alternative text) to a chart, which helps you better explain what a chart is about.

Creating Charts

If you used an older version of Excel before version 2019, or the version for Microsoft Office 365, you may have used Chart Wizard to create a chart. In that case, you will be disappointed to learn that the Chart Wizard is not included in the latest versions of Excel.

Even so, Microsoft still makes it easy to create charts in the latest versions of Excel. You can build a chart, both within an existing worksheet and as a separate worksheet within your workbook, so that it's easier for readers to move back and forth quickly between a worksheet with data and a worksheet with a chart, which references that data.

Building Charts

So, how do you build a chart? After you open a workbook that contains a worksheet with numerical data, here's how to find the chart you want and add it to your worksheet:

1. Select the cells you want to use to create a chart.

2. Click the Insert menu option.

3. In the Charts section in the Insert ribbon, click the Recommended Charts icon, as shown in Figure 11.1.

FIGURE 11.1   The Recommended Charts icon in the Insert ribbon

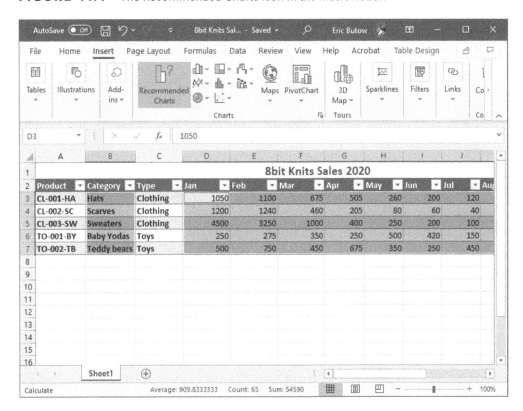

4. In the Insert Chart dialog box that appears in Figure 11.2, scroll up and down the list of recommended charts in the Recommended Charts tab. Click a chart type in the list to view a sample of how the chart will look as well as a description of what the chart is about and when to use it.

5. Select the All Charts tab to view a list of all charts. The Column category is selected in the list on the left side of the dialog box (see Figure 11.3).

   The column chart area appears at the right side of the dialog box; the column type icon is selected at the top of the area.

6. Move the mouse pointer over the column type to view a larger preview of the chart.

7. For this example, select the Recommended tab and add the Clustered Column chart that you saw in Figure 11.2.

8. Click OK.

   The chart appears below the table in the example, as shown in Figure 11.4.

FIGURE 11.2 The Insert Chart dialog box

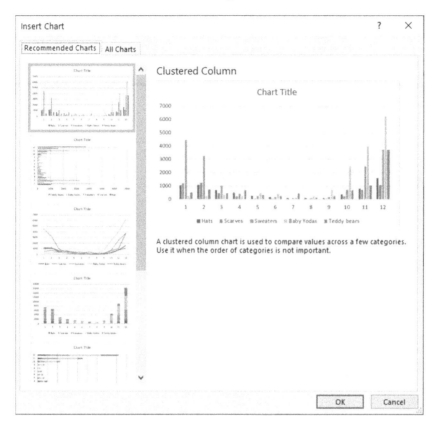

Now your text is in the table, though you may have to do some more tweaking to get it to appear the way you want it to look.

You can resize the chart by clicking and holding one of the circular sizing handles and then dragging the chart in the direction that you want. If you want to resize both the horizontal and vertical size of the chart, click and drag one of the corner sizing handles.

Working with Chart Sheets

When you don't want to have a chart appear with the same worksheet, Excel makes it easy to create a new chart in a new worksheet. Microsoft calls this a *chart sheet*, and you may find it most useful if you are creating a chart from a large amount of data.

For example, instead of having your viewers scroll around your worksheet to find the chart, you can make it easy for them to view the chart with one click of the worksheet tab that contains your chart sheet.

FIGURE 11.3   The Column category in the All Charts tab

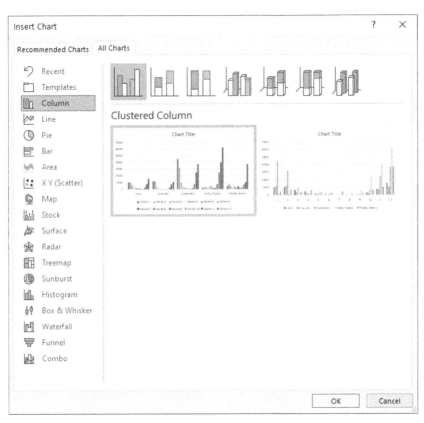

Create a chart sheet by following these steps:

1. Create a chart as you learned to do earlier in this chapter. I will use the chart I created earlier in this chapter for this example.

2. Click anywhere in the chart.

3. Click the Chart Design menu option.

4. In the Location section in the Chart Design ribbon, click the Move Chart icon, as shown in Figure 11.5.

5. In the Move Chart dialog box (see Figure 11.6), click the New Sheet radio button.

6. Type a new name if you want by pressing the Backspace key and then typing the new name in the New Sheet text box. For this example, leave the default Chart1 name.

7. Click OK.

FIGURE 11.4   The chart in the worksheet

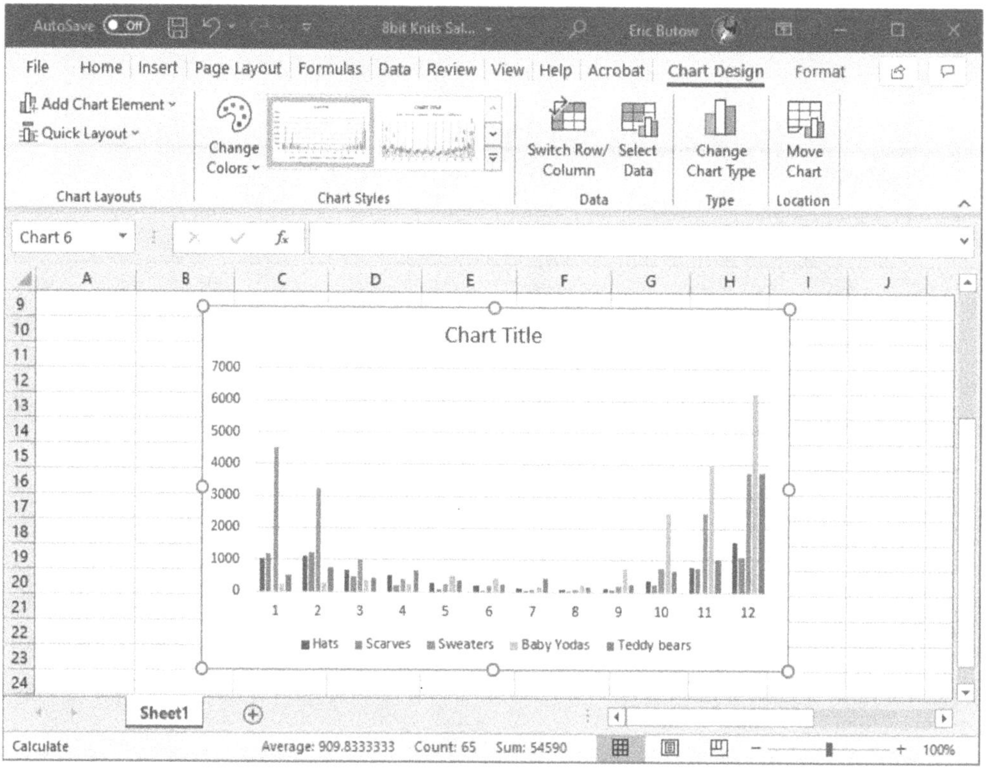

A new worksheet appears, as shown in Figure 11.7, and the chart takes up the entirety of the worksheet space.

The chart sheet tab appears to the left of the worksheet tab. Click the worksheet tab to view the worksheet data without the chart.

> **NOTE**   Though there are sizing handles that bound the chart in the chart sheet, you cannot resize the chart using those sizing handles.

EXERCISE 11.1

Creating Charts

1. Open a new workbook.

2. In the worksheet, add a header row with text in four columns.

3. Add numbers into four rows within all the columns.

4. Create a Clustered Column chart for the entire table.

5. Move the chart to a new chart sheet.

6. Save the workbook.

FIGURE 11.5   Move Chart icon in the Chart Design ribbon

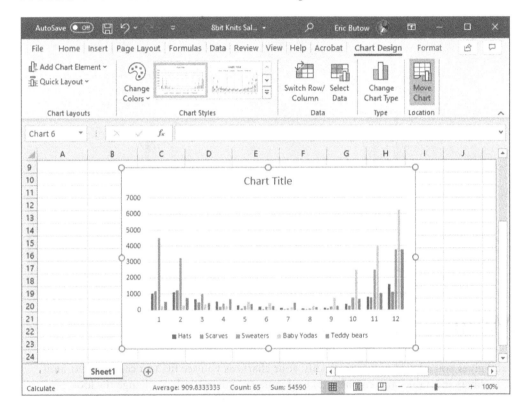

FIGURE 11.6   Move Chart dialog box

FIGURE 11.7   The chart in a new tab

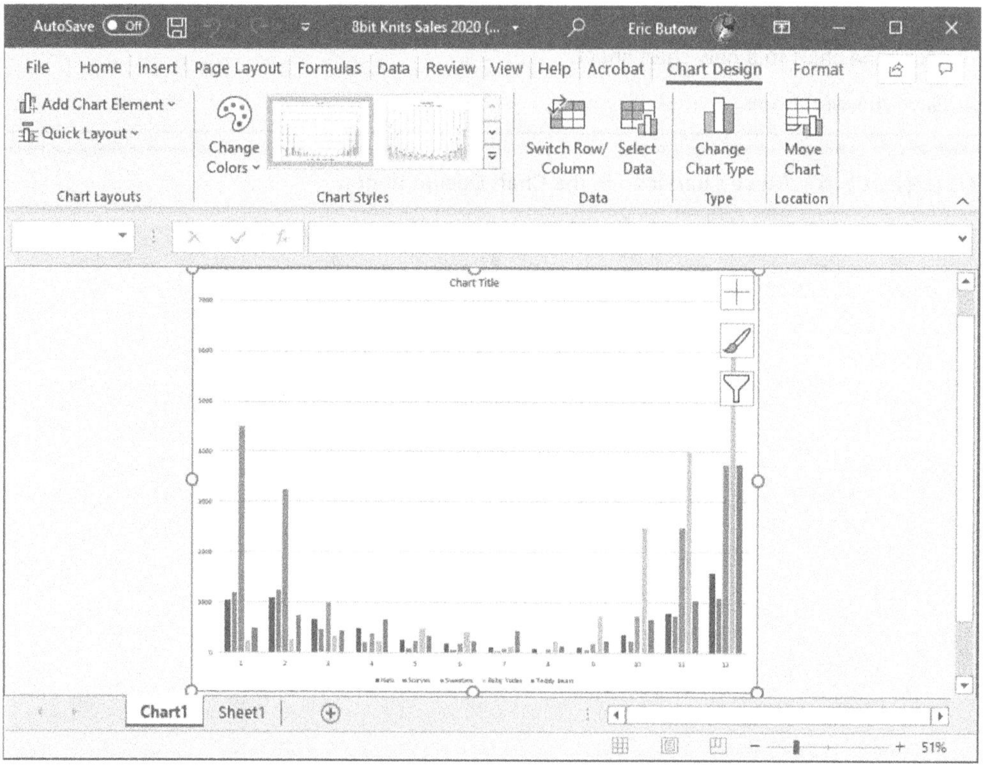

Modifying Charts

Excel gives you a lot of power to modify your charts as you see fit. You can sort text and/or numbers in a table. You can also take advantage of more tools to change the look of the text and graphics in your chart, align your chart in the worksheet, and even change the chart type.

Adding Data Series to Charts

A *data series* is one or more rows and/or columns in a worksheet or table that Excel uses to build a chart. After you add a chart, you may want to add more information to the worksheet and have Excel update the chart accordingly. It's easy to do this in the same worksheet chart and in a chart sheet.

Add a Data Series in the Same Worksheet Chart

Follow these steps to add a data series to a chart in the same worksheet:

1. Click the chart if necessary. The corresponding rows and/or columns of data appear in the worksheet or table.

2. In the worksheet or table, click and hold the sizing handle at the bottom right of the selection that you want to add.

3. Drag the sizing handle to place the selection over the data you want to include.

4. Release the mouse button.

The selection box in the worksheet or table now reflects your changes, and the chart shows new bars that reflect the data in column F (see Figure 11.8).

FIGURE 11.8   The updated chart and expanded selection area in the table

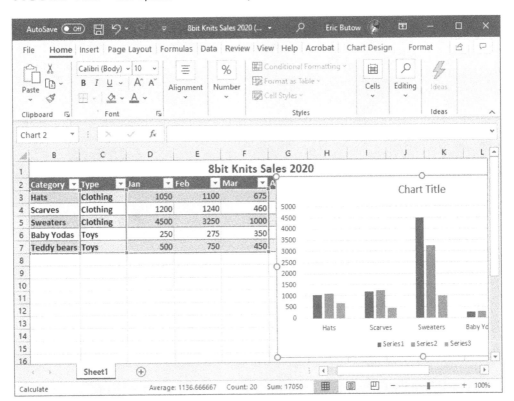

Add a Data Series to a Chart Sheet

When you have a chart sheet based on data in another worksheet, and you have a lot of data in that worksheet, then selecting a large range may not be a practical option. In this case, Excel allows you to add a data series within the chart sheet. Here's how to do it:

1. At the bottom of the Excel window, click the sheet tab that contains the chart. In this example, the chart sheet name is Chart1.

2. In the Data section in the Chart Design menu ribbon, click Select Data.

3. The Select Data Source dialog box opens, and the worksheet with your data appears in the Excel window (see Figure 11.9).

FIGURE 11.9   Select Data Source dialog box and selected table cells

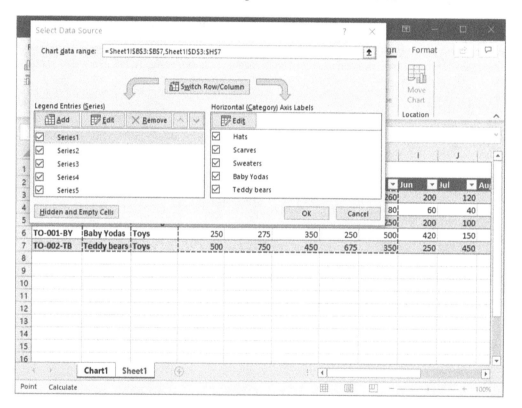

4. Press and hold the Ctrl key as you click and drag on more cells that you want to add to the chart.

5. When you select all the cells in the worksheet or table, release the Ctrl key and the mouse button.

6. Click OK in the Select Data Source dialog box.

In this example, the updated chart with the added bars for the month of June appears in the chart sheet (see Figure 11.10).

FIGURE 11.10   Updated chart in chart sheet

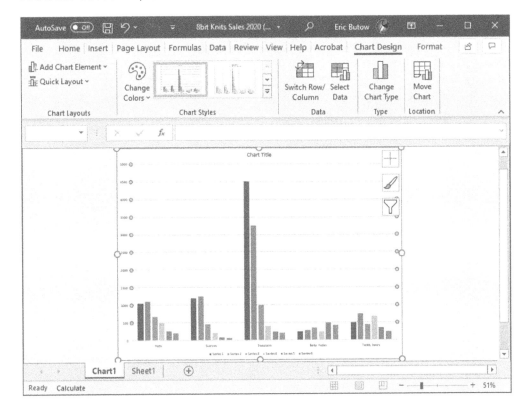

Switching Between Rows and Columns in Source Data

Excel follows one rule when it creates a chart: the larger number of rows or columns is placed in the horizontal axis. For example, if there are 12 columns and 5 rows, then columns are along the horizontal axis.

But what if you want the rows to appear in the horizontal axis? Excel makes it easy. Start by clicking the chart in your worksheet or in the chart sheet. In the Data section in the Chart Design menu ribbon, click Switch Row/Column.

Now the axes have switched, as you can see in Figure 11.11, so you can determine whether you like it. If you don't, click Switch Row/Column in the Chart Design ribbon again.

What happens if you have equal numbers of rows and columns in your worksheet or table? Excel uses the same layout as rows and columns in a worksheet: columns for the horizontal axis and rows for the vertical axis.

FIGURE 11.11   Row titles in the horizontal axis

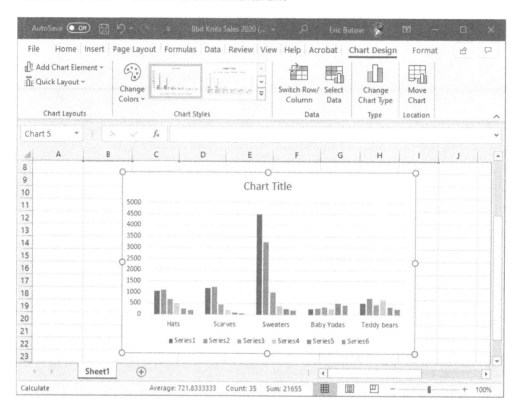

Adding and Modifying Chart Elements

It's easy to add and modify the elements you see in a chart. You can view a list of elements that you can add to the chart by clicking anywhere in the chart and then clicking the Chart Elements icon at the upper-right corner of the chart.

A list of the elements appears, with check boxes to the left of each element name, as shown in Figure 11.12.

Selected check boxes indicate that the element is currently applied. Cleared check boxes mean that the element is not applied. When you move the mouse pointer over the element in the list, you see how the element will appear in the chart—that is, if the element is not already applied.

The following is a list of the elements you can add and remove from your chart:

Axes   These are the horizonal and vertical units of measure in the chart. In the sample chart shown in Figure 11.12, the horizontal units represent products sold and the vertical units represent sales in increments of 1,000. Excel shows the axes by default.

FIGURE 11.12   Chart elements list

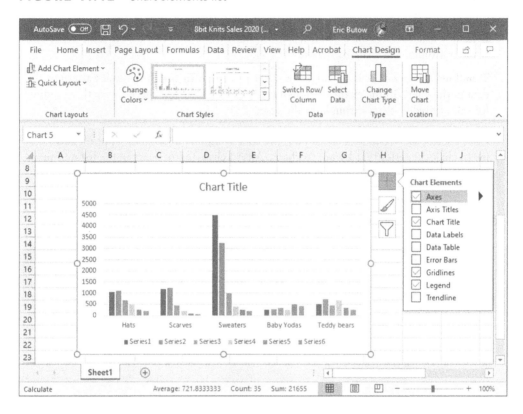

Axis Titles   These are the titles for the vertical and horizontal axes. The default name of each title is Axis Title. You can change the title after you add it by double-clicking within the title, selecting the text, and then typing your own text.

Chart Title   Excel automatically shows the title of your chart, which is Chart Title by default. You can change this title by double-clicking Chart Title, selecting the text, and then typing a new title.

Data Labels   These add the number in each cell above each corresponding point or bar in the chart. If your points or bars are close together, having data labels can be difficult to read because the numbers can overlap.

Data Table   This places your selected cells in a table below the chart. If you have a large table, then you may need to enlarge the size of the chart in the worksheet.

Error Bars   If you have a chart with data that has margins of error, such as political polls, you can add *error bars* to your chart to show those margins. Error bars also work when you want to see the standard deviation, which measures how widely a range of values are from the mean.

Gridlines   This displays the gridlines behind the lines or bars in a graph. Gridlines are active by default.

Legend   Excel shows the *legend*, which explains what each line or bar color represents, at the bottom of the chart by default.

Trendline   A *trendline* is a straight or curved line that shows the overall pattern of the data in the chart. In the example shown in Figure 11.13, I can check to see the trendline for sales of teddy bears throughout the year.

Once I select the Trendlines check box, the Add Trendline dialog box appears and asks me to click the series that I want to check. After I click Teddy Bears in the list and then click OK, the dashed line appears and the trendline also appears in the legend (see Figure 11.13).

FIGURE 11.13   Trend line for teddy bears

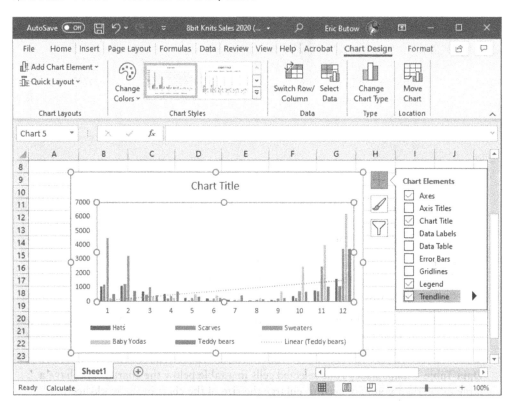

Change Elements More Precisely

An arrow appears to the right of each element name. When you click the arrow, a secondary menu with more precise options, as well as an option for viewing even more options, appears. For example, you can hide the vertical axis label but keep the horizontal axis label.

When you click More Options in the secondary menu, the Format panel appears at the right side of the Excel window so that you can make even more specific changes, such as making the chart title text outlined instead of solid.

EXERCISE 11.2

Modifying Charts

1. Open the workbook that you created in Exercise 11.1 if it's not already open.

2. Add a new column to the worksheet.

3. Populate the column with text in the first row and numbers in the remaining rows.

4. Add the new column to the chart.

5. Reverse the axes.

6. Add a trendline.

Formatting Charts

When you need to format your chart, click within the chart to view the two formatting ribbons:

- Click the Chart Design menu option to add and change chart styles. The Chart Design ribbon appears after you create your chart.
- Click the Format menu option to change formats of the various elements in your ribbon.

When you click in an area outside of your chart and then click the chart again, Excel remembers the menu ribbon that you last used and opens that ribbon automatically.

Microsoft has identified three common tasks when you create a chart, and so those tasks are in the MO-200 exam: apply a chart layout, apply chart styles, and add alternative text, which is also known by the shorthand term *Alt text*.

Using Chart Layouts

After you create a chart, Excel applies its default layout to the chart. Microsoft realizes that you may not want this layout, but you also may not want to take the time to create your own custom layout. So, Excel contains not only the default layout but also 10 other built-in layouts that you can apply to a chart. Follow these steps to apply a chart layout:

1. Click the chart if necessary. The corresponding rows and/or columns of data appear in the worksheet or table.

2. Click the Chart Design menu option if necessary.

3. In the Chart Layouts section in the Chart Design ribbon, click the Quick Layout icon.

4. Move the mouse pointer over the layout tile in the drop-down menu. As you move the mouse pointer over each layout, the chart style in your worksheet or chart sheet changes so that you can see how the style looks (see Figure 11.14).

FIGURE 11.14 Excel previews the layout in the chart.

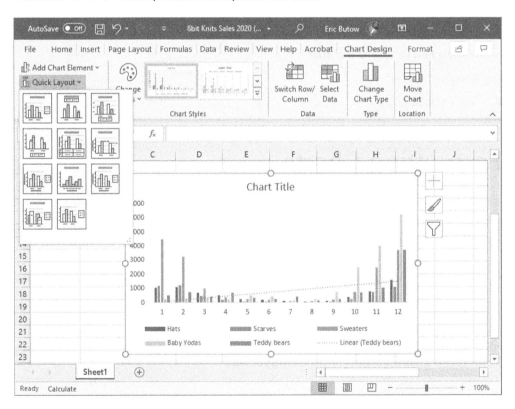

5. When you find a chart layout, click the tile in the drop-down menu.

Excel applies the chart layout that you previewed into the chart.

Create Your Own Chart Layout

You may like some parts of the built-in layout that you selected but not others. Excel gives you the ability to change different parts of your chart layout to suit your needs.

Start by clicking the chart and then clicking the Format menu option if necessary. In the Format ribbon, which is shown in Figure 11.15, you can select options within the following seven ribbon sections.

FIGURE 11.15   Format ribbon sections

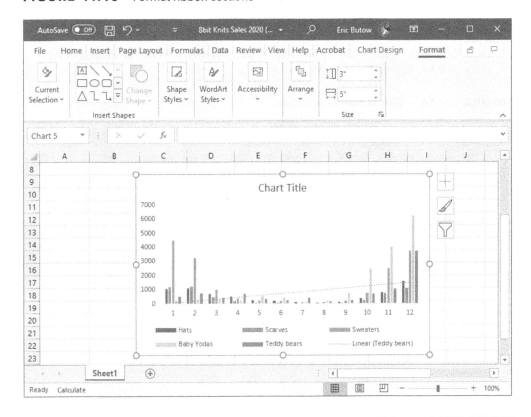

As you work with the Format ribbon, keep the following in mind:

- In the screenshots shown in this chapter, the width of the Excel window is 800 pixels. If your window is wider, however, then you will see most or all of the options in each section without having to click the section name.

- Different parts of the ribbon will be disabled depending on the portion of the chart that you want to edit. For example, when you click the chart title, the width and height setting options in the Size section are disabled.

- The Format ribbon changes when you perform certain actions. For example, when you add a shape, the Shape Format ribbon replaces the Format ribbon so that you can edit the shape. Shape formatting options are beyond the purview of this book.

Current Selection

In the Current Selection section on the left side of the ribbon (see Figure 11.16), you can change the following settings:

Chart Area: The current area that you're editing appears in the area box. Click the down arrow to the right of the box to view a drop-down list of all the areas that you can edit. Select an area to edit by clicking the area in the list.

Format Selection: Click Format Selection to open the Format pane on the right side of the Excel window and make more precise edits, such as the background fill color for the horizontal axis.

Reset To Match Style: Discard your changes and revert to the built-in settings of the chart style by clicking Reset To Match Style.

FIGURE 11.16 Current Selection section

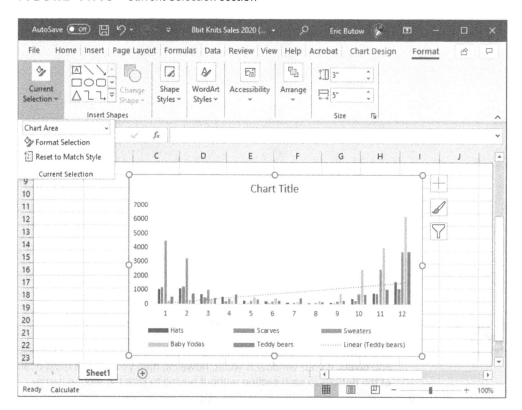

Insert Shapes

In the Insert Shapes section, shown in Figure 11.17, you can insert shapes as separate elements in the chart by clicking the shape icon.

FIGURE 11.17   Insert Shapes section

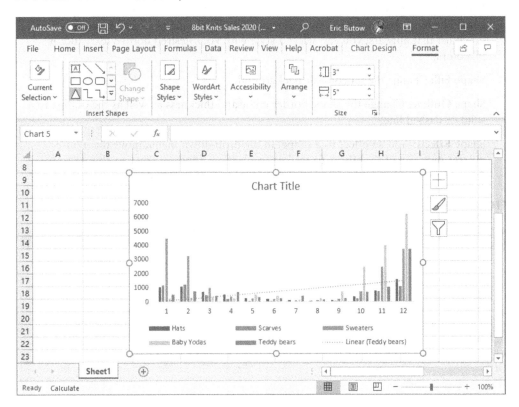

If you don't see the shape you want, click the More button to the right of the icons. (The More button looks like a down arrow with a line above it.) Then you can select the shape icon from the drop-down list.

Add the shape by following these steps:

1. Move the mouse pointer where you want to add the shape.
2. Click and hold down the mouse button.
3. Drag the mouse pointer until the shape is the size you want.
4. Release the mouse button.

Once you add a shape, you can make changes to your shape in the Shape Format ribbon.

Shape Styles

The Shape Styles area, shown in Figure 11.18, allows you to apply the following features to a shape:

Shape Styles: Click one of the seven shape style icons to change the shape border color. If you don't like any of those style colors, click the More button to the right of the icon row. (The More button looks like a down arrow with a line above it.) From the drop-down list that appears, you can select a style with your desired border, text, and/or fill colors.

Shape Fill: Change the fill color or background.

Shape Outline: Change the shape border color and thickness as well as the outline to a solid or dashed line.

Shape Effects: Add an effect to a shape. In the drop-down menu, move the mouse pointer over one of the effects to see how each effect appears. You can choose from Preset, Shadow, Reflection, Glow, Bevel, 3-D Rotation, or Transform.

FIGURE 11.18   Shape Styles section

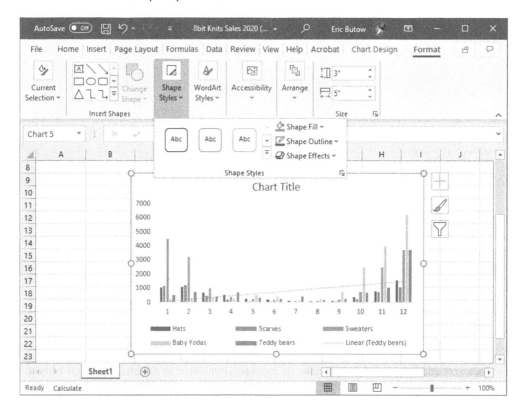

WordArt Styles

WordArt is Microsoft's term for special effects applied to text in Word, Outlook, Power-Point, and Excel. In the WordArt Styles section, click one of the three built-in text effect icons (see Figure 11.19).

FIGURE 11.19   WordArt Styles section

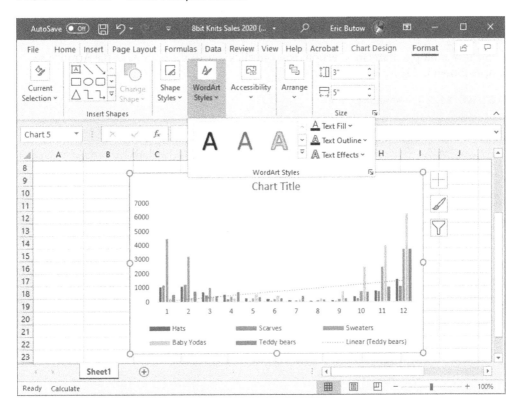

You can view more styles by clicking the More button to the right of the text effect icon row. (The More button looks like a down arrow with a line above it.) Then you can select the style from the drop-down list.

If you want to create your own style, click one of the following icons:

Text Fill: Change the text color in the drop-down menu.

Text Outline: Add an outline, including color and outline line width, using the drop-down menu.

Text Effects: View and add other effects to the text. In the drop-down menu, move the mouse pointer over one of the effects to see how the effect appears in your photo. You can choose from Preset, Shadow, Reflection, Glow, Bevel, 3-D Rotation, and Transform.

Accessibility

Click the Alt Text icon to add alternative text to your chart. This information is important enough that I will discuss this topic in its own section later in this chapter.

Arrange

If you have multiple charts in a section, you can click one of the options in the Arrange section, as shown in Figure 11.20.

FIGURE 11.20   Arrange section

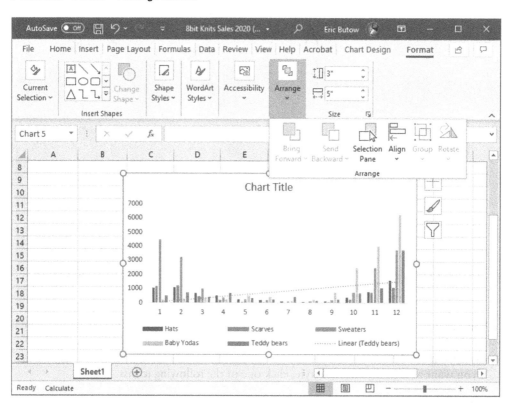

For example, click Selection Pane to open the Selection panel on the right side of the Excel window so that you can see all the charts, and choose to hide a chart for some reviewers who don't need to see it but show the chart again if you want to display the chart for other reviewers.

Size

Change the exact height and width by clicking the Height and the Width box, respectively (see Figure 11.21).

FIGURE 11.21   Size section

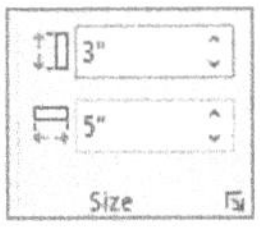

You can type the height and width in inches as precise as hundredths of an inch. To the right of the Height and Width boxes, click the up and down arrows to increase or decrease the height by one tenth of an inch.

When you select the entire chart and then make changes, all of those changes are made within that chart. However, if you make changes to one area of the chart, such as the vertical axis, then the changes apply only to the one area that you edited.

Align Multiple Charts in a Worksheet

You have two charts in a worksheet that you're going to share with the executives in your company. Although you want to make the charts easy to read, you don't want to take the time to move each chart and get them aligned in the way you want.

You can take advantage of the alignment features in Excel to align multiple charts as follows:

1. Select both charts by holding down the Shift key and then selecting each chart.

2. Click the Shape Format menu option.

3. In the Arrange section in the Shape Format ribbon, click Align.

Now you can align the charts vertically (left, center, and right) or horizontally (top, middle, or bottom). If both charts have similar horizontal and/or vertical positions, as shown in the screenshot here, then your alignment may result in one chart overlapping the other.

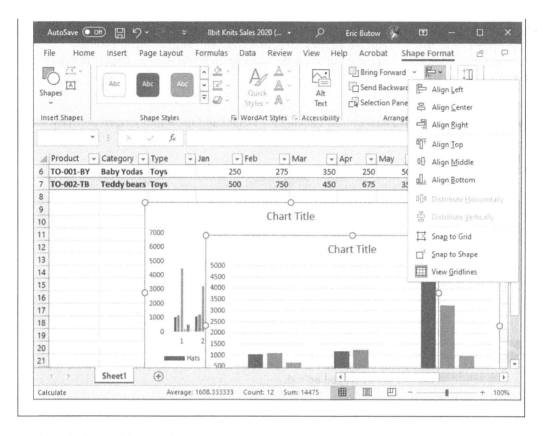

Applying Chart Styles

When you create a chart, Excel applies its default style for the type of chart you select in the Insert Chart dialog box that you learned about earlier in this chapter. If you don't like that style, you can add one of an additional 13 styles.

Excel also allows you to make changes to a style to make the chart look the way you want. Before you can make changes to a style, you must apply the built-in style.

Apply a Built-In Chart Style

Here's how to apply one of the built-in styles to your chart:

1. Click the chart if necessary. The corresponding rows and/or columns of data appear in the worksheet or table.

2. Click the Chart Design menu option if necessary.

3. In the Chart Styles section in the Chart Design ribbon, click the More button to the right of the last chart style tile in the row. (The More button looks like a down arrow with a line above it.)

4. Move the mouse pointer over the style tile in the drop-down menu. As you move the mouse pointer over each style, the chart style in your worksheet or chart sheet changes so that you can see how the style looks (see Figure 11.22).

FIGURE 11.22   The preview of the style in the chart

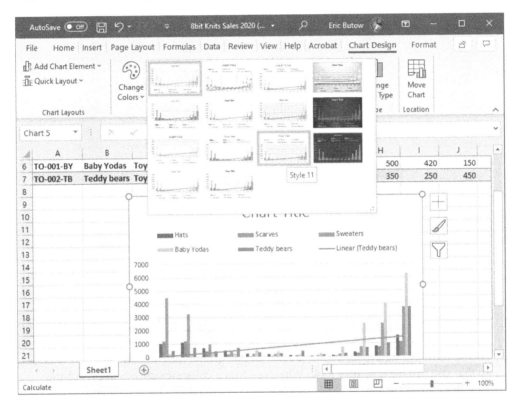

5. When you find a chart style, click the tile in the drop-down menu.

Excel applies the chart style that you previewed into the chart.

Create Your Own Chart Style

After you apply a chart style, you can modify it in only one way: the color scheme. To do that, follow these steps:

1. Click the chart if necessary. The corresponding rows and/or columns of data appear in the worksheet or table.

2. Click the Chart Design menu option if necessary.

3. In the Chart Styles section in the Chart Design ribbon, click the Change Colors icon.

4. Swipe up and down in the list of color swatch groups. There are six colors in each swatch group (see Figure 11.23).

FIGURE 11.23 Six swatch colors in the selected swatch group

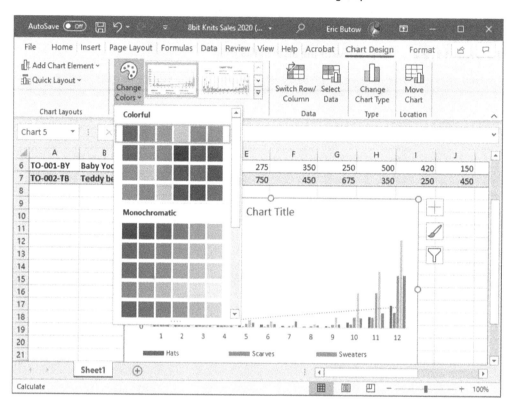

5. As you move the mouse pointer over each swatch group, the colors in the chart change so that you can see how they look. When you find a color swatch you like, click the swatch group in the list.

Excel applies the color swatch group to all elements in the chart.

You can edit specific colors in a chart, such as bars for one series of data, by clicking the color in the chart and then clicking the Format menu option. Then you can change the color as you learned to do earlier in this chapter.

Adding Alternative Text to Charts for Accessibility

Alt text, or alternative text, tells anyone who views your document in Excel what the chart is when the reader moves their mouse pointer over it. If the reader can't see your document, then Excel will use text-to-speech in Windows to read your Alt text to the reader audibly.

Here's how to add Alt text:

1. Click the chart if necessary.

2. Click the Format menu option if necessary.

3. In the Accessibility section in the Format ribbon, click the Alt Text icon. (If your Excel window isn't very wide, you may need to click the Accessibility icon and then click Alt Text.)

4. In the Alt Text pane on the right side of the Excel window (see Figure 11.24), type one or two sentences in the text box to describe the object and its context.

FIGURE 11.24   AltText pane

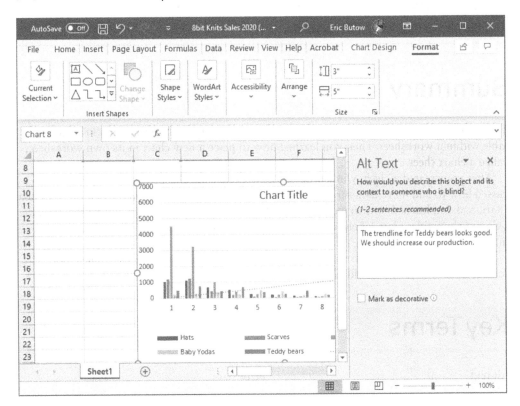

5. Click the Mark As Decorative check box if your chart adds visual interest but doesn't require a description.

6. When you're done, close the pane.

EXERCISE 11.3

Formatting Charts

1. Open a workbook that contains numerical data.

2. Create a chart in the worksheet, if necessary.

3. Change the chart style to another one of your choice.

4. Add a new shape of your choice into the chart.

5. Change the shape style to another one of your choice.

6. Apply a new color scheme to your chart.

7. Add Alt text that describes your chart.

Summary

This chapter started by showing you how to create a chart from selected data in a range or table within a worksheet. Then you learned how to place a new chart in its own worksheet, called a chart sheet.

After you created a chart, you learned how to modify the chart to suit your needs. I discussed how to add more data series to a chart. Next, you learned how to switch the axes in a chart, and you learned how to modify the look and feel of your chart, including the axes, the axis and chart titles, data labels, the data table, error bars, gridlines, the legend, and trendlines.

Finally, you learned how to use and apply chart layouts, apply and change the color scheme in chart styles, and add alternative text to a chart.

Key Terms

Alt text	error bars
chart	legend
chart sheet	trendline
data series	WordArt

Exam Essentials

Understand how to create a chart.　Know how to create a chart by accessing the Insert Chart dialog box and then selecting either a recommended chart or one of the many chart types Excel has available.

Know how to create a chart sheet.　Understand how to create a chart that appears separately within an entire worksheet.

Understand how to add a data series to a chart.　Know how to add additional cells in a worksheet or a table into a chart after you have already created the chart.

Know how to switch between row and column data in a chart.　Understand how Excel places data series in the horizontal and vertical axes as well as how to switch those axes in a chart.

Understand how to add and modify chart elements.　Know how to add chart elements to your chart—including axes, axis titles, the chart title, data labels in the chart, a data table in the chart, error bars, gridlines, a legend, and a trendline—and be able to modify those elements.

Be able to apply chart layouts.　Know how to apply a different chart layout using the Quick Layout menu in the Chart Design ribbon.

Know how to select and change chart styles.　Know how to apply a chart style from the Chart Design ribbon as well as change the color scheme for the style.

Understand how to add Alt text.　Know why Alt text is important for your readers and how to add Alt text to a chart.

Review Questions

1. How do you view a list of all charts that you can create?

   A. Click the Change Chart Type icon in the Chart Design ribbon.

   B. Click a new style tile in the Chart Design ribbon.

   C. Select the All Charts tab in the Insert Chart dialog box.

   D. Click the Chart Elements icon in the upper-right corner of the selected chart.

2. If you create a chart from a worksheet or table that has equal numbers of columns and rows, what does Excel use as the horizontal axis?

   A. A dialog box appears and asks you if you want to use rows or columns.

   B. Columns

   C. Rows

   D. An error message appears in a dialog box.

3. What types of styles can be applied when you format a chart? (Choose all that apply.)

   A. Shapes

   B. Chart area

   C. WordArt

   D. Size

4. What do you need to add to a chart that explains what each line or bar color represents?

   A. Legend

   B. Data labels

   C. Data table

   D. Axis titles

5. What shape attributes can you change with a built-in style? (Choose all that apply.)

   A. Border color

   B. Text size

   C. Text color

   D. Background color

6. How do you change a data element in your chart more precisely?

   A. Click Add Chart Element in the Chart Design ribbon and then click the type of element that you want to edit.

   B. Click Format Selection in the Format ribbon.

   C. Click the right arrow next to the element name in the Chart Elements list.

   D. Click Quick Layout in the Chart Design ribbon and then select the appropriate layout from the drop-down menu.

7. How do you resize a chart in the chart sheet?

    A. Click and drag one of the sizing handles at the boundary of the chart.

    B. You can't resize it.

    C. Set the measurement in the Format ribbon.

    D. Resize the chart in the worksheet before you move the chart to its own chart sheet.

8. Why do you add a trendline in a bar chart?

    A. To better show the levels of a bar in a chart

    B. Because Excel requires it before you can save the chart

    C. To see the overall trend of data over time

    D. To show the margins of error in a chart

9. What is the difference between a chart layout and a chart style?

    A. They're the same thing.

    B. The chart layout lets you change the type of chart, and the chart style changes the look and feel of the chart.

    C. The chart layout applies the chart style elements to the chart.

    D. A chart layout shows chart elements, and chart styles change how the chart looks.

10. Why should you add Alt text to a chart?

    A. Because it's required for all charts in an Excel workbook

    B. To help people who can't see the chart know what the graphic is about

    C. Because Excel won't save your workbook until you do

    D. Because you want to be as informative as possible

PowerPoint Exam MO-300

PART

III

Chapter

12

Creating Presentations

MICROSOFT EXAM OBJECTIVES COVERED IN THIS CHAPTER:

✓ **Manage presentations**

- Modify slide masters, handout masters, and note masters

  - Change the slide master theme or background

  - Modify slide master content

  - Create slide layouts

  - Modify slide layouts

  - Modify the handout master

  - Modify the notes master

- Change presentation options and views

  - Change slide size

  - Display presentations in different views

  - Set basic file properties

- Configure print settings for presentations

  - Print all or part of a presentation

  - Print notes pages

  - Print handouts

  - Print in color, grayscale, or black and white

- Configure and present slide shows

  - Create custom slide shows

  - Configure slide show options

  - Rehearse slide show timing

  - Set up slide show recording options

  - Present slide shows by using Presenter View

- Prepare presentations for collaboration
    - Mark presentations as final
    - Protect presentations by using passwords
    - Inspect presentations for issues
    - Add and manage comments
    - Preserve presentation content
    - Export presentations to other formats

Greetings, and welcome to this Microsoft Office Specialist Study Guide for PowerPoint, which is designed to help you study for and pass the MO-300 Microsoft PowerPoint (PowerPoint and PowerPoint 2019) exam and become a certified Microsoft Office Specialist: PowerPoint Associate. If you have your favorite beverage on your desk and you're comfortable, let's get started.

In this chapter, I'll start by showing you how to modify master slides, handouts, and notes in PowerPoint. Next, I'll show you how to change presentation options and views so that your presentation will look the way you want.

After we finish creating a presentation, I'll show you how to configure the presentation to be printed in case you want to have your audience follow along with your presentation using a printed version. You'll also learn how to configure your presentation to get it ready to be presented to your audience.

Finally, I'll show you how to share your presentation with others so that they can provide their feedback and allow you to manage the review process.

I'll have an exercise at the end of every section in this chapter so that you can practice doing different tasks. Then, at the end of this chapter, you'll find a set of Review Questions that mimic the test questions you'll see on the MO-300 exam.

Modifying Slide Masters, Handout Masters, and Note Masters

You may be familiar with *styles* in Word, which are small files that contain formatting information that you can apply to selected text just by clicking on the style name. Though PowerPoint doesn't have styles, they use their equivalent: *masters*. That is, masters allow you to create one slide with information that you always use in a slide, such as your company logo and text with a specific font. You can also create more than one *slide master*, so when you create a new slide, you can quickly apply the appropriate master.

Microsoft realizes that you may also want to give your audience handouts of the presentation so that they can follow along and make notes of their own on the pages with each slide. PowerPoint allows you to make handout masters with information on each page of the handout, such as your company logo in the lower-right corner of each page.

PowerPoint wouldn't be a program worthy of the name presentation software if it didn't allow you to make notes that you can use to keep you on track during your presentation. You can also create note masters with a format that works best for you as you give your presentation.

Design Your Masters First

When you create a new presentation, it's a good idea to design all the masters first so that you can figure out what everything is going to look like. Once you set up your masters, you will find that slide creation goes more quickly. (It's a lot like preparing a wall properly before you start painting.)

If you edit any of the slide masters, PowerPoint does not make any changes to the affected slides with those masters. Instead, you need to reapply the new master to a slide. So, if you find that you need to make changes, do so early in the slide creation process. That way, you won't have to apply your master changes to very many slides and you save some time.

Changing the Slide Master Theme or Background

When you open a blank PowerPoint presentation, you see placeholders for adding a title and subtitle. You also see the Design Ideas panel on the right side of the PowerPoint window. When you want to change the slide master theme and/or background for your needs, you can create a new master in Slide Master view.

Open the Slide Master screen by clicking the View menu option, and then click Slide Master in the View menu ribbon (see Figure 12.1).

The Slide Master screen shows a variety of slide master templates on the right side of the PowerPoint window, the slide itself on the right side, and options in the Slide Master menu ribbon, as shown in Figure 12.2.

Within the Slide Master ribbon, you can change both the style theme as well as the background.

FIGURE 12.1   Slide Master option in the Master Views section

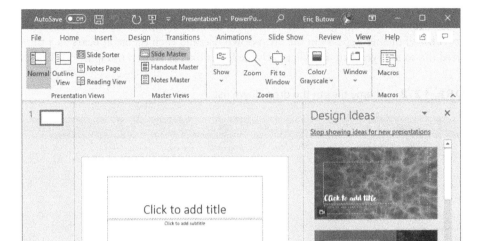

FIGURE 12.2   Slide Master screen

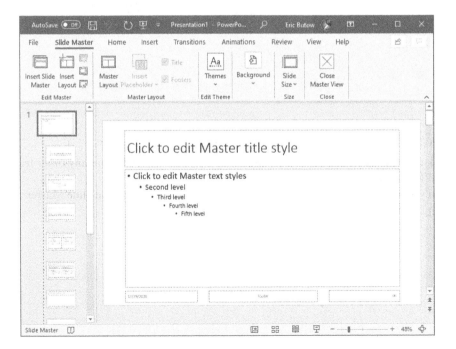

Apply a Slide Master theme

A slide master *theme* is a saved group of format and layout settings for your slides. Apply a slide master theme by clicking the Themes icon in the Edit Theme section in the Slide Master ribbon. A list of themes appears in the drop-down list, and each theme appears as a thumbnail-sized tile so that you can see what each tile looks like, as shown in Figure 12.3.

FIGURE 12.3   Theme tiles in the drop-down list

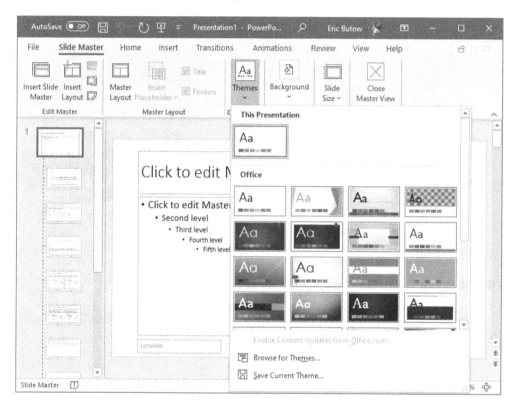

Scroll up and down in the list to view all the themes. When you find one that you want to use, click the tile. The slide shows the font, background for the slide, and any other features, such as a footer area that you can click to change the footer text.

When you're satisfied with the theme, click Close Master View in the Slide Master ribbon to return to editing an individual slide.

If you have an existing style theme that you use for your slideshows, such as one that your company requires you to use, you can open the theme by clicking Browse For Themes at the bottom of the drop-down list. Then you can browse to the appropriate folder and open the file, which will be added to the tiles within the Themes drop-down menu.

Change the Slide Master Background

If your master slide has a blank background or a background that's part of a theme, you can change just the background to one that's more to your liking. Start by opening the Slide Master menu ribbon, which you learned to do earlier in this chapter.

Next, change the background style by clicking Background Styles in the Background section in the Slide Master ribbon. A dozen tiles with different background types appear in the drop-down menu, as shown in Figure 12.4.

FIGURE 12.4   Background tiles in the drop-down list

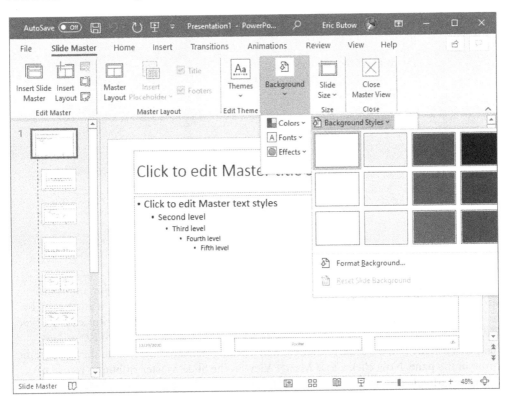

Move the mouse pointer over a tile to preview how the background will look in the slide. Click a tile to apply the background to the slide master.

If none of the background tiles meets your fancy, select Format Background at the bottom of the drop-down list. The Format Background pane appears at the right side of the Power-Point window (see Figure 12.5).

FIGURE 12.5 Format Background pane

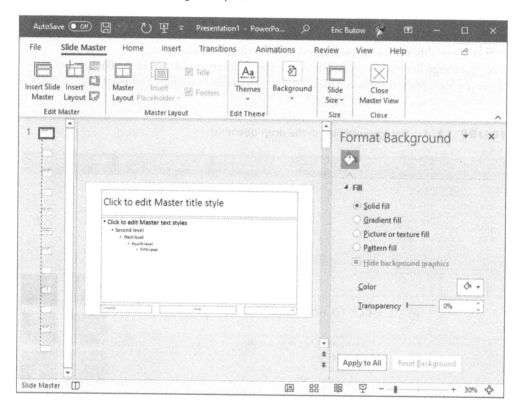

By default, the Solid Fill option is selected so that you can change the color and transparency of the fill. You can also add a gradient fill, picture or texture fill, or a pattern fill by clicking the appropriate button. The options for editing the fill are different for each fill type.

As you make changes, your changes appear within the slide. When you finish making changes, close the Format Background pane by clicking the Close (X) icon in the upper-right corner of the pane. Now click Close Master View in the Slide Master ribbon to return to editing an individual slide.

Modifying Slide Master Content

A new *slideshow* contains one master slide and 11 *layouts* within that master slide. These layouts have different formatting so that you can quickly apply one layout for a particular slide.

So why have a slide master? One good reason is that you can't apply a background to all layouts in a master—only the background in the selected layout. If you want to have the background apply to all layouts, and if you want to put the same features (like footers) in all layouts, then you must alter the slide master itself. Here's how to do that:

1. Click the View menu option.

2. In the Master Views section in the View ribbon, click the Slide Master icon.

3. In the Slide Master pane on the left side of the PowerPoint window, click the thumbnail-sized master slide at the very top of the pane. (You may need to scroll up to see it.)

4. Click the Slide Master menu option.

5. In the Master Layout section in the Slide Master ribbon, click Master Layout, as shown in Figure 12.6.

FIGURE 12.6   Master Layout icon in the ribbon

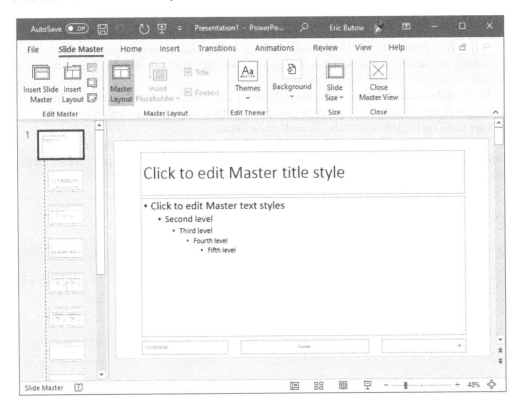

6. In the Master Layout dialog box, shown in Figure 12.7, select one of the check boxes to hide the feature in the master slide and all of the layouts.

7. When you're done, click OK.

FIGURE 12.7 Master Layout dialog box

The features that you decided to hide no longer appear in the slide master or in the layouts. When you want to return to editing individual slides, click the Close Master View icon in the View ribbon.

Creating Slide Layouts

If you need to create another slide layout within a master slide, PowerPoint makes this task easy. Start by clicking the View menu option and then click the Slide Master icon in the Master View section in the View ribbon.

In the Slide Master ribbon, as shown in Figure 12.8, click the Insert Layout icon in the Edit Master area. A new layout appears underneath the selected layout within the Slide Master pane on the left side of the PowerPoint window.

The new layout on the right side of the PowerPoint window shows the title area and other page elements contained in the slide master. Now you can add more placeholder areas, rename the layout, or delete the layout.

FIGURE 12.8   Insert Layout icon

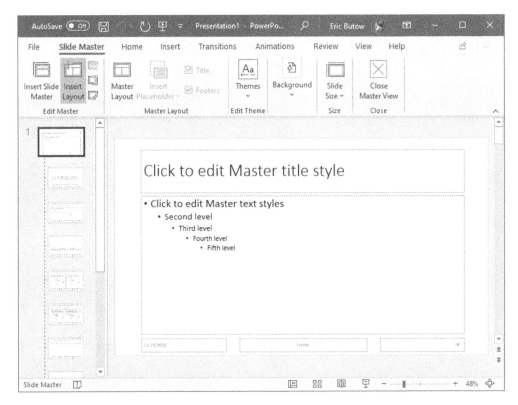

Add Placeholder Areas

You can add more *placeholder areas* for text and graphics that you can then edit either within the layout or within an individual slide that has the layout applied to it. Here's how to add a placeholder area in a layout:

1.   Click Insert Placeholder in the Master Layout section in the Slide Master ribbon.

2.   Select one of the eight content type options from the drop-down menu (see Figure 12.9).

FIGURE 12.9 Eight content type options in the drop-down menu

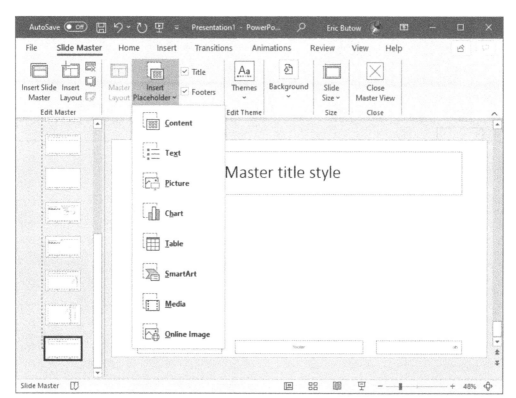

3. Move the cursor over the layout slide. When you do, the cursor changes to a cross.

4. Click, hold, and drag across the area where you want to draw the placeholder area.

5. Release the mouse button.

The information that appears in the placeholder area depends on the content type that you selected in step 2. For example, if you selected Content from the drop-down menu, then you see sample text in five different levels of a bulleted list.

You can resize a placeholder within the slide by clicking and holding on one of the sizing handles around the edge of the placeholder, and then dragging the placeholder to the size that you want. If you want to resize both the vertical and horizontal dimensions of the placeholder, click and hold on one of the corner sizing handles.

You can also move a placeholder area by clicking and holding within the placeholder area and then dragging to a new location in the slide. The cursor changes to a four-headed arrow when you move the mouse pointer over the area and when you drag it. PowerPoint also snaps the placeholder to specific points on the slide grid so that your content will be aligned properly in the layout.

Rename the Layout

You can give a new layout its own unique name so that you can find it easily when you apply the layout to a slide. Change the layout name by clicking Rename in the Edit Master section in the Slide Master ribbon. (If the width of your PowerPoint window is limited, click the Rename icon in the Edit Master section.) The Rename Layout dialog box has the default name selected within the Layout Name box (see Figure 12.10).

FIGURE 12.10   Rename Layout dialog box

Press the Backspace key, type the new name, and then click Rename. PowerPoint makes no visible changes, but when you apply the layout to an individual slide, you will see the new layout name in the list. You will learn more about applying a layout to a slide in Chapter 13, "Managing Slides."

Delete the Layout

If you want to delete a layout, you have two ways to do it:

- Click on the layout in the Slide Master pane on the left side of the PowerPoint window. Then press Delete on your keyboard.

- Click on the layout in the Slide Master pane, and then click Delete in the Edit Master area in the Slide Master ribbon, as shown in Figure 12.11. (If the width of your PowerPoint window is limited, click the Delete icon in the Edit Master section.)

FIGURE 12.11   Delete icon in Slide Master ribbon

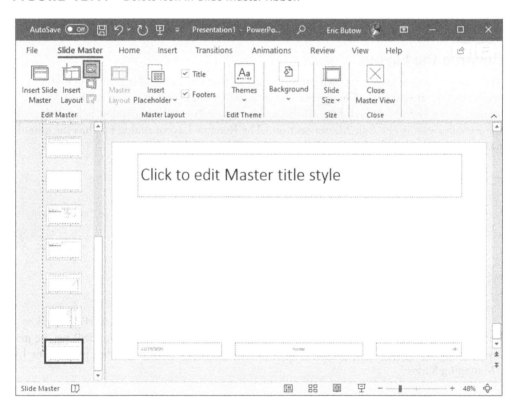

In both cases, PowerPoint deletes the layout and displays the layout directly underneath the deleted layout in the list.

Modify Slide Layouts

You can modify slide layouts using many of the tools that were already discussed in this chapter, including adding a placeholder, changing the theme, and changing the background. The Slide Master ribbon also contains several other options for changing layout features.

Title and Footers Check Boxes   In the Master Layout section, select the Title and/or Footers check boxes, as shown in Figure 12.12, to hide the title section and/or the footers section in a layout, respectively. You can clear the check boxes to display the title and/or footer in the layout.

FIGURE 12.12   Title and Footers check boxes

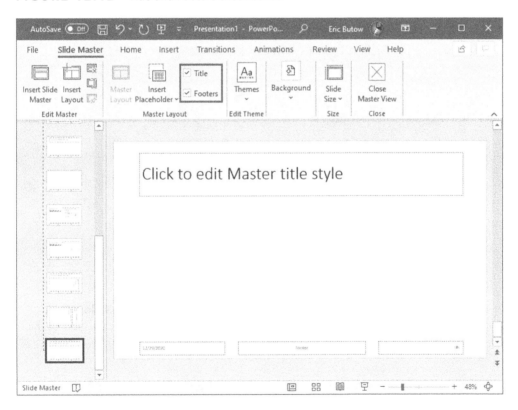

Colors   Click Colors in the Background area to open the drop-down list of color schemes that you can apply to a layout (see Figure 12.13). Scroll up and down in the list to view all the schemes and click a scheme to apply it to the layout. As you move the mouse pointer over the color scheme, the scheme appears in the layout so that you can preview how the colors look before you commit to the scheme.

FIGURE 12.13   Color scheme drop-down list

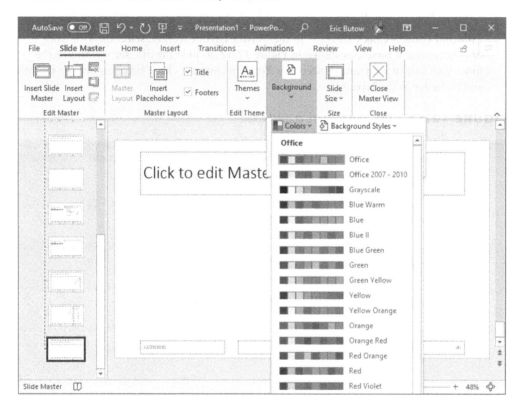

You can also set custom colors for your layout by selecting Customize Colors from the bottom of the drop-down list, but customizing colors is beyond the purview of the exam.

Fonts   Click Fonts in the Background area to show the drop-down list of font schemes that you can apply to a layout, as shown in Figure 12.14. The scheme is listed with the title font above the font for the rest of the text in the layout.

FIGURE 12.14   Font scheme drop-down list

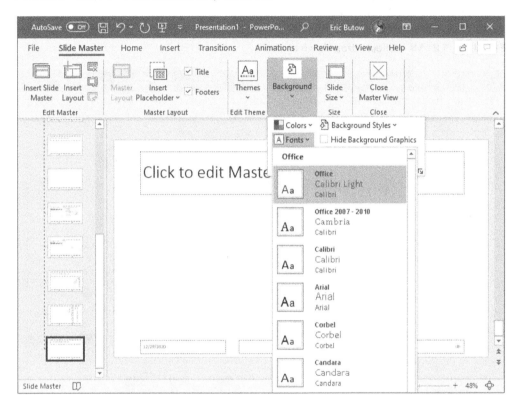

Scroll up and down in the list to view all the schemes and click a scheme to apply it to the layout. As you move the mouse pointer over the font scheme, the scheme appears in the layout so that you can preview how the fonts look before you commit to the scheme.

You can also set custom fonts for your layout by selecting Customize Fonts from the bottom of the drop-down list, but customizing fonts is not covered on the MO-300 exam.

Effects   Click Effects in the Background area to show a drop-down list of effects (see Figure 12.15) that you can apply to graphics in a layout, such as Inset to give your graphics a beveled look.

FIGURE 12.15   Effects drop-down list

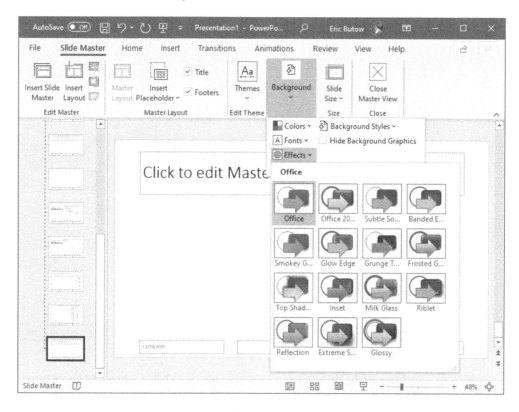

If you have any graphics in the layout, then as you move the mouse pointer over the effect, PowerPoint applies the effect to the graphic so that you can preview how the graphic looks in the layout before you apply the effect.

Hide Background Graphics   If you don't want to show graphics in the background of your layout and any slides that have the layout applied, select the Hide Background Graphics check box, as shown in Figure 12.16. If you decide that you want to show the background graphic(s) at any point in the future, clear the check box.

FIGURE 12.16 Hide Background Graphics check box

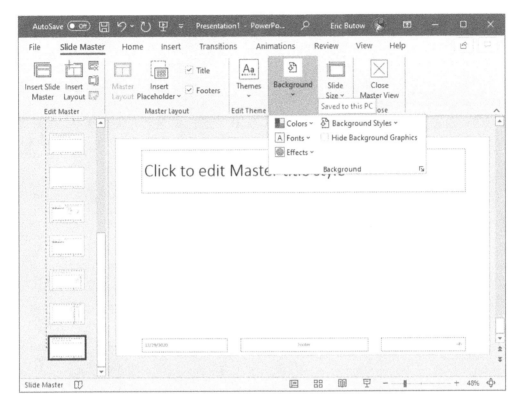

Modifying the Handout Master

The layout requirements for slides, handouts, and notes are different, so it's no surprise that PowerPoint has separate functions for changing masters for all three categories. The Handout Master screen allows you to edit how your handouts look, including the layout, headers, footers, and the background.

 When you make changes to a handout master, the changes appear on all pages of the handout when you print it to paper or to a PDF file.

Modify the Handout Master by clicking the View menu option and then clicking Handout Master in the Master Views section in the View ribbon, as shown in Figure 12.17.

FIGURE 12.17   The Handout Master option

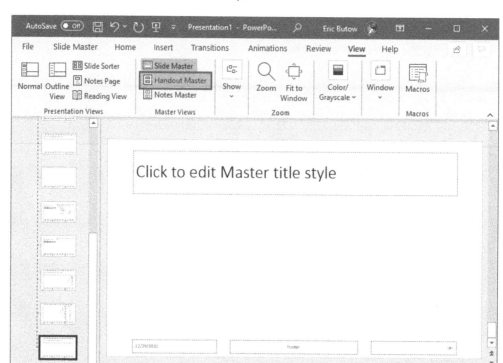

The Handout Master menu ribbon opens by default (see Figure 12.18), so you can select one of the following options in the ribbon:

Handout Orientation   Select the orientation of handout pages: Portrait (8.5 inches wide by 11 inches high) and Landscape (11 inches wide by 8.5 inches high). The default orientation is Portrait.

Slide Size   Change the size of each slide on handout pages between Widescreen (a 16:9 aspect ratio) or Standard (a 4:3 aspect ratio). The default size is Widescreen. You can also set a custom screen size, which you will learn about later in this chapter.

Slides Per Page   Choose how many slides you want to place on each handout page. The default is 6 slides, as shown in Figure 12.19. However, you can also choose between 1, 2, 3, 4, and 9 slides on a page. You can also display only the slideshow outline without any slides.

FIGURE 12.18   Handout Master ribbon

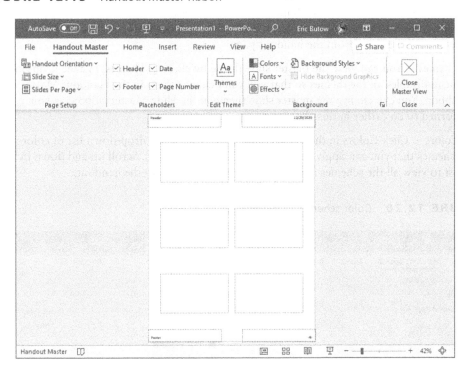

FIGURE 12.19   Slides Per Page drop-down list

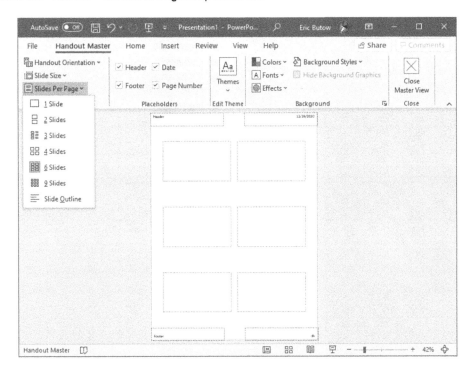

Placeholders   In the Placeholders section, the Header, Footer, Date, and Page Number check boxes are selected, which means that those features appear on each handout page. Select one or more of the check boxes to hide those features on the page, and the feature(s) disappear from the handout page.

Themes   You can view the master slide theme by clicking Themes, but the drop-down menu disables all the themes so that you can't change them in the Handout Master ribbon. You can change the master slide theme in the Slide Master ribbon, as you learned to do earlier in this chapter.

Colors   Click Colors in the Background area to show the drop-down list of color schemes that you can apply to a handout (see Figure 12.20). Scroll up and down in the list to view all the schemes and click a scheme to apply it to the handout.

FIGURE 12.20   Color scheme drop-down list

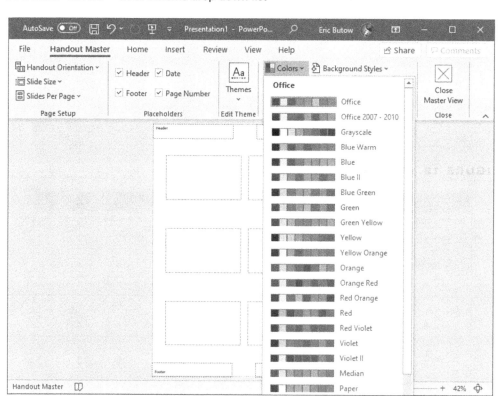

You can also set custom colors for your layout by selecting Customize Colors from the bottom of the drop-down list, but customizing colors is not covered on the MO-300 exam.

Fonts   Click Fonts to show the drop-down list of font schemes that you can apply to a layout, as shown in Figure 12.21. The scheme is listed with the title font above the font for the rest of the text in the layout.

FIGURE 12.21   Font schemes in the drop-down list

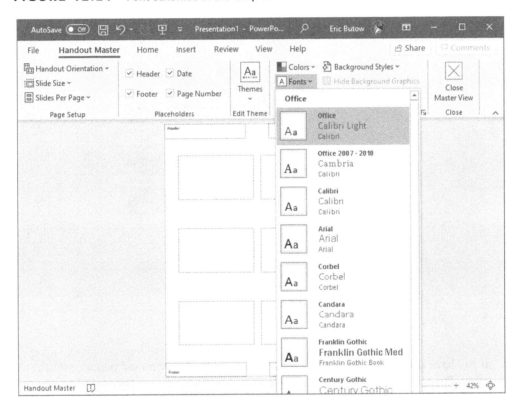

Scroll up and down in the list to view all the schemes and click a scheme to apply it to the layout. When you click the scheme, the fonts change on the page.

You can also set custom fonts for your layout by selecting Customize Fonts from the bottom of the drop-down list, but customizing fonts is not covered on the MO-300 exam.

Effects   Click Effects to show a drop-down list of effects (see Figure 12.22) that you can apply to graphics in a handout.

FIGURE 12.22   Effects drop-down list

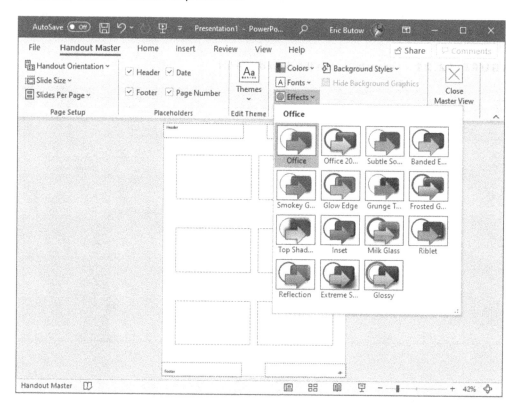

If you have any graphics in the handout, then as you move the mouse pointer over the effect, PowerPoint applies the effect to the graphic so that you can preview how the graphic looks in the handout before you apply the effect.

Background   Change the background style in the handout by clicking Background Styles. A dozen tiles with different background types appears in the drop-down menu, as shown in Figure 12.23.

FIGURE 12.23   Background tiles in the drop-down list

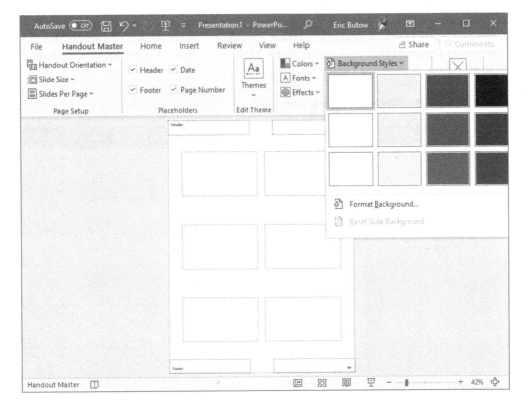

Move the mouse pointer over a tile to preview how the background will look in the slide. Click a tile to apply the background to the Handout Master.

If none of the background tiles meets your fancy, select Format Background from the bottom of the drop-down list. Formatting Handout Master backgrounds is beyond the scope of the exam.

Hide Background Graphics   If you don't want to show graphics in the background of your layout and any slides that have the layout applied, select the Hide Background Graphics check box. If you decide that you want to show the background graphic(s) at any point in the future, clear the check box.

Close Master View   Click the Close Master View icon to stop editing the Handout Master and to return to editing individual slides.

Modifying the Notes Master

When you want to refer to notes as you give your presentation, you can format your notes so that they appear in the way you want them. Modify the Notes Master by clicking the View menu option and then clicking the Notes Master icon in the Master Views section in the View ribbon, as shown in Figure 12.24.

FIGURE 12.24 The Notes Master icon

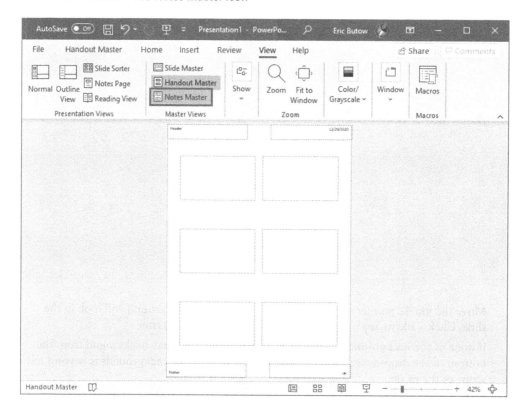

The Notes Master menu ribbon opens by default (see Figure 12.25) so that you can select one of the following options in the ribbon.

FIGURE 12.25   Notes Master ribbon

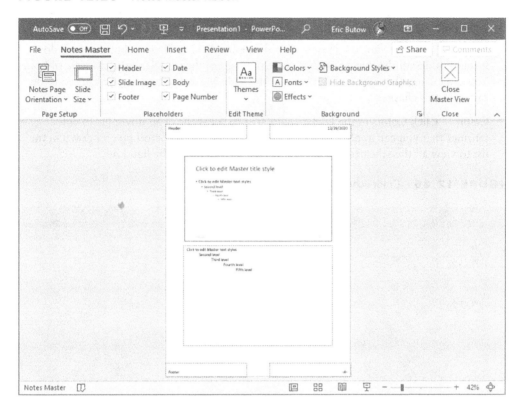

Notes Page Orientation   Select the orientation of notes pages: Portrait (8.5 inches wide by 11 inches high) or Landscape (11 inches wide by 8.5 inches high). The default orientation is Portrait.

Slide Size   Change the size of each slide on handout pages between Widescreen (a 16:9 aspect ratio) or Standard (a 4:3 aspect ratio). The default size is Widescreen. You can also set a custom screen size, which you will learn about later in this chapter.

Placeholders   In the Placeholders section, the Header, Slide Image, Footer, Date, Body, and Page Number check boxes are selected, which means that those features appear on each handout page.

Clear one or more of the check boxes to hide those features on the page, and the feature(s) disappear from the handout page. For example, clear the Slide Image check box to hide slides from each notes page.

Themes You can view the master slide theme by clicking Themes, but the drop-down menu disables all the themes so that you can't change them in the Notes Master ribbon. You can change the master slide theme in the Slide Master ribbon as you learned to do earlier in this chapter.

Colors Click Colors in the Background area to show the drop-down list of color schemes that you can apply to a handout (see Figure 12.26). Scroll up and down in the list to view all the schemes and click a scheme to apply it to the handout.

FIGURE 12.26 Color scheme drop-down list

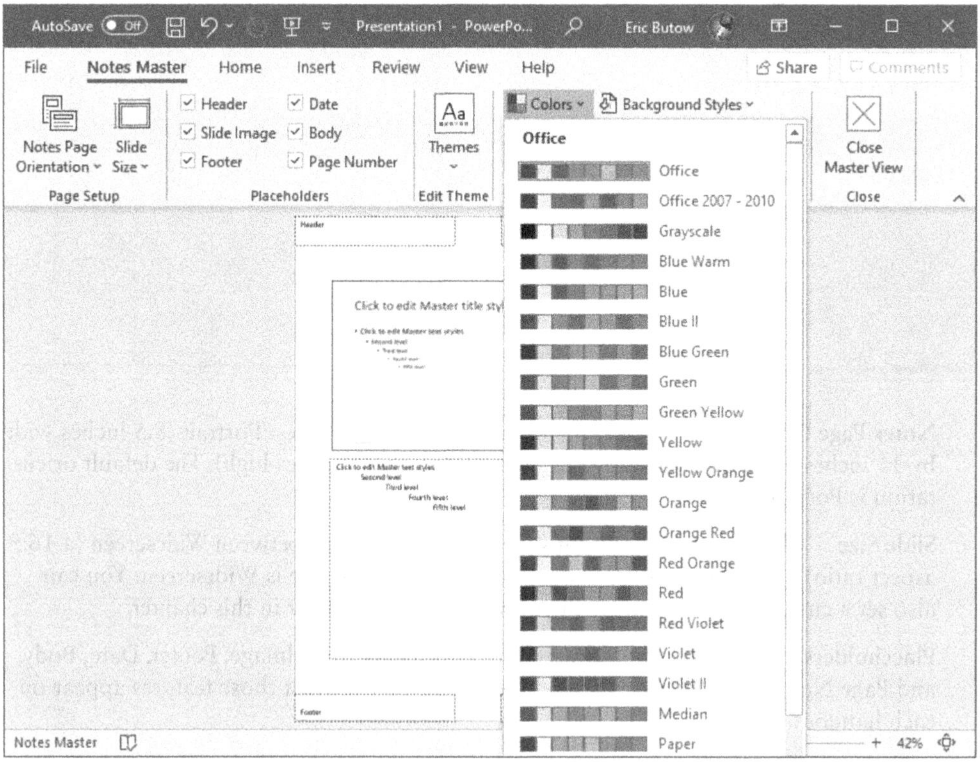

You can also set custom colors for your layout by selecting Customize Colors from the bottom of the drop-down list, but customizing colors is not included on the MO-300 exam.

Fonts   Click Fonts to show the drop-down list of font schemes that you can apply to a layout, as shown in Figure 12.27. The scheme is listed with the title font above the font for the rest of the text in the layout.

FIGURE 12.27   Font schemes in the drop-down list

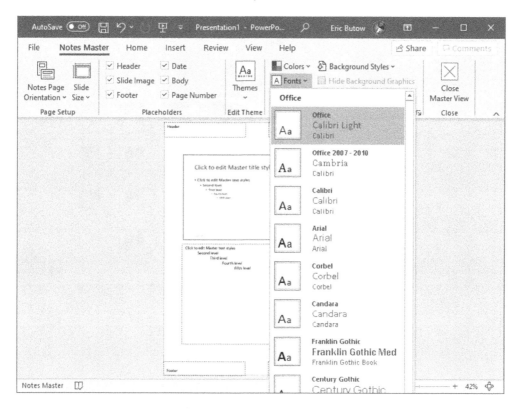

Scroll up and down in the list to view all the schemes and click a scheme to apply it to the layout. When you click the scheme, the fonts change on the page.

You can also set custom fonts for your layout by selecting Customize Fonts from the bottom of the drop-down list, but customizing fonts is beyond the purview of the exam.

Effects Click Effects to show a drop-down list of effects (see Figure 12.28) that you can apply to graphics in a handout.

FIGURE 12.28 Effects drop-down list

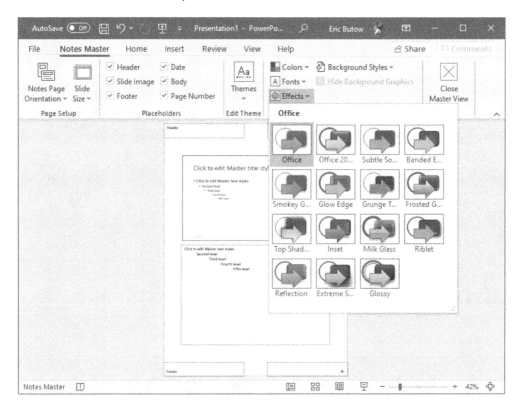

If you have any graphics in the handout, then as you move the mouse pointer over the effect, PowerPoint applies the effect to the graphic so that you can preview how the graphic looks in the handout before you apply the effect.

Background Change the background style in the handout by clicking Background Styles. A dozen tiles with different background types appear in the drop-down menu, as shown in Figure 12.29.

FIGURE 12.29   Background tiles in the drop-down list

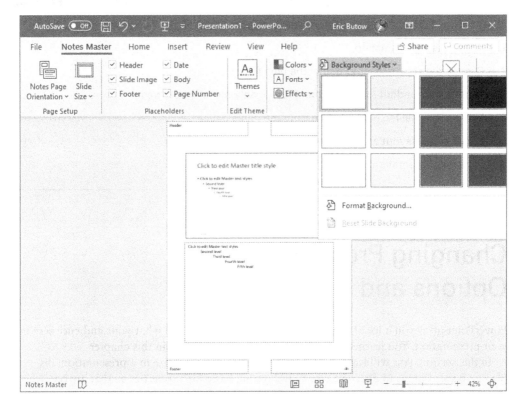

Move the mouse pointer over a tile to preview how the background will look in the slide. Click a tile to apply the background to the handout master.

If none of the background tiles meets your fancy, select Format Background from the bottom of the drop-down list. Formatting handout master backgrounds is not covered on the MO-300 exam.

Hide Background Graphics   If you don't want to show graphics in the background of your layout and any slides that have the layout applied, select the Hide Background Graphics check box. If you decide that you want to show the background graphic(s) at any point in the future, clear the check box.

Close Master View   Click the Close Master View icon to stop editing the handout master and return to editing individual slides.

Modifying Slide Masters, Handout Masters, and Note Masters

1. Open a new presentation.

2. Change the slide master to one of the blue themes.

3. Change the handout master so that there is only one slide per page.

4. In the notes master, hide the date from the notes pages.

5. Create a new layout and place a text placeholder in the layout.

6. Save the presentation.

Changing Presentation Options and Views

PowerPoint gives you a lot of power to change what you see and what your audience sees in your presentation. You learned a little about some of this earlier in this chapter.

In this section, you will learn more about changing the slide size in a presentation, displaying presentations in different views, and setting basic file properties so that anyone who wants more information about the creation of the slideshow can view it.

Changing the Slide Size

When you don't want to go through the trouble of having to change the screen size for your presentation within the slide master, you can change the size of all the slides when you edit individual slides. Here's how to do this:

1. Click the Design menu option.

2. In the Customize section in the Design ribbon, click Slide Size. (If the width of your PowerPoint window is limited, click the Customize icon and then click Style Size.)

3. Select Standard (4:3) or Widescreen (16:9) from the drop-down list, as shown in Figure 12.30.

FIGURE 12.30   Slide Size drop-down list

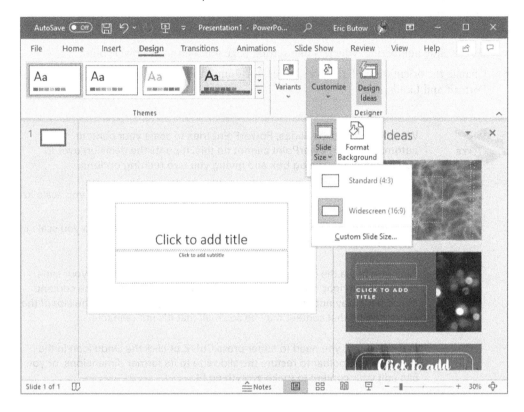

FIGURE 12.31   Slide Size dialog box

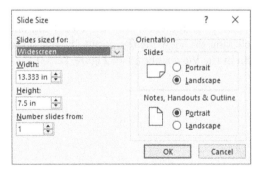

You can also customize the slide size by clicking Custom Slide Size at the bottom of the menu. The Slide Size dialog box, shown in Figure 12.31, allows you to do the following:

- Select a preexisting size from the Slides Sized For area. Just click the down arrow to the right of the Widescreen box to view the sizes in the drop-down list.
- Set a custom width and height.
- Set the slide numbering, which is like setting page numbering in PowerPoint.
- Change the orientation of all slides, notes, handouts, and the outline pages between Portrait and Landscape.

When you resize the slides, PowerPoint tries to scale your content automatically. If PowerPoint cannot do this, it punts the decision over to you by opening a dialog box and giving you two resizing options:

- Click Maximize to increase the size of the slide content when you scale to a larger slide size.
- Click Ensure Fit to decrease the size of the slide content when you scale to a smaller slide size.

After you make the changes, you should check to make sure that your slide content looks right. For example, when you increase the size of the content, the content may not fit on the slide. Conversely, if you decrease the size of the slide content, that content may be so small that it's not readable.

In those cases, you need to either press Ctrl+Z or click the Undo icon in the Quick Access Toolbar to restore the slide size to its former dimensions, or you can edit your content to make everything fit.

Displaying Presentations in Different Views

As with any other Microsoft 365 program, PowerPoint allows you to change views to match your needs as well as those of your audience. You can select from one of five different views that you can display by clicking the View menu option. The five option icons appear in the Presentation Views section in the View ribbon (see Figure 12.32).

FIGURE 12.32   Icons in the Presentation Views section

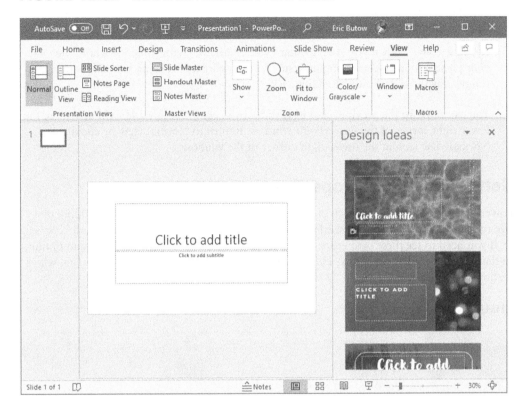

By default, PowerPoint selects Normal view, which shows you the list of slides in the pane on the left and the current slide you're editing in the pane on the right. You can change your view by clicking one of the following four icons:

Outline View   Shows the outline text in the left pane in outline form so that you can begin typing your text. When you finish typing the first entry in your outline, press Enter to continue to the next line. Each line in the outline is a new slide.

Press Tab to create a bulleted, indented entry below the main level (or Level 1) entry. This new bulleted entry is also the first bullet in the associated slide.

Slide Sorter   The Slide Sorter view shows thumbnail images of your slides so that you can review them quickly. You can reorder the slides by clicking and holding on a slide and then dragging to a new location within the window. As you move the slide, other slides move aside to make room for your moved slide. Double-click a slide to edit it in Outline view.

Notes Page   Add notes quickly to your presentation by clicking the Notes Page icon in the ribbon. The first slide appears at the top of the page. Below the slide is a text box. Click within the text box to start typing notes associated with the slide.

Reading View   When you need to share your slideshow with someone who is viewing your presentation on their computer, such as a coworker reviewing your slideshow, you can display the slideshow in Reading view.

You can move to the previous and next slides by clicking the left and right arrows in the lower-right corner of the PowerPoint window. Return to Normal view by clicking the Normal view icon in the lower-right corner of the window.

Setting Basic File Properties

PowerPoint constantly keeps track of basic properties about your slideshow, including the size of the slideshow file, who last edited it, and when the slideshow was last saved.

If you need to see these properties and add some of your own, click the File menu option. In the menu on the left side of the File screen, click Info. Now you see the Info screen, which is shown in Figure 12.33.

FIGURE 12.33   Info screen

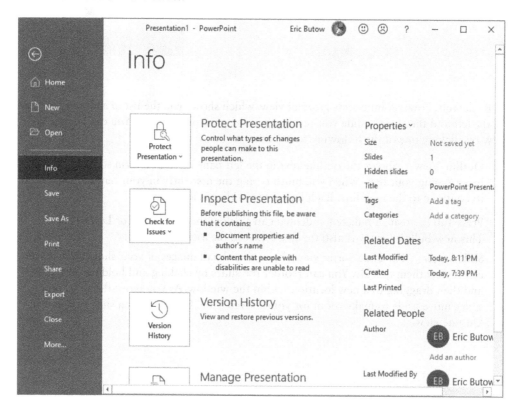

The Properties section appears at the right side of the screen. Scroll up and down in the Info screen to view more properties. PowerPoint doesn't show all properties by default, but you can reveal the hidden properties by clicking the Show All Properties link at the bottom of the Properties section.

You can also add properties, including a slideshow title, a tag (which is the Microsoft term for a keyword), and a category. For example, click Add A Tag in the Properties section and type one or more tags in the box.

EXERCISE 12.2

Changing Presentation Options and Views

1. Open a new presentation.

2. Change the slide size to Standard.

3. Add three slides with text information in Outline view.

4. View your slideshow in Reading view.

5. Return to Normal view and save your presentation.

Configuring Print Settings for Presentations

You may want to print your slideshow to look at it on paper (or have people comment on the printed copies tacked to a wall). Printing handouts is also a common task in PowerPoint; for example, you can copy a master and distribute the copies to your attendees. If you prefer not to use a second computer or to have your screen split, you may want to print your notes as well.

PowerPoint has you covered. You can print all slides or some of the slides within a slideshow, print some or all notes pages, and decide if you want to print in color or monochrome (if you have a color printer, that is).

Printing All or Part of a Presentation

When you want to print some slides or all slides from your slideshow, follow these steps:

1. Click the File menu option.

2. On the File screen, click Print in the menu on the left side of the screen.

3. Click the Print All Slides button to view the print options in the drop-down menu, as shown in Figure 12.34.

FIGURE 12.34 Print options

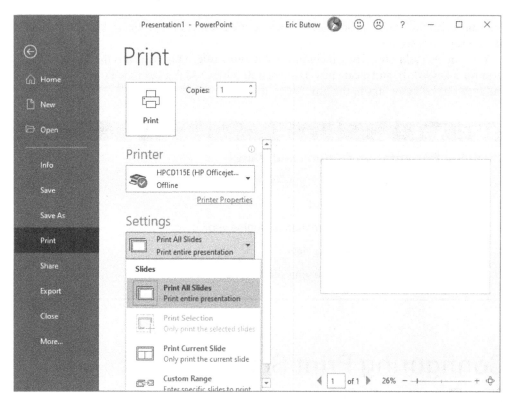

Now you can select from one of the following options to print your presentation in the Print screen:

Print All Slides: This is the default option that prints all slides in your slideshow.

Print Selection: After you click this option, the button changes to Print Selection. Now you can print one or more slides by typing the slide number(s) in the Slides box that appears directly underneath the Print Selection box.

Print Current Slide: After you click this option, the button changes to Print Current Slide. This means PowerPoint only prints the current slide shown in the print preview pane on the right side of the Print screen. The slide in the print preview pane shows its associated slide number.

Custom Range: After you click this option, the button changes to Custom Range. Type the slide number(s) that you want to print in the Slides box directly underneath the Custom Range box.

In the Slides box, indicate groups of slides by placing a hyphen between the slide numbers. For example, **4-6** means that you will print slides 4, 5, and 6 in your slideshow. Separate individual or groups of slides with commas, such as **1,3,5-9,11**. You do not need to add a space after each comma.

Printing Notes Pages

When you want to print one slide and all the notes for that slide on each printed page, here's what to do:

1. Click the File menu option.
2. On the File screen, click Print in the menu on the left side of the screen.
3. Click the Full Page Slides button to view the print layout options in the drop-down menu, as shown in Figure 12.35.

FIGURE 12.35   Print Layout options

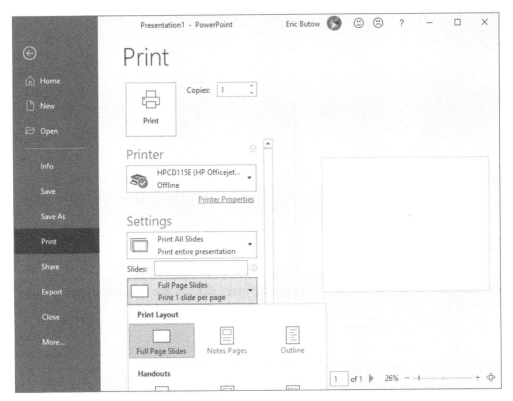

Select Notes Pages from the drop-down list. The button changes to Notes Pages, and the slide in the print preview area shows the slide at the top and the notes area at the bottom (see Figure 12.36).

FIGURE 12.36   Notes area below the slide on the page

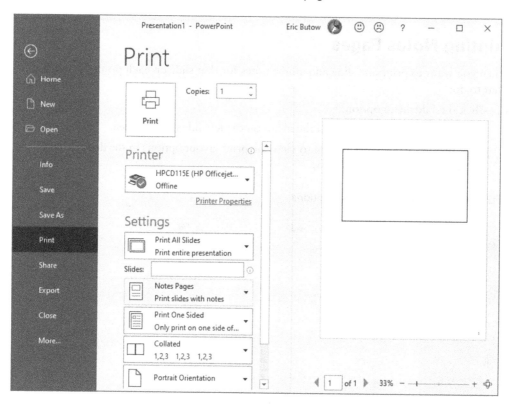

Printing Handouts

Perhaps the most common printouts from PowerPoint are handouts that you distribute to your audience so that they can follow along and make notes of their own. Print handouts by following these steps:

1. Click the File menu option.

2. On the File screen, click Print in the menu on the left side of the screen.

3. Click the Full Page Slides button to view print layout options in the drop-down menu.

4. In the Handouts section, shown in Figure 12.37, click one of the nine handout print option icons.

FIGURE 12.37   Handouts section icons

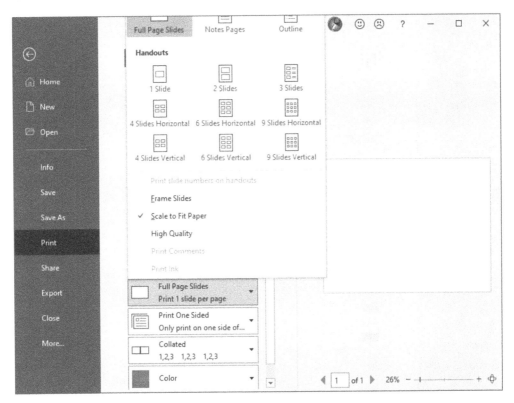

Each icon shows you how the slides will appear in the handout. Only the 3 Slides option has lines to the right of each slide so that people who receive the handout can write notes on those lines. The rest only show one to as many as nine slides on one page.

Printing in Color, Grayscale, or Black and White

If you have a color printer, you have the option of printing your presentation in full and vibrant color. You can also print in grayscale, which approximates colors into various shades of gray, or you can print in black and white. That is, any colors automatically print with black ink—even text to which you applied the gray color.

Choose your print color style by opening the Print screen as you learned to do earlier in this chapter. Now click the Color button in the Settings section. The drop-down menu with your color options appears, as shown in Figure 12.38.

The default setting is color, but when you click Grayscale or Pure Black and White, the slide in the print preview area changes to show you what the slide will look like with the setting applied.

FIGURE 12.38   Color settings list

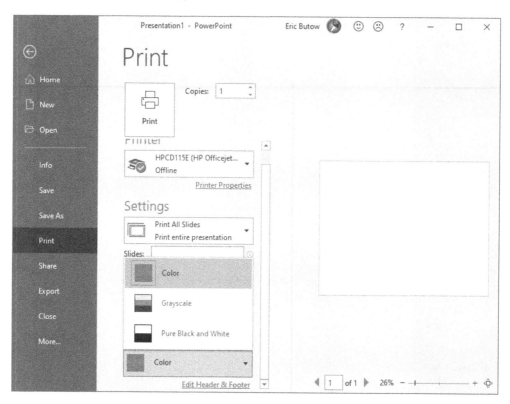

Configuring Print Settings for Presentations

1. Open a new slideshow.

2. Create three slides and add text in each slide.

3. Select slides 1 and 3 for printing.

4. Print the handouts with note lines next to each slide.

5. Print the slides.

6. Save the slideshow by pressing Ctrl+S.

Configuring and Presenting Slideshows

When you're ready to present your slideshow, PowerPoint gives you several options to customize slideshows for your audience. You can also rehearse your slideshow *timing* so that each new slide appears in time with recorded audio, and you can set up recording options. Once you're done, you can present your slideshow in Presenter View.

Creating Custom Slideshows

You can show a certain number of slides of a slideshow for a specific audience only. For example, you may want to show the slides with financial charts in a presentation to the sales team. PowerPoint creates a custom show so that you can place specific slides in your slideshow within the custom show.

You can create two types of custom slideshows. The first is a simple custom slideshow that appears on your computer, and the other is a custom slideshow that contains a hyperlink to a group of slides. The latter is useful if you have slides that you want to show to all employees and then have specific links for specific company departments.

Once you set up your custom slideshow, you can present it to your audience, either on your computer or from another website such as a company intranet.

Create a Simple Custom Slideshow

When you want to create a custom slideshow that you are going to bring with you on a laptop to share in a live presentation, follow these steps:

1. Click the Slide Show menu option.
2. In the Start Slide Show section in the Slide Show ribbon, click Custom Slide Show (see Figure 12.39).
3. Select Custom Shows from the drop-down menu.
4. In the Custom Shows dialog box, click New.
5. In the Define Custom Show dialog box, shown in Figure 12.40, press Backspace and then type the new slideshow name in the Slide Show Name box.
6. In the Slides In Presentation box, select the check boxes to the left of the names of slides that you want to add.
7. Click the Add button. The slides appear in the Slides In Custom Show list.
8. Click OK. The dialog box closes, and the custom show appears in the Custom Shows dialog box.
9. Click Close.

FIGURE 12.39   Custom Slide Show option in the ribbon

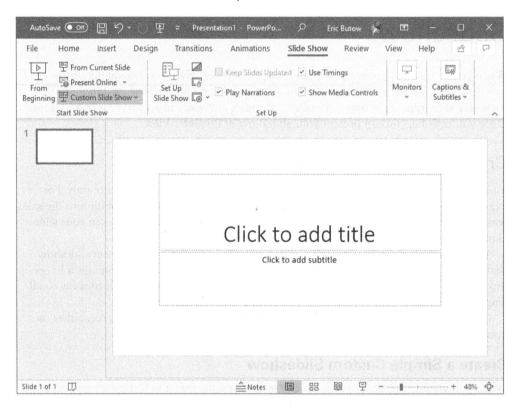

FIGURE 12.40   Define Custom Show dialog box

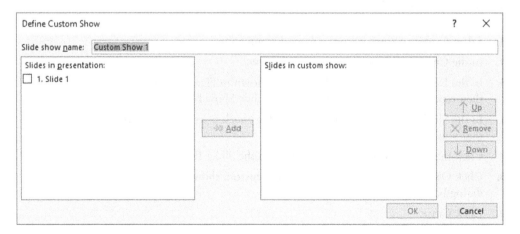

Create a Hyperlinked Custom Slideshow

After you create a custom slideshow for a specific audience, you can link text from one slide to those custom slides. Here's how to do that:

1. Go to the slide in your slideshow into which you want to place the link.

2. Click the Insert menu option.

3. In the Links section in the Insert ribbon, click Link (see Figure 12.41). (If the width of your PowerPoint window is limited, click the Links icon and then click Link.)

FIGURE 12.41   The Link option in the drop-down menu

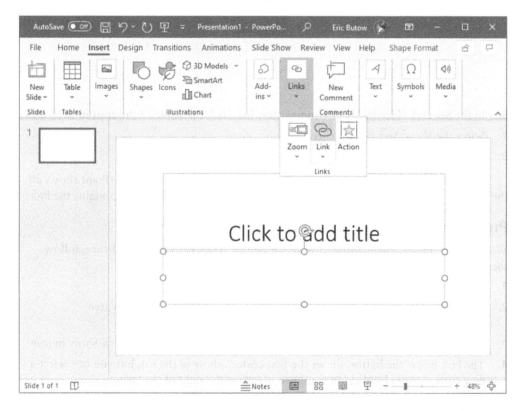

4. Select Insert Link from the drop-down menu.

5. In the Insert Hyperlink dialog box, as shown in Figure 12.42, click the Place In This Document icon.

FIGURE 12.42   The Place In This Document icon in the Link To section

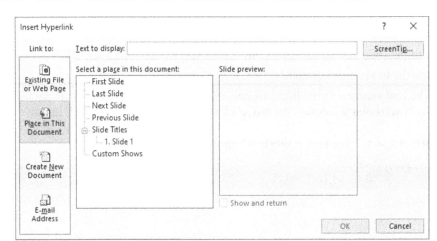

6. In the Select A Place In This Document tree list, click the name of the custom slideshow.

7. Select the Show And Return check box.

8. Click OK.

When you run the presentation and you click the link in the slide, PowerPoint shows all the slides in your custom slideshow and then returns you to the slide that contains the link.

Present a Custom Slideshow Setup

When you're ready to set up your custom slideshow to present to your audience, follow these steps:

1. Click the Slide Show menu option.

2. In the Set Up section in the Slide Show ribbon, click Set Up Slide Show (see Figure 12.43).

3. In the Set Up Show dialog box, shown in Figure 12.44, click the Custom Show button.

4. The box below the button shows the first custom show in the list, but you can select a new custom show by clicking the down arrow to the right of the custom show name and then selecting the custom show in the list.

5. Click OK.

FIGURE 12.43   Set Up Slide Show option in the ribbon

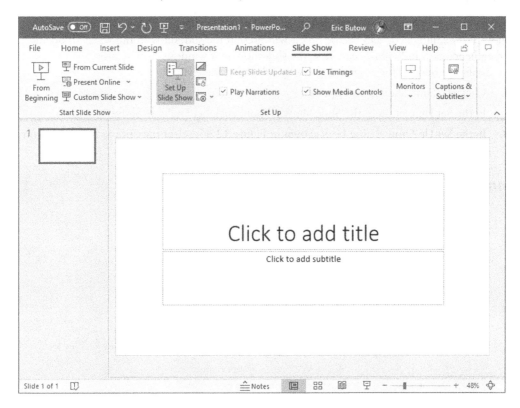

FIGURE 12.44   Custom Show button

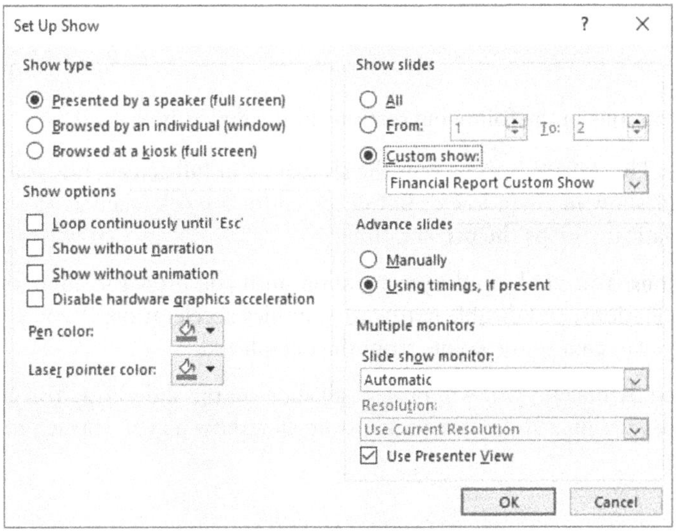

Configuring Slideshow Options

You may need to configure other slideshow options aside from preparing a custom slide-show. For example, you can decide if you will present the slideshow in full-screen mode to an audience or if individuals can view the slideshow in a window.

Configure options for your slideshow by following these steps:

1. Click the Slide Show menu option.

2. In the Set Up section in the Slide Show ribbon, click Set Up Slide Show.

3. In the Set Up Show dialog box, shown in Figure 12.45, select the options that you want to change.

FIGURE 12.45   Set Up Show dialog box

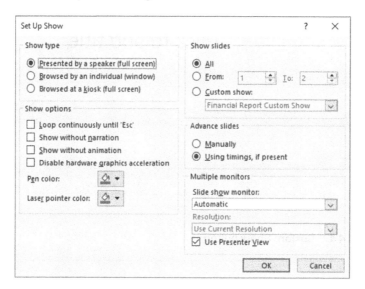

You can set options in the following sections in the dialog box:

Show Type: The default is to present the slideshow in full screen, but you can also present the slideshow in a window or in full screen for a kiosk (such as at a trade show) that automatically loops the presentation.

Show Options: You can loop the presentation until you press Esc, mute the narration, hide all animations, and disable hardware graphics acceleration. If you use a pen or laser pointer, you can change the colors from the default red.

Show Slides: By default, you will present all slides in the slideshow. You can show only specific slides within a slideshow or a custom slideshow as you learned to do earlier in this chapter.

Advance Slides: PowerPoint advances slides using timings if you have set them. You will learn how to change slide timing in the next section. You can also advance slides manually.

Multiple Monitors: You automatically present your slideshow on the default monitor. However, if your computer is connected to another device, such as a large TV or a projection system, you can change the default monitor and the video resolution. You can also present the slideshow in Presenter View, which you will learn about later in this chapter.

Rehearsing Slideshow Timing

When you record audio narration, or you feel confident that when you talk in a live presentation your slides will move in time with you, PowerPoint allows you to set the timing for your slides to move from one to the other.

Once you set the timing for each slide, PowerPoint makes it easy for you to rehearse and tweak your timing to match your audio narration or where you think you'll stop talking about one slide and you'll be ready to move to the next one.

Rehearse Your Timings

You can rehearse your slideshow timings by clicking the Slide Show menu option and then clicking the Rehearse Timings icon in the Set Up section in the Slide Show ribbon (see Figure 12.46). (If the width of your PowerPoint window is limited, click the Delete icon in the Edit Master section.)

The recording dialog box appears in the upper-left corner of the PowerPoint window and starts the clock, as shown in Figure 12.47, so you can start timing your first slide.

In the Recording dialog box, the recording time for the current slide is shown in the white box. The total recording time for the entire presentation is at the right side of the dialog box.

If you want to pause the recording, click the Pause icon to the left of the current time. When you're ready to resume, click Resume Recording in the PowerPoint dialog box in the center of the screen.

You can start the recording back at the beginning by clicking the Repeat icon immediately to the right of the recording time for the current slide. PowerPoint pauses the recording immediately so that you can get ready, and then you can click Resume Recording in the PowerPoint dialog box in the center of the screen.

When you're done, click the Next icon (it's a right arrow) to start recording the next slide.

After you finish rehearsing your timings, click the Close icon in the upper-right corner of the dialog box. A new dialog box appears in the center of the screen that tells you the length of the recording and asks if you want to save the slide timings. Click Yes to save the timings to the slideshow or No to reject them.

You can also stop recording by pressing the Esc key instead of clicking the Close icon.

FIGURE 12.46 Rehearse Timings icon in the ribbon

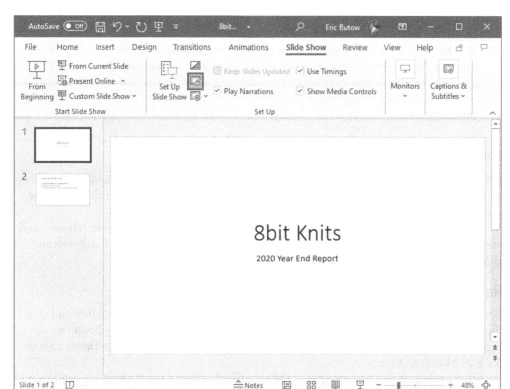

FIGURE 12.47 Recording dialog box

View and Turn Off Slideshow Timings

When you need to view your slideshow timings, click the View menu option and then click the Slide Sorter icon in the Presentation View section in the View ribbon. The recording time appears below the thumbnail image for each slide, as shown in Figure 12.48.

But what happens if you change your mind, or the presentation isn't going as you expected and you have to turn the timings off? There are two ways to do that.

Change the Timing Setup

Click the Slide Show menu option, and then click the Slide Show icon in the Set Up section in the Slide Show ribbon. In the Set Up Show dialog box, click the Manually button and then click OK (see Figure 12.49).

FIGURE 12.48   The time underneath Slide 1

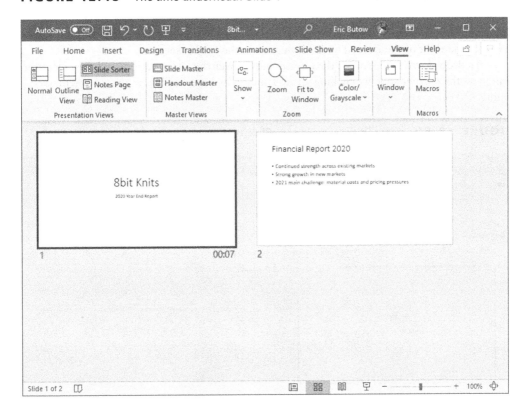

FIGURE 12.49   Manually button

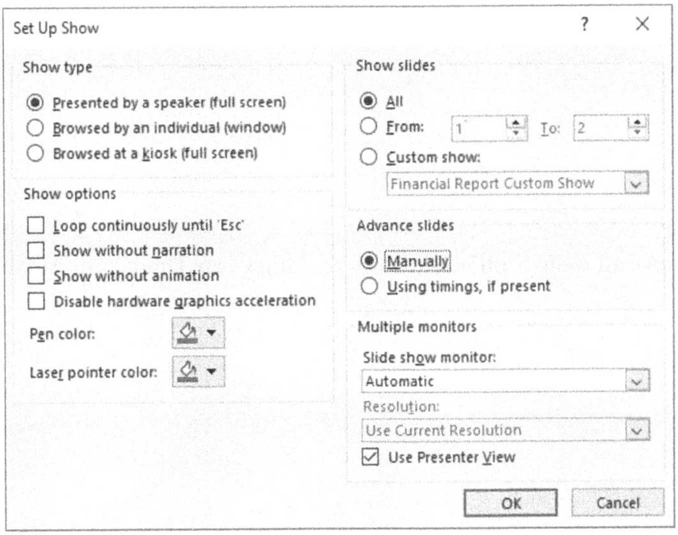

Remove the Timing Setup

Click the Slide Show menu option, and then click Record Slide Show in the Set Up section in the Slide Show ribbon. (If the width of your PowerPoint window is limited, click the down arrow to the right of the Record Slide Show icon in the Set Up section.)

In the drop-down menu, move the mouse button over the Clear option, and then clear the timing on the current slide by clicking Clear Timing On Current Slide in the side menu (see Figure 12.50).

FIGURE 12.50   Clear Timing On Current Slide option

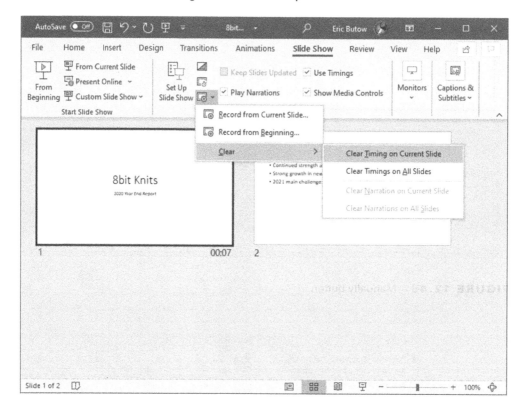

You can remove all timings on all slides by clicking Clear Timing On All Slides in the side menu.

Setting Up Slideshow Recording Options

An easier way to set your timings and make your presentation more professional is to narrate the audio for your presentation. In some cases, such as when you have an automated presentation in a kiosk, narration is a requirement if you want to use audio. You can also use recorded audio for presentations that people can view at any time, such as a new employee presentation that will be viewed by new employees over a period of months.

Record Audio Narration

Microsoft realized that you probably don't want to buy additional software to record your voice and then take that recording and import it into PowerPoint. Instead, you can record audio narration from within PowerPoint by following these steps:

1. Click the Slide Show menu option.
2. In the Set Up section in the Slide Show ribbon, click Record Slide Show. (If the width of your PowerPoint window is limited, click the down arrow to the right of the Record Slide Show icon in the Set Up section.)
3. Click Record From Beginning to start recording from the first slide (see Figure 12.51).

FIGURE 12.51   Record From Beginning option

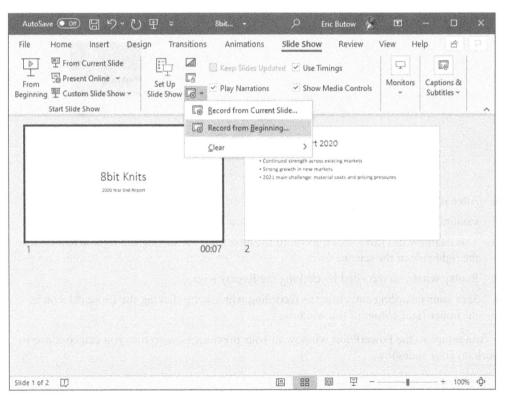

4. In the recording screen, shown in Figure 12.52, click Record, wait three seconds as PowerPoint counts down from three seconds down to zero, and then start speaking into your microphone.

FIGURE 12.52 Audio recording screen

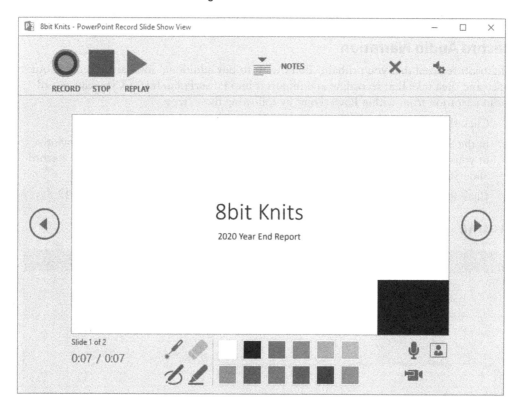

5. After you finish talking, click the Pause icon.
6. Continue recording by clicking the Record icon.
7. This example has three slides; move to the next slide by clicking the right arrow icon at the right side of the screen.
8. Replay what you recorded by clicking the Replay icon.
9. Save your recording and close the recording window by clicking the Close (X) icon in the upper-right corner of the window.

You return to the PowerPoint window in your previous view so that you can continue to work on your slideshow.

If your slides transition automatically, then PowerPoint turns off audio recording during the transition. There are two ways to get around this. The first is to stop speaking during the transition. The other way is to make all transitions manual, at least while you record, by changing the transition method to Manual, as you learned to do earlier in this chapter.

Your audio recording is not saved until you save the slideshow. You can do this by clicking the File menu option and then clicking Save on the File screen, or by pressing Ctrl+S.

Playing and Removing the Audio Recording

After you attach an audio recording to the slide, a black box appears in the lower-right corner of the slide. When you click the slide in Normal or Slide Sorter view and then move the mouse pointer over the black box, a playback bar appears (see Figure 12.53).

FIGURE 12.53   Playback bar

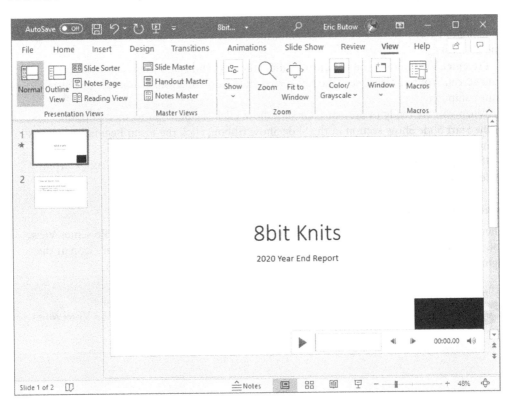

Play the audio by clicking the Play icon on the left side of the playback bar. If you decide that you don't like the audio and want to re-record it, you need to remove the audio and re-record it. (You can also remove the audio if you don't want it anymore.)

Click the black box within the slide. You know the audio recording box is selected when you see the sizing handles around the border of the box. There are two ways that you can delete the audio narration from the slide:

- Press Del (or Delete) on your keyboard to delete the audio from the slide.

- Click the Slide Show menu option, and then click Record Slide Show in the Set Up section in the Slide Show ribbon. In the drop-down menu, move the mouse button over the Clear option, and then clear the timing on the current slide by clicking Clear Narration On Current Slide in the side menu.

You can also delete audio narrations from all slides by clicking Clear Narrations On All Slides in the side menu.

Presenting Slideshows by Using Presenter View

When you present your slideshow, the Presenter View opens automatically and gives you an enhanced version of the PowerPoint interface, which PowerPoint calls speaker view, on one monitor.

Presenter View shows you the current slide, the next slide, and the speaker notes on your screen. Your audience sees the full-screen slideshow on another monitor connected to your computer.

When you are ready to present your slideshow, click the Slide Show menu option. In the Start Slide Show section in the Slide Show ribbon, click the From Beginning icon, as shown in Figure 12.54. (You can also press F5.)

If you prefer to start playing the slideshow from the current slide, click From Current Slide instead.

Start Presenter View

The full screen slide appears on your screen. When you move the mouse in Presenter View, you see a row of icons at the bottom-left corner of the screen. Click the More icon at the right side of the row, and then click Show Presenter View (see Figure 12.55).

These icons may be difficult to see, especially against a white background, so this may affect your decision to use Presenter View when presenting your slideshow.

FIGURE 12.54   From Beginning icon

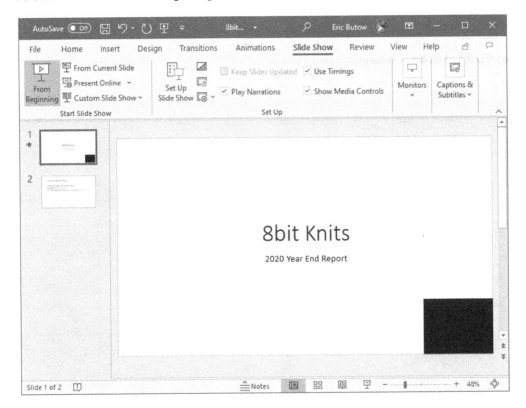

FIGURE 12.55   Full Screen View controls

Now you see the Presenter View screen (see Figure 12.56), which shows the current slide on the left pane, the next slide in the upper-right pane, and any notes for the slide in the lower-right pane.

FIGURE 12.56   Presenter View screen

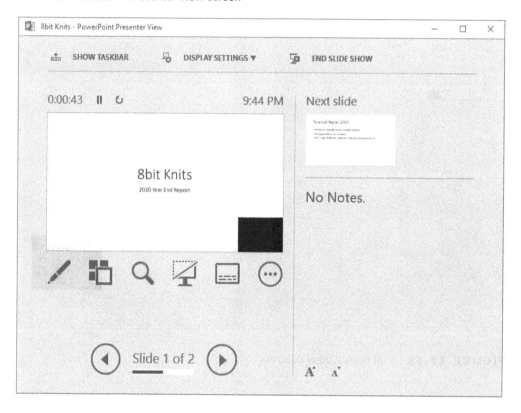

 The Presenter View screen is a separate screen within Windows. You can move between the Presenter View screen, full-screen slideshow screen, and the PowerPoint window by pressing Alt+Tab to switch between them.

Use Presenter View Controls

The main control options in Presenter View are in three areas: at the top of the screen, below the slide in the left pane, and at the bottom of the left pane.

Top of Screen

In the menu bar at the top of the screen, you can show and hide the Windows taskbar, change display settings, and end the slideshow.

 When you end the slideshow, you close both the Presenter View and full-screen slideshow screens and return to the PowerPoint window.

Below the Slide in the Left Pane

In the icon row just below the slide, click one of the following icons, from left to right:

- Change laser pointer and pen settings to annotate your slides.
- See a thumbnail view of all slides.
- Zoom into the slide.
- Make the entire slide black in case you want to hide it for any reason. Unhide the slide by clicking the icon again.
- Toggle subtitles on and off.
- View more options in the drop-down menu, including the ability to end the slideshow.

At the Bottom of the Left Pane

Click the left arrow icon to move to the previous slide, and click the right arrow icon to move to the next slide. The current slide number and total number of slides appear between the two arrow icons.

Set Monitor and Presenter View Settings

PowerPoint allows you to change the monitor settings and turn Presenter View on and off easily. Start by clicking the Slide Show menu option. In the Monitors section in the Slide Show ribbon, as shown in Figure 12.57, you can change one of the following options:

- In the Monitor area, click the Automatic box and then select the primary monitor to present your slideshow in the drop-down list.
- Clear the Use Presenter View check box to turn off Presenter View when you present a video. You can activate Presenter View by selecting the check box.

FIGURE 12.57   Monitors area in the Slide Show ribbon

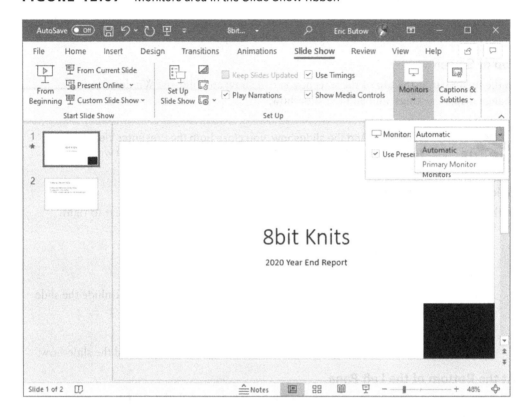

 NOTE   If the width of your PowerPoint window is limited, click the Monitors icon and then select Automatic from the drop-down menu.

 **Real World Scenario**

Make Your Notes Bigger

You're getting close to giving your presentation when you become irritated by the small size of the Notes pane in the Presenter View. Fortunately, PowerPoint makes it easy to change the size of the pane as well as the size of the font so that you can focus on the notes and not the slides.

To perform both tasks, do the following:

1. Click the Slide Show menu option.

2. In the Slide Show ribbon, click the From Beginning icon.

3. On the full-screen presentation screen, click the More icon.

4. Select Show Presenter View from the drop-down menu.

5. Click and hold on the vertical line between the current slide and the notes. The cursor changes to a double-headed arrow.

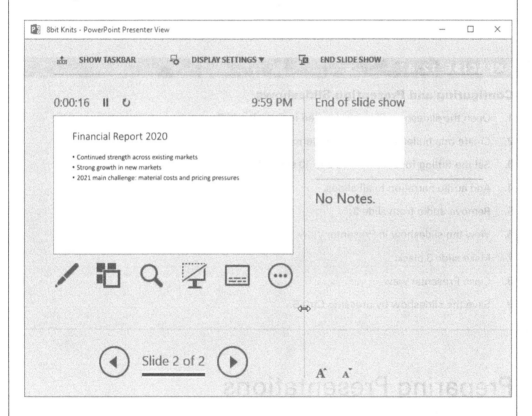

6. Drag the cursor to the left so that the notes are the size you want.

7. In the right pane, click and hold on the horizontal line between the slide above and the notes below. The cursor changes to an up and down double-headed arrow.

8. Drag the cursor up and down until the Notes pane is the size you want.

9. Click the Make The Text Larger icon (a large A) at the bottom of the Notes pane. Click this icon as many times as needed until the text size is somewhat larger than what you want.

10. Click the Make The Text Smaller icon (a smaller A) at the bottom of the Notes pane to shrink the size of the text. Click this icon as many times as needed until the text size is what you want.

Now that you have set the Notes pane and text size, close Presenter View. PowerPoint saves this setting so that you can use it with the current slideshow or a new slideshow.

EXERCISE 12.4

Configuring and Presenting Slideshows

1. Open the slideshow that you created in Exercise 12.3.

2. Create one bulleted list with four items.

3. Set the timing for slides 1 and 2 to 10 seconds.

4. Add audio narration to all slides.

5. Remove audio from slide 3.

6. View the slideshow in Presenter View.

7. Make slide 3 black.

8. Close Presenter View.

9. Save the slideshow by pressing Ctrl+S.

Preparing Presentations for Collaboration

PowerPoint makes it easy to share slideshows with other people, such as C-level executives in the company who need information displayed visually and succinctly.

Before you share your slideshow, you must finalize your presentation. If you share your presentations for review but you don't want people changing the presentation content, PowerPoint allows you to protect a slideshow with a password. You also need to check your slideshow for any issues that will prevent viewers from seeing your slideshow as you intend for it to be seen.

You can accept comments from reviewers within PowerPoint much as you do in a Word document. If you have slide masters in your slideshow but you don't want PowerPoint to delete them because you plan to use them when you add slides later, you can preserve those slide masters. When you're ready to share your slideshow, you can export the slideshow to other formats as well as external media, including CDs and USB drives.

Mark Presentations as Final

Before you prepare your presentation to share with others, take care to mark the presentation as final. When you or someone else opens a file, a yellow warning bar appears below the menu bar that tells you the presentation has been marked as final to discourage any further editing.

Here's how to mark your presentation as final:

1. Click the File menu option.
2. Click Info in the menu bar on the left side of the File screen.
3. On the Info screen, click the Protect Presentation button.
4. Select Mark As Final from the drop-down menu (see Figure 12.58).

FIGURE 12.58 Mark As Final option

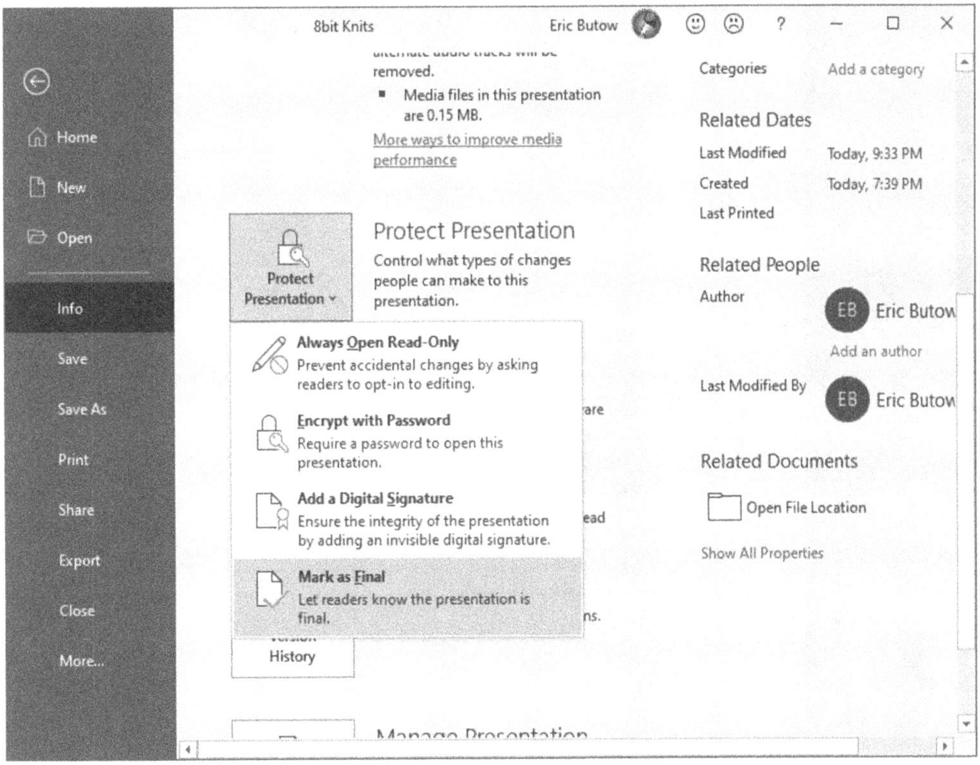

5. Click OK in the dialog box.

6. In the dialog box that tells you the slideshow has been marked as final, click OK.

The yellow warning bar appears below the menu bar. The warning bar appears every time that you open the file.

Protecting Presentations by Using Passwords

Unfortunately, anyone can edit a slideshow marked as final by clicking the Edit Anyway button in the warning bar, or by simply going to the Info screen and selecting Mark As Final from the Protect Presentation drop-down menu. You can secure your slideshow from edits by adding a password to your PowerPoint file.

Follow these steps to add a password:

1. Click the File menu option.

2. Click Info in the menu bar on the left side of the File screen.

3. On the Info screen, click the Protect Presentation button.

4. Select Encrypt With Password from the drop-down menu, as shown in Figure 12.59.

FIGURE 12.59 Encrypt With Password option

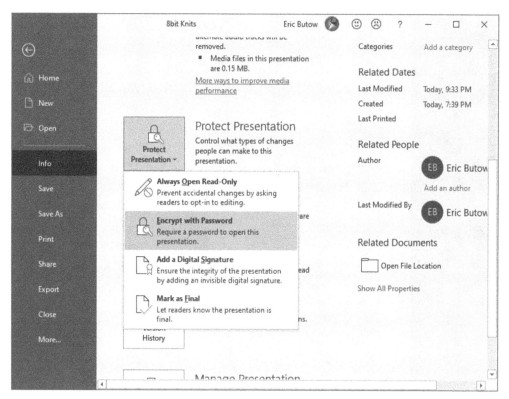

5. In the Encrypt Document dialog box, type the case-sensitive password in the Password box (see Figure 12.60).

FIGURE 12.60 Encrypt Document dialog box

6. Click OK.

7. In the Confirm Password dialog box, type the password again in the Reenter Password box.

8. Click OK.

The Protect Presentation option on the Info screen is highlighted in yellow to let you know that a password is required to open the presentation.

Apply the password by clicking Save in the menu on the left side of the PowerPoint window.

If you decide that you don't want a password, repeat steps 1–4. Then, in the Encrypt Document dialog box, delete the password in the Password box and then click OK. The Protect Presentation option is no longer highlighted in yellow, so now you know the slideshow is not password protected.

Inspecting Presentations for Issues

Before you share a slideshow with other people, such as in an email attachment, you should take advantage of the Document Inspector in PowerPoint to find information that you may not realize is saved with your slideshow. For example, PowerPoint saves author information, and you may not want to share that information when you share the slideshow with someone outside your company.

Before you inspect your slideshow and perhaps remove some information, you may want to save a copy of your slideshow and remove the information from that copy. PowerPoint may not be able to restore data when you click Undo in the Quick Access Toolbar or press Ctrl+Z, so it's better to be safe than sorry.

Start by clicking the File menu option. Click Info in the menu bar on the left side of the File screen. Now that you're on the Info screen, click the Check For Issues button. From the drop-down list, select Inspect Document.

If you haven't saved your slideshow, a dialog box will appear that prompts you to do so. Click Yes to save the slideshow.

Now you see the Document Inspector dialog box, as shown in Figure 12.61. Scroll up and down the list of content that Windows will inspect.

FIGURE 12.61 Document Inspector dialog box

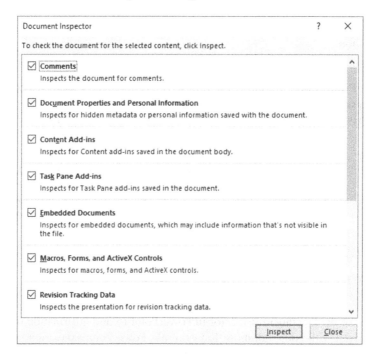

By default, the following check boxes next to the content category names are selected:

- Comments
- Document Properties And Personal Information
- Content Add-Ins
- Task Pane Add-Ins
- Embedded Documents
- Macros, Forms, And ActiveX Controls
- Revision Tracking Data
- Custom XML Data
- Invisible On-Slide Content (This is content on slides that has been formatted not to show up on the slide, such as white text on a white background, but it does not include objects covered by other objects.)
- Presentation Notes

These check boxes mean that the Document Inspector will check content in all those areas.

Select the Ink check box if you want to check whether someone has written in the slideshow with a stylus, such as the Microsoft Surface Pen. If you want to check for invisible objects that are not visible because they are outside the slide area (excluding animated objects), select Off-Slide Content.

When you decide what you want PowerPoint to check out, click Inspect. Once PowerPoint finishes its inspection, you can review all the results in the dialog box.

The results show all content categories that look good by displaying a green check mark to the left of the category name. If PowerPoint finds something that you should check out, you see a red exclamation point to the left of the category. Under the category name, PowerPoint lists everything it found. Remove the offenders from your slideshow by clicking the Remove All button to the right of the category name.

You can reinspect the slideshow by clicking Reinspect as often as you want until you see that all the categories are okay. When you're done, click the Close button to return to the Info screen.

Adding and Managing Comments

During the review process, other people (and even you) may want to add comments to the slideshow. A comment is an easy way to get the attention of reviewers without affecting text or images in slides. Comments appear in a slide as a text bubble icon.

Insert Comments

Here's how to insert a comment into a slideshow:

1. Select the text or image on the slide on which you want to comment.

2. Click the Review menu option.

3. In the Review menu ribbon, click New Comment in the Comments section.

PowerPoint shows your comment with a red outline in the Comments pane on the right side of the PowerPoint window (see Figure 12.62).

FIGURE 12.62   A new comment

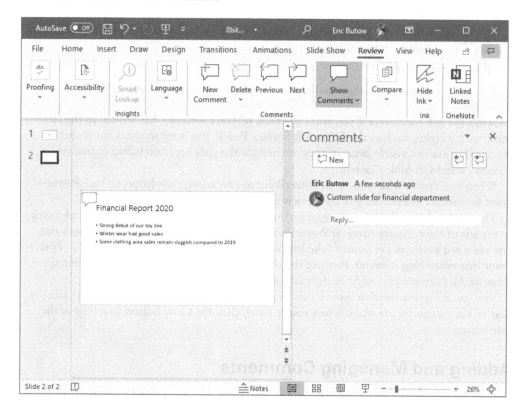

The red outline represents the default color of the primary reviewer. (That's you.) PowerPoint assigns different colors to different commenters automatically. When you finish typing the comment, press Enter. The comment appears in the margin. You can type a new comment by clicking the New button at the top of the Comments pane.

At the top of the comment box, PowerPoint displays your Microsoft 365 username, your avatar, and how long ago you wrote the comment. An avatar is an icon that you created for yourself when you created a Microsoft 365 account. If you don't have one, then PowerPoint shows a placeholder avatar.

View, Review, and Reply to Comments

When you want to view a comment, you can click on the text bubble icon in the slide to open the Comments pane (if it isn't already open) and view the associated comment. Selected comment icons in a slide have a solid color background, such as red. A comment that is not selected has an icon with a white background.

You can review comments by scrolling through the slideshow, but you can also use the Review menu ribbon to go to the next comment. Start by clicking the Review menu option. In the Review menu ribbon, click Next in the Comments section to see the next comment in the Comments pane (see Figure 12.63).

FIGURE 12.63 The next comment

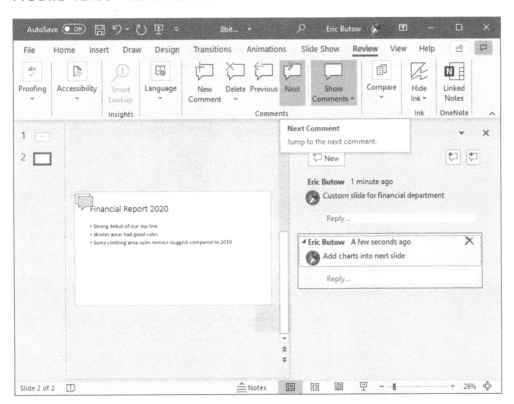

PowerPoint takes you to the slide that contains the next comment in the document. Go to the previous comment in the slideshow by clicking Previous in the ribbon, as shown in Figure 12.63.

If you see a comment from someone else (or even yourself) and you want to reply, click Reply in the comment box and then enter your reply. When you're finished, click in the document. You see the reply indented underneath the first comment.

 Anyone who can access your slideshow can edit your comments, not just the information in each slide.

Delete Comments

Here's how to delete one or more comments when you decide that you no longer need them:

1. Click in the comment box.
2. Click the Review menu option, if necessary.
3. In the Review menu ribbon, click the Delete icon in the Comments section (see Figure 12.64).

FIGURE 12.64   Deleting a comment

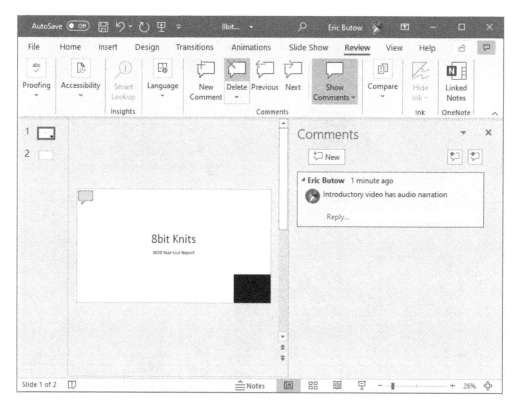

PowerPoint deletes the comment and any replies within that comment.

You can delete all comments in the slideshow, even without selecting a comment, by clicking the down arrow underneath the Delete icon in the ribbon. From the drop-down menu, select Delete All Comments In This Presentation. After you click Yes in the dialog box that appears, all comments in the slideshow disappear.

Print One or More Comments

When you want to print one or more comments for yourself or share with someone else, follow these steps:

1. Click the File menu option.

2. Click Print in the menu bar on the left side of the File screen.

3. On the Print screen, click the Full Page Slides button.

4. Select Print Comments from the drop-down list, as shown in Figure 12.65.

FIGURE 12.65   Print Comments option

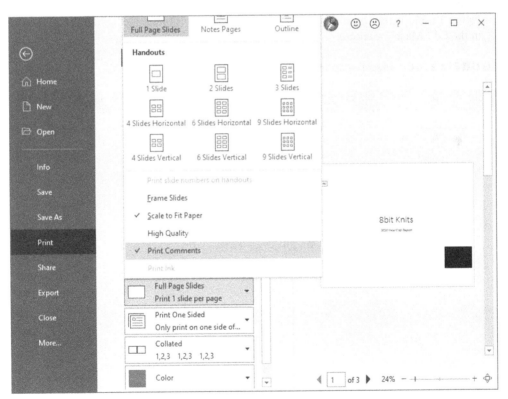

PowerPoint may have this option checked by default; in that case you can click Print Comments to remove the check mark if you don't want to print comments with your slideshow.

Once you ensure that Print Comments is on, you can print the slideshow and all comments by clicking the Print button on the Print screen.

Preserving Presentation Content

Over time, PowerPoint will try to be helpful and delete any master slides that the program detects you haven't used for a while. If you want to keep a master slide for use later, PowerPoint allows you to preserve the slide master, which tells the program not to delete it.

Preserve the master by following these steps:

1. Click the View menu option.
2. In the Master Views section in the View ribbon, click Slide Master.
3. Click the master slide that you want to preserve in the left pane.
4. In the Edit Master section in the Slide Master ribbon, click Preserve, as shown in Figure 12.66. (If the width of your PowerPoint window is limited, click the Preserve icon in the Edit Master section.)

FIGURE 12.66   Preserve option and pushpin icon

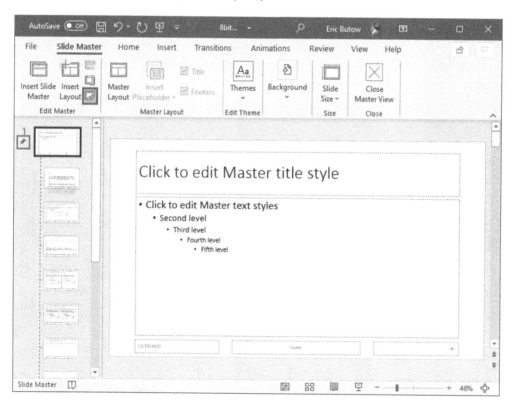

A pushpin icon appears to the left of the slide master, as you can see in Figure 12.66. Now you can rest easier knowing that PowerPoint won't try to help you and automatically delete that slide master.

Exporting Presentations to Other Formats

If you want to share your slideshow with other people but they want to have it in a different format, such as a video file, PowerPoint makes it easy to export your slideshow to video as well as many other formats.

Start by clicking the File menu option, and then click Export in the menu bar on the left side of the File screen. On the Export screen, shown in Figure 12.67, you can click one of the six export options.

FIGURE 12.67   Export options on the Export screen

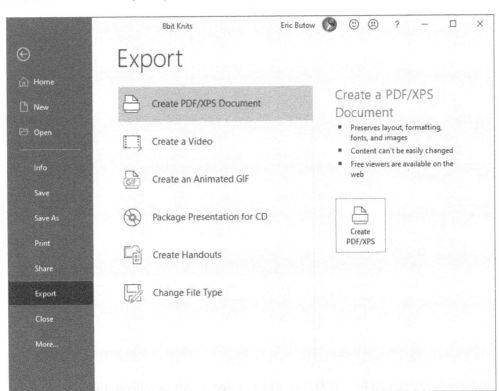

Export to a PDF or XPS Document

The Create PDF/XPS Document option is selected by default. You can export to the Adobe PDF format or the Open XML Paper Specification, better known by its file extension .xps.

Here's how to export the file to PDF or XPS:

1. Click the Create PDF/XPS button, which you saw in Figure 12.67.

2. In the Publish As PDF Or XPS dialog box, navigate to the folder where you want to save the file. The filename of the slideshow is the default filename in the File Name box.

3. In the Save As Type area, click the PDF button and then select either PDF or XPS Document from the drop-down list, as shown in Figure 12.68. (If you want PDF, then you can skip this step.)

4. Click Publish.

FIGURE 12.68   Save As Type drop-down list

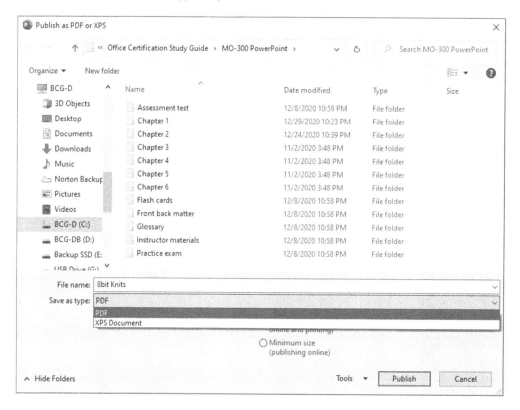

Your default program to view PDF or XPS files opens automatically so that you can see how the slideshow looks.

Export a Slideshow as a Video

Click Create A Video on the Export screen to view the Create A Video export options (see Figure 12.69).

FIGURE 12.69   Video export options

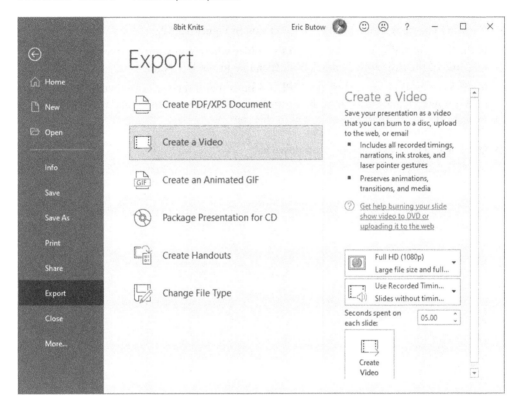

You can click one of the following three boxes to change how your slideshow is exported to a video:

Full HD (1080p)   Change the video resolution, which by default is 1080p. From the drop-down menu, you can select Standard (480p), HD (720p), or Ultra HD (4K). Each option includes the pixel dimensions for each setting.

Use Recorded Timings And Narrations   The exported video file will include the slide timings and the audio narrations contained in the slideshow. You can turn this option off by selecting Don't Use Recorded Timings And Narrations, which means that the exported video will use PowerPoint default timing settings and will not export audio narrations.

Seconds Spent On Each Slide   If you don't use recorded timings but want to have a custom time spent on each slide, this box shows a default of five seconds on each slide. Type the number of seconds as precise as to the hundredths of a second in the box, or click the up and down arrows to increase and decrease, respectively, the time by one second.

Once you finish changing settings, create the video by following these steps:

1. Click the Create A Video button that you saw in Figure 12.69.

2. In the Save As dialog box, navigate to the folder where you want to save the file. The filename of the slideshow is the default filename in the File Name box.

3. In the Save As Type area, click the MPEG-4 button and then select either MPEG-4 Video or Windows Media Video from the drop-down list, as shown in Figure 12.70. (If you want MPEG-4 Video, then you can skip this step.)

FIGURE 12.70   Save As Type drop-down list

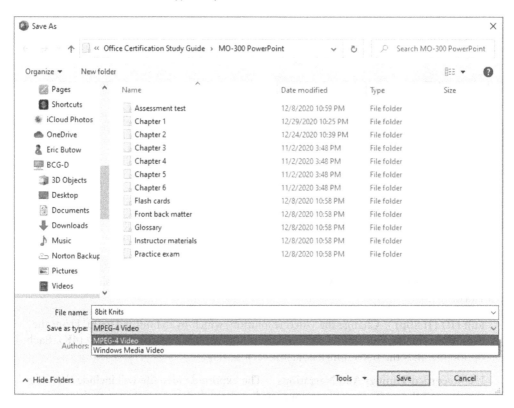

4. Click Save.

You need to open File Explorer and navigate to the folder with the video file to double-click the file and view it in your default video player program.

The next option in the Export list is Create An Animated GIF, but that task is not covered on the MO-300 exam.

Package a Presentation to Save to a CD-R or CD-RW

If you want to package a slideshow to save to a recordable compact disc (CD-R) or compact disc rewritable (CD-RW)—for example, when you want someone to take home a copy of the presentation so that they can view it on their computer at their leisure—PowerPoint allows you to burn your slideshow directly to a CD-R or CD-RW.

After you insert a blank CD-R or CD-RW and navigate to the File screen, as you learned to do earlier in this chapter, follow these steps:

1. Click Package Presentation For CD on the Export screen.
2. Click the Package For CD button, as shown in Figure 12.71.

FIGURE 12.71   Package For CD button

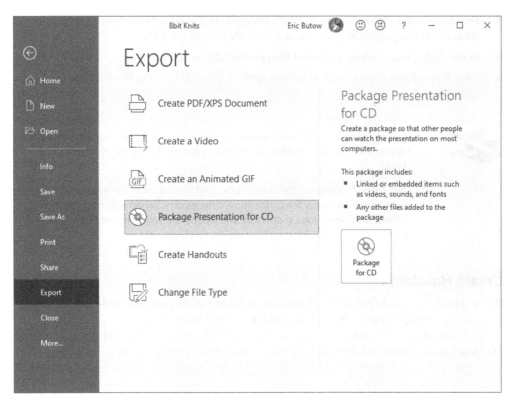

3. In the Package For CD dialog box, shown in Figure 12.72, select the default PresentationCD name in the Name The CD box and type in a new CD name.

FIGURE 12.72   Package For CD dialog box

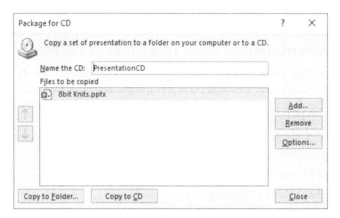

4. For this example, leave the current slideshow file in the Files To Be Copied area as is without clicking any other options and then click Copy To CD.

5. In the dialog box, include all linked files on the CD by clicking Yes.

6. After PowerPoint copies your slideshow to the CD, click Close in the Package For CD dialog box.

In the Package For CD dialog box, you can also package your slideshow to be placed in another folder, such as on your company intranet or a USB drive.

Click Copy To Folder in the dialog box, and then change the presentation name and browse to a new folder location if necessary. When you click OK, PowerPoint publishes your slideshow and opens the folder in the File Explorer window.

Create Handouts

If you want to edit and format your handouts in Word before you present them to others, you can export the handout files to Word directly within PowerPoint.

After you open the Export screen, as you learned to do earlier in this chapter, click Create Handouts in the menu and then click the Create Handouts button, as shown in Figure 12.73.

FIGURE 12.73   Create Handouts button

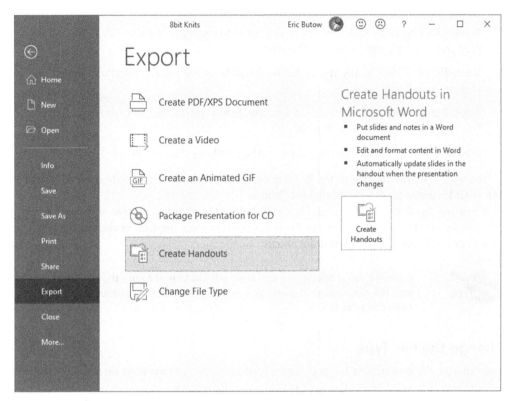

In the Send To Microsoft Word dialog box, shown in Figure 12.74, you can set up your handout page layout in one of five ways:

FIGURE 12.74   Send To Microsoft Word dialog box

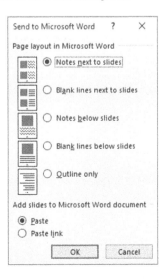

Notes Next To Slides: Notes appear to the right of each slide on the page. This is the default setting.

Blank Lines Next To Slides: Blank lines appear to the right of each slide if you want your recipients to write notes on those lines.

Notes Below Slides: Notes appear below the slide on the page. PowerPoint places one slide on each page.

Blank Lines Below Slides: Blank lines appear below each slide. As with notes, Power-Point places one slide on each page.

Outline Only: Print only the slideshow outline without slides or notes.

You also paste the slides into the Word document by default. If you only want to export a link to slides instead, click the Paste Link button.

When you finish making changes, click OK. PowerPoint exports the file and opens Microsoft Word so that you can click in the Word window (or click the icon in the taskbar) and view your handouts in a new Word document.

Save the Word file before you start editing to make sure that you don't lose the document, because you never know when a computer or power failure may strike.

Change the File Type

You can save the PowerPoint file in different formats in one of two ways on the File screen:

- Click Save As and then select the file format on the Save As screen.

- Click Export and then click Change File Type on the Export screen. A list of common presentation and image file types appears in the Change File Type list, as shown in Figure 12.75.

FIGURE 12.75   Change File Type list

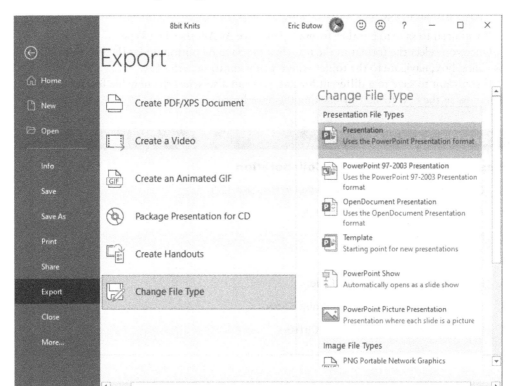

The default file type is Presentation, which is a current PowerPoint file. You can also save the file in seven other formats:

- PowerPoint 97-2003 Presentation for older versions of PowerPoint
- An OpenDocument Presentation
- A PowerPoint template to use as the basis for other slideshows
- PowerPoint Show to open the PowerPoint file automatically as a slideshow
- A PowerPoint Picture Presentation where PowerPoint saves each slide as its own picture file

- PNG-format image files for each slide
- JPEG-format image files for each slide

If you need to save to another format, click Save As Another File Type.

Once you select the format in the list, click the Save As button under the list. In the Save As dialog box, navigate to the folder where you want to save the file.

If you want to save to a different format, you can also select the new file format. Save the slideshow in the new format by clicking the Save button.

EXERCISE 12.5

Preparing Presentations for Collaboration

1. Open the slideshow that you created in Exercise 12.3.

2. Add two comments to the first slide.

3. Mark the slideshow as final.

4. Inspect the slideshow for issues.

5. Export the slideshow as a PDF file.

6. Save the slideshow as a PowerPoint Show.

7. Save the slideshow by pressing Ctrl+S.

Summary

This chapter started by showing you how to change the slide master theme and background in PowerPoint. Then you saw how to modify content in a slide master. You learned how to create and modify slide layouts. You also learned how to modify handouts and notes masters.

After you created and modified masters, you learned how to change the slide size. Next, you saw how to display your presentation in one of five different views. You also learned how to find and change basic properties in your PowerPoint file.

Then you learned how to print all or part of a slideshow, notes pages, and handouts. You also saw how to tell PowerPoint to print a slideshow in color, grayscale, or pure black and white.

Next, I discussed how to create a custom slideshow. You learned how to configure your slideshow options. After that, I discussed how to rehearse your slideshow timing and set up slideshow recording options. You also learned how to present slideshows in Presenter View.

Finally, you learned several important things about preparing your slideshow to share with others, including marking a slideshow as final, using a password to prevent edits, inspecting presentations for issues, adding and managing comments, preserving slide masters, and exporting a slideshow to other formats.

Key Terms

handouts	presentation
layouts	slide master
masters	slideshow
notes	theme
placeholder areas	timing

Exam Essentials

Understand how to modify slide masters.   Know how to select a prebuilt theme for your slide master as well as how to change the background of a slide master whether you applied a theme to the master or not.

Know how to create and modify slide layouts.   Understand how to create a layout within a master slide, how to add more placeholder areas within a layout, and how to rename and delete a layout.

Understand how to modify handout and notes masters.   Know how to format handout and notes masters, and understand why these masters are different from style masters.

Know how to change the slide size.   Understand how to change the size of a slide between the built-in standard and widescreen sizes, as well as how to resize your content to a resized slide.

Understand how to display presentations in different views.   Know how to use the five built-in PowerPoint views to display a slideshow in the way that you want.

Be able to set basic file properties.   Know how to open the Info screen, view the properties of your PowerPoint file, and make changes to various properties, such as tags and categories.

Know how to print all or part of a presentation.   Understand how to print an entire slideshow or specific slides within the slideshow.

Understand how to print notes pages and handouts.   Know how to print notes and handouts from the Print screen.

Know how to print in color, grayscale, and black and white.   Understand how to tell PowerPoint to print in color, grayscale, or black and white, no matter what type of printer you have.

Understand how to create custom slideshows.   Know how to create a custom slideshow that you can present only to certain audiences, as well as how to connect a custom slideshow with an existing slideshow.

Be able to configure slideshow options.   Know how to select the right slideshow option between the default Show Type as well as how to change show options, show slides, advance slides, and use multiple monitors connected to your computer.

Know how to rehearse slideshow timing.   Know how to rehearse the timing between slides so that you can ensure that the slides move when you expect them to move during your presentation, or to synchronize your slides with your audio narration.

Understand how to set up slideshow recording.   Know how to record audio narration within PowerPoint, play your recent audio recording, and delete the narration if you don't like it.

Know how to present slideshows in Presenter View.   Understand how to open Presenter View and use the controls in Presenter View, such as to make the notes area larger when you present your slideshow to an audience.

Understand how to mark presentations as final.   Know why you need to mark a slideshow as final, how to mark your slideshow as final, and the limitations of marking a slideshow as final.

Know how to use passwords to keep others from editing your slideshow.   Understand how to enter a password in your PowerPoint file to keep reviewers from editing text and images in the slideshow.

Understand how to inspect presentations for issues.   Know how to use the Document Inspector to inspect your slideshow for any issues that could cause problems viewing the slideshow for some people who view it.

Be able to add and manage comments.   Know how to add comments and manage comments added to your slideshow by reviewers.

Know how to preserve slide masters.   Understand why you need to preserve an inactive slide master so that PowerPoint does not delete it automatically.

Understand how to export presentations to other formats.   Know how to export your slideshow to other presentation, graphic, and documentation formats, such as PDF.

Review Questions

1. What are some options for changing a slide layout? (Choose all that apply.)

   A. Fonts

   B. Themes

   C. Colors

   D. Headers

2. What view does PowerPoint use by default?

   A. Reading view

   B. Normal

   C. Outline view

   D. Notes Page

3. When you type **3-8,10,12** in the Slides box within the Print menu, what slides does Power-Point print? (Choose all that apply.)

   A. All slides from 3 through 12

   B. Slides 3 through 8

   C. Slides 10 through 12

   D. Slides 10 and 12

4. When you want to set up a slideshow so that it loops continuously, what section in the Set Up Show dialog box must you go to?

   A. Advance Slides

   B. Show Options

   C. Show Type

   D. Show Slides

5. Why would you protect a slideshow with a password instead of marking a slide-show as final?

   A. You need to mark a slideshow as final before you can add a password.

   B. Marking and saving with a password are the same thing.

   C. Because PowerPoint won't allow you to share a document until you add a password

   D. Because marking a slideshow still gives others the ability to edit the slideshow

6. What happens when you apply changes to a handout master?

   A. The handout pages remain the same until you apply the master.

   B. A dialog box appears asking if you want to apply the changes to all handout pages.

   C. PowerPoint applies the changes to all pages in the handout.

   D. PowerPoint does not apply the changes until you save the slideshow.

7. What are the standard slide sizes? (Choose all that apply.)

    A. Standard (4:3)

    B. On-screen Show (16:10)

    C. Overhead

    D. Widescreen (16:9)

8. How many handout print options can you choose from?

    A. Five

    B. Nine

    C. Eight

    D. Six

9. In Presenter View, where do you look to see what slide you're on?

    A. In the top menu bar

    B. At the top of the left pane

    C. At the bottom of the left pane

    D. In the top-right pane

10. What are the video resolutions that you can select when you export a slideshow to a video? (Choose all that apply.)

    A. HD (720p)

    B. Standard (4:3)

    C. 1080p

    D. Widescreen (16:9)

Chapter

13

Managing Slides

MICROSOFT EXAM OBJECTIVES COVERED IN THIS CHAPTER:

✓ **Manage slides**

- Insert slides
    - Import Word document outlines
    - Insert slides from another presentation
    - Insert slides and select slide layouts
    - Insert Summary Zoom slides
    - Duplicate slides
- Modify slides
    - Hide and unhide slides
    - Modify individual slide backgrounds
    - Insert slide headers, footers, and page numbers
- Order and group slides
    - Create sections
    - Modify slide order
    - Rename sections

Chapter 12, "Creating Presentations," contained information about how to modify slide masters and a high-level overview of how to set up a slideshow. In this chapter, I will take a deeper dive into the various ways of inserting slides into a slideshow.

I will then show you how to modify slides by hiding and unhiding slides, modifying backgrounds in individual slides, as well as inserting headers and footers into slides, including page numbers.

Finally, I will show you how you can change the order of your slides and add sections so that you can group related slides. You will also learn how to rename sections to match what the slides in the section are about.

At the end of each section in this chapter, I will provide an exercise so that you can test yourself and see if you can apply what you've learned.

Inserting Slides

Microsoft PowerPoint allows you to insert slides in a variety of ways. You can import an outline that you created in Word into PowerPoint and build your presentation from there. If you want to use slides from another presentation in your current one, you can reuse slides. You can also add a blank slide yourself and apply a layout to it before you start editing the slide.

Once you insert your slides and order them in the way you want, you can use the Summary Zoom feature to go to different slides quickly as you give your presentation. And when you need to duplicate one or more existing slides within your presentation to speed up the creation process, PowerPoint has a built-in tool to do that, too.

Importing Word Document Outlines

If you create an outline in Word that you want to use in a presentation, such as an outline for a report that needs to be presented to the board of directors, PowerPoint allows you to import an outline directly from Word. Here's how to do that:

1. Open a new or existing presentation in PowerPoint.

2. Click the slide where you want to insert a new slide. That new slide will appear after your selected slide.

3. Click the Home menu option (if necessary).

4. In the Slides section in the Home ribbon, click New Slide. (If the PowerPoint window has a small width, click Slides in the ribbon and then select New Slide from the drop-down menu.)

5. Select Slides From Outline from the drop-down menu, as shown in Figure 13.1.

FIGURE 13.1   Slides From Outline option at the bottom of the drop-down menu

6. In the Insert Outline dialog box, shown in Figure 13.2, navigate to the folder that contains the outline.

FIGURE 13.2   Insert Outline dialog box

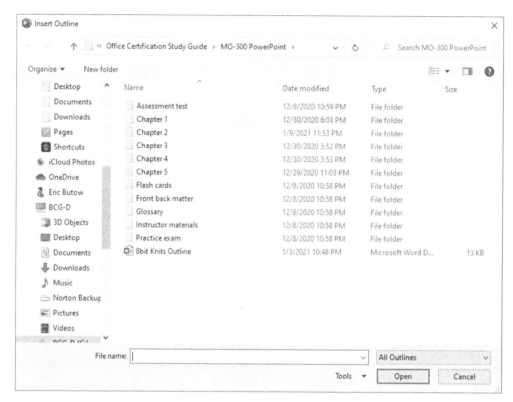

7.   Click the filename in the list.

8.   Click Insert.

The outline appears within the slide shown in Figure 13.3. If there is more information in the outline than can fit on one slide, PowerPoint creates additional slides to accommodate the text automatically.

Within Word, you can create the outline in Outline view or as paragraphs with heading styles. You can save a document in Outline view, just as you can with any other document.

If the outline is in paragraph form and contains no heading style, PowerPoint creates a slide for each paragraph in the Word outline.

FIGURE 13.3 The outline appears within the slide.

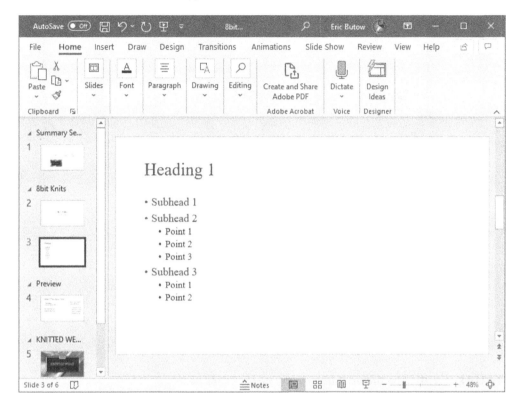

Inserting Slides from Another Presentation

When you have slides in another presentation that you want to use, such as notes about the confidentiality of the information, you can reuse slides from another presentation. Follow these steps:

1. Open a new or existing presentation in PowerPoint.
2. Click the slide below which you want to insert the slide from the other presentation.
3. Click the Home menu option (if necessary).
4. In the Slides section in the Home ribbon, click New Slide. (If the PowerPoint window has a small width, click Slides in the ribbon and then select New Slide from the drop-down menu.)
5. Select Reuse Slides from the drop-down menu, as shown in Figure 13.4.
6. In the Reuse Slides pane at the right side of the PowerPoint window (see Figure 13.5), click the Browse button.

FIGURE 13.4   Reuse Slides option at the bottom of the drop-down menu

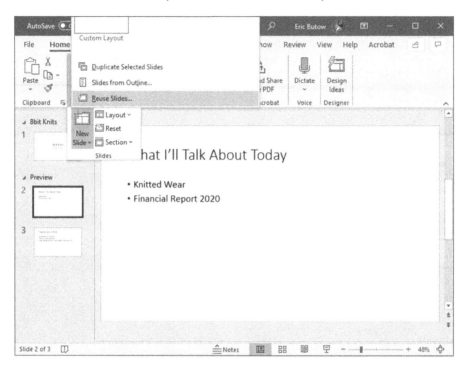

FIGURE 13.5   The Browse button in the Reuse Slides pane

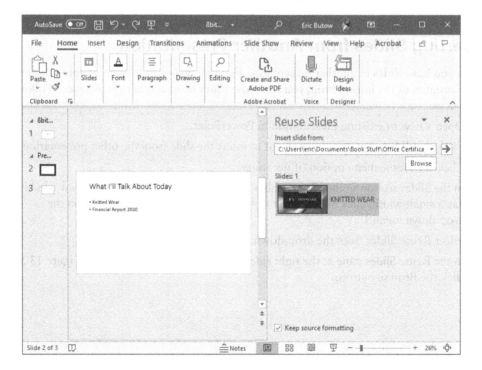

7. In the Browse dialog box, navigate to the folder that contains the PowerPoint file, click the filename, and then click Open.

8. Select the Keep Source Formatting check box to keep the format of the slide.

9. Click the slide in the Reuse Slides pane.

The inserted slide with its source formatting appears after the selected slide, as shown in Figure 13.6.

FIGURE 13.6   The inserted slide

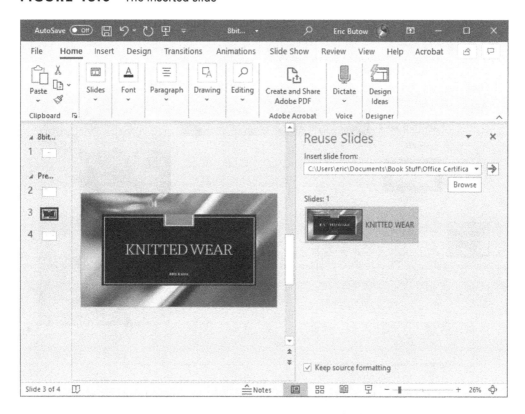

Now you can close the Reuse Slides pane by clicking the Close (X) icon in the upper-right corner of the pane.

Inserting Slides and Selecting Slide Layouts

When you just want to insert a blank slide and then apply an existing slide layout to it, follow these steps:

1. Click the slide below which you want to insert the new slide.

2. Click the Home menu option, if necessary.

3. In the Slides section in the Home ribbon, click New Slide. (If the PowerPoint window has a small width, click Slides in the ribbon and then select New Slide from the drop-down menu.)

4. In the drop-down list (see Figure 13.7), click the slide layout icon.

FIGURE 13.7 Slide layout icons in the list

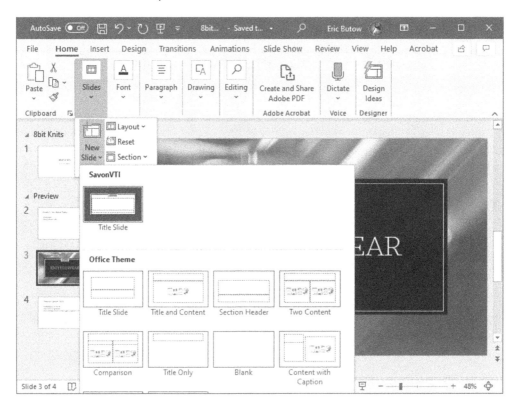

The new slide with its layout formatting appears after the selected slide. Now you can click the new slide and make changes to it.

 If you reused a slide that has a different layout, that layout also appears within the list shown in Figure 13.7.

Inserting Summary Zoom Slides

When you need to see all of your slides at once and display a specific slide during your presentation, such as a slide that will reinforce a point you're trying to make when answering a question, you can create a *Summary Zoom* slide. Here's how:

1. Click the Insert menu option.
2. In the Links section in the Insert ribbon, click Zoom. (If the PowerPoint window has a small width, click Links in the ribbon and then select Zoom from the drop-down menu.)
3. Select Summary Zoom from the drop-down menu, as shown in Figure 13.8.

FIGURE 13.8   The Summary Zoom option

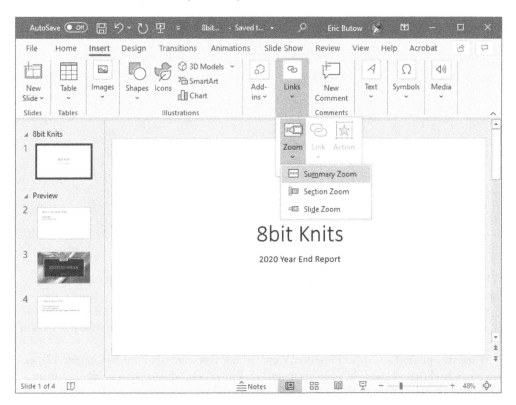

4. In the Insert Summary Zoom dialog box (see Figure 13.9), click all the slides that you want to add to your Summary Zoom slide. As you click each slide, the check box underneath the thumbnail-sized slide is selected.

5. Click Insert.

FIGURE 13.9 Insert Summary Zoom dialog box

PowerPoint creates the Summary Zoom slide at the top of the list of slides in the left pane, and it appears in the right pane (see Figure 13.10).

Within the list of slides in the left pane, each slide in the Summary Zoom is placed inside its own section with a section title above the slide. PowerPoint displays one slide per section within a Summary Zoom slide.

When you present a slide in Presenter View (which you learned about in Chapter 12), as you move to different slides in your presentation, PowerPoint displays an animation from the Summary Zoom slide in the slide in full-screen mode.

The downside to this approach is that once you move to the next slide, you go back to the Summary Zoom slide, so click the Next icon in the icon row in the lower left of the screen, press Page Down, or press the down arrow on your keyboard to move to the next slide.

FIGURE 13.10   The Summary Zoom slide in the right pane

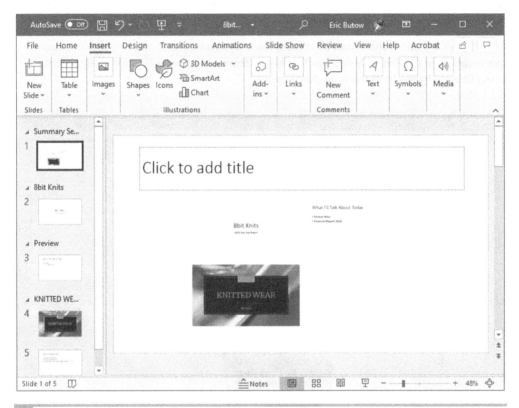

> **NOTE** If you don't include a slide within the Summary Zoom slides, that slide is still a part of your presentation. However, any slides excluded from the Summary Zoom slide are not included in a section unless you click and drag that excluded slide underneath a section name. In that case, any slides below the excluded slide within the section are no longer included in the Zoom slide.

 Real World Scenario

Changing a Summary Zoom Slide to an Image

Your boss likes the Summary Zoom slide as a way for potential new clients to understand why they should buy from your company. But the opening slide is just text, and your boss wants to see the company logo there. How do you replace the Summary Zoom slide with a logo but keep the original slide as text?

In the Summary Zoom slide, start by clicking the thumbnail-sized slide. Then click the Zoom menu option. In the Zoom Options section in the Zoom ribbon, click Change Image. Now select Change Image from the drop-down menu.

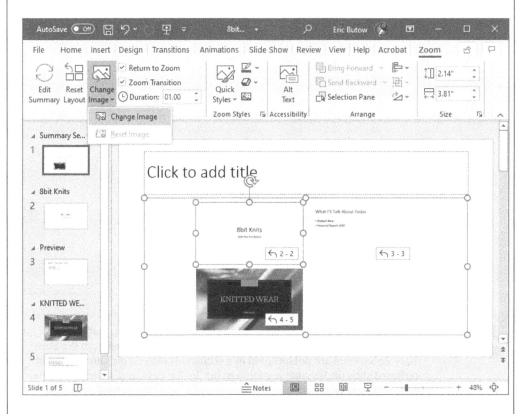

In the Insert Pictures dialog box, you can insert a picture from a file, a picture from stock images, an online picture from cloud-based storage services like OneDrive, or a picture from the PowerPoint icon collection.

The next dialog box you see depends on the type of picture you add. Once you add a picture, it replaces the text thumbnail-sized slide in the Summary Zoom slide. However, when you look at the slide in the left pane, the slide still has text in it, and when you click that slide, it appears in the right pane.

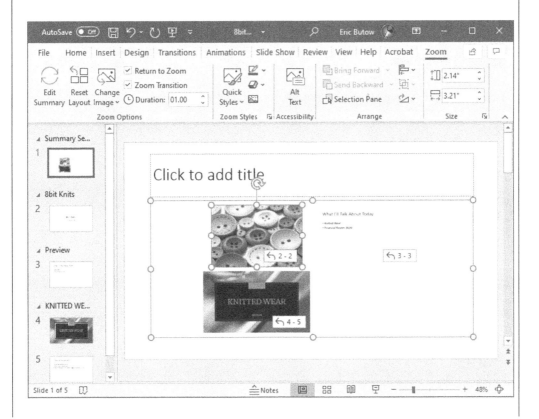

You can delete the picture and display text in the slide again by clicking the picture in the Summary Zoom slide, clicking Change Image in the Zoom Options section in the Zoom ribbon, and then selecting Reset Image from the drop-down menu.

Duplicating Slides

You may find that you want to duplicate a slide to other slides, especially if you have the same background and/or text that you want to apply to other slides.

When you need to duplicate a slide, follow these steps:

1. Click the thumbnail-sized slide in the left pane.
2. Click the Home menu option, if necessary.
3. In the Slides section in the Home ribbon, click New Slide. (If the PowerPoint window has a small width, click Slides in the ribbon and then select New Slide from the drop-down menu.)
4. Select Duplicate Selected Slides from the drop-down menu, as shown in Figure 13.11.

FIGURE 13.11 The Duplicate Selected Slides option

The duplicated slide is selected underneath the original slide in the list, and the duplicated slide appears in the right pane so that you can edit it.

When you want to select multiple slides to duplicate, you can do so in one of two ways. One is to select a contiguous group of slides by clicking on the first slide in the left pane, pressing and holding the Shift key, and then clicking the last slide in the pane. After you click Duplicate Selected Slides, as shown in step 4 earlier, the first selected slide, last selected slide, and all slides in between appear below the last selected slide.

You can also click the first slide in the left pane, press and hold the Ctrl key, and then click the slides that you want to duplicate. After you click Duplicate Selected Slides, as shown in step 4 earlier, the selected slides appear below the last slide in the slideshow regardless of whether the last slide has been selected.

EXERCISE 13.1

Inserting Slides

1. Open a new slideshow.

2. Add three slides with text in each one.

3. Insert a new slide after the second one and apply a layout to it.

4. Add a Summary Zoom slide for all four slides.

5. Replace the first slide in the Summary Zoom slide with a picture.

6. Duplicate slide 2 and slide 4.

7. Save the slideshow.

Modifying Slides

As you work on your slideshow, you may find that you need to modify your slides to make them look the way you want, as well as hide slides that don't apply to one or more of your audiences.

PowerPoint gives you the power to hide slides and show them again. You can also modify your slides by changing the background graphic and text, including the header, footer, and slide number, which PowerPoint calls a *page number*.

Hiding and Unhiding Slides

When you find that you need to hide slides during a presentation, such as those that discuss detailed financial information that are not of interest to the marketing department, you can hide slides. You can also tell PowerPoint to show those slides again when you want.

Here's how to hide a slide:

1. In the left pane, click the thumbnail-sized slide that you want to hide.
2. Click the Slide Show menu ribbon.
3. In the Set Up section in the Slide Show ribbon, click the Hide Slide icon.

In the left pane, the hidden slide appears with faded text and graphics and the slide number has a line through it (see Figure 13.12).

In the Slide Show ribbon, the Hide Slide icon is also in gray to show the slide is hidden. When you give your presentation and you show each slide, PowerPoint skips the hidden slide and moves to the next one.

FIGURE 13.12 The hidden slide in the left pane

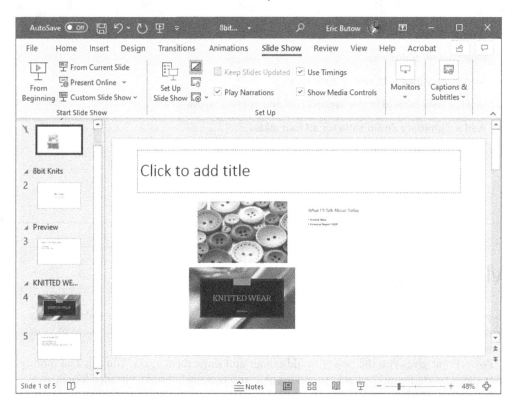

When you want to show the slide again, click the hidden slide in the left pane and then repeat steps 2 and 3. The gray shading in the slide disappears, and PowerPoint will show your slide during your presentation.

Showing a Hidden Slide During Your Presentation

If you find that you need to show a hidden slide as you give your presentation, such as in response to a question from the head of marketing about a specific line item on a financial slide that you hid, PowerPoint allows you to show a hidden slide within Presenter View as follows:

1. Click the Slide Show menu option if necessary.

2. In the Start Slide Show area in the Slide Show ribbon, click From Beginning.

3. When you see the first slide on the screen, right-click the screen.

4. Click Show All Slides in the pop-up menu.

5. In the list of thumbnail-sized slides, click the hidden slide that you want to show.

Now you can move to the next slide by clicking the down arrow or Page Down on your keyboard, or you can move to the previous slide by clicking the up arrow or Page Up on your keyboard.

Modifying Individual Slide Backgrounds

Though you can set backgrounds for your entire slideshow as you learned about in Chapter 12, you can also change a background for an individual slide. Here's how to do that:

1. Click the View menu option.

2. In the Presentation Views section in the View ribbon, click Normal (if necessary).

3. In the left pane, click the thumbnail-sized slide that you want to edit.

4. Click the Design menu option.

5. In the Customize section in the Design ribbon, click Format Background, as shown in Figure 13.13. (If the PowerPoint window has a small width, click Customize in the ribbon and then select Format Background from the drop-down menu.)

FIGURE 13.13 The Format Background option

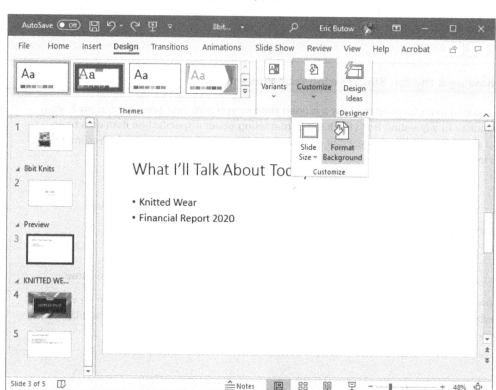

The Format Background pane appears on the right side of the PowerPoint window, as shown in Figure 13.14.

By default, the Solid Fill button is selected so that you can change the background fill color as well as the level of transparency from 0 percent (the default) to 100 percent, which means the color is invisible.

You can also click one of the three other buttons in the pane:

Gradient Fill: Set the color of the fill, the gradient type and direction, the gradient position, as well as the gradient transparency and brightness.

Picture or Texture Fill: Insert a picture or a textured background, change the transparency, and set the position of the picture or texture.

Pattern Fill: Select a pattern background from one of the 48 pattern swatches as well as the pattern foreground and background colors.

FIGURE 13.14   The Format Background pane

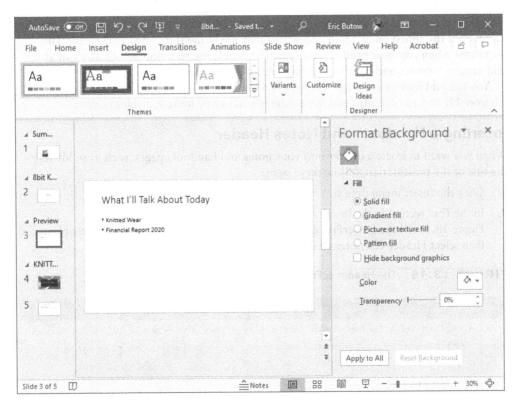

If you don't want to display graphics in the background, select the Hide Background Graphics check box.

As you make background changes, the slide changes so that you can see what each change looks like. If a change doesn't look good to you, press Ctrl+Z or click the Undo icon in the Quick Access Toolbar at the left side of the PowerPoint window title bar.

When you finish making changes, click the Close (X) icon in the upper-right corner of the Format Background pane.

If you want to apply your changes to all slides, click the Apply To All button at the bottom of the Format Background pane. You can also delete all of your background changes and start again by clicking the Reset Background button at the bottom of the pane.

Inserting Slide Headers, Footers, and Page Numbers

Slide footers and page numbers are good features to add when you want to let your audience know what the slideshow is about and where they are in the slideshow. This is especially important when you have printed handouts that people use to follow along. You can also add headers to notes and handouts, though not to a slide itself.

You can add footers and page numbers in a master slide, as you learned about in Chapter 12, and you can also add these elements in one or more individual slides.

Inserting a Handouts and Notes Header

When you want to insert a *header* into your notes and handouts pages, such as to identify the title of the presentation, follow these steps:

1. Click the Insert menu option.

2. In the Text section in the Insert ribbon, click Header & Footer, as shown in Figure 13.15. (If the PowerPoint window has a small width, click Text in the ribbon and then select Header & Footer from the drop-down menu.)

FIGURE 13.15 The Header & Footer icon

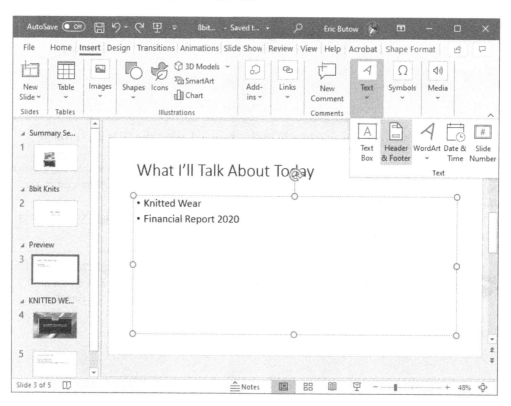

3. In the Header And Footer dialog box (see Figure 13.16), click the Notes And Handouts tab.

FIGURE 13.16   The Notes And Handouts tab

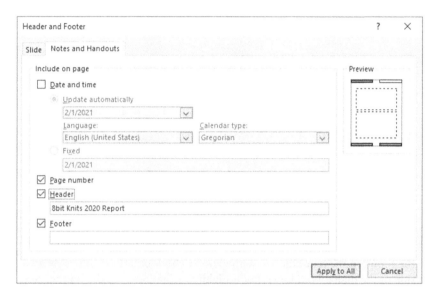

4. Select the Header check box. In the Preview area on the right side of the dialog box, PowerPoint highlights the header in the upper-left corner of the page.

5. Type the header in the text box below the Header check box.

6. Click Apply To All.

The dialog box closes, but you see no changes in any slide. You must print notes or handouts to display the header on the page.

Inserting a Slide Footer

Follow these steps to insert a *footer* into one or more slides:

1. Click the Insert menu option.

2. In the Text section in the Insert ribbon, click Header & Footer. (If the PowerPoint window has a small width, click Text in the ribbon and then select Header & Footer from the drop-down menu.)

3. In the Header And Footer dialog box, shown in Figure 13.17, select the Footer check box.

FIGURE 13.17 The Footer check box

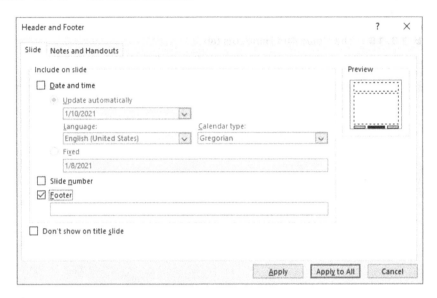

4. Type the footer in the text box below the Footer check box. In the Preview area on the right side of the dialog box, PowerPoint highlights the footer at the bottom center of the slide.

5. Click Apply to All to apply the footer to all slides.

There is more that you can do with a slide footer by selecting one or more of the following check boxes:

Date And Time Add the current date and/or time. You can either have PowerPoint update this information every time you save the slideshow, or you can have a fixed date. In the Preview area, the footer on the left side of the slide appears so that you see where the date and time will be placed.

Slide Number Add the page number to the slide, which you will learn how to do in the next section.

Don't Show On Title Slide Don't show any footer information on the title slide.

Click Apply To All to apply the footer to all slides. If you have the Don't Show On Title Slide check box selected, then the footer will appear on all slides except the title slide.

Inserting a Page Number

PowerPoint includes all slides, including hidden slides, in the slide count. You can add the *page number* at the bottom of each slide as follows:

1. Click the Insert menu option.

2. In the Text section in the Insert ribbon, click Header & Footer. (If the PowerPoint window has a small width, click Text in the ribbon and then select Header & Footer from the drop-down menu.)

3. In the Header And Footer dialog box, shown in Figure 13.18, select the Slide Number check box.

FIGURE 13.18   The Slide Number check box

In the Preview area on the right side of the dialog box, PowerPoint highlights the header in the lower-right corner of the page.

Click Apply to apply the slide number to the current slide. Click Apply To All to apply the slide numbers to all slides.

EXERCISE 13.2

Modifying Slides

1. Open the slideshow that you created in Exercise 13.1.

2. Hide one of the slides, but not the Summary Zoom slide.

3. Apply a different background color to another slide.

4. Insert a slide number for all slides except the title slide.

5. Unhide the hidden slide.

6. Save the slideshow.

Ordering and Grouping Slides

As you create more slides, you may find that it becomes unwieldy to manage all of those slides. PowerPoint makes the process easier by providing tools to order and group your slides.

You can place your slides into sections, modify the order of slides, and rename your sections easily.

Creating Sections

Earlier in this chapter, you learned how PowerPoint automatically creates sections when you create a Summary Zoom slide. You can also create a *section* yourself to group slides in different categories.

Create a section by following these steps:

1. Click the slide where you want to insert a section.

2. Click the Home menu option, if necessary.

3. In the Slides section in the Home ribbon, click Section. (If the PowerPoint window has a small width, click Slides in the ribbon and then click Section in the drop-down menu.)

4. From the drop-down menu shown in Figure 13.19, select Add Section.

5. In the Rename Section dialog box, as shown in Figure 13.20, press Backspace to delete the default section name in the Section Name box and then type the new name.

FIGURE 13.19 The Add Section option

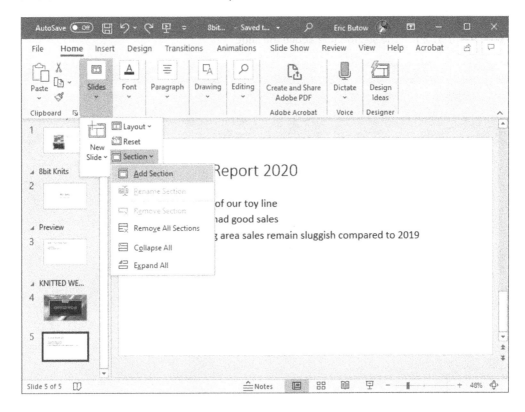

FIGURE 13.20 Rename Section dialog box

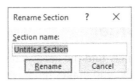

6. Click Rename. In the left pane, the slide is now contained within the section that has the new name (see Figure 13.21).

FIGURE 13.21   The section title above the slide

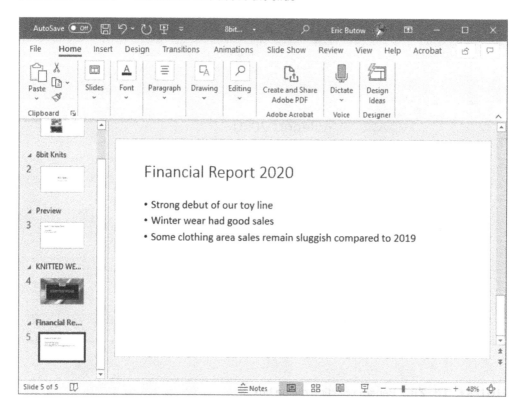

Modifying the Slide Order

As you create your slideshow, you may find the need to modify the order of slides so that your slideshow flows more smoothly (and makes more sense to your audience). You can also move a section that contains one or more slides.

Modify an Individual Slide

Modify the order of individual slides by following these steps:

1. Click the View menu option.

2. In the Presentation Views section in the View ribbon, click Normal (if necessary).

3. In the left pane, click and hold on the thumbnail-sized slide you want to edit.

4. Drag the slide up and down until the slide is where you want it.

5. When the slide is in your desired location, release the mouse button.

As you drag the selected slide in between other slides, the other slides move aside to make room for the slide you're moving.

 You can move multiple slides by pressing and holding the Ctrl key, clicking multiple slides in the left pane, and then clicking and dragging the slides to the new location.

Move a Section

When you want to move an entire section to another location, follow these steps:

1. Click the View menu option.
2. In the Presentation Views section in the View ribbon, click Normal (if necessary).
3. In the left pane, click and hold on the section title.
4. Drag the section title and move the sections up and down. All the slides disappear, and you only see the slide titles (see Figure 13.22).
5. When the section is where you want it, release the mouse button.

FIGURE 13.22   The selected slide in the left pane

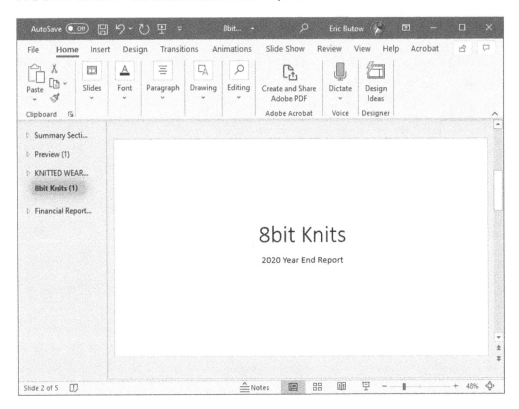

After you release the mouse button, the slides reappear. PowerPoint highlights the section title and the first slide within the section.

Renaming Sections

As you move slides and sections around, you may decide that a different section name better describes the slides within that section. You can rename a section by following these steps:

1. Click the Home menu option, if necessary.

2. In the left pane, click the section name you want to rename.

3. In the Slides section in the Home menu ribbon, click Section. (If the PowerPoint window has a small width, click Slides in the ribbon and then select Section from the drop-down menu.)

4. Select Rename Section from the drop-down menu, as shown in Figure 13.23.

FIGURE 13.23 Rename Section option

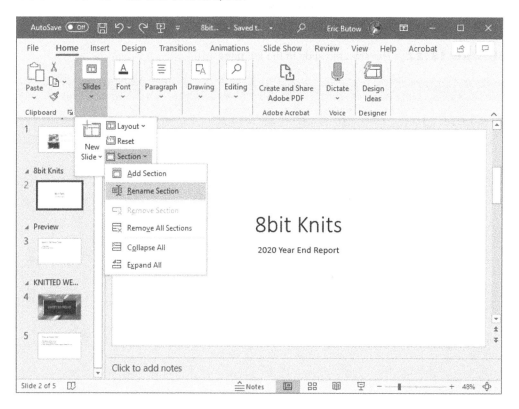

5. In the Rename Section dialog box (see Figure 13.24), press Backspace to delete the old section name in the Section Name text box.

FIGURE 13.24 Rename Section dialog box

6. Type the new name in the text box.
7. Click Rename.

The selected section name shows your new name.

EXERCISE 13.3

Ordering and Grouping Slides

1. Open the slideshow that you created in Exercise 13.1.

2. Click the last slide (slide 4) in the slideshow.

3. Add a new slide (slide 5), as you learned to do earlier in this chapter.

4. Create a new section for slide 5.

5. Move one slide from one location to another.

6. Change the section name for slide 5.

7. Save the slideshow.

Summary

I started this chapter by showing you how to add slides from other files, including Word document outlines and slides from another PowerPoint slideshow. Then you learned how to insert slides from within your slideshow in PowerPoint and select a slide layout. Next you learned how to insert Summary Zoom slides. You also learned how to duplicate one or more slides.

Next, you saw how to hide and unhide slides within a slideshow. Then you learned about modifying individual slide backgrounds and inserting master slide backgrounds, which I discussed in Chapter 12. You also learned how to insert slide headers, footers, and page numbers.

You further learned about applying styles that Word provides automatically in new documents, which builds on what I discussed in Chapter 12. I finished that section by telling you how to clear all your formatting and start fresh without losing your text (and your time).

Finally, you learned how to order and group slides. I talked a bit about these tasks in Chapter 12. In this chapter, however, you learned much more, including how to create sections, modify the slide order in a slideshow, and rename sections.

Key Terms

headers	sections
footers	Summary Zoom

Exam Essentials

Understand how to import outlines.   Know how to import outlines created in Microsoft Word for use in creating a PowerPoint slideshow.

Understand how to import slides from another slideshow.   Know how to import slides from an existing PowerPoint slideshow into the open slideshow.

Understand how to insert slides and backgrounds.   Understand how to insert individual slides and set backgrounds for one or all slides in your slideshow.

Know how to insert Summary Zoom slides.   Understand what a Summary Zoom slide is, how to insert a Summary Zoom slide into your slideshow, and how to add one or more slides to the Summary Zoom slide.

Be able to duplicate slides.   Know how to duplicate one or more slides and place the slide(s) at another point within the slideshow.

Know how to modify slides.   Understand how to hide and unhide slides, set and change individual slide backgrounds, insert slide headers and footers, and place page numbers into one or all slides.

Understand how to order and group slides.   Know how to modify the order of slides in a slideshow as well as create and rename sections.

Review Questions

1. When you add more pages of an outline than will fit on a slide, what happens?

   A. A dialog box appears telling you that the outline was too long.

   B. You only see the outline text that fits in the slide.

   C. PowerPoint creates additional slides to accommodate the text.

   D. A dialog box appears that says PowerPoint cannot add the outline because it's too long.

2. How do you know a slide is hidden in the list of slides in the left pane?

   A. The slide no longer exists in the list.

   B. The hidden slide appears with a gray background, and the slide number has a line through it.

   C. The hidden slide number has a line through it, but the slide no longer exists in the list.

   D. Click Slide Sorter in the View ribbon.

3. When you create a section, what option do you click in the Slides drop-down menu?

   A. Section and then click Remove Sections

   B. Layout and then click Blank Slide

   C. New Slide and then click Section Header

   D. Section and then click Add Section

4. How do you keep the formatting contained in an imported slide when you import it into your slideshow?

   A. After you import the slide, a dialog box asks you if you want to keep the formatting when you import it.

   B. Right-click the imported slide in the Reuse Slides pane and then click Keep Source Formatting in the menu.

   C. Select the Keep Source Formatting check box in the Reuse Slides pane.

   D. Click Browse in the Reuse Slides pane and then select the correct file type in the Browse dialog box.

5. What other types of fills can you add to a slide background? (Choose all that apply.)

   A. Gradient fill

   B. Solid fill

   C. Pattern fill

   D. Hide background graphics

6. What key do you press and hold to select more than one slide to move?

   A. Ins

   B. Alt

    C. Shift

    D. Ctrl

7. When you click a slide in the list of slides in Normal view, where does a new slide appear?

    A. Above the selected slide

    B. Below the selected slide

    C. As the first slide in the slideshow

    D. As the last slide in the slideshow

8. Where does a page number appear in a slide?

    A. Bottom-right corner

    B. Bottom-left corner

    C. Bottom and centered

    D. Top-right corner

9. What menu option do you click to rename a section?

    A. Design

    B. Insert

    C. Home

    D. Review

10. How many slides does PowerPoint add to a Summary Zoom slide?

    A. All the slides

    B. The first three

    C. You can choose the slides you want to add in a dialog box that appears after you create the Summary Zoom slide.

    D. One slide per section

Chapter
14

Inserting and Formatting Text, Shapes, and Images

MICROSOFT EXAM OBJECTIVES COVERED IN THIS CHAPTER:

✓ **Insert and format text, shapes, and images**

- ▪ Format text
  - ▪ Apply formatting and styles to text
  - ▪ Format text in multiple columns
  - ▪ Create bulleted and numbered lists
- ▪ Insert links
  - ▪ Insert hyperlinks
  - ▪ Insert Section Zoom links and Slide Zoom links
- ▪ Insert and format images
  - ▪ Resize and crop images
  - ▪ Apply built-in styles and effects to images
  - ▪ Insert screenshots and screen clippings
- ▪ Insert and format graphic elements
  - ▪ Insert and change shapes
  - ▪ Draw by using digital ink
  - ▪ Add text to shapes and text boxes
  - ▪ Resize shapes and text boxes
  - ▪ Format shapes and text boxes
  - ▪ Apply built-in styles to shapes and text boxes
  - ▪ Add Alt text to graphic elements for accessibility

- Order and group objects on slides
    - Order shapes, images, and text boxes
    - Align shapes, images, and text boxes
    - Group shapes and images
    - Display alignment tools

PowerPoint gives you the ability to communicate your message effectively using both text and graphics in your slides. After you place your text and/or graphics in your slideshow, you can use the built-in formatting tools to make the text and graphics look the way you want.

This chapter starts by showing you how to add and format text in slides that will help you communicate your message with various styles, columns, and lists. You can also add hyperlinks to external sources, such as websites, and insert links to Section Zoom and Slide Zoom slides.

Next, I'll show you how to insert images, either from your own computer or from stock libraries installed with PowerPoint. After you add an image, you can resize it, add styles, and apply effects. What's more, you can add screenshots of your computer and place screen clippings, which are a portion of your screen, into your slideshow.

I also talk about adding and formatting shapes and images, adding text boxes, adding text to graphic elements, and positioning those images so that they look good on the page. You will also learn how to add alternative, or Alt, text to images and photos so that people who cannot see them can read a description.

Finally, you will learn how to order your text boxes, shapes, and images to place them where you want on one or more slides.

Formatting Text

PowerPoint makes it easy to add text to a Slide Master or an individual slide and then format the style the way you want. That can include things as basic as changing the font from normal to bold, or you can apply built-in styles to make your text pop.

You can also format your text in ways that are similar to Microsoft Word, including laying out the text in multiple columns, bulleted lists, or numbered lists.

Applying Formatting and Styles to Text

PowerPoint has several tools at the ready so that you can apply formatting and styles to your text. These include the Format Painter, the ability to set line and paragraph spacing, the ability to indent a paragraph, and built-in styles. You can also clear formatting that you've made at any time.

Applying Formatting by Using Format Painter

The *Format Painter* feature is a quick and easy way to apply formatting from selected text or an entire paragraph to another block of text or a paragraph. Follow these steps to get started:

1. Select the text or click text in a slide that has the formatting you want to copy.

2. Click the Home menu option if it's not selected already.

3. In the Home ribbon, click the Format Painter icon in the Clipboard area, as shown in Figure 14.1.

FIGURE 14.1   Format Painter icon

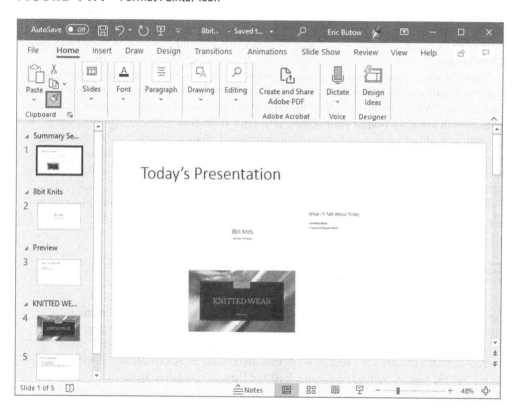

The mouse pointer changes to a cursor icon combined with a paintbrush. Now you can select a block of text or click inside a paragraph. The text or paragraph that you selected now shows the format that you copied.

This process works only once, but you can change the format of multiple blocks of text or paragraphs. After you select the text with the formatting that you want to copy, double-click the Format Painter icon in the Home toolbar and then select the text and/or paragraphs. When you're done, press the Esc key.

Setting Line Spacing

You may need to change spacing between lines so that your audience has no trouble reading the text on your slide. When you want to set line spacing, place the cursor where you want to start the different line spacing, or select the text that will have the different line spacing. In the Home ribbon, click the Line Spacing icon in the Paragraph area. (If your PowerPoint window width is small, click the Paragraph icon and then click the Line Spacing icon.)

Now you can select one of the built-in line spacing amounts, as shown in Figure 14.2. For example, selecting 2.0 means that you will see double-spaced lines as you type.

FIGURE 14.2   Line Spacing drop-down menu

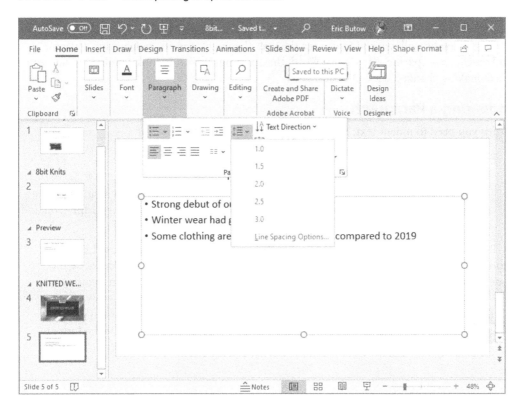

Below the list of built-in line spacing amounts, select Line Spacing Options to open the Paragraph dialog box (see Figure 14.3) to change specific line spacing settings.

FIGURE 14.3   Paragraph dialog box

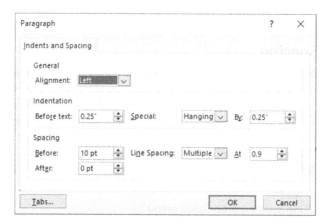

The dialog box allows you to change the text alignment, specific indentation settings, and specific line spacing. (If you use Word, these settings probably look familiar.) When you finish making changes, click OK.

Indenting a Paragraph

When you need to indent text, follow these steps:

1. Place the cursor in the text that you want to change.

2. Click the Home menu option if it's not selected already.

3. In the Home ribbon, click the Increase List Level icon in the Paragraph area, as shown in Figure 14.4. (If your PowerPoint window width is small, click the Paragraph icon and then click the Line Spacing icon.)

PowerPoint indents the text by 0.5 inches. Whenever you click the Increase List Level icon, PowerPoint increases the indent by an additional 0.5 inches. You can decrease the indent by 0.5 inches by clicking the Decrease List Level icon that you saw in Figure 14.4.

 If you indent a bullet or numbered list, the line reflects the formatting for the next list level. If you decrease the indent, the line reflects the formatting for the previous list level.

FIGURE 14.4 Decrease List Level (left) and Increase List Level (right) icons

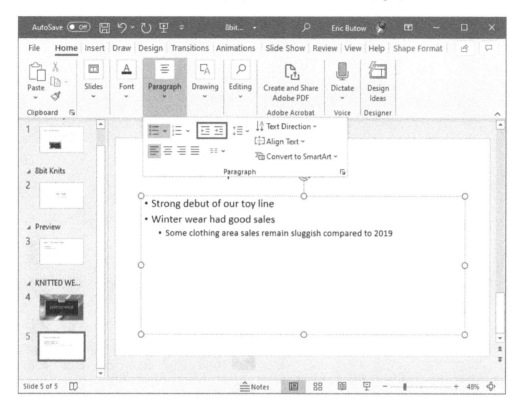

Applying Built-In Styles to Text

When you open a new document, PowerPoint includes 77 different styles for you to apply to text. You can view and apply these styles to text by clicking the Home menu option if it's not already active.

In the Drawing area in the Home ribbon, click Quick Styles in the ribbon, as shown in Figure 14.5. (If your PowerPoint window width is small, click the Drawing icon and then click Quick Styles.)

As you move the mouse pointer over each style, the slide area that contains the text changes to reflect the style. When you find a style that you like, click the style in the drop-down menu. PowerPoint closes the drop-down menu so that you can see the slide with the style applied to the slide area.

FIGURE 14.5   The Quick Styles drop-down menu

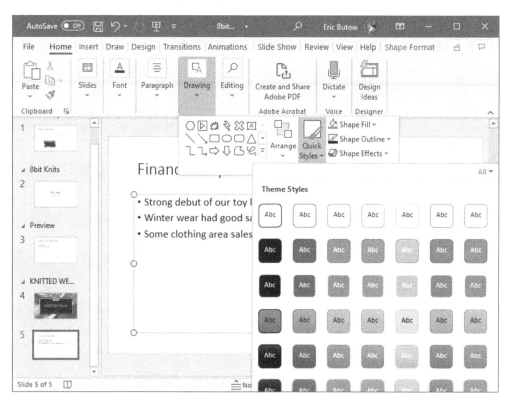

 If you want a different background for the slide area, move the mouse pointer over Other Theme Fills at the bottom of the drop-down menu, and then move the mouse pointer over one of the 12 background color tiles to see how each color will look in the slide area. If you like one, select the tile to close the drop-down menu.

Clearing Formatting

You can clear formatting in selected text by clicking the Home menu option (if necessary). In the Font area in the Home ribbon, click the Clear All Formatting icon, as shown in Figure 14.6. (If your PowerPoint window width is small, click the Font icon and then click the Clear All Formatting icon.)

The text reverts to the default Normal paragraph style. However, if this text has other paragraph formatting—for example, it's in a bulleted or numbered list—the paragraph formatting remains intact.

FIGURE 14.6 Clear All Formatting icon

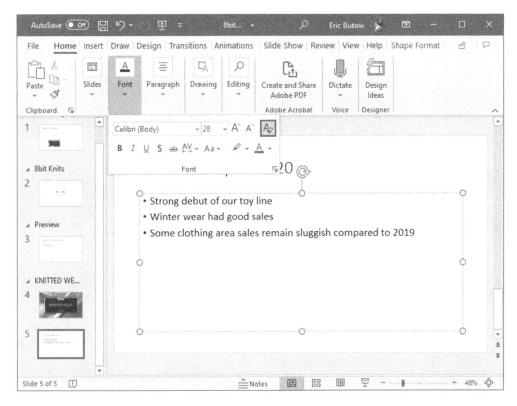

 What if you want to clear the formatting of all the text in a slide area? Press Ctrl+A to select all the text and then click Clear All Formatting in the Font section in the Home ribbon.

Formatting Text in Multiple Columns

If you want to put text into more than one column on a slide to make it easier to read, here are the steps to add multiple columns in a PowerPoint slide:

1. In the slide area that contains the text, click anywhere in the text.

2. Click the Home menu option, if necessary.

3. In the Paragraph section in the Home ribbon, click the Add Or Remove Columns icon. (If your PowerPoint window width is small, click the Paragraph icon and then click the Line Spacing icon.)

4. Select the number of columns from the drop-down list (see Figure 14.7). The default is One. You can select as many as Three.

FIGURE 14.7   Add Or Remove Columns menu

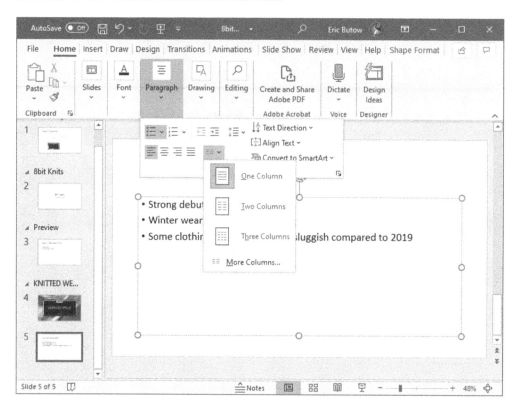

If you want even more control over your columns, click More Columns in the drop-down list. The Columns dialog box appears so that you can change the number of columns and the spacing between each column.

Creating Bulleted and Numbered Lists

An entry in a list, whether it's a few words or a few sentences, is treated as a paragraph. PowerPoint makes it easy to change a paragraph to a numbered list or a bulleted list.

Create a List

You don't need to do anything special to create a numbered or bulleted list.

Start a numbered list by typing **1**, a period (**.**), a space, and then your text. When you finish typing your text, press Enter. PowerPoint formats the first entry in your list and places you on the next line in the numbered list with the number 2.

Create a bulleted list by typing an asterisk (*), a space, and then your text. When you're done typing, press Enter. The asterisk changes to a black circle and places you on the next line with another black circle to the left so that you can continue working on your list.

You can also start a numbered or bulleted list from within the Home ribbon. If you don't see it, click the Home menu option. In the ribbon, click the Bullets or the Numbering icon in the Paragraph section, as shown in Figure 14.8. (If your PowerPoint window width is small, click the Paragraph icon and then click the Bullets or Numbering icon.)

FIGURE 14.8 Bullets (left) and Numbering (right) icons

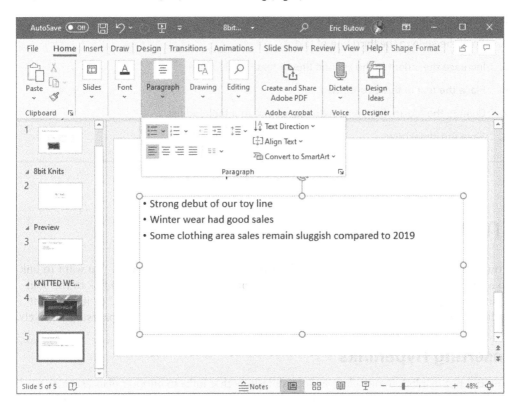

Now you see the number 1 or a bullet circle to the left of your cursor, and you can start typing your list. When you reach the last item in your list, press Enter twice to switch the bullets or numbering off.

Create a List from Existing Text

Using the Home ribbon, you can easily create a list from text you've already written. Start by selecting the text you want to convert to a list, and then click the Bullets or Numbering icon in the Paragraph section. Each paragraph in the text appears as a separate number or bullet in the list.

You can continue the list by clicking the last item in the list and then pressing Enter. If the list is fine as is, click outside the selection.

EXERCISE 14.1

Formatting Text

1. Create a new slideshow.

2. In the first slide, type six lines of text.

3. Apply a style to the first line of text.

4. Copy the style to the third line of text.

5. Increase the indent in the second line of text to 0.5 inches.

6. Place the text in three columns.

7. Change the fourth, fifth, and sixth line of text to a bulleted list.

8. Save the slideshow.

Inserting Links

PowerPoint allows you to add a hyperlink to your document, such as when you want to link to an external web page that you want your audience to see. If you want to link to the Summary Zoom page that you learned about in Chapter 13, "Managing Slides," or if you want to link to selected slides, you can link to Summary Zoom and Slide Zoom pages, respectively.

Inserting Hyperlinks

You can put in a link in one place in your slideshow that links to another place, such as a link on Slide 3 that will take you to the slide that contains the list of topics covered in your presentation.

Here's how to add a link:

1. Click the text in the slide that you want to use in the link.

2. Click the Insert menu option.

3. In the Links section in the Insert ribbon, click the Link icon. (If your PowerPoint window width is small, click the Links icon and then click the Link icon.)

4. Select Insert Link from the drop-down menu.

5. In the Insert Hyperlink dialog box, shown in Figure 14.9, click the Place In This Document option under Link To.

FIGURE 14.9 Insert Hyperlink dialog box

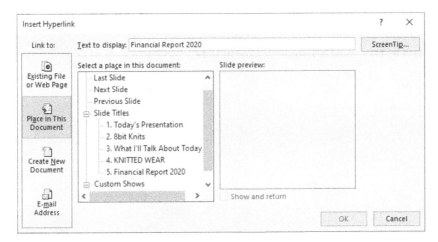

6. Click what you want to link to. In this example, click Financial Report 2020 in the Select A Place In This Document list box.

7. Click OK.

The link in the text is blue with an underline. When you run your slideshow and click the link, the linked slide appears on the screen.

Inserting Section Zoom Links and Slide Zoom Links

When you create a Section Zoom or Slide Zoom, you can link to those zoom slides easily. Although Chapter 13 didn't cover adding a Slide Zoom, I will show you how to create a new Slide Zoom in this section and then link to it.

Linking to a Summary Zoom Slide

Link to a *Summary Zoom* slide by following these steps:

1. Click the text in the slide that you want to use in the link.

2. Click the Insert menu option.

3. In the Links section in the Insert ribbon, click the Link icon. (If your PowerPoint window width is small, click the Links icon and then click the Link icon.)

4. Select Insert Link from the drop-down menu.

5. In the Insert Hyperlink dialog box, click the Place In This Document option under Link To.

6. Select the Summary Zoom slide you want to link to, which is the first slide in this example. The Summary Zoom slide has only the name of the slide, which is Slide 1 (see Figure 14.10).

7. Click OK.

FIGURE 14.10   Selected Summary Zoom slide

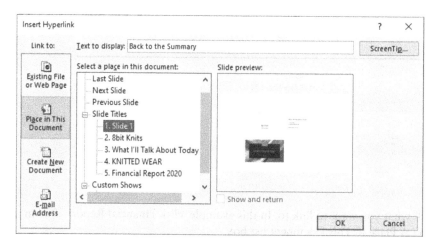

The link in the text is blue and underlined. When you run your slideshow and click the link, the Summary Zoom slide appears on the screen.

Creating a Slide Zoom Slide

A *Slide Zoom* is good to use when you have a small slideshow so you can have links to all of your slides from within the Slide Zoom slide. Before you can link to a slide with a Slide Zoom, you need to create the Slide Zoom first. Here's how to do that:

1. Click the slide below which the Slide Zoom slide will appear.

2. Click the Insert menu option.

3. In the Slides section in the Insert ribbon, click New Slide.

4. Select the Blank thumbnail-sized slide template from the drop-down list.

5. In the Links section in the Insert ribbon, click the Zoom icon. (If your PowerPoint window width is small, click the Links icon and then click the Zoom icon.)

6. Select Slide Zoom from the drop-down menu.

7. In the Insert Slide Zoom dialog box, shown in Figure 14.11, click the thumbnail-sized slide(s) that you want to include in the Slide Zoom slide.

8. Click Insert.

FIGURE 14.11   Insert Slide Zoom dialog box

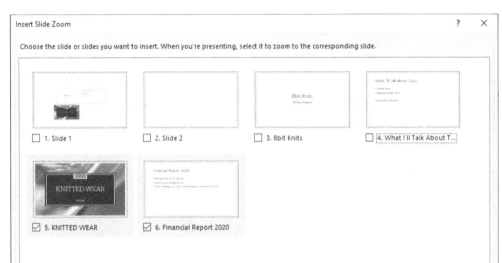

Thumbnail-sized slides appear within the slide (see Figure 14.12) tiled one atop another. You can move slides around by clicking the part of the slide that you want to move and then clicking and dragging the slide to a new location on the parent slide.

When you click one of the thumbnail-sized slides in the Slide Zoom slide, sizing handles appear around the slide so that you can click one of the handles and drag the handle to resize the slide within the parent slide.

Linking to a Slide Zoom Slide

Now that you have created a Slide Zoom slide, you can link to it from another slide. The process is similar to linking to a Summary Zoom slide:

1. Click the text in the slide that you want to use in the link.
2. Click the Insert menu option.
3. In the Links section in the Insert ribbon, click the Link icon. (If your PowerPoint window width is small, click the Links icon and then click the Link icon.)
4. Select Insert Link from the drop-down menu.
5. In the Insert Hyperlink dialog box, click the Place In This Document option under Link To.

FIGURE 14.12   Thumbnail-sized slides within the Slide Zoom

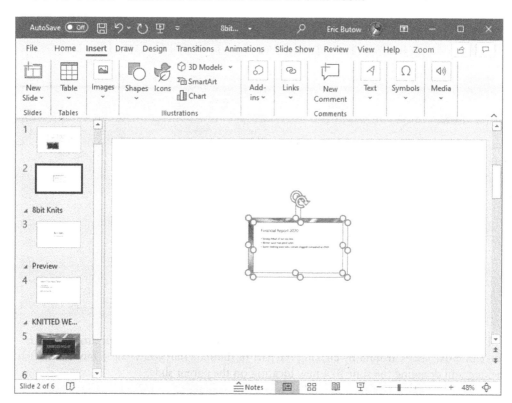

6. Select the Slide Zoom slide you want to link to, which is the second slide in this example. The Slide Zoom slide has only the name of the slide, which is Slide 2 (see Figure 14.13).

7. Click OK.

FIGURE 14.13   Selected Slide Zoom slide

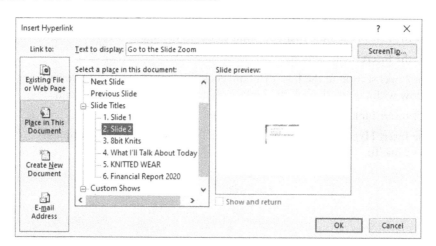

Like other text links, the link text is blue and underlined. When you run your slideshow and click the link, the Slide Zoom slide appears on the screen.

EXERCISE 14.2

Inserting Links

1. Open the slideshow that you created in Exercise 14.1.

2. In Slide 4, add text (if necessary) and then add a hyperlink to Slide 1 in the text.

3. Create a Slide Zoom slide after Slide 1 in the slideshow.

4. In Slide 5, add text (if necessary) and then add a hyperlink to the Slide Zoom slide in the text.

5. Save the slideshow.

Inserting and Formatting Images

PowerPoint makes it easy to add images, apply styles and effects to those images, as well as add screenshots and clippings of your screen into a slide so that you don't have to switch back and forth between your presentation and another window or your Windows desktop.

You can add pictures stored on your computer, stock images that were installed with PowerPoint, or pictures available on the http://office.com website. Here's how:

1. In the slide, place your cursor where you want to insert the image.

2. Click the Insert menu option.

3. In the Insert ribbon, click Pictures in the Images section. (If your PowerPoint window width is small, click the Images icon and then click Pictures.)

4. From the drop-down menu, shown in Figure 14.14, select one of the following options:

   This Device: Click this option to browse for and select a photo from your computer.

   Stock Images: Click this option to view and open a stock image on your computer.

   Online Pictures: Click this option to view and open an image from Office.com.

   For this example, I'll open a stock image. By default, the Images dialog box opens with the stock images displayed selected, as shown in Figure 14.15.

5. Scroll up and down in the list of thumbnail images until you find the one that you want, and then click the image.

6. Click Insert.

FIGURE 14.14 Pictures drop-down menu

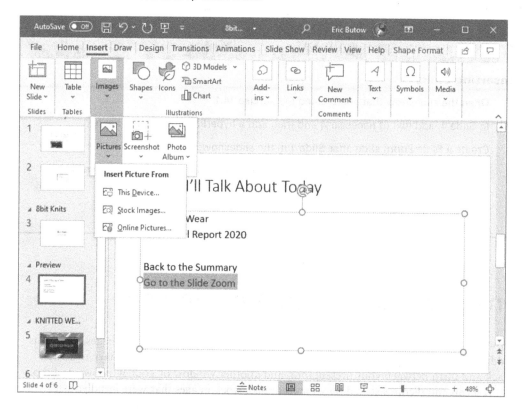

FIGURE 14.15 Images dialog box

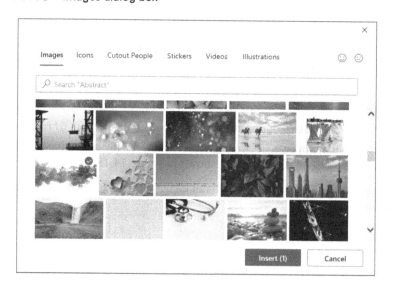

The image appears in the document, and text moves underneath the image. You'll learn how to move the image and change the text wrapping style later in this chapter.

Resizing and Cropping Images

If an inserted image is smaller than the size of the slide, then PowerPoint places the entire image in the center of the slide. If the image is larger than the size of the slide, PowerPoint automatically resizes the image so that the height of the image is the same as the slide height.

PowerPoint makes it easy to resize images in a slide. When you want to crop an image to focus on a specific area of an image, you can crop an image to remove many of the features that you find extraneous.

Resize an Image

Once you click an image, you have two ways to resize it:

- Click and drag one of the sizing handles to change the width or height. If you want to change both the width and height, then click and drag one of the corner sizing handles.

- In the Picture Format ribbon that appears after you click the image, type the height and width in the Shape Height and Shape Width boxes, respectively, in the Size section (see Figure 14.16).

FIGURE 14.16   Shape Height (top) and Width (bottom) boxes

Crop an Image

Crop an image within a slide by following these steps:

1. Click the image in the slide.

2. In the Size section in the Picture Format ribbon, click Crop.

3. From the drop-down menu, shown in Figure 14.17, select Crop.

FIGURE 14.17 The Crop menu option

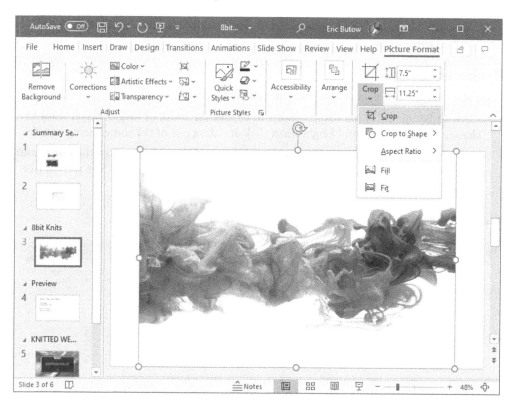

4. Click and hold the mouse button on one of the black resizing handles around the perimeter of the image.

   The cursor changes to a T- or L-shaped bar depending on the handle that you select.

5. Drag the mouse pointer until the cropped image appears the way that you want.

   As you drag, the image area that you are removing appears in dark gray.

6. When you're done, release the mouse button.

7. In the Size section in the Picture Format ribbon, click the Crop icon (see Figure 14.18).

   PowerPoint replaces the crop handles with sizing handles around the cropped image.

FIGURE 14.18   The Crop icon in the Picture Format ribbon

Applying Built-In Styles and Effects to Images

PowerPoint also allows you to set effects from within the Picture Format ribbon. However, if you don't need to have fine-tuned effects on your picture, PowerPoint has prebuilt styles for you that you can apply to the selected picture by clicking the appropriate tile in the ribbon.

Apply a Picture Style

Apply a *picture style* from the ribbon by following these steps:

1. Click the image in the slide.

2. In the Picture Styles section in the Picture Format ribbon, move the mouse pointer over the thumbnail-sized style tiles in the Picture Styles section, as shown in Figure 14.19. (If the PowerPoint window isn't very wide, click Quick Styles in the ribbon to view a drop-down ribbon with the style icons.)

    As you move the pointer over every style icon, the picture in your document changes to reflect the style.

3. Apply the style by clicking the icon.

FIGURE 14.19 Quick Styles style tiles

If you don't like any of the styles, move the icon away from the row of styles and the picture reverts to its default state.

Add a Picture Effect

Here's how to choose and add a *picture effect*:

1. Click the picture.

2. In the Picture Styles section in the Picture Format ribbon, click Picture Effects.

3. In the drop-down menu, move the mouse pointer to one of the seven effects that you want to add. I selected Shadow in this example.

4. In the side menu, move the mouse pointer over the tile that contains the shadow style. The style is applied to the picture in your slide so that you can see what it looks like (see Figure 14.20).

5. When you find an effect that you like, click the tile in the menu.

FIGURE 14.20   Offset: Center shadow style applied to the picture

If you want to change the effect, select Options from the bottom of the menu. For example, in Shadow, select Shadow Options. The Format Picture pane appears on the right side of the PowerPoint window so that you can make more detailed changes, such as the color of the shadow.

Inserting Screenshots and Screen Clippings

You can take a photo of another window and add it directly into your document from within PowerPoint. You can also clip a portion of your screen within PowerPoint and add it to your document automatically.

Screenshot

Add a *screenshot* to your document by following these steps:

1. Place your cursor where you want to insert the screenshot.

2. Click the Insert menu option.

3. In the Insert ribbon, click Screenshot in the Images section. (If your PowerPoint window width is small, click the Images icon and then click Screenshot.) If any windows are open, PowerPoint scans your computer and places thumbnail-sized images of the windows within the drop-down list, as shown in Figure 14.21.

FIGURE 14.21 Screenshots drop-down list

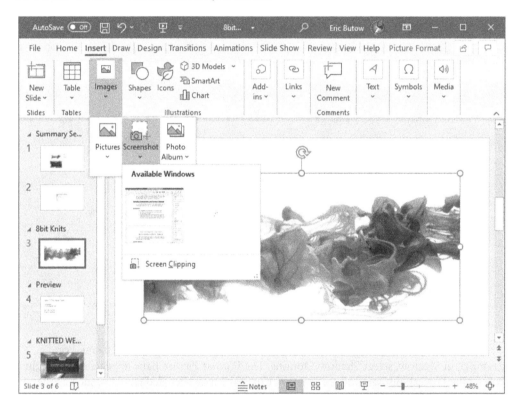

The currently open PowerPoint window is one of the windows that PowerPoint finds. When you click the window in the list, PowerPoint places the screenshot at the insertion point in your document.

Screen Clipping

You can clip the entire screen or a portion of it. Here's how to add a *screen clipping*:

1. Place your cursor where you want to insert the screenshot.
2. Click the Insert menu option.

3. In the Insert ribbon, click Screenshot in the Images section. (If your PowerPoint window width is small, click the Images icon and then click Screenshot.)

4. Select Screen Clipping from the drop-down list. PowerPoint automatically opens the last window that you had open prior to using PowerPoint. If you didn't have a window open, you see the desktop. The screen has a transparent white overlay, and the mouse pointer changes to a cross, which means that PowerPoint is ready for you to capture the screen.

5. Move the cursor to the location where you want to start capturing the screen.

6. Hold down the mouse button and drag until you've captured your selection (see Figure 14.22).

FIGURE 14.22   Capture area

7. Release the mouse button.

The clipped image appears within the slide and the Design Ideas pane appears at the right side of the PowerPoint window so that you can view suggestions for placing the screen clipping and any other images within the slide. You can apply the suggested design by clicking the thumbnail image within the Design Ideas pane.

EXERCISE 14.3

Inserting and Formatting Images

1. Open the slideshow that you created in Exercise 14.1.

2. In Slide 1, add a new stock image.

3. Resize the image to a smaller size of your choosing in the slide.

4. Apply a picture style to the image.

5. Go to Slide 3.

6. Add a screenshot to the slide.

7. Save the slideshow.

Inserting and Formatting Graphic Elements

PowerPoint makes it easy to choose and insert shapes and text boxes, and even annotate your slides with handwriting, which is what PowerPoint calls *digital ink*.

After you add a shape, text box, or handwriting, PowerPoint gives you plenty of tools to format them to make them look the way you want and then place them where you want on the page. You can even convert a handwritten drawing into a shape.

Inserting and Changing Shapes

PowerPoint contains many built-in shapes that you can add to your document, from lines to callouts like the speech balloons that you find in graphic novels and comic strips. When you add a shape, you place the item on the slide and then size the shape to your needs.

Add a shape by following these steps:

1. Select the slide where you want to add the shape.

2. Click the Insert menu option.

3. In the Insert ribbon, click Shapes in the Illustrations section.

4. Select a shape icon from the drop-down list (see Figure 14.23). The mouse pointer changes from an arrow to a cross.

FIGURE 14.23   The shapes drop-down list

5. Move the pointer to the location in your slide where you want to add the shape.

6. Hold down the mouse button, and then drag the shape to the size you want.

7. When you're done, release the mouse button.

The shape appears in front of the text in the slide. You can resize the shape by clicking and dragging one of the sizing handles around the perimeter of the shape.

You can also add an *action button*, which is a button in your slide that performs a specific function when you click it. For example, when you insert the Play button, you can change what the Play button does.

Adding an action button is beyond the purview of the MO-300 exam, but you can still add one and see what it looks like by clicking and dragging one of the buttons from the action button section at the bottom of the shapes drop-down list that you saw in Figure 14.23.

Drawing by Using Digital Ink

If you ever need to annotate your slides in a presentation or in notes, and you would rather not type those annotations, you can write them within the slide using what Microsoft calls *digital ink*. Handwritten annotations are free form, so you can write words and draw pictures.

Turn On the Draw Menu Option

You use the Draw menu option to draw on a slide, and PowerPoint automatically adds that option to the menu when you work on a computer with a touch-enabled screen. If you don't see the Draw menu option, you can add it yourself by following these steps:

1. Click the File menu option.

2. Click Options at the bottom-left corner of the PowerPoint window.

3. In the PowerPoint Options dialog box, click Customize Ribbon in the menu on the left side of the dialog box.

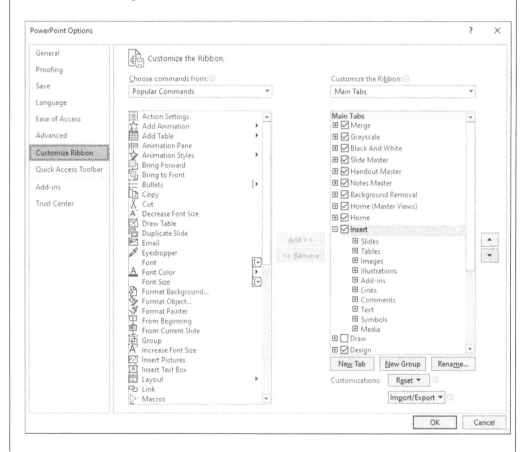

4. In the Customize The Ribbon list on the right side of the dialog box, select the Draw
    check box.

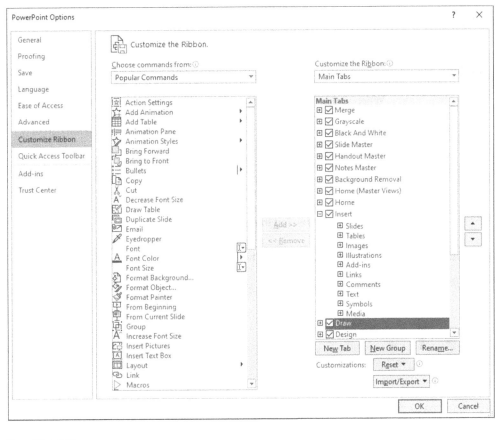

5. Click OK.

The Draw menu option appears between Insert and Design in the menu bar.

Draw on a slide using digital ink by following these steps:

1. Click the slide you want to draw on in the left pane.

2. Click the Draw menu option.

3. In the Drawing Tools section in the Draw ribbon, click one of the three drawing icons:
    Pen (Black), Pen (Red), or Highlighter.

4. Move the mouse pointer over the slide.

5. Click and hold on the spot where you want to start drawing, and then drag to draw.

6. When you're finished, release the mouse button.

Your drawing appears on the slide. Repeat steps 5 and 6 to draw in other areas within the slide.

Here are two things to keep in mind as you draw on a slide:

- When you click a drawing icon in the Draw ribbon, the pen icon becomes larger and a down arrow appears to the lower-right of the icon. Click the icon to open a drop-down menu that allows you to change the pen or highlighter thickness and color.

- If you want to erase anything you've drawn on a slide, click the Eraser icon in the Draw ribbon that you saw in Figure 14.24. Then click on the drawing (such as a not-so-straight line) and PowerPoint deletes that drawing. Click on every drawing in the slide with the Eraser tool to remove each drawing that you added.

FIGURE 14.24   The Draw ribbon and digital ink on the slide

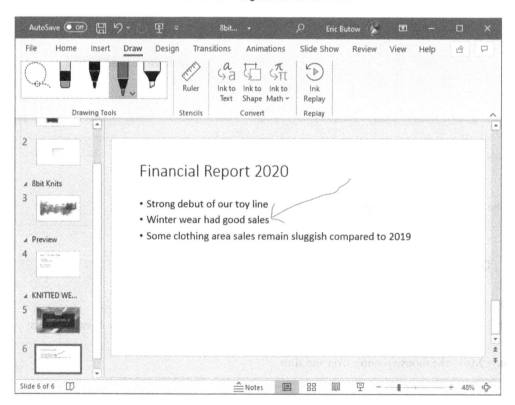

Adding Text to Shapes and Text Boxes

After you add a shape, PowerPoint gives you the ability to add text to a shape. And after you add a text box, PowerPoint makes it easy to add text within the box.

Add Text to a Shape

In a shape, start by right-clicking anywhere in your shape and then clicking Edit Text in the context menu, as shown in Figure 14.25.

FIGURE 14.25   Edit Text option

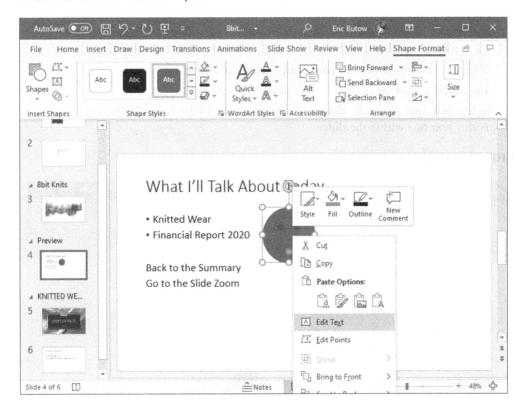

The cursor appears in the center of the shape so that you can type your text. When you finish typing, click outside the text box or the shape.

Add a Text Box

Before you can add text to a text box, you need to know how to add a text box first, so follow these steps:

1. In the left pane, click the slide in which you want to add the text box.

2. Click the Insert menu option.

3. In the Text section in the Insert ribbon, click Text Box. (If your PowerPoint window width is small, click the Text icon and then click Text Box.)

4. Move the mouse pointer over the slide. The cursor changes to a straight line with a small perpendicular line near the bottom, which makes the cursor look like a little sword.

5. Click and hold on the spot where you want to add the text box and then drag the mouse. As you drag, the cursor changes to a cross and you see the boundary of the text box.

6. When the text box is the size you want, release the mouse button.

7. The cursor is blinking in the text box so that you can start typing text.

The text box appears on the slide, as shown in Figure 14.26. Repeat steps 5 and 6 to create another text box within the slide.

FIGURE 14.26 The text box in the slide

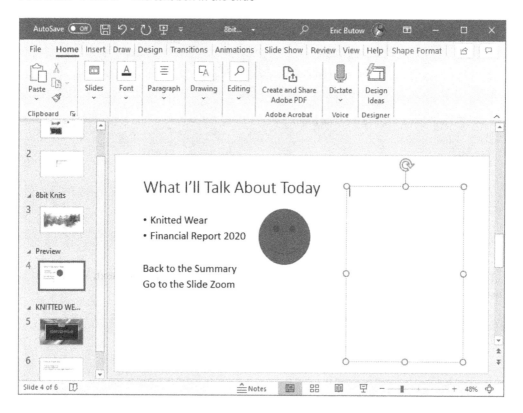

Resizing Shapes and Text Boxes

PowerPoint makes it easy to resize shapes and text boxes. You can do so in one of two ways: clicking and dragging one of the handles around the boundary of the shape or text box, or changing the size in the Shape Format ribbon.

Resize a Shape

All you need to do to resize a shape manually is to click the shape, click and hold one sizing handle around the boundary of the shape, and then drag the shape until it's the size you want.

If you want to set the exact height and/or width of the shape, type the measurement in inches in the Height and/or Width boxes in the Size section in the Shape Format ribbon, as shown in Figure 14.27. (If your PowerPoint window width is small, click the Size icon and then type the height and/or width.)

FIGURE 14.27   Height and Width boxes

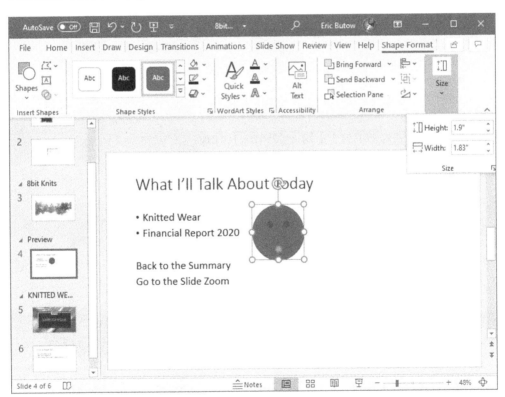

You can set the height and/or width as precisely as in hundredths of an inch. After you type the height and/or width and then press Enter, the size of the shape changes in the slide.

Resize a Text Box

You can resize a text box manually by clicking anywhere in the text box, clicking and holding one sizing handle around the boundary of the text box, and then dragging the text box until it's the size you want.

If you want to set the exact height and/or width of the shape, type the measurement in inches in the Height and/or Width boxes, as shown in Figure 14.28. (If your PowerPoint window width is small, click the Size icon in the Shape Format ribbon and then type the height and/or width.)

FIGURE 14.28 Height and Width boxes in the Size section

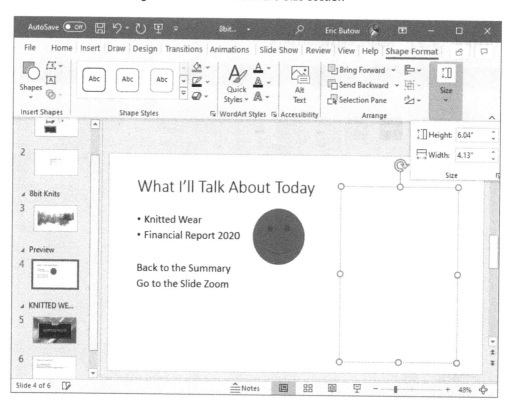

You can set the height and/or width as precisely as in hundredths of an inch. After you type the height and/or width and then press Enter, PowerPoint changes the size of the text box in the slide.

Formatting Shapes and Text Boxes

When you want to format shapes and text boxes, you can do so by clicking the shape or text box and then clicking the Shape Format menu option.

Shapes

Within the Shape Format menu ribbon, shown in Figure 14.29, you can make a variety of changes to the shape, including the following:

FIGURE 14.29   Shape Format ribbon

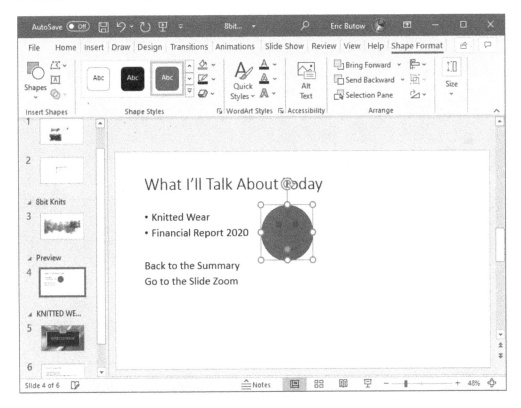

- Changing the shape or editing points in the shape by clicking Edit Shape in the Insert Shapes section
- Changing shape styles, including the shape fill, outline, and effects, in the Shape Styles section
- Changing the size of the shape by typing the height and/or width in the Size section as discussed earlier in this chapter

Text Boxes

If you want to format other features of your text, such as the font and paragraph settings, you can format text in a text box just as you would in the rest of your document.

Start by selecting the text in the text box that you want to edit. Next, click the Home menu option (if necessary). In the Home ribbon, shown in Figure 14.30, you can change the font and paragraph as you see fit within the Font and Paragraph options. (If your PowerPoint window width is small, you need to click the Font or Paragraph icon to open the drop-down menus and view the editing options.)

FIGURE 14.30 Font and Paragraph icons in the Home ribbon

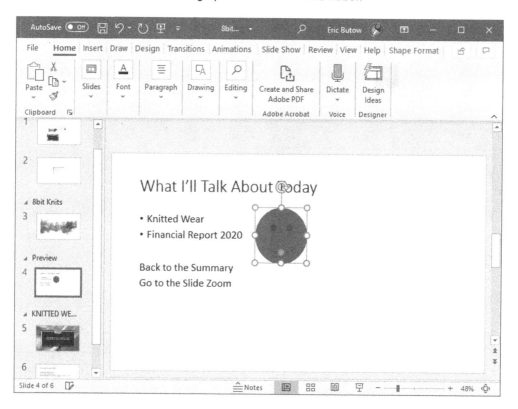

Placing Your Graphics for Easy Reading

Your boss has reviewed your slideshow and she likes it—mostly. She wants to add more shapes on slides so that people can get different representations of each function of the great new product that the company is rolling out. For example, she wants circles with text inside so that each circle points out an important new feature.

There is a limit to the number of graphics that you should add to a document so as not to overwhelm viewers and leave them wondering where they should look . . . or ignore the graphics completely. A reader's eyes follow a pattern as they look across a slide—from the upper-left corner to the lower-right corner, and then to the lower-left corner.

So, if you want to get the attention of your customers (and please your boss), position your graphics in one or more of those locations in your document. When readers visually scan those graphics, they will likely pick up on some of the text that you have in your slide, too.

Applying Built-In Styles to Shapes and Text Boxes

After you add a shape or a text box, you can change the style of the shape. If you have text within a shape or text box, you can change the text within the shape or text box as well as how the text appears.

Apply a Shape Style

You can apply a shape style in the Shape Styles section, as shown in Figure 14.31.

FIGURE 14.31   Shape Styles section

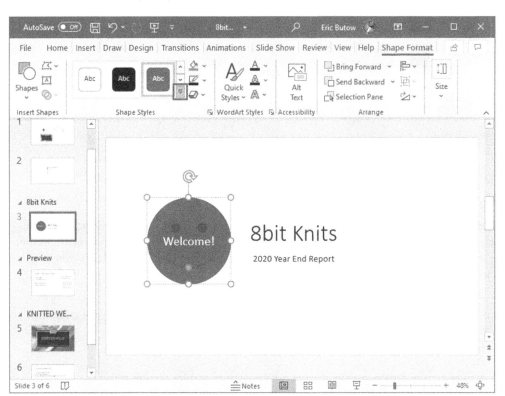

Each style in the style row shows different shape backgrounds, borders, and text colors. If you don't see the style you want, click the More button to the right of the last tile in the style row highlighted in Figure 14.31. It looks like a down arrow with a line above it.

The complete list of built-in style tiles in the drop-down menu appears (see Figure 14.32). Select one of the tiles in the list to apply it to the shape.

FIGURE 14.32 Shape Styles drop-down list

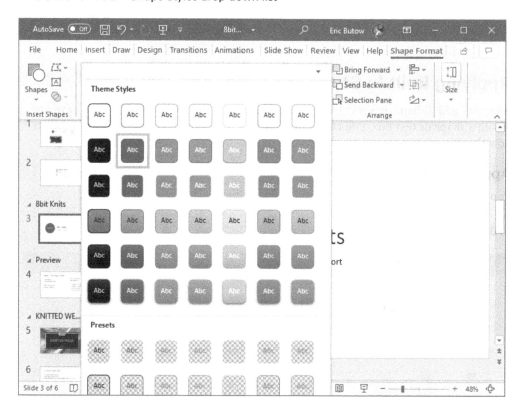

Apply WordArt Styles

With both shapes and text boxes, you can apply WordArt styles to the text inside them by selecting the text in the shape or text box and then clicking the Shape Format menu option.

In the WordArt Styles section in the Shape Format ribbon (see Figure 14.33), you can choose one of three built-in text effects:

- Select Text Fill from the drop-down menu to change the text color.

- Select Text Outline from the drop-down menu to add an outline, including color and outline line width.

- Select Text Effects to view and add other effects to the text. In the drop-down menu, move the mouse pointer over one of the effects to see how each effect appears in your photo. You can choose from Shadow, Reflection, Glow, Bevel, 3-D Rotation, and Transform.

FIGURE 14.33   WordArt Styles section

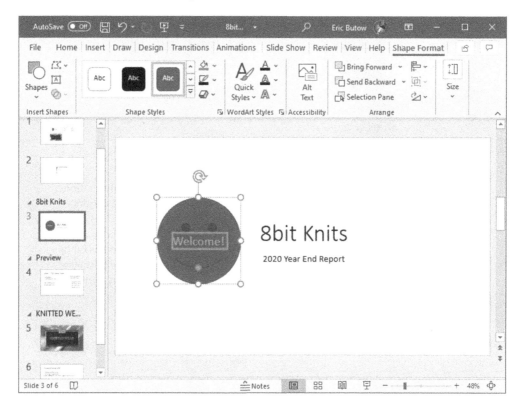

Change Text Appearance

You can change the text appearance in your shape or text box by clicking the shape or text box and then clicking the Home menu option (if necessary).

In the Paragraph section in the Home ribbon, shown in Figure 14.34, you can change the text appearance in one of three ways:

- Click Text Direction to rotate the text 90 degrees or 270 degrees. You can also click Stacked to display the text with all letters stacked on top of each other in a vertical line.

- Click Align Text to align the text vertically with the Top, Middle, or Bottom of the shape. The default is Middle.

- Click Convert To SmartArt to display your text in one of 20 built-in graphic layout formats, such as an organizational chart.

FIGURE 14.34   Paragraph section

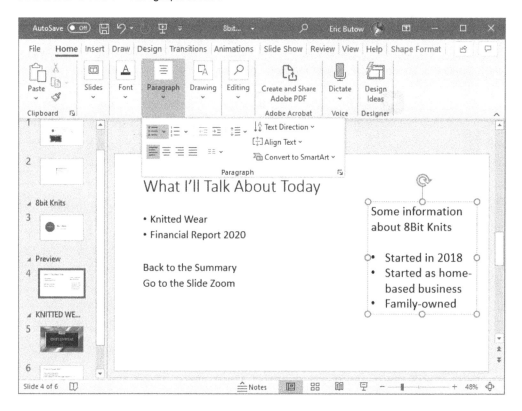

If your PowerPoint window width is small, you need to click the Paragraph icon to open the drop-down menus and view paragraph editing options.

Adding Alt Text to Graphic Elements for Accessibility

Alt text, or alternative text, tells anyone who views your document in PowerPoint what the picture or shape is when the reader moves their mouse pointer over it. If the reader can't see your document, then PowerPoint will use text-to-speech in Windows to read your Alt text to the reader audibly.

Here's how to add Alt text:

1.   Click the picture or shape.
2.   Click the Shape Format or Picture Format menu option.

3. In the Shape Format or Picture Format ribbon, click the Alt Text icon in the Accessibility section.

4. In the Alt Text pane on the right side of the PowerPoint window (see Figure 14.35), type one or two sentences in the text box to describe the object and its context.

FIGURE 14.35 Alt Text pane

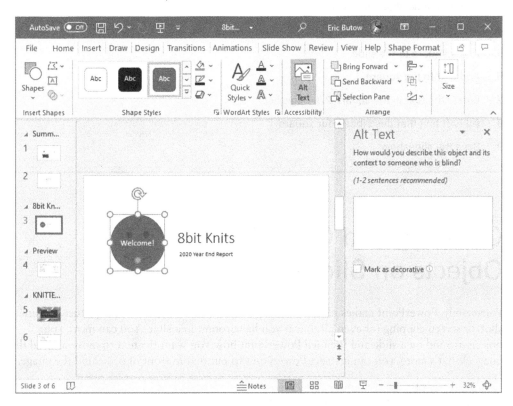

Some images, especially stock images, already have this information in the text box, but you can change it.

5. Click the Mark As Decorative check box if your image, shape, or SmartArt graphic adds visual interest but isn't informative, such as a line.

6. When you're done, close the pane by clicking the Close (X) icon in the upper-right corner of the pane.

EXERCISE 14.4

Inserting and Formatting Graphic Elements

1. Open the slideshow that you created in Exercise 14.1.

2. In the left pane, click the slide where you want to add a shape.

3. Add a triangle shape to the slide.

4. Add text to the square.

5. Add a square to the slide.

6. Add text to the square.

7. Rotate the text in the square 270 degrees.

8. Add Alt text that describes your square.

9. Save the slideshow.

Ordering and Grouping Objects on Slides

Fortunately, PowerPoint makes it easy to change where you can put a shape, picture, screenshot, or screen clipping (or even all four if you have room) in a slide. You can move your objects around on a slide and then tell PowerPoint how you want the text to move around the image. What's more, you can instruct PowerPoint to put text in front of or behind the image.

Ordering Shapes, Images, and Text Boxes

When you add a new shape, image, or text box, the object appears in front of the rest of the text on the page, if any. Now you can move the shape, image, or text box in your document by moving the mouse pointer over the image, holding down the mouse button, and then moving the image.

If you want the shape, image, or text box to appear in front of or behind other elements, including text, shapes, and images, you can do so by clicking the Home menu option (if necessary). Within the Drawing section, click Arrange. (If your PowerPoint window isn't very wide, click the Drawing icon and then click Arrange.)

The Drawing drop-down list appears, as shown in Figure 14.36.

FIGURE 14.36   Drawing drop-down list options

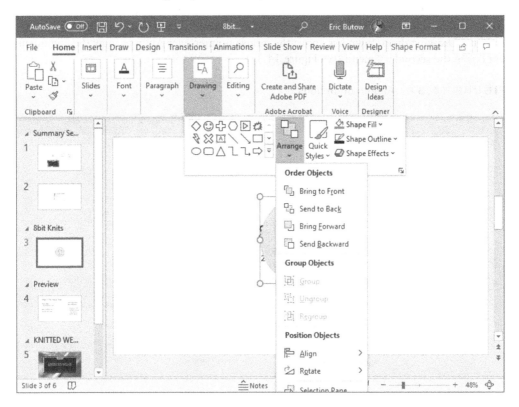

Within the Order Objects section at the top of the drop-down list, you can change the stacking order of a shape, image, or text box in a slide in one of four ways:

Bring To Front: Moves the object to the top layer in the stack. Every other object appears behind the object in front.

Send To Back: Moves the object to the bottom layer in the stack. All other objects appear in front of the object at the bottom layer.

Bring Forward: Moves the object up one layer in the stack

Send Backward: Moves the object down one layer in the stack

Aligning Shapes, Images, and Text Boxes

When you add a new shape, image, or text box, the object appears in front of the rest of the text on the page, if any. Now you can move the shape or image in your document by moving the mouse pointer over the image, holding down the mouse button, and then moving the image.

If you need to align your shape, image, or text box within a slide, start by clicking the Home menu option (if necessary). Within the Drawing section, click Arrange. (If your PowerPoint window isn't very wide, click the Drawing icon and then click Arrange.)

In the Drawing drop-down list, move the mouse pointer over Align to view the alignment options in the secondary menu (see Figure 14.37).

FIGURE 14.37 Alignment options

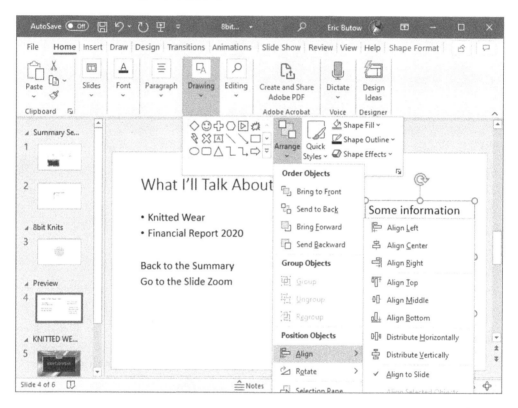

You can change the alignment of a shape, image, or text box in a slide by clicking one of the following six options:

Align Left: Aligns the object at the left side of the slide

Align Center: Aligns the object vertically in the center of the slide

Align Right: Aligns the object at the right side of the slide

Align Top: Aligns the object at the top of the slide

Align Middle: Aligns the object horizontally in the middle of the slide

Align Bottom: Aligns the object at the bottom of the slide

You can click more than one option to align the object both horizontally and vertically within the slide. For example, click Align Center and then click Align Bottom to align the object horizontally in the center bottom of the slide.

Grouping Shapes and Images

You can move several images or shapes by grouping them together. Start by selecting the first object, and then hold down the Ctrl key. Next, select the other images and/or shapes that you want to group.

Now click the Home menu option (if necessary). Within the Drawing section, click Arrange. (If your PowerPoint window isn't very wide, click the Drawing icon and then click Arrange.)

From the Drawing drop-down list, select Group in the Group Objects section (see Figure 14.38).

FIGURE 14.38   Group option in the drop-down menu

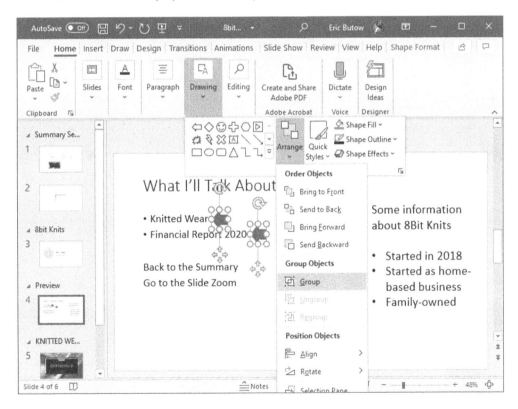

Now you can move all the grouped objects around the slide. You can ungroup them by clicking Arrange in the Home ribbon and then selecting Ungroup from the drop-down menu.

Displaying Alignment Tools

To figure out where you want to align your shape, image, and/or text box within a slide, you can display *guides* and *gridlines* to have PowerPoint give you a good idea of where it places objects. You can also display *rulers* above and to the left of the slide, just as you can in Word.

Display the rulers, guide, and gridlines by following these steps:

1. Click the View menu option.

2. In the Show section in the View ribbon, select the Ruler check box. (If your PowerPoint window isn't very wide, click the Show icon and then select the Ruler check box.)

3. Select the Gridlines check box.

4. Select the Guides check box.

Now you see the rulers, the gridlines with dotted lines throughout the slide, and the guides with dashed lines through the vertical and horizontal center of the slide (see Figure 14.39).

FIGURE 14.39 The ruler, gridlines, and guides

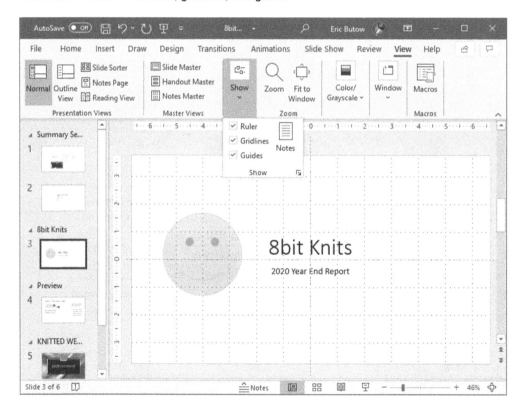

As you move an object around the slide, the object will snap to a point in the slide and highlight the gridline or guide. For example, if you move a shape to the horizontal center of the slide, the horizontal guide appears in red when the object snaps to the guide.

You can hide the rulers, gridlines, and/or guides by repeating steps 2, 3, and/or 4 depending on what you want to hide.

EXERCISE 14.5

Ordering and Grouping Objects on Slides

1. Open the slideshow that you created in Exercise 14.4, if necessary.

2. Align the triangle at the top center of the slide.

3. Align the square at the middle center of the slide.

4. Order the shapes so that the triangle is in front of the square.

5. Select and group both shapes.

6. Display the guides in the slide.

7. Position the group so that the shapes appear in the center of the slide, both vertically and horizontally.

8. Save the slideshow.

Summary

This chapter started with a discussion on how to format shapes, images, and text boxes. You learned how to apply formatting and styles to text within shapes and text boxes, format text in your slide within multiple columns, as well as create bulleted and numbered lists.

I followed up by discussing how to insert hyperlinks, Section Zoom links, and Slide Zoom links. Then you learned how to resize and crop images in a slide, add built-in styles and effects to images, insert screenshots, and add screen clippings to a slide.

Next, you learned how to insert and format shapes and text boxes, draw on a slide, add text to shapes and text boxes, and add Alt text to a graphic object to ensure that people who can't see that object will know what that image, shape, screenshot, or screen clipping is about.

Finally, you learned how to order shapes and images on a slide, including ordering, aligning, and grouping shapes and images. You also learned how to display alignment tools on a slide to help you place the shape and/or image.

Key Terms

Alt text	pictures
digital ink	rulers
Format Painter	screen clippings
gridlines	screenshots
guides	Section Zoom
indent	Slide Zoom
picture effect	spacing
picture style	

Exam Essentials

Understand how to format text.   PowerPoint allows you to apply styles and other text formatting, format text in multiple columns, and create both bulleted and numbered lists.

Know how to insert different types of links.   Understand how to insert hyperlinks, Section Zoom links, and Slide Zoom links, and know the differences between all three link types.

Be able to add and format different types of graphics.   PowerPoint allows you to add a variety of shapes and photos to your slideshow. You need to know how to add shapes, pictures, screenshots of open windows, and clip portions of your screen to your slideshow. You also need to know how to resize and crop images as well as apply built-in styles and effects to an image.

Know how to draw on a slide.   Be able to use digital ink within PowerPoint to draw directly onto a slide to make a point and/or annotate a slide.

Understand how to insert and format shapes and text boxes.   Know how to add a shape, resize and format a shape, apply built-in styles to a shape, and insert text into a shape.

Know how to add and format text boxes.   Understand how to add a text box that is separate from other text on a page, modify a text box, and format text in a text box.

Be able to add Alt text.   Understand why Alt text is important for your readers and know how to add Alt text to a graphic or picture.

Understand how to order and group shapes, images, and text boxes on slides.   Know how to order objects so that they appear above or below other objects, align objects in a slide, group shapes and images, and display alignment tools including rulers, gridlines, and guides.

Review Questions

1. How do you apply a format from one selected block of text to another block?

    A. By clicking the Format Painter icon in the Home ribbon and selecting the other block

    B. By seeing what style the block of text has in the Home ribbon or Styles text

    C. By searching for the special character in the Navigation pane

    D. From the Symbol window

2. How does a link appear in your slide?

    A. Blue text

    B. Bold text

    C. Blue and underlined text

    D. Underlined text

3. How do you apply a specific picture style in the Picture Format ribbon?

    A. Click the Corrections icon.

    B. Click one of the picture styles tiles in the Picture Styles area.

    C. Click Picture Effects.

    D. Click Change Picture.

4. Why should you add a text box?

    A. Because it's easier to read

    B. Because you need to add one before you can start typing text in the slide

    C. You don't need to add one because you can add text directly on a slide

    D. To have text separate from the rest of the text in your slideshow

5. What ordering tool do you use when you want to move an object down a level in the stack?

    A. Send To Back

    B. Align Bottom

    C. Send Backward

    D. Align Middle

6. When you add a link to a Summary Zoom slide, what options do you have to select in the Insert Hyperlink dialog box? (Choose all that apply.)

    A. Existing File Or Web Page

    B. Place In This Document

    C. The first named slide title in the page

    D. The numbered slide that corresponds to the Summary Zoom slide

7. What menu option do you click to change the indentation and spacing of text in a slide?

    A. Home

    B. Shape Format

    C. View

    D. Design

8. How do you add text to a shape?

    A. Use the Shape Format ribbon.

    B. Click the Draw ribbon.

    C. Use the Insert ribbon.

    D. Right-click the shape.

9. Why should you add Alt text to shapes and images?

    A. Because it's required for all images in a PowerPoint slideshow

    B. To help people who can't see the shape or image know what the shape or image is about

    C. Because PowerPoint won't save your document until you do

    D. Because you want to be as informative as possible

10. What are the three alignment tools that you can display in a slide? (Choose all that apply.)

    A. Guides

    B. Gridlines

    C. Slide Master

    D. Rulers

Chapter

15

Inserting Tables, Charts, SmartArt, 3D Models, and Media

MICROSOFT EXAM OBJECTIVES COVERED IN THIS CHAPTER:

✓ **Insert tables, charts, SmartArt, 3D models, and media**

- Insert and format tables
    - Create and insert tables
    - Insert and delete table rows and columns
    - Apply built-in table styles
- Insert and modify charts
    - Create and insert charts
    - Modify charts
- Insert and modify SmartArt graphics
    - Insert SmartArt graphics
    - Convert lists to SmartArt graphics
    - Add and modify SmartArt graphic content
- Insert and modify 3D models
    - Insert 3D models
    - Modify 3D models
- Insert and manage media
    - Insert audio and video clips
    - Create and insert screen recordings
    - Configure media playback options

Tables are effective in conveying information in a slide that your audience can digest easily. This chapter begins by showing you how to create tables. You will also learn how to insert and delete rows and columns from a table, as well as apply built-in table styles.

Then I will show you how to create a chart in a slide. You will also see how to modify charts by adding data series, switch between rows and columns, and add and modify various chart elements.

Next you will learn about custom diagrams—which Microsoft calls SmartArt—so that you can add things like organization and process charts easily. You will also learn how to convert lists to SmartArt graphics as well as add and modify SmartArt content.

I will then show you how to insert 3D models, either from your own computer or from stock libraries installed with PowerPoint.

Finally, you'll learn how to insert and manage different types of media in a PowerPoint slideshow, including audio and video; how to create screen recordings; and how to configure media playback options.

Inserting and Formatting Tables

PowerPoint makes it easy for you to create a table within a slide. When you need to change your table, PowerPoint provides plenty of tools to make your table look the way you want, including inserting and deleting rows and columns and the ability to add built-in table styles.

Creating and Inserting Tables

Insert a *table* into a slide by following these steps:

1. In the left pane, click the slide in which you want to create a chart, or create a new slide, as you learned to do in Chapter 13, "Managing Slides."

2. Place your cursor in the content section of the slide (the large section underneath the smaller title section).

3. Click the Insert menu option.

4. Click the Table icon.

5. Move your mouse pointer over the grid in the drop-down menu. Cells in the grid light up as you move the pointer so that you can see the size of the table in terms of *rows* and *columns*.

The table also appears in your slide so that you can see what the table will look like as you move the mouse pointer over the grid in the drop-down menu.

6. When the table is the size you want, click the highlighted cell, as shown in Figure 15.1.

FIGURE 15.1   The selected table cells

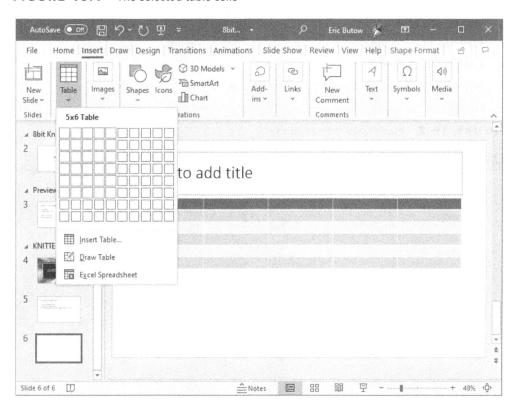

Now the table appears on the page with the number of rows and columns you selected in the grid.

Inserting and Deleting Table Rows and Columns

The Insert Table grid gives you the ability to create a maximum table size of only 10 columns and 8 rows. You can insert as many as 75 rows and 75 columns into a table. You can also insert and delete one or more rows or columns in a table.

Create a Larger Table

If you need more rows or columns than what the Insert Table grid will allow, follow these steps:

1. In the left pane, click the slide in which you want to create a chart, or create a new slide, as you learned to do in Chapter 13.

2. Place your cursor in the content section of the slide (the large section underneath the smaller title section).

3. Click the Insert menu option (if you haven't done so already).

4. Click the Table icon.

5. Select Insert Table from the drop-down menu, as shown in Figure 15.2.

FIGURE 15.2 Insert Table menu option

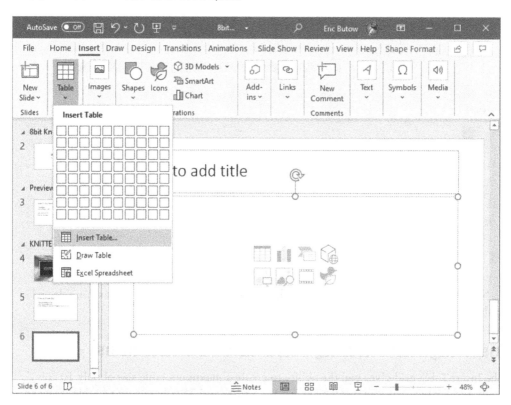

6. In the Insert Table dialog box (see Figure 15.3), specify the number of columns and rows that you want in the Number Of Columns and Number Of Rows boxes, respectively. The default is five columns and two rows.

FIGURE 15.3   Insert Table dialog box

Insert Rows and/or Columns

If you need to insert rows and/or columns after you have created a table, follow these steps:

1. Click a cell within the table. The cursor blinks in your cell within the row or column.

2. Click the Layout menu option.

3. In the Rows & Columns section in the Layout ribbon, shown in Figure 15.4, click one of the four insertion options.

FIGURE 15.4   Insertion options in the Rows & Columns section

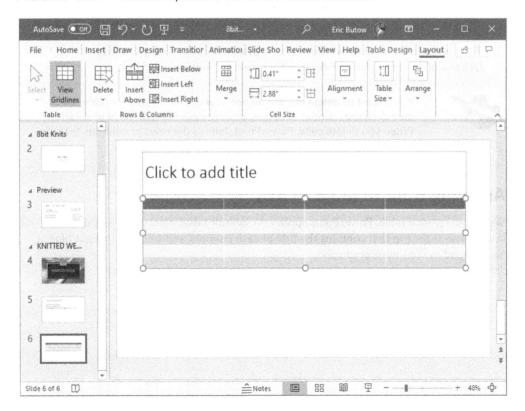

The four insertion options are (from left to right):

Insert Above: Insert a new row above the selected cell.

Insert Below: Insert a new row below the selected cell.

Insert Left: Insert a new column to the left of the selected cell.

Insert Right: Insert a new column to the right of the selected cell.

 If you want to add more than one row or column, click a table cell and then drag the number of row or column cells that you want to add. When you add cells, PowerPoint adds the number of rows or columns. For example, if you select three cells in a column and then insert rows below the selected cells, PowerPoint adds three new rows under the selected cells.

Delete Rows and/or Columns

When you need to delete a row or column, PowerPoint also makes this easy to do. Here's how:

1. Click a cell within the table. The cursor blinks in your selected cell within the row or column.

2. Click the Layout menu option.

3. In the Rows & Columns section in the Layout ribbon, click Delete.

4. From the drop-down menu (see Figure 15.5), select Delete Rows or Delete Columns.

   When you click Delete Rows, PowerPoint deletes the row with your selected cell. Click Delete Columns to delete the column that contains your selected cell.

 If you want to delete more than one row or column, click a table cell and then drag the number of row or column cells that you want to delete. When you delete cells, PowerPoint deletes the rows or columns that contain the cells.

Applying Built-In Table Styles

When you create a table, PowerPoint applies the default table style, which is a dark blue header row at the top that contains the title of each column, and cells with a light blue background in even-numbered rows.

FIGURE 15.5   Delete options

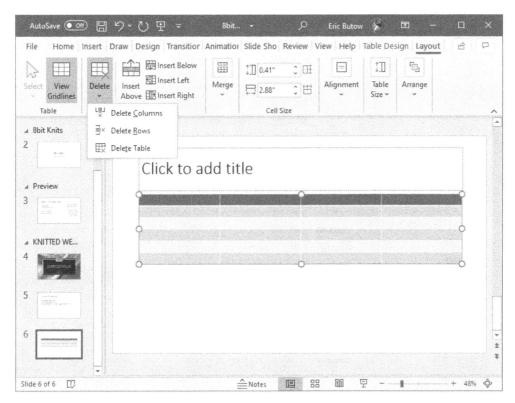

If you prefer to apply a different table style, apply another built-in table style by following these steps:

1. Click a cell within the table.

2. Click the Table Design menu option.

3. In the Table Styles section in the Table Design ribbon, click the More button to the right of the row of table style tiles. (The More button looks like a down arrow with a horizontal line above it.)

4. From the Table Styles drop-down list, shown in Figure 15.6, select one of the table style tiles.

FIGURE 15.6 Table style tiles

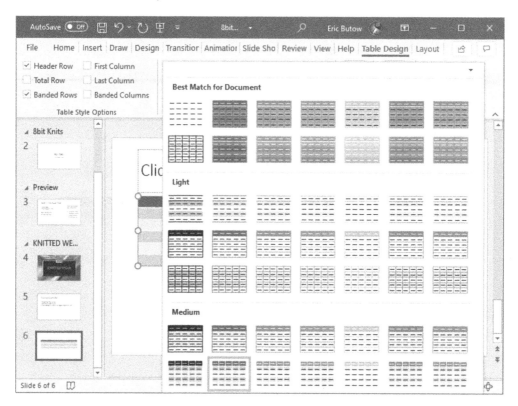

As you move the mouse pointer over each style tile, the table on the slide changes so that you can see what the style will look like before you select it. If you decide that you like the current table style after all, click outside the drop-down menu to close the menu.

EXERCISE 15.1

Inserting and Formatting Tables

1. Open a new slideshow.

2. Create a new Title And Content slide, as you learned to do in Chapter 13.

3. In the content area of the slide, create a new table with six rows and five columns.

4. Click in the third row in the table.

5. Add a new row below the current row.

6. Delete the column.

7. Apply a different style to the table.

8. Save the slideshow.

Inserting and Modifying Charts

PowerPoint is a visual medium, so it should come as no surprise that you can add a chart into a slideshow. After you insert a chart, the built-in chart tools let you modify it, such as adding data series, changing how data is presented, and adding more elements.

Creating and Inserting Charts

So, how do you build a chart? After you open a slideshow and either open a slide or create a new one to place your chart into, follow these steps:

1. In the left pane, click the slide in which you want to create a chart, or create a new slide, as you learned to do in Chapter 13.

2. Place your cursor in the content section of the slide (the large section underneath the smaller title section).

3. Click the Insert menu option.

4. In the Illustrations section in the Insert ribbon, click the Chart icon, as shown in Figure 15.7.

FIGURE 15.7 The Chart icon in the Insert ribbon

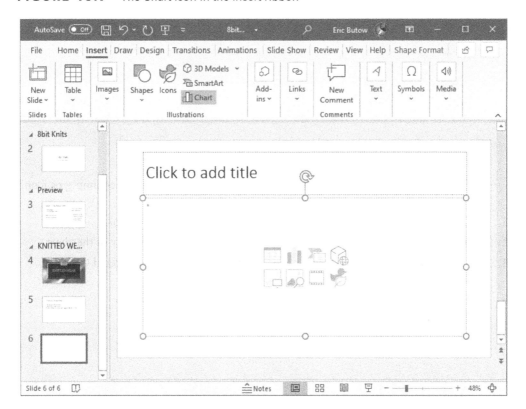

5. In the Insert Chart dialog box that appears (see Figure 15.8), the Column category is selected in the list on the left side of the dialog box.

FIGURE 15.8 The Column category in the Insert Chart dialog box

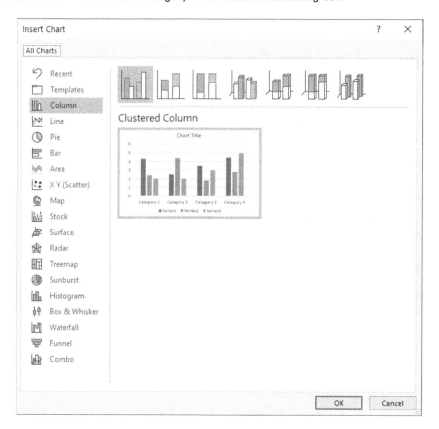

The column chart area appears at the right side of the dialog box; the column type icon is selected at the top of the area.

6. Click a chart type in the list to view a sample of how the chart will look.

7. Move the mouse pointer over the column type to view a larger preview of the chart.

8. For this example, click the Column chart type to add the default Clustered Column chart that you saw in Figure 15.8.

9. Click OK.

The chart appears in the slide, as shown in Figure 15.9.

FIGURE 15.9   The chart in the worksheet

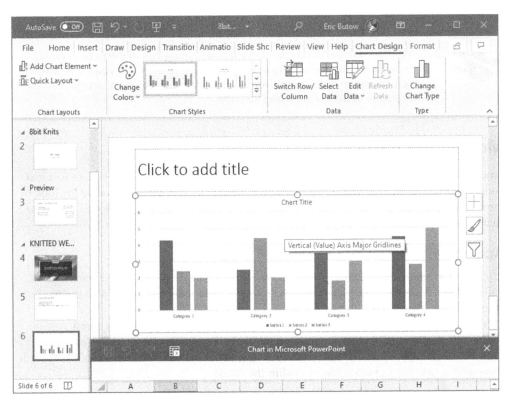

A Chart In Microsoft PowerPoint window appears underneath the chart and on top of the PowerPoint window (see Figure 15.10). That shows you a small spreadsheet with all of the numeric values in the chart selected.

FIGURE 15.10   The selected chart entries in the spreadsheet window

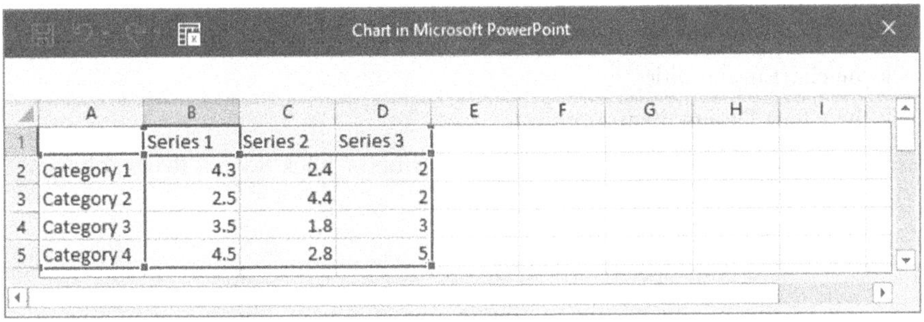

The window remains on the screen even if you click outside the chart or even on another slide. You can close the window by clicking the Close (X) icon at the right side of the window title bar that you saw in Figure 15.10.

 You can resize the chart by clicking and holding one of the circular sizing handles and then dragging the chart in the direction that you want. If you want to resize both the horizontal and vertical size of the chart, click and drag one of the corner sizing handles.

Modifying Charts

PowerPoint gives you a lot of power to modify your charts as you see fit. You can sort text and/or numbers in a table. You can also take advantage of more tools to change the look of the text and graphics in your chart, align your chart in the worksheet, and even change the chart type.

Adding Data Series to Charts

A *data series* is one or more rows and/or columns in a worksheet that PowerPoint uses to build a chart. After you add a chart, you may want to add more information to the worksheet and have PowerPoint update the chart accordingly.

Start by clicking the chart if necessary. Then type text and/or numbers in a new row or column. PowerPoint adds a new element to the chart that reflects the new data automatically. In the example shown in Figure 15.11, a new series of data in column E of the spreadsheet adds a new bar in each category within the chart.

 In Figure 15.11, the spreadsheet window has been moved above the chart so that you can see both the spreadsheet and the chart.

Switching Between Rows and Columns in Source Data

PowerPoint follows one rule when it creates a chart: the larger number of rows or columns is placed in the horizontal axis. For example, if there are 12 columns and 5 rows, then columns are along the horizontal axis.

But what if you want the rows to appear in the horizontal axis? Here's what to do:

1. Click the chart in the slide.
2. Click the Chart Design menu option.
3. In the Data section in the Chart Design menu ribbon, click Switch Row/Column.

FIGURE 15.11   The updated chart and expanded selection area in the spreadsheet

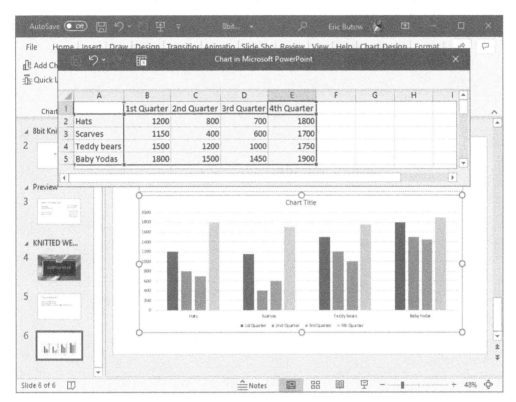

Now the axes have switched, as you can see in Figure 15.12, so that you can determine whether you like it. If you don't, click Switch Row/Column in the Chart Design ribbon again.

As you switch between rows and columns, keep the following in mind:

- If the Switch Row/Column icon is disabled, it means that you don't have the Chart In Microsoft PowerPoint window open. You can open this window by right-clicking in the chart and then clicking Edit Data in the pop-up menu.

- What happens if you have equal numbers of rows and columns in your worksheet or table? PowerPoint uses the same layout as rows and columns in a worksheet: columns for the horizontal axis and rows for the vertical axis.

FIGURE 15.12 Column titles in the horizontal axis

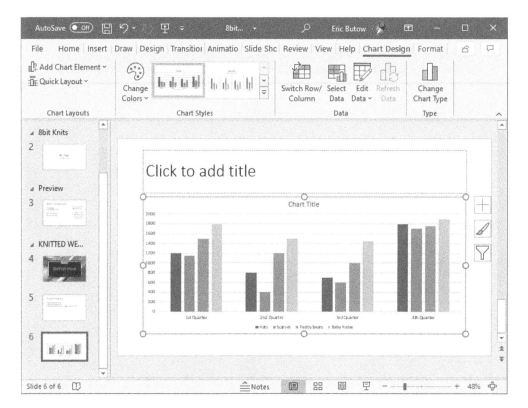

Adding and Modifying Chart Elements

It's easy to add and modify the elements that you see in a chart. You can view a list of elements that you can add to the chart by clicking anywhere in the chart and then clicking the Chart Elements icon at the upper-right corner of the chart.

A list of the elements appears, with check boxes to the left of each element name, as shown in Figure 15.13.

Selected check boxes indicate that the element is currently applied. Cleared check boxes mean that the element is not applied. When you move the mouse pointer over the element in the list, you see how the element will appear in the chart—that is, if the element is not already applied.

The following is a list of the elements that you can add and remove from your chart:

Axes These are the horizontal and vertical units of measure in the chart. In the sample chart shown in Figure 15.13, the horizontal units represent products sold and the vertical units represent sales in increments of 200. PowerPoint shows the axes by default.

FIGURE 15.13   Chart elements list

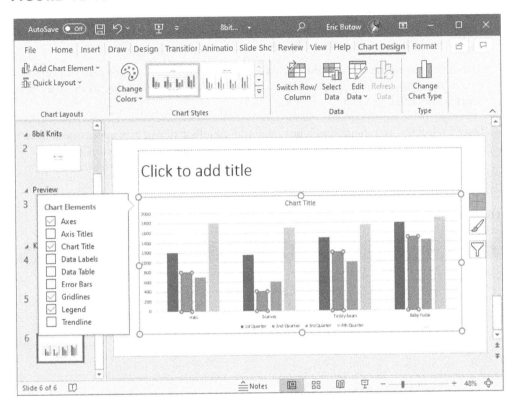

Axis Titles   These are the titles for the vertical and horizontal axes. The default name of each title is Axis Title. You can change the title after you add it by double-clicking within the title, selecting the text, and then typing your own text.

Chart Title   PowerPoint automatically shows the title of your chart, which is Chart Title by default. You can change this title by double-clicking Chart Title, selecting the text, and then typing a new title.

Data Labels   These add the number in each cell above each corresponding point or bar in the chart. If your points or bars are close together, having data labels can be difficult to read because the numbers can overlap.

Data Table   PowerPoint places your selected cells in a table below the chart. If you have a large table, then you may need to enlarge the size of the chart in the worksheet.

Error Bars   If you have a chart with data that has margins of error, such as political polls, you can add *error bars* to your chart to show those margins. Error bars also work when you want to see the standard deviation, which measures how widely a range of values are from the mean.

Gridlines This displays the gridlines behind the lines or bars in a graph. Gridlines are active by default.

Legend PowerPoint shows the *legend,* which explains what each line or bar color represents, at the bottom of the chart by default.

Trendline A *trendline* is a straight or curved line that shows the overall pattern of the data in the chart. In the example shown in Figure 15.14, I can view the trendline for first quarter sales of all products.

Once I select the Trendlines check box, the Add Trendline dialog box appears and asks me to click the series that I want to check. After I click Quarter 1 in the list and then click OK, the dashed line appears and the trendline also appears in the legend (see Figure 15.14).

FIGURE 15.14 Trendline for first quarter sales

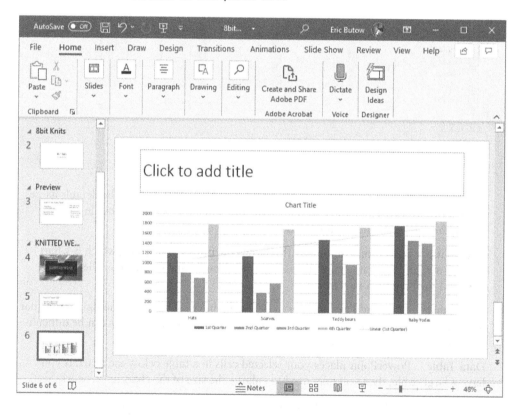

Change Elements More Precisely

An arrow appears to the right of each element name. When you click the arrow, a secondary menu with more precise options, as well as an option for viewing even more options, appears, as shown in Figure 15.13. For example, you can hide the vertical axis label but keep the horizontal axis label.

When you click More Options in the secondary menu, the Format panel appears at the right side of the PowerPoint window so that you can make even more specific changes, such as making the chart title text outlined instead of solid.

EXERCISE 15.2

Inserting and Modifying Charts

1. Open the slideshow that you created in Exercise 15.1 if it's not already open.

2. Create a new Title And Content slide, as you learned to do in Chapter 13.

3. Insert a new slide into the content area of the slide.

4. Add a new chart spreadsheet in the Chart window that includes five rows and four columns.

5. Add text in the first row and in the first column.

6. Add numbers into the remaining cells in the spreadsheet.

7. Create a Clustered Column chart for the entire table.

8. Reverse the axes.

9. Add a new column and populate it with text in the first row and numbers in the other four rows.

10. Add a trendline.

11. Save the slideshow.

Inserting and Formatting SmartArt Graphics

SmartArt graphics are built-in art types for conveying specific kinds of information, such as a flowchart to show a process or a decision tree to show a hierarchy. PowerPoint allows you to create a SmartArt graphic quickly and insert it into a slide. Then you can use built-in tools to format your SmartArt graphic easily.

Inserting SmartArt Graphics

Follow these steps to add a SmartArt graphic:

1. In the left pane, click the slide in which you want to add a SmartArt graphic, or create a new slide, as you learned to do in Chapter 13.

2. Place your cursor in the content section of the slide (the large section underneath the smaller title section).

3. Click the Insert menu option.

4. In the Illustrations section in the Insert ribbon, click SmartArt (see Figure 15.15).

5. In the Choose A SmartArt Graphic dialog box, shown in Figure 15.16, select a category from the list on the left side of the dialog box.

   The default is All, which shows all the SmartArt graphics from which you can choose. The list of SmartArt graphic type icons in the center of the dialog box depends on the category you chose. For this example, I chose Hierarchy.

6. Click the graphic type that you want to insert. A description of the graphic type appears at the right side of the dialog box.

7. Click OK.

The graphic appears in the content section of the slide. You'll learn how to set up a graphic to look the way you want, as well as change the text wrapping style, later in this chapter.

Converting Lists to SmartArt Graphics

When you have a bulleted or numbered list that you want to show graphically, PowerPoint makes it easy to convert a list to a SmartArt graphic. Here's how:

1. In the left pane, click the slide in which you want to add a SmartArt graphic, or create a new slide, as you learned to do in Chapter 13.

2. Place your cursor in the content section of the slide (the large section underneath the smaller title section).

FIGURE 15.15   SmartArt option in the Insert ribbon

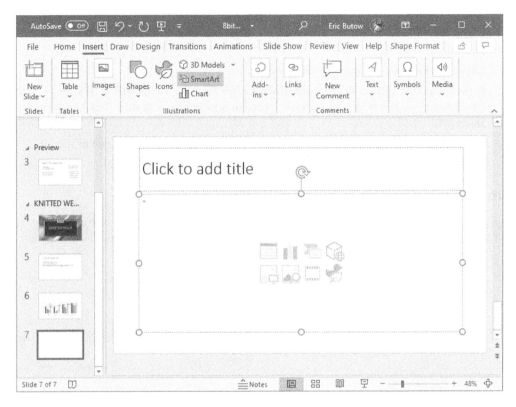

FIGURE 15.16   SmartArt categories

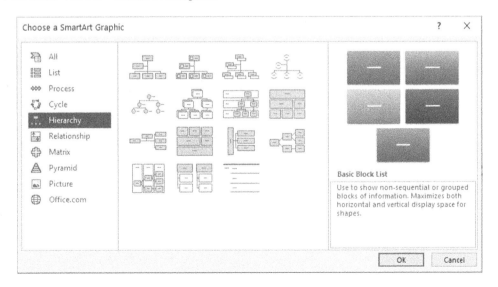

3. If necessary, type a bulleted list with three entries.

4. Indent the second bullet once.

5. Indent the third bullet twice.

6. Select the entire list.

7. Click the Home menu option, if necessary.

8. In the Paragraph section in the Insert ribbon, click Convert To SmartArt. (If your PowerPoint window width is small, click the Paragraph icon and then click Convert To SmartArt.)

9. In the drop-down list (see Figure 15.17), move the mouse pointer over one of the 20 SmartArt graphic tiles to see how your converted list will appear.

FIGURE 15.17   The Convert To SmartArt drop-down list

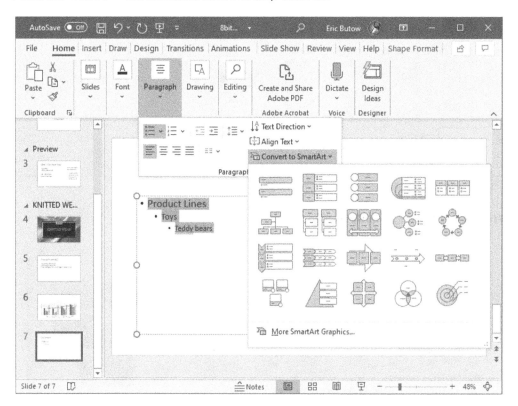

10. When you find a graphic you like, click it.

The graphic appears in the content section of the slide.

If you don't find a SmartArt graphic that you like, click More SmartArt Graphics at the bottom of the drop-down list. The Choose A SmartArt Graphic dialog box appears so that you can find a graphic to your liking, as you learned about earlier in this chapter.

Adding and Modifying SmartArt Graphic Content

After you add SmartArt, the Type Your Text Here box appears to the left of the image. You can type the text that will appear in the image by clicking [Text] in each bullet line and replacing that template text with your own (see Figure 15.18).

FIGURE 15.18   The Type Your Text Here box

The SmartArt Design ribbon appears by default so that you can make any changes you want. The type of SmartArt you added determines the options that appear in the ribbon.

For example, I created an organization chart, shown in Figure 15.19, and in the ribbon, I can change the following:

- The layout of the chart in the Create Graphic section
- The layout type in the Layouts section
- The chart box colors and styles in the SmartArt Styles section

Remove all graphic style changes that you made and return the graphic to its original style by clicking the Reset Graphic icon.

When you finish making any changes to your SmartArt graphic, click the page outside the graphic to deselect it.

FIGURE 15.19 Designing an organization chart using SmartArt

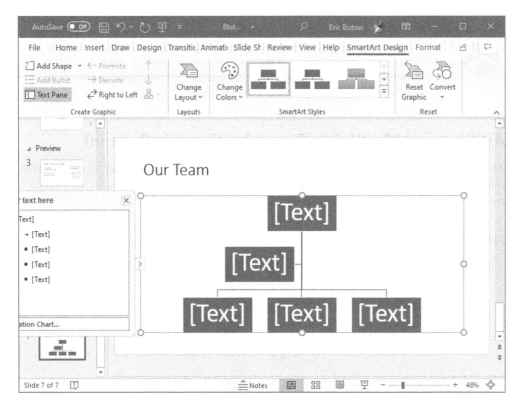

As you modify your SmartArt graphic, remember these points:

- Once you stop editing your SmartArt graphic and deselect it, you won't be able to remove any previous changes that you made to the graphic.

- Convert the SmartArt graphic to a text or shape by clicking Convert in the Reset section in the SmartArt Design ribbon.

- You can change the size of a SmartArt graphic or screen clipping image by clicking the image, moving the mouse pointer over one of the circular handles on the perimeter of the image, holding down the mouse button, and dragging the image. When the image is the size you want, release the mouse button.

Inserting and Formatting SmartArt Graphics

1. Open the slideshow that you created in Exercise 15.1 if it's not already open.

2. Create a new Title And Content slide, as you learned to do in Chapter 13.

3. Click within the content area of the slide.

4. Create a bulleted list with four entries.

5. Convert the list to a Vertical Block List SmartArt graphic.

6. Change two of the text entries in the SmartArt graphic.

7. Change the SmartArt Style into a Subtle Effect in the SmartArt Design ribbon.

8. Save the slideshow.

Inserting and Modifying 3D Models

PowerPoint, Word, and Excel all have access to the Microsoft library of Office graphics. One category of graphics are 3D models.

3D models are graphics that appear three-dimensional on the screen. You can also rotate them by 360 degrees within PowerPoint so that you can have the 3D model oriented the way you want. For example, you may want to have a dinosaur walking away from you rather than toward you.

Inserting 3D Models

You can insert a 3D model into a slide and then change the orientation. Follow these steps:

1. In the left pane, click the slide in which you want to add a SmartArt graphic, or create a new slide, as you learned to do in Chapter 13.

2. Place your cursor in the content section of the slide (the large section underneath the smaller title section).

3. Click the Insert menu option.

4. In the Insert ribbon, click 3D Models in the Illustrations section.

5. You can search for 3D models on your computer or stock 3D models that were installed with PowerPoint. For this example, I'll click Stock 3D Models.

6. In the Online 3D Models dialog box (see Figure 15.20), scroll up and down the list of categories and then click the category tile that you want. I selected the Winter category.

7. Click the 3D model you want and then click Insert.

   The model appears in the slide, as shown in Figure 15.21.

FIGURE 15.20   3D model category list

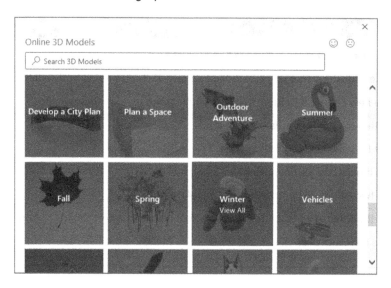

FIGURE 15.21   A 3D hat model

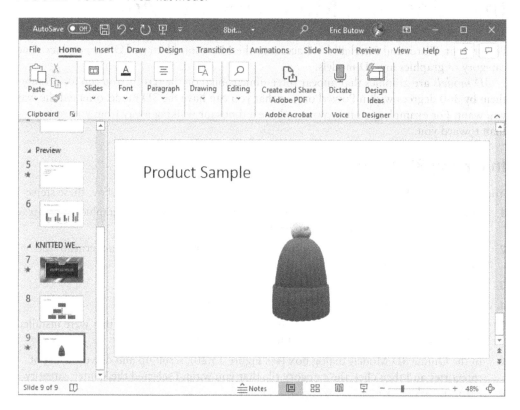

If you have any text on the slide, the model appears in front of the text. You'll learn how to modify the location and position of the 3D model, as well as change the text wrapping style, later in this chapter.

Modifying 3D Models

You can change the size of a 3D model by clicking the model, clicking one of the circular sizing handles on the perimeter of the selection box, holding down the mouse button, and then dragging. When the model is the size you want, release the mouse button.

Rotate the 3D model 360 degrees in any direction by clicking and holding down the Rotate icon in the middle of the model graphic (see Figure 15.22) and then dragging the mouse pointer to see how the model moves. When the model looks the way you want on the slide, release the mouse button.

FIGURE 15.22   The Rotate icon in the 3D model

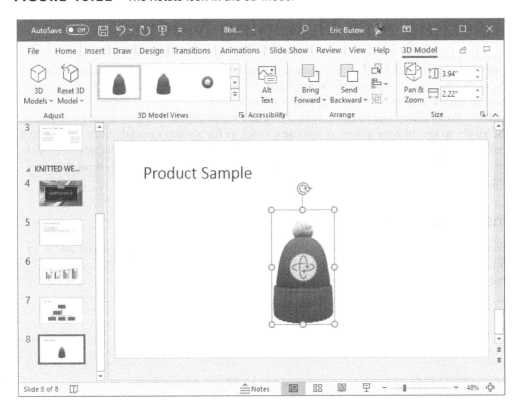

EXERCISE 15.4

Inserting and Modifying 3D Models

1. Open the slideshow that you created in Exercise 15.1 if it's not already open.

2. Create a new Title And Content slide, as you learned to do in Chapter 13.

3. Click within the content area of the slide.

4. Add a new 3D model of your choice.

5. Rotate the model until it looks the way that you want.

6. Save the slideshow.

Inserting and Managing Media

PowerPoint is not just for showing static slides with text and graphics. You can insert different types of media into your slideshow so that you don't have to go back and forth between your slideshow and an external application to run media.

PowerPoint allows you to insert both audio and video clips into a slideshow, gives you the ability to record your screen as you use it (such as for a video tutorial about how to do a task), and then insert the screen recording into a slide. Once you insert media into your slide, you can configure the playback options so that the media plays the way you want it to during your presentation.

Inserting Audio and Video Clips

You can insert just an audio clip into a slide or insert a video clip with or without audio. In either case, PowerPoint includes playback controls within the slide so that you can pause and play the clip during the presentation as needed.

Supported Audio and Video Formats

PowerPoint will insert several different formats of audio and video files, and Microsoft recommends specific audio and video format files for the best results.

For audio files, Microsoft recommends that you insert M4A format files encoded with AAC audio. PowerPoint will also insert audio with the following formats and their associated file extensions:

> **AIFF audio file:** `.aiff`
>
> **AU audio file:** `.au`
>
> **MIDI:** `.mid` or `.midi`
>
> **MPEG3 audio file:** `.mp3`
>
> **MPEG4 audio file:** `.mp4`
>
> **Windows audio file:** `.wav`
>
> **Windows Media audio file:** `.wma`

For video clips, Microsoft recommends that you insert MP4 format files encoded with H.264 video and AAC audio. You can also insert a file with the following formats and their associated file extensions:

> **Windows Video file:** `.asf` or `.avi`
>
> **MP4 video file:** `.m4v` or `.mov`
>
> **MPEG movie file:** `.mpg` or `.mpeg`
>
> **Windows Media Video file:** `.wmv`

If you need more information, search for PowerPoint supported file formats on the Microsoft Support website at `support.microsoft.com`.

Adding an Audio Clip

Insert an audio clip by following these steps:

1. In the left pane, click the slide in which you want to insert the audio clip, or create a new slide, as you learned to do in Chapter 13.

2. Place your cursor in the content section of the slide (the large section underneath the smaller title section).

3. Click the Insert menu option.

4. In the Insert ribbon, click Audio in the Media section. (If your PowerPoint window width is smaller, click Media in the ribbon and then select Audio from the drop-down menu.)

5. Click Audio On My PC (see Figure 15.23).

FIGURE 15.23 Audio On My PC menu option

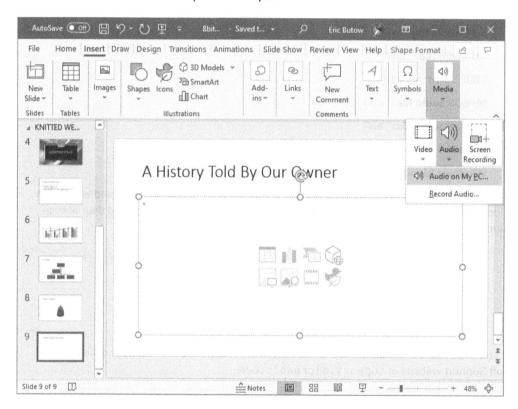

6. In the Insert Audio dialog box, navigate to the folder that contains the audio file you want to insert.

7. Click the name in the list and then click Insert (see Figure 15.24).

FIGURE 15.24 The Insert button in the dialog box

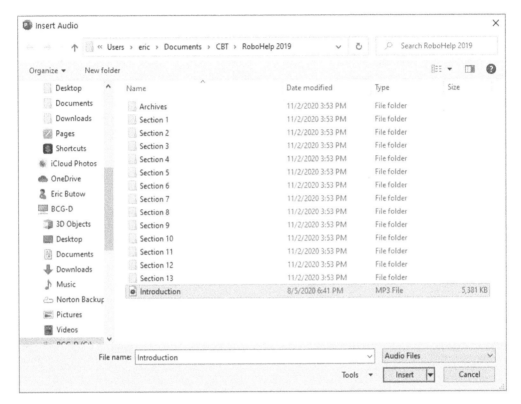

The audio icon appears in the center of the slide with a playback bar underneath it so that you can start playing the audio by clicking the play button (the triangle pointing to the right) at the left side of the playback bar, as shown in Figure 15.25.

After you insert the audio clip, you see sizing handles around the edge of the audio icon. You can resize the size of the icon by clicking and holding on one of the circular sizing handles and then dragging the icon until it's the size you want. This does not affect the playback ability of the audio clip.

The sizing handles also tell you that the audio clip is selected. After you click the audio clip to select it, delete the clip by pressing Delete on your keyboard.

FIGURE 15.25 The audio file in the slide

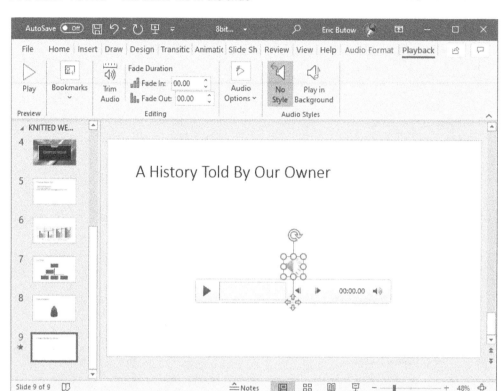

Adding a Video Clip

PowerPoint allows you to embed a video that you have on your computer hard drive or a network into a slide. Insert a video clip by following these steps:

1. In the left pane, click the slide in which you want to insert the video clip, or create a new slide, as you learned to do in Chapter 13.

2. Place your cursor in the content section of the slide (the large section underneath the smaller title section).

3. Click the Insert menu option.

4. In the Insert ribbon, click Video in the Media section. (If your PowerPoint window width is smaller, click Media in the ribbon and then click Video in the drop-down menu.)

FIGURE 15.26   Video On My PC menu option

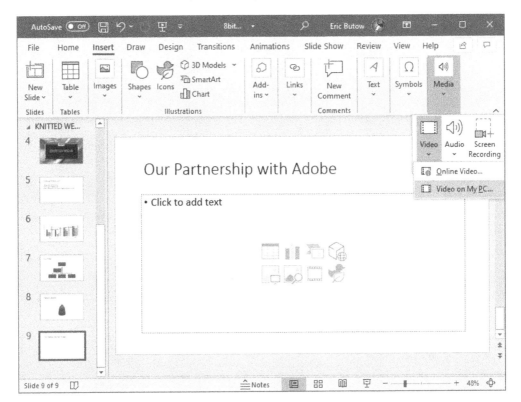

5. Click Video On My PC, as shown in Figure 15.26.

6. In the Insert Video dialog box, navigate to the folder that contains the audio file that you want to insert.

7. Click the name in the list and then click Insert (see Figure 15.27).

FIGURE 15.27   The Insert button in the dialog box

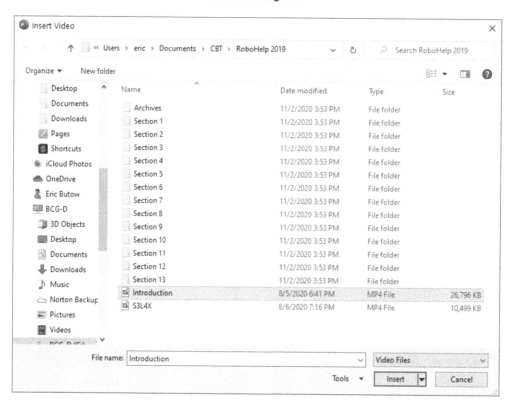

The first frame in the video file appears in the center of the slide with a playback bar underneath it so that you can start playing the video by clicking the play button (the triangle pointing to the right) at the left side of the playback bar (see Figure 15.28).

After you insert the video clip, you see sizing handles around the edge of the video icon. You can resize the size of the icon by clicking and holding on one of the circular sizing handles and then dragging the icon until it's the size that you want. This does not affect the playback ability of the video clip.

The sizing handles also tell you that the video clip is selected. After you click the video clip to select it, delete the clip by pressing Delete on your keyboard.

FIGURE 15.28   The video file in the slide

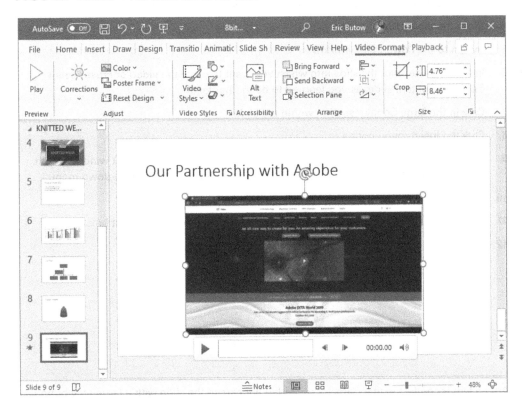

Real World Scenario

Insert Online Video from YouTube

Your boss has seen a video on YouTube that she thinks would be a great addition to the presentation scheduled to be made to the board of directors the next day. She's given you a mission: embed that YouTube video onto a new slide and save the slideshow on the company intranet so that she can review it.

After you work with your boss and/or anyone else in your company (like the legal department) to make sure that you have permission to use that video in your presentation, PowerPoint makes the rest of the job easy. Just follow these steps:

1. Open the video on YouTube.

2. Click the Share icon underneath the viewer.

3. Click Copy in the Share dialog box. A small box in the lower-left corner of the browser window informs you that the URL has been copied to the Clipboard.

4. Close the dialog box.

5. Switch to the PowerPoint window.

6. In the left pane, click the slide into which you want to place the video or create a new Title And Content slide, as you learned to do in Chapter 13.

7. Click in the large Content section within the slide.

8. Click the Insert menu option.

9. In the Media Section in the Insert ribbon, click Video. (If your PowerPoint window width is smaller, click Media in the ribbon and then select Video from the drop-down menu.)

10. From the Video drop-down list, select Online Video.

11. In the Online Video dialog box, paste the URL from YouTube into the text box.

12. Click Insert.

After a few seconds, the title frame of the video appears in the slide with a large play button in the center. Play the video by clicking the Play button.

When you play the video, all of the YouTube video controls appear within the window so that you can change the volume, move the playback slider, and use all the other standard features found in the viewer on the YouTube website.

Creating and Inserting Screen Recordings

If you want to record a screen that shows you doing something in Windows and then insert that recording into a slide, you don't need to use a separate program to do that. PowerPoint has all of the built-in tools so that you can record video and/or audio, as well as audio only.

The directions in this section presume that you have a microphone so that you can record audio.

Recording Audio Clips

Here's how to use audio clips to create and insert an audio recording:

1. In the left pane, click the slide in which you want to insert the audio clip, or create a new slide, as you learned to do in Chapter 13.

2. Place your cursor in the content section of the slide (the large section underneath the smaller title section).

3. Click the Insert menu option.

4. In the Insert ribbon, click Audio in the Media section. (If your PowerPoint window width is smaller, click Media in the ribbon and then select Audio from the drop-down menu.)

5. Click Record Audio (see Figure 15.29).

FIGURE 15.29   Record Audio menu option

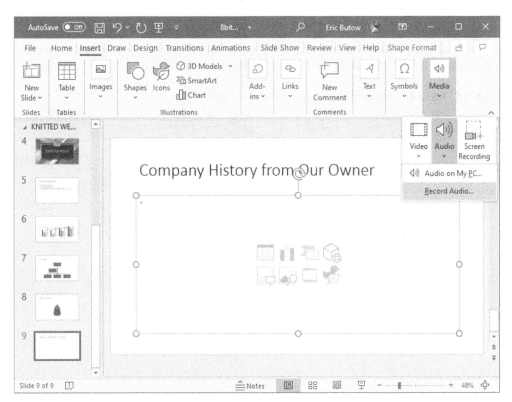

6. In the Record Sound dialog box, shown in Figure 15.30, delete the default Recorded Sound name in the Name box and replace it with a name of your choosing.

7. Click the Record button, which has a red circle icon.

FIGURE 15.30 Record Sound dialog box

8. Talk into your microphone. As you speak, the Total Sound Length counter starts counting the number of seconds in your recording.

9. When you're done, click the Stop button. (It has a red square icon.)

10. Play back the recording by clicking the Play button, which has a green triangle icon, or resume recording by clicking the Record button.

11. When you finish recording, click OK.

A gray audio icon appears in the center of the slide. Click the icon to show the playback bar underneath it so that you can start playing the audio by clicking the play button (the triangle pointing to the right) at the left side of the playback bar, as shown in Figure 15.31.

FIGURE 15.31 The recorded audio file in the slide

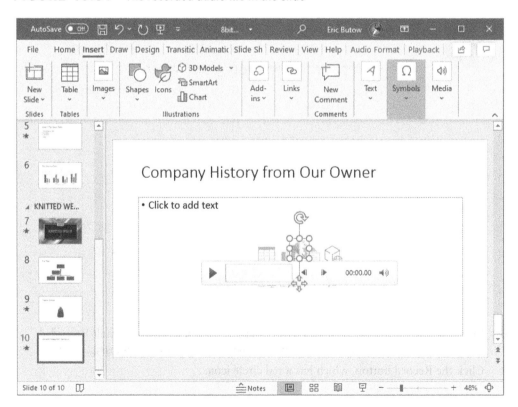

You can move the clip by clicking and holding the audio icon and then dragging the icon to a different location on the slide. If you use more than one audio file on a slide but you want to have your selected audio file appear on multiple slides, it's a good rule of thumb to put that selected audio file in the same location on the slide because PowerPoint doesn't label each individual audio clip.

Recording Video Clips

Record a video clip from within PowerPoint by following these steps:

1. In the left pane, click the slide in which you want to insert the audio clip, or create a new slide, as you learned to do in Chapter 13.

2. Place your cursor in the content section of the slide (the large section underneath the smaller title section).

3. Click the Insert menu option.

4. In the Insert ribbon, click Screen Recording in the Media section, as shown in Figure 15.32. (If your PowerPoint window width is smaller, click Media in the ribbon and then select Audio from the drop-down menu.)

FIGURE 15.32   Screen Recording icon

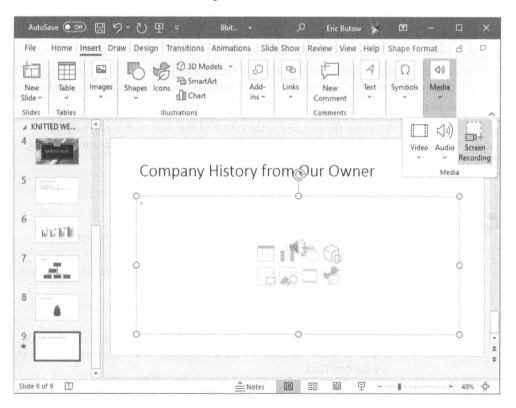

5. In the *Control Dock* box, shown in Figure 15.33, select an area to record by clicking Select Area.

FIGURE 15.33   Control Dock box

PowerPoint adds a slightly opaque white overlay to the entire screen.

6. Click and hold a section in the screen and then drag to select the area to record, which is bounded by a red dashed line.

7. Click Audio to turn off audio recording as you record your video.

8. Click Record Pointer to hide the mouse pointer as you record your video.

9. Click Record.

A large orange box appears in the center of the screen and counts down from three seconds to zero to give you a little time to prepare. Once you start recording, the Control Dock moves up and off the top of the screen.

10. When you're done recording, move the mouse pointer over the top edge of the screen and then click the Stop icon, which is a square.

The recording timer underneath the Stop icon continues to count the number of seconds and/or minutes. Once you click the icon, you return to the screen you were recording.

11. Switch to the PowerPoint window.

The first frame in the video file appears in the center of the slide with a playback bar underneath it so that you can start playing the video by clicking the play button (the triangle pointing to the right) at the left side of the playback bar (see Figure 15.34).

As you create a video recording, note the following:

■ You need to record a screen area that is at least 64 pixels high by 64 pixels wide.

■ If your video recording contains audio, then a gray audio icon appears in the center of the video in the slide.

■ If you prefer to stop recording using your keyboard, press and hold Windows logo key+Shift+Q.

■ You can keep the Control Dock from disappearing as you record by clicking the pin icon, which looks like a thumbtack, in the lower-right corner of the Control Dock.

FIGURE 15.34 The video recording and playback bar in the slide

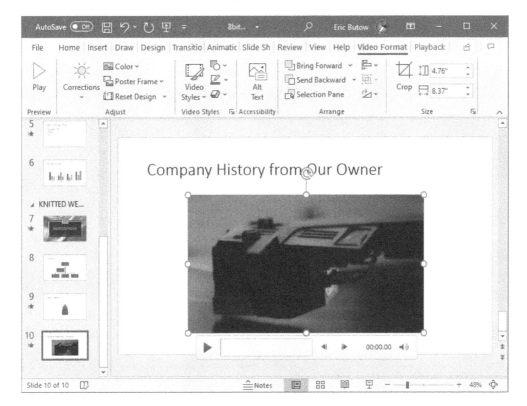

Configuring Media Playback Options

You may not be happy with the audio and/or video you just recorded. For example, you may want to trim off a section at the end of audio that has no sound. PowerPoint gives you rudimentary tools for editing audio and video clips.

Editing Audio Clips

When you click the audio icon in the slide, PowerPoint displays the Playback and Audio Format menu options and displays the Playback ribbon by default (see Figure 15.35).

Within the ribbon, you can click one or more options in the following sections. If your PowerPoint window width is smaller, you may need to click the section name in the ribbon and then select one of the options from the drop-down menu.

FIGURE 15.35 Playback ribbon

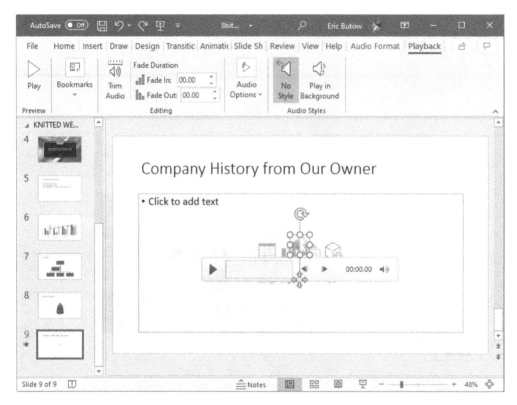

Preview   Click the Play icon to play the audio clip.

Bookmarks   Add a bookmark within the timeline in the playback bar. The timeline is the long bar to the right of the Play button. When you click each bookmark in the timeline, you jump to that point in the audio file.

Trim   Trim the audio by deleting certain parts of the audio file in the Trim Audio dialog box, which is beyond the purview of the MO-300 exam.

Editing   Type the number of seconds to add a fade-in effect at the beginning of the audio clip and/or a fade-out effect at the end of the clip in the Fade In and Fade Out boxes, respectively. You can specify the time as precisely as hundredths of a second.

Audio Options   In this section, you can change the volume, determine how Power-Point should start playing the audio clip, how the audio clip plays, and if the audio icon should be hidden when you play your slideshow.

Audio Styles   Click No Style to reset the playback options to their default settings. You can have the audio play in the background across all slides by clicking Play In Background.

Changing Video Playback Settings

When you insert a video, PowerPoint displays the Video Format and Playback menu options and displays the Video Format ribbon by default. Click the Playback menu option to view the Playback ribbon, as shown in Figure 15.36.

FIGURE 15.36   The Playback ribbon for videos

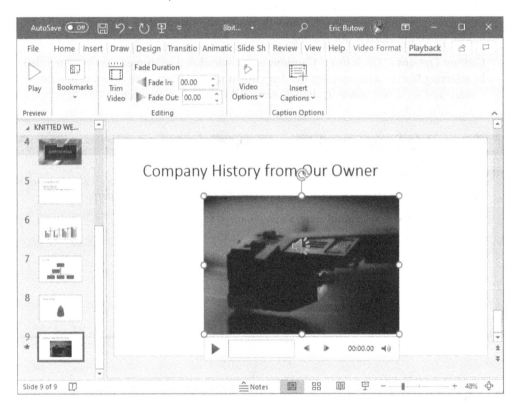

Within the ribbon, you can click one or more options in the following sections. If your PowerPoint window width is smaller, you may need to click the section name in the ribbon and then select one of the options from the drop-down menu.

Preview   Click the Play icon in the Preview section to play the video clip.

Bookmarks   Add a bookmark within the timeline in the playback bar. The timeline is the long bar to the right of the Play button. When you click each bookmark in the time-line, you jump to that point in the video.

Trim   Trim the audio by deleting certain parts of the audio file in the Trim Video dialog box, which is outside the scope of this book and the MO-300 exam.

Editing   Type the number of seconds to add a fade-in effect at the beginning of the video and/or a fade-out effect at the end of the video in the Fade In and Fade Out boxes, respectively. You can specify the time as precisely as hundredths of a second.

Video Options   In this section, you can change the volume, determine how PowerPoint should start playing the audio clip, how the audio clip plays, and if the video should be hidden when the video is not playing.

Caption Options   Click Insert Captions to include closed captioned text in your video by selecting Insert Captions from the drop-down menu. If you have closed captioning in a video and want to remove it, click Remove All Captions in the menu.

EXERCISE 15.5

Inserting and Managing Media

1. Open the slideshow that you created in Exercise 15.1 if it's not already open.

2. Create a new Title And Content slide, as you learned to do in Chapter 13.

3. Add an audio file to the slide.

4. Record a video clip on the slide.

5. Play the video from within the Playback ribbon.

6. Save the slideshow.

Summary

This chapter started by showing you how to create a table and place it in a slide, insert and delete rows and columns within a table, and format your table by applying a built-in table style.

After you created a table, you learned how to create, insert, and modify charts, including adding data series, switching between rows and columns in the chart, and applying a variety of other chart elements.

Next, I discussed how to insert built-in SmartArt graphics to convey your message graphically. You also learned how to convert lists to SmartArt graphics as well as how to add and modify content in a SmartArt graphic.

Then you learned how to insert built-in 3D models into a slide and rotate the orientation of the 3D model.

Finally, you learned how to insert and manage audio and video clips, insert screen recordings, and configure playback options for audio and/or video in a slide.

Key Terms

3D models	legend
chart	rows
columns	SmartArt
Control Dock	Tables
data series	trendline
error bars	

Exam Essentials

Know how to create a table.   Understand how to use the Table option in the Insert menu to insert a table into a slide.

Understand how to modify a table.   Know how to add and delete rows and columns in a table as well as how to change the style of a table by applying a built-in table style.

Know how to add a data series to a chart.   Understand how to add additional cells in a worksheet or a table into a chart after you have already created the chart.

Understand how to switch between row and column data in a chart.   Know how PowerPoint places data series in the horizontal and vertical axes as well as how to switch those axes in a chart.

Know how to add and modify chart elements.   Understand how to add chart elements to your chart—including axes, axis titles, the chart title, data labels in the chart, a data table in the chart, error bars, gridlines, a legend, and a trendline—and be able to modify those elements.

Be able to apply chart layouts.   Know how to apply a different chart layout using the Quick Layout menu in the Chart Design ribbon.

Understand how to select and change chart styles.   Know how to apply a chart style from the Chart Design ribbon as well as how to change the color scheme for the style.

Understand how to add different types of media.   PowerPoint allows you to add a variety of graphics to a slide, including 3D models, SmartArt graphics, audio, and video. You need to know how to add those graphics, audio, and video; modify 3D models and SmartArt graphics; and change audio and video playback options.

Review Questions

1. How do you create a table with built-in styles?
   - **A.** Click the Table icon in the Insert ribbon.
   - **B.** Open the Styles panel.
   - **C.** Click the Insert ribbon, click Table, and then move the mouse pointer over Quick Tables in the drop-down menu.
   - **D.** Click the Columns icon in the Layout menu.

2. If you create a chart that has equal numbers of columns and rows, what does PowerPoint use as the horizontal axis?
   - **A.** A dialog box appears and asks you if you want to use rows or columns.
   - **B.** Columns
   - **C.** Rows
   - **D.** An error message appears in a dialog box.

3. How do you clear style and text changes that you made to a SmartArt graphic?
   - **A.** Use the SmartArt Design menu ribbon.
   - **B.** Delete the SmartArt graphic.
   - **C.** Click the Undo icon in the title bar.
   - **D.** Use the Format menu ribbon.

4. How do you rotate a selected 3D model?
   - **A.** Click one of the icons in the 3D Model Views section in the 3D Model menu ribbon.
   - **B.** Click and drag the handles on the selection box around the model.
   - **C.** Click and drag the icon in the middle of the model.
   - **D.** Click the Position icon in the 3D Model menu ribbon.

5. What keys do you press to stop recording a video? (Choose all that apply.)
   - **A.** Windows logo key+Q
   - **B.** Ctrl+Shift+Q
   - **C.** Windows logo key+Ctrl+Q
   - **D.** Windows logo key+Shift+Q

6. What menu options appear when you click inside a table?
   - **A.** Table Design and Layout
   - **B.** Shape Format
   - **C.** Format and Table Design
   - **D.** Chart Design

7. Why do you add a trendline in a chart?

   A. To show the levels of a bar in a chart better

   B. Because PowerPoint requires it before you can save the chart

   C. To see the overall trend of data over time

   D. To show the margins of error in a chart

8. How do you add a pyramid chart to your document using the Insert menu ribbon?

   A. Click Shapes.

   B. Click SmartArt.

   C. Click Chart.

   D. Click Pictures.

9. When you want to resize a 3D model, what do you select in the 3D Model ribbon? (Choose all that apply.)

   A. Align

   B. Height box

   C. Pan & Zoom

   D. Width box

10. Why do you add bookmarks in an audio or video clip?

   A. To tell you where to trim the clip later

   B. You need to add a bookmark so you can add fade-in and fade-out effects.

   C. Because PowerPoint will not save your slideshow if you don't add at least one bookmark

   D. So you can jump to a particular point in an audio or video clip

Chapter

16

Applying Transitions and Animations

MICROSOFT EXAM OBJECTIVES COVERED IN THIS CHAPTER:

✓ **Apply transitions and animations**

- Apply and configure slide transitions
  - Apply basic and 3D slide transitions
  - Configure transition effects
- Animate slide content
  - Animate text and graphic elements
  - Animate 3D models
  - Configure animation effects
  - Configure animation paths
  - Reorder animations on a slide
- Set timing for transitions
  - Set transition effect duration
  - Configure transition start and finish options

Once you have your slides in order, you may decide that you want to add some pizzazz to your slideshow. PowerPoint allows you to apply built-in options for animating transitions between slides as well as animate models in a slide.

The chapter begins with a discussion about applying various types of slide transitions and how to configure transition effects built into PowerPoint.

Next, I talk about how to animate content in your slide, including text, graphics, and 3D models. You will also learn how to configure animation effects and paths, as well as how to reorder your animations on a slide.

Finally, you'll learn how to change the duration for transition effects between slides and how to configure the transition start and finish options.

Applying and Configuring Slide Transitions

PowerPoint has many built-in slide transitions so that you can transition from one slide to another in a way that will (maybe) impress your audience. Once you add a transition, you can change the transition effects to one of the many built-in effect styles that come with PowerPoint.

The instructions in this section presume that you are working in Normal view within PowerPoint. You can learn more about views in Chapter 12, "Creating Presentations."

Applying Basic and 3D Slide Transitions

When you want to add a transition between slides, follow these steps:

1. In the left pane, click the slide to which you want to add the transition.
2. Click the Transitions menu option.
3. In the Transitions To This Slide section in the Transitions ribbon, click the More button to the right of the row of transition slides. (The More button looks like a down arrow with a line above it.)
4. In the drop-down list, as shown in Figure 16.1, click the transition effect icon from one of three sections: Subtle, Exciting, and Dynamic Content.

FIGURE 16.1   The drop-down list of transition effects

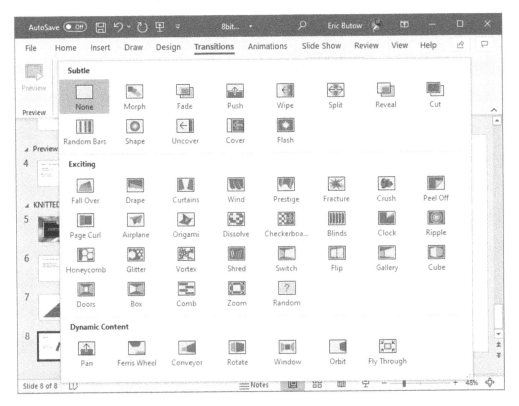

If you need more information about what an effect does, hover the mouse pointer over the transition effect icon. After a second or two, a tooltip describes what the effect does.

For this example, I used the Rotate effect in the Dynamic Content section, which is an example of a 3D slide transition—that is, the effect makes it appear that the slide is three-dimensional as it rotates from the current slide to the next one.

When you first apply the effect, you see the effect in the slide. However, this effect may go too quickly. You can preview the effect at any time by clicking the Preview icon in the Transitions ribbon (see Figure 16.2).

If you decide that you no longer want to have any effect applied to the slide, click the More button in the Transitions ribbon and then click None in the Subtle section (which is as subtle as it gets).

FIGURE 16.2   Preview icon

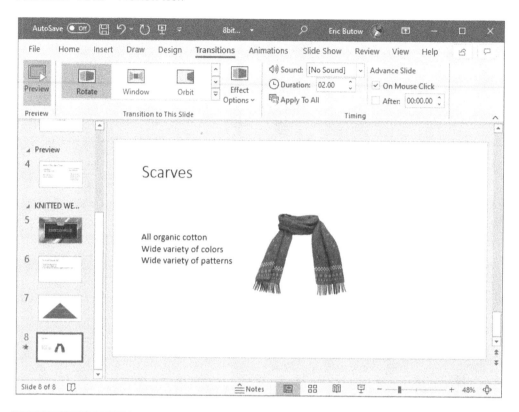

 The effect that you select applies only to the current slide. If you want the effect to apply to all slides, click Apply To All in the Timing section in the Transitions ribbon.

Configuring Transition Effects

After you add a transition effect, many (but not all) effects allow you to configure the effect to behave in different ways. Configure a transition effect by following these steps:

1. In the left pane, click the slide that contains the transition you created in the previous section.

2. Click the Transitions menu option.

3. In the Transitions To This Slide section in the Transitions ribbon, click the More button to the right of the row of transition slides. (The More button looks like a down arrow with a line above it.)

4. Click one of the transition options in the drop-down menu. For this example, I choose the Airplane transition (see Figure 16.3).

FIGURE 16.3   Airplane transition in the drop-down list

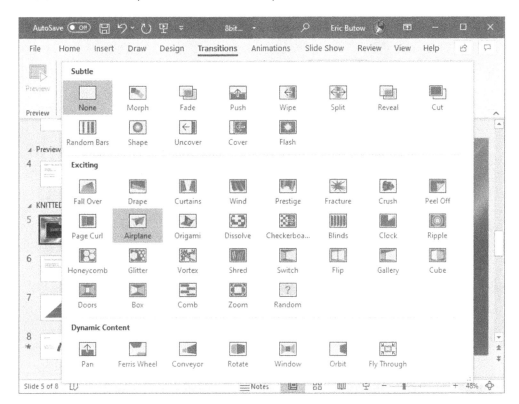

PowerPoint previews the transition so that you can see how the Airplane effect works.

5. In the Transitions To This Slide section in the Transitions ribbon, click Effect Options.

What you see in the Effect Options drop-down list depends on the transition that you select. For the Airplane effect, the default direction of the airplane is Right.

6. Click Left to have the previous slide fold into a paper airplane and fly off the left side of the slide (see Figure 16.4).

PowerPoint animates the slide so that you can see how the transition will appear in your presentation. The duration of the transition may affect how quickly the new effect plays in the slide, and you may need to change the transition timing accordingly.

FIGURE 16.4 The Left icon in the drop-down list

If the Effect Options icon in the Transitions ribbon is disabled, this means there are no options that you can set for that effect.

Real World Scenario

Add Sounds, Not Just Effects

Your boss likes the effect that you chose for all of your slides. However, she wants to have a sound play during the transition from the first slide to the second. This, she says, will help get the audience to perk up a bit during the early morning presentation.

PowerPoint has you covered with more than a few built-in sounds that you can add to a transition quickly. Here's how to do that:

1. In the left pane, click the slide that contains the transition.

2. Click the Transitions menu option.

3. In the Timing section in the Transitions ribbon, click the down arrow to the right of the No Sound box.

4. In the drop-down menu, click one of the sound effects in the list.

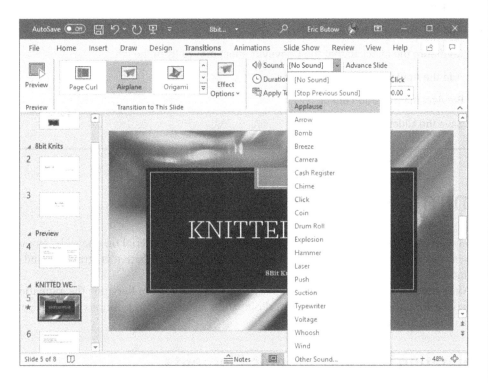

You can listen to the sound with the transition by clicking Preview in the Transitions ribbon.

If you want to add your own sound, such as the company jingle stored on the company intranet, click Other Sound at the bottom of the drop-down menu. You can navigate to the file and insert it within the Add Audio dialog box.

Applying and Configuring Slide Transitions

1.   Open a new slideshow.

2.   Add one slide in addition to the current one. If you need to know how to add slides, refer to Chapter 13, "Managing Slides."

3.   Add text to both slides.

4.   Click the first slide in the left pane.

5.   Add the Conveyor transition effect.

6.   Configure the effect so that the Conveyor effect moves from the left.

7.   Add the Applause sound to the slide.

8.   Preview the transition effect.

9.   Save the slideshow.

Animating Slide Content

When you want to get your audience to pay attention to the material on one slide, animating content can be effective. PowerPoint gives you the option to animate text, graphics, and even 3D models.

After you animate your content, you may find that you need to fine-tune the animation to make it look the way you want. PowerPoint contains many effect options to make your animation(s) look the way you want.

Animating Text and Graphic Elements

You can animate text in one of two ways: have one line appear at a time or have one letter appear at a time. You can also animate individual shapes and SmartArt graphics, modify the animation in the Animation pane, reverse the animation order, and remove an animation.

Making Text Appear One Line at a Time

When you want to animate each line of text to appear on the slide one at a time instead of all at once, follow these steps:

1.   In the left pane, click the slide with the text that you want to animate.

2.   Click in the section of the slide that contains the text.

3.   Click the Animations menu option.

4. In the Animation section in the Animations ribbon, click the More button to the right of the row of transition slides. (The More button looks like a down arrow with a line above it.)

If your PowerPoint window width is small, click the Animation Styles icon in the Animations ribbon.

5. In the drop-down list, shown in Figure 16.5, click an animation style icon. For this example, I'll click Float In.

FIGURE 16.5 Animation styles in the drop-down list

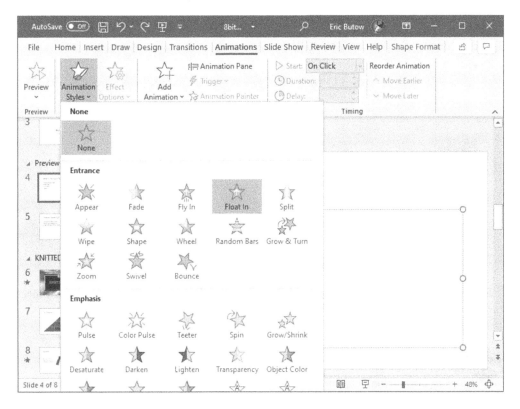

6. In the Animations ribbon, click Effect Options.

By default, PowerPoint shows the Float In effect appearing one line at a time, but the following steps show you how to return to this default option if the effect option is different.

7. At the bottom of the menu, click As One Object to make the text float in at one time.

8. Click Effect Options in the Animations ribbon.

9. Reapply the Float In effect to have the text appear one line at a time by clicking By Paragraph (see Figure 16.6).

FIGURE 16.6 By Paragraph at the bottom of the drop-down list

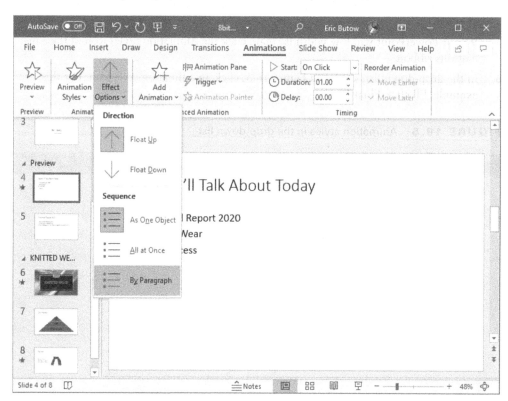

PowerPoint animates the text on the slide so that each line of text floats in one at a time, starting with the top line.

As you create animations, take note of the following features:

- Numbered orange boxes, or *markers*, appear at the left side of each slide that show you how many animations are in the slide and the order of the animations. That is, the number 1 marker means that the first animation runs before the second animation denoted by the number 2 marker.

- Markers on a slide don't appear in your presentation.

- In the left pane, you see a little star icon to the left of the thumbnail-sized slide in the list. Click this icon to play all of the animations in the slide.

- You can also preview all of the animations in the slide by clicking the Preview icon in the Animations ribbon.

Making Text Appear One Letter at a Time

When you make text appear on a slide one letter at a time, this gives your audience the illusion that you're typing text directly into the slide. Follow these steps to add this effect:

1. In the left pane, click the slide with the text that you want to animate.

2. Click in the section of the slide that contains the text.

3. Click the Animations menu option.

4. In the Advanced Animation section in the Animations ribbon, click Animation Pane.

    The Animation Pane appears on the right side of the PowerPoint menu (see Figure 16.7).

FIGURE 16.7   Animation Pane

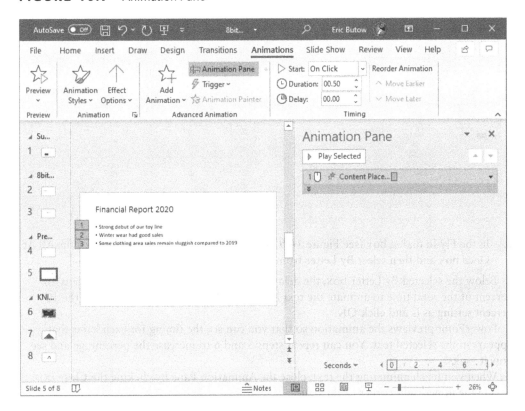

5. Click the down arrow to the right of the text that you want to animate in the list, and then select Effect Options from the drop-down menu, as shown in Figure 16.8.

FIGURE 16.8 Effect Options in the drop-down menu

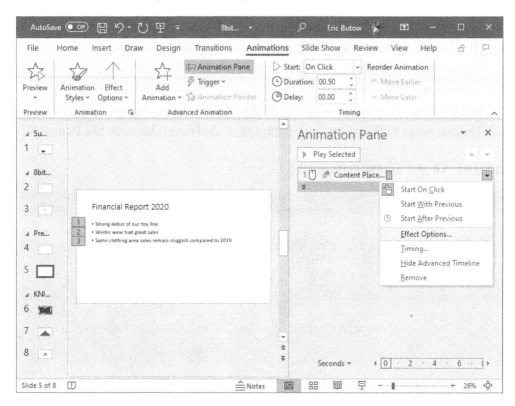

6. In the Fly In dialog box (see Figure 16.9), click the down arrow to the right of the All At Once box and then select By Letter from the drop-down list.

Below the selected By Letter box, the delay between letters appearing in the slide is 10 percent of the total time to animate the text by default. For this example, I'll keep the 10 percent setting as is and click OK.

PowerPoint previews the animation so that you can see the timing for each letter that appears in the selected text. You can repeat steps 5 and 6 to increase the percentage and see how it looks.

When you finish animating the text, close the Animation Pane by clicking the Close (X) icon in the upper-right corner of the pane.

If the animation went by too quickly for you, preview it again by clicking Preview in the Animations ribbon.

FIGURE 16.9   By Letter option in the Animate Text drop-down menu

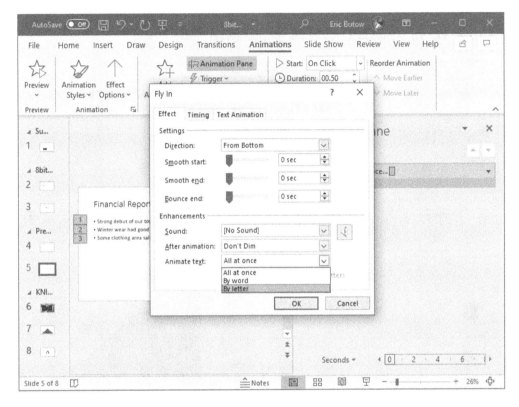

Animating SmartArt Graphics

PowerPoint allows you to animate SmartArt graphics and individual shapes within them. For example, you may want to animate one part of a graphic at a time to help make a point.

Here's how to add a SmartArt graphic and animate it:

1. In the left pane, click the slide in which you want to add the SmartArt graphic.

2. Click in the slide and then click the Insert menu option.

3. In the Illustrations section in the Insert ribbon, click SmartArt.

4. Select the graphic that you want to add in the Choose A SmartArt graphic and then click OK. This example uses a pyramid.

5. Click the Animations menu option.

6. In the Animation section in the Animations ribbon, click the More button to the right of the row of transition slides. (The More button looks like a down arrow with a line above it.)

   If your PowerPoint window width is small, click the Animation Styles icon in the Animations ribbon.

7. In the drop-down list, as shown in Figure 16.10, click an animation style icon. For this example, I'll click Wipe.

FIGURE 16.10 The Wipe style in the drop-down list

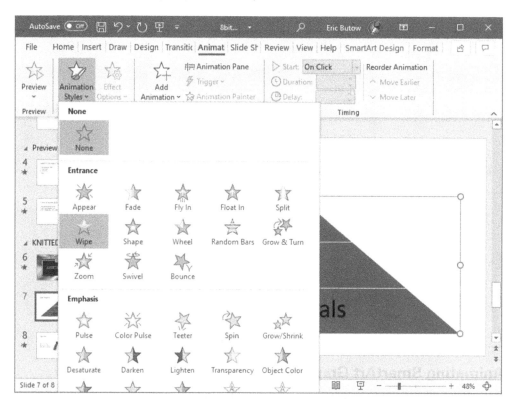

You can select an animation style from one of three sections: Entrance, Emphasis, and Exit. The Wipe style icon in this example is in the Entrance section.

After you click Wipe, PowerPoint animates the SmartArt graphic so that you can see how it will look in your presentation. You will learn how to configure animation effects for a SmartArt graphic later in this chapter.

 You can get more information about adding a SmartArt graphic in Chapter 15, "Inserting Tables, Charts, SmartArt, 3D Models, and Media."

Animating Shapes in a SmartArt Graphic

Now that you have animated an entire SmartArt graphic, you can animate individual shapes within it. In the pyramid example I created, I will animate the various levels of the pyramid by clicking Effect Options in the Animation section in the Animation ribbon.

From the drop-down list shown in Figure 16.11, select One By One.

FIGURE 16.11   One By One option in the Sequence section

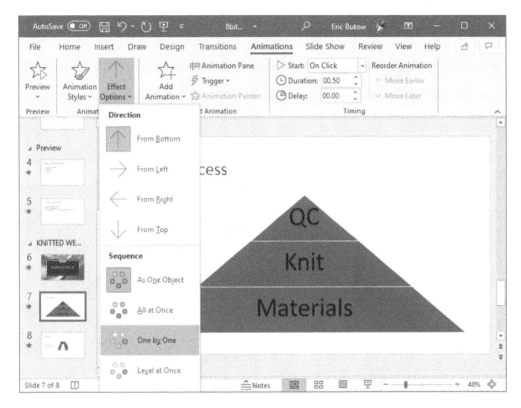

PowerPoint previews the animation on the slide so that you can see each shape gradually appear in the SmartArt graphic. You will learn how to control the timing of the animation later in this chapter.

Reverse the Order of an Animation

In this example, the animation appears with each level in the pyramid appearing from top to bottom, and each level appears from the bottom to the top. You can reverse the order of the animation so that the pyramid appears from the bottom to the top by following these steps:

1. Click the SmartArt graphic in the slide, if necessary.
2. Click the Animations menu option, if necessary.
3. In the Animation section in the Animations ribbon, click the Show Additional Effects Options icon in the lower-right corner of the section (see Figure 16.12).
4. In the Wipe dialog box, shown in Figure 16.13, click the SmartArt Animation tab.
5. Click the Reverse Order check box.
6. Click OK.

FIGURE 16.12   The Show Additional Effects Options icon

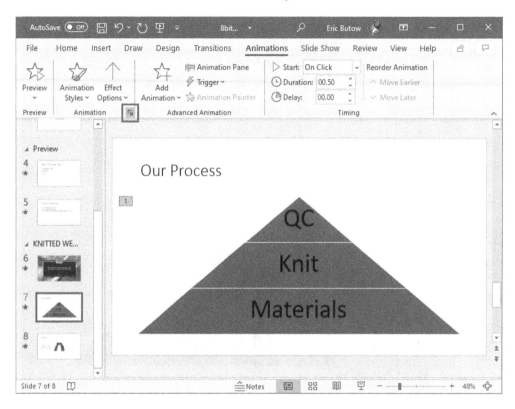

FIGURE 16.13   The Wipe dialog box

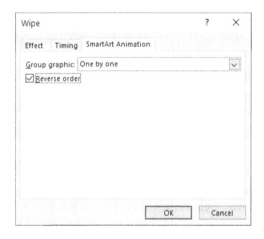

After you click OK, PowerPoint previews the animation that shows each level appearing from the bottom to the top.

 You cannot reverse the animation for an individual shape within a SmartArt graphic. You can only reverse all of the shapes.

Removing an Animation

When you want to remove an animation from one or all levels of an animation, such as all the levels of a pyramid in this example, follow these steps:

1. Click the SmartArt graphic in the slide, if necessary.
2. Click the Animations menu option, if necessary.
3. Click the Animations menu option.
4. In the Advanced Animation section in the Animations ribbon, click Animation Pane.
5. Click the down arrow to the right of the text for level 1 (see Figure 16.14).
6. Select Remove from the drop-down menu, as shown in Figure 16.15.

FIGURE 16.14 Level 1 in the Animation Pane

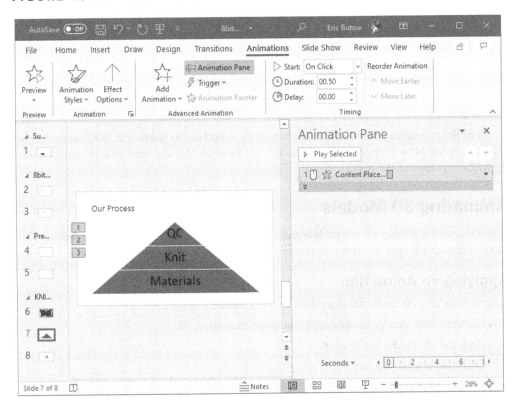

FIGURE 16.15 Remove option in the drop-down menu

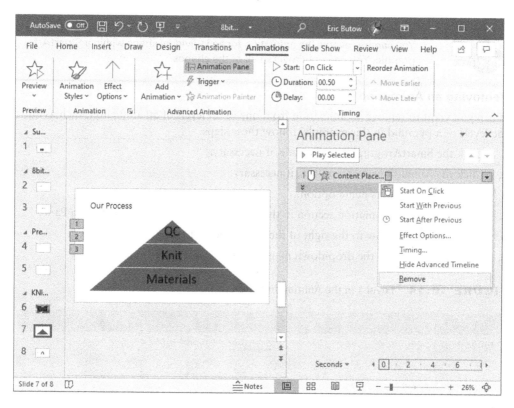

All of the animations listed in the Animation pane and the animation number boxes in the slide disappear. Now you can close the Animation Pane by clicking the Close (X) icon in the upper-right corner of the pane.

Animating 3D Models

When you add a 3D model, as you learned to do in Chapter 15, you can not only rotate a model but also animate it. After you animate a model, you can change its effects.

Applying an Animation

Follow these steps to apply an animation to a 3D model:

1. Click the slide that contains the 3D model, if necessary.
2. Click the 3D model in the slide.
3. Click the Animations menu option.

4. In the Animation section in the Animations ribbon, click the More button to the right of the row of transition slides. (The More button looks like a down arrow with a line above it.)

    If your PowerPoint window width is small, click the Animation Styles icon in the Animations ribbon.

5. In the drop-down list, as shown in Figure 16.16, click an animation style icon in the 3D section at the top of the list. For this example, I'll click Turntable.

FIGURE 16.16   The Turntable style in the drop-down list

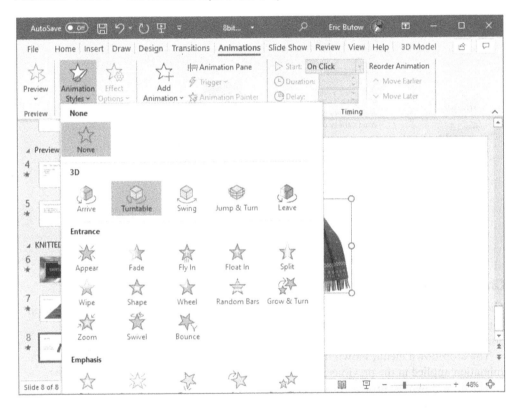

After you click Turntable, PowerPoint previews the SmartArt graphic animation. In this example, you see the 3D model of a scarf (see Figure 16.17) rotate around the x-axis in the slide.

FIGURE 16.17   The rotating scarf with the Turntable effect applied

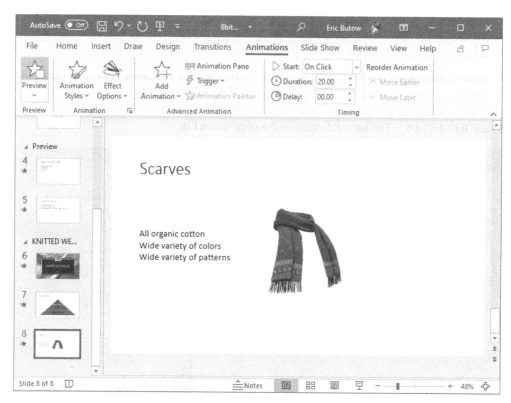

Changing Animation Effects

The animation effects that you can change in a 3D model depend on the type of animation you choose. Start by clicking Effect Options in the Animation section in the Animations ribbon.

The drop-down menu, shown in Figure 16.18, reflects the options for the Turntable animation applied in the previous section.

The drop-down list groups the options into three categories: Direction, Amount, and Rotation Axis. (You may see options in the Intensity category for some effects.) By default, the options for the Turntable effects are to rotate to the right, do a full spin of the 3D model, and spin on the View Center rotation axis.

Change one of these options by clicking the option(s) in the drop-down menu. For example, click Down to rotate the 3D model on the z-axis. After you click the option, PowerPoint previews the new animation effect in the slide.

FIGURE 16.18   Animation effect options for the Turntable style

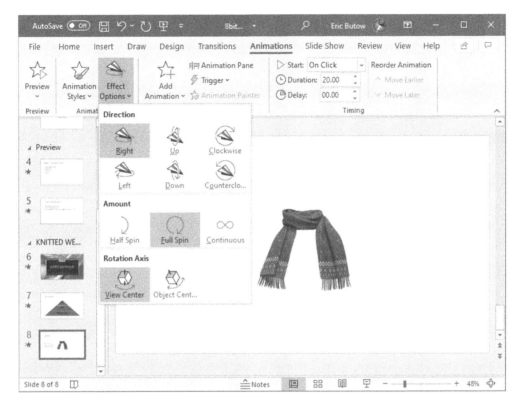

Configuring Animation Effects

When you need to fine-tune your SmartArt animation, you can change the animation effects. Start by clicking the slide in the left pane that contains the SmartArt graphic, and then click the SmartArt graphic in the slide.

In the Advanced Animation section in the Animations ribbon, click Animation Pane. The Animation Pane appears on the right side of the PowerPoint menu. Now click the down arrow to the right of the animation in the list and then select Effect Options from the drop-down menu (see Figure 16.19).

In this example, the Wipe dialog box appears because I applied the Wipe animation pyramid SmartArt graphic earlier in this chapter. Click the SmartArt Animation tab, as shown in Figure 16.20.

FIGURE 16.19   Effect Options menu option

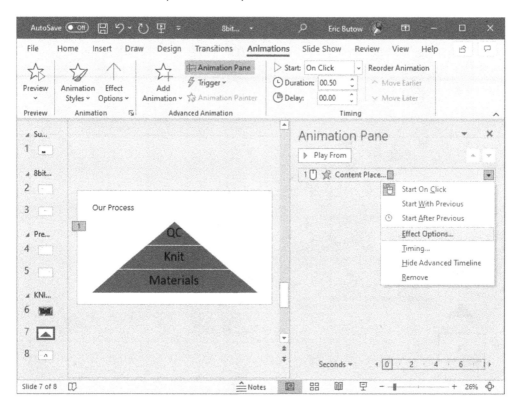

FIGURE 16.20   Wipe dialog box

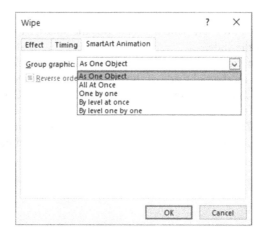

In the Group Graphic section, click the down arrow to the right of the As One Object box. Now you can choose from one of the following sequence options:

As One Object   The default option animates the SmartArt graphic as one object. For example, when you use the Wipe animation with a pyramid SmartArt graphic, the first shape grows to its full height before the next shape above or below it grows.

All At Once   Animate each shape in the SmartArt graphic at the same time. For example, when you use the Wipe animation with a pyramid SmartArt graphic, all three shapes grow to their full height simultaneously.

One By One   Animate each shape individually. When one shape finishes its animation, PowerPoint animates the next shape.

By Level At Once   Animate all shapes with the same text level at the same time, starting with level 1. For example, if you have some shapes in a SmartArt graphic with level 1 bulleted text and other shapes with level 2 bulleted text, PowerPoint animates the shapes with level 1 bulleted text first. Once those shapes have been animated, Power-Point animates all of the shapes with level 2 bulleted text.

By Level One By One   Animate all shapes with the same text level one after the other, starting with level 1. For example, if you have some shapes in a SmartArt graphic with level 1 bulleted text and other shapes with level 2 bulleted text, PowerPoint animates shapes with level 1 bulleted text one after the other. Once those shapes have been animated, PowerPoint animates all of the shapes with level 2 bulleted text one after the other.

Once you select the option in the list, click OK. PowerPoint previews the new animation effect in the slide.

Differences in Animation Behavior

When you apply an animation style to a SmartArt graphic, pay attention to how PowerPoint applies animation styles:

- When you animate a SmartArt graphic all at once, you will likely find that each shape in the graphic goes at different speeds so that all shapes finish their animations at the same time. When you animate a graphic as one option, the entire graphic animates at the same speed.

- If your graphic has a background, PowerPoint does not animate the background, only the slides.

- If you pick any effect other than As One Object, the background of the graphic will show on your slide when you run the slideshow.

Configuring Animation Paths

If you want to animate a shape so that it appears to follow a path within a slide, such as if you want to have a SmartArt graphic or 3D model move out of the way so that you can display text underneath it, PowerPoint allows you to use two different tools: *motion paths* and *morph*.

Adding a Motion Path

When you want to add a motion path to a SmartArt graphic, follow these steps:

1. Click the slide that contains the SmartArt graphic or 3D model, if necessary. For this example, I will click a pyramid SmartArt graphic.

2. Click the SmartArt graphic in the slide.

3. Click the Animations menu option.

4. In the Animation section in the Animations ribbon, click the More button to the right of the row of transition slides. (The More button looks like a down arrow with a line above it.)

    If your PowerPoint window width is small, click the Animation Styles icon in the Animations ribbon.

5. In the drop-down list, shown in Figure 16.21, click a motion path icon in the Motion Paths section near the bottom of the list. For this example, I'll click Turns.

FIGURE 16.21   The Turns motion path in the drop-down list

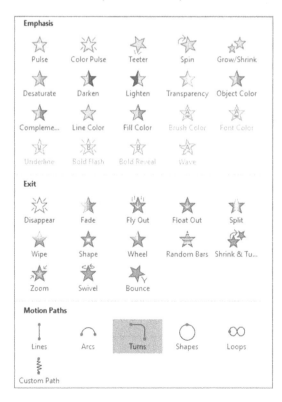

The Turns option icon shows you the path the SmartArt graphic will take—that is, the graphic will move from its current position signified by the green dot and make a turn downward to its ending point on the slide signified by the red dot.

Here are a few important points to remember as you apply a motion path:

- Though Figure 16.21 does not show these colors, they do appear in color on the screen.

- You can draw a custom motion path on the slide by selecting Custom Path from the drop-down menu, as shown in Figure 16.21, but a custom menu path is beyond the purview of the MO-300 exam.

- You can select from more motion paths by clicking More Motion Paths at the bottom of the drop-down menu, as shown in Figure 16.21. This information is not covered in this book or the MO-300 exam.

After you click Turns, PowerPoint previews the SmartArt graphic animation. In this example, the graphic moves to the lower-right area of the slide, and some of the graphic disappears from the slide (see Figure 16.22).

FIGURE 16.22   The truncated graphic in the slide

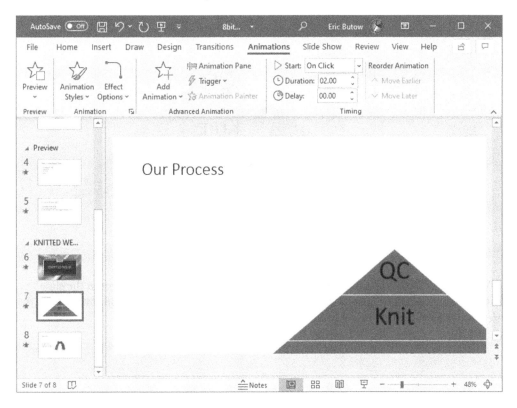

When you start the slideshow and view the slide, click the SmartArt graphic in the slide to move the graphic along the motion path.

Editing a Motion Path

PowerPoint allows you to change the motion path in different directions. Start by clicking the SmartArt graphic in the slide. In the Animation section in the Animations ribbon, click Effect Options.

The drop-down list with a list of options appears, and the options reflect the Turns motion path selected in the previous section (see Figure 16.23).

FIGURE 16.23   Effect Options drop-down menu

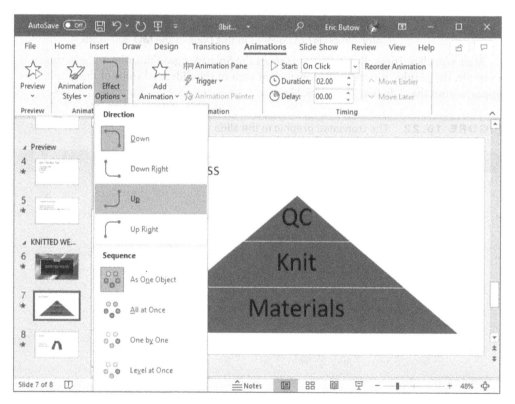

When I click Up in the list, PowerPoint previews the new animation effect in the slide that shows the SmartArt graphic moving right on the slide and then up. You can preview the effect again by clicking Preview in the Animations ribbon.

Creating a Morph Transition

The morph feature allows you to animate an object automatically including a SmartArt graphic, shape, or even text. To do this, you need to duplicate a slide; move the graphic, shape, or text in the duplicated slide to a new location; and then apply the morph transition.

 You cannot use the morph transition to animate a chart.

Create a morph transition by following these steps:

1. In the left pane, click the slide that you want to duplicate. This example uses a slide with text.

2. Click the Home menu option.

3. In the Slides section in the Home ribbon, click New Slide.

   If your PowerPoint window width is small, click the Slides icon in the Home ribbon and then select New Slide from the drop-down menu.

4. Select Duplicate Selected Slides from the drop-down menu, as shown in Figure 16.24.

   The duplicated slide appears in the right pane.

FIGURE 16.24   The Duplicate Selected Slides option

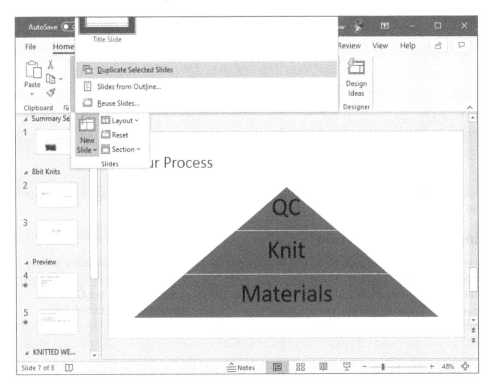

5. Move the text in the duplicated slide to a different location within the slide.

6. Click the Transitions menu option.

7. In the Transition To This Slide section in the Transitions ribbon, click Morph (see Figure 16.25).

FIGURE 16.25 The Morph icon in the ribbon

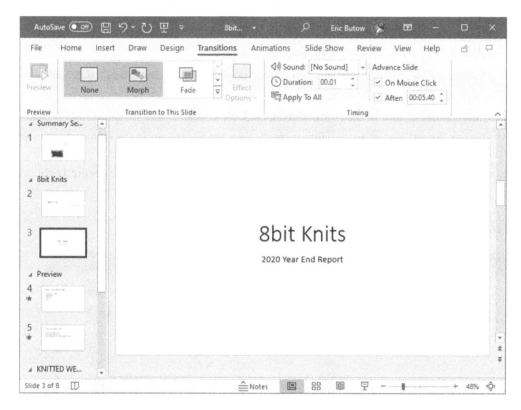

PowerPoint moves the text from the location in the first slide to the location in the second slide, so it appears that the text is animated.

Editing a Morph Transition

If you want to edit the morph effect, start by clicking the duplicated slide and then clicking the Transitions menu option (if necessary).

In the Transitions To This Slide section in the Transitions ribbon, click Effect Options. The drop-down menu you see depends on the type of morph transition you added. In the example shown in Figure 16.26, the effects are for morphing text.

FIGURE 16.26   Effects drop-down menu

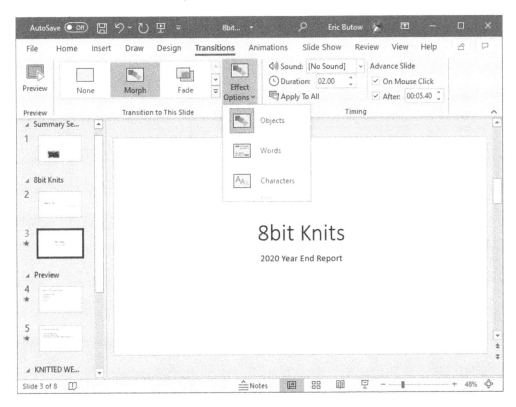

The default option in the menu is to morph the words as objects. You can morph objects and individual words by clicking Words, and you can morph objects and individual letters by clicking Characters. If you morph words or characters, the text in both the original and duplicated slide must have the same capitalization.

Reordering Animations on a Slide

When you have multiple animations on a slide, each marker has a number that tells you which animations will appear in the sequence. You can change the order of the sequence by clicking the animation marker in a slide (see Figure 16.27).

Click the Animations menu option if necessary. In the Timing section in the Animations ribbon, click one of the two options in the Reorder Animation section:

Move Earlier: Move the animation so that it appears earlier in the animation sequence.

Move Later: Move the animation so that it appears later in the sequence.

FIGURE 16.27   Animation marker on the slide

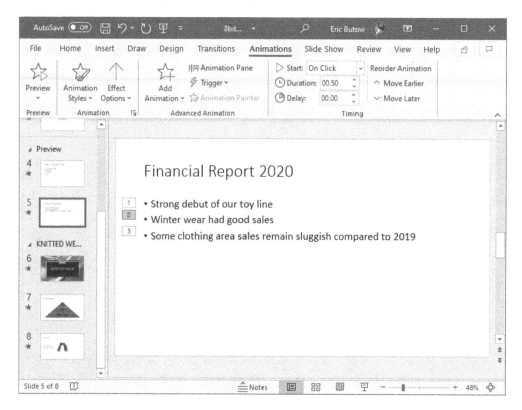

After you click the option, the marker numbers change in the slide. For example, if you move marker 2 to the first animation in the sequence, the number of this marker changes to 1. The marker that formerly had the number 1 changes to number 2.

Animating Slide Content

1. Open the slideshow that you created in Exercise 16.1.

2. Add a new slide, which is the third slide in the slideshow, with a Title And Content theme. If you need to know how to add slides, refer to Chapter 13.

3. Add a SmartArt graphic to the content section of the slide.

4. Animate the graphic with the Fly In effect.

5. Add a Turns motion path to the graphic.

6. Change the effect turn direction to Up Right.

7. Add a new slide, which is the fourth slide in the slideshow, with a Title And Content theme.

8. In the content area of the slide, add text and move it to the left side of the slide.

9. Duplicate the fourth slide.

10. In the duplicated slide, move the text to the right side of the slide.

11. Morph the text in the slide.

12. Save the slideshow.

Setting Timing for Transitions

PowerPoint allows you to customize your slide transitions by setting timing, effect, and start and finish options. You can also specify a time to advance to the next slide automatically during your presentation.

Setting Transition Effect Duration

By default, each effect has a default transition time, but if you have not specified a transition the default speed is Auto. Each effect has a different duration.

You can change the duration to a speed you want from within the Transitions ribbon by following these steps:

1. In the left pane, click the slide for which you want to change the transition speed.

2. Click the Transitions menu option.

3. In the Timing section in the Transitions ribbon, click in the Duration box, as shown in Figure 16.28.

   This example uses the Morph transition, so the Duration box shows 02.00, which is the default two-second duration.

4. Press Backspace and then type the number of seconds in the form ss.ff, where *ss* is the number of seconds and *ff* is a fraction of a second, such as 25 for one-quarter of a second.

You can set the duration as precisely as in hundredths of a second. Increase and decrease the duration by 0.25 seconds at a time by clicking the up and down arrows, respectively, to the right of the Duration box.

After you add the duration, you can apply that duration to all of your slide transitions by clicking Apply To All in the Timing section in the Transitions ribbon.

FIGURE 16.28   The Duration box

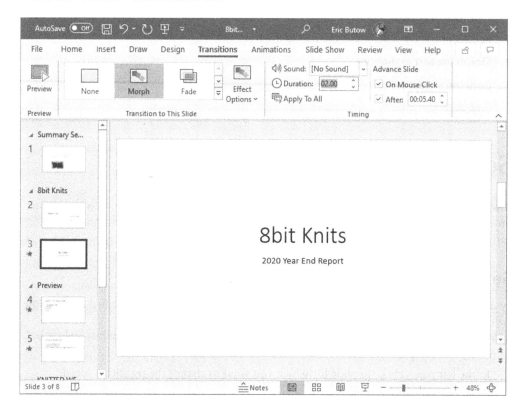

Configuring Transition Start and Finish Options

PowerPoint lets you advance your slides yourself by default—that is, you can advance to the next slide with just the click of your left mouse button.

However, if you want to change the advancement time for your slide—for example, if you have an unattended slideshow that will loop continuously during a trade show—you can set the transition timing by following these steps:

1. In the left pane, click the slide that contains the transition.

2. Click the Transitions menu option.

3. In the Timing section in the Transitions ribbon, clear the On Mouse Click check box.

4. Select the After check box, as shown in Figure 16.29.

5. Click the time box to the right of the After check box. The default time advancement period is 00:00.00.

6. Press Backspace and then type the number of seconds in the form mm:ss.ff, where *mm* is the number of minutes, *ss* is the number of seconds, and *ff* is a fraction of a second such as 25 for one-quarter of a second.

FIGURE 16.29   After check box in the Transitions ribbon

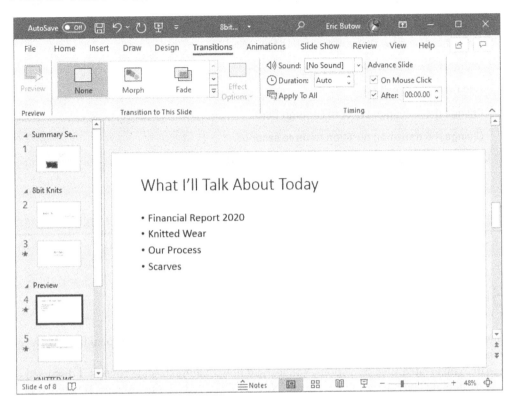

You can set the duration as precisely as in hundredths of a second. Increase and decrease the duration by one second at a time by clicking the up and down arrows, respectively, to the right of the time box.

After you set the time, click Preview at the left side of the Transitions ribbon to see the previous slide and how quickly it transitions to your selected slide.

Keep the following in mind as you configure your start and finish options:

- After you set the advancement time for the current slide, you can apply this time to all slides in your slideshow by clicking Apply To All in the Timing section in the Transitions ribbon.

- You can enable advance timing by using the mouse or automatically by clicking the On Mouse Click and After check boxes. This gives you the flexibility of being able to advance a slide with a left mouse click before PowerPoint advances the slide automatically.

EXERCISE 16.3

Setting Timing for Transitions

1. Open the slideshow that you created in Exercise 16.1.

2. In the left pane, click the third slide.

3. Add the Fade transition.

4. Change the transition effect to Through Black.

5. Change the transition duration to three seconds.

6. Change the advancement After time to six seconds.

7. Preview the transition.

8. Save the slideshow.

Summary

This chapter started by showing you how to apply basic and three-dimensional (3D) slide transitions. You also learned how to configure transition effects.

After you created slide transitions, you learned how to animate slide content. I discussed how to animate text and graphic elements. Next, you learned how to animate 3D models in a slide. I explained how to configure both animation effects and animation paths, and you learned how to reorder animations on a slide.

Finally, you learned how to set the transition effect duration, as well as how to configure transition start and finish options.

Key Terms

3D	motion paths
markers	transitions
morph	

Exam Essentials

Understand how to apply basic and 3D slide transitions.   Know how to open the drop-down list of built-in transition types and apply one to the selected slide.

Know how to configure transition effects.   Understand how to access the list of effects for a transition and apply the effect to a slide.

Understand how to animate text, graphic elements, and 3D models.   Know how to make text appear one line at a time or one letter at a time, animate SmartArt graphics as well as individual shapes within them, animate 3D models, and change 3D model animation effects.

Be able to configure animation effects and paths.   Know how to configure animation effects; configure animation paths, including adding and editing a motion path; and create a morph transition.

Know how to reorder animations on a slide.   Understand how to select an animation marker in the slide and reorder the order of animations.

Understand how to configure transition timing.   Know how to set the transition effect duration as well as start and finish timing options.

Review Questions

1. How do you apply a slide transition to all slides?

   A. A dialog box appears after you add the transition asking you to which slides you wish to apply the transition.

   B. Copy and paste the slide formatting in the Home ribbon.

   C. Click Apply To All in the Transitions ribbon.

   D. Apply the transition in the Slide Master.

2. What ways can you animate text in a slide? (Choose all that apply.)

   A. One word at a time

   B. One letter at a time

   C. One line at a time

   D. One slide at a time

3. After you change the transition duration, how do you see the duration in action?

   A. Click Preview in the Animations ribbon.

   B. Run the slideshow from the current slide in the Slides ribbon.

   C. Click Preview in the Transitions ribbon.

   D. Click Reading view in the View ribbon.

4. What are the three types of slide transitions that you can add? (Choose all that apply.)

   A. Subtle

   B. 3D

   C. Basic

   D. Exciting

5. What menu ribbon do you use to add effects between slides?

   A. Animations

   B. Transitions

   C. Design

   D. View

6. How do you find out how many animations are within the slide? (Choose all that apply.)

   A. Click the Animations menu option.

   B. Click the View menu option.

   C. Look at the marker numbers.

   D. Click the Design menu option.

7. How do you know what a transition effect does?

 A. By right-clicking the transition name

 B. From a description in a tooltip

 C. From the name below the effect icon

 D. By clicking the Help menu option

8. What effect option do you select to animate each shape in a graphic sequentially?

 A. Level One By One

 B. One By One

 C. Size

 D. As One Object

9. What is the default duration for a slide effect?

 A. Auto

 B. Two seconds

 C. It depends on the effect.

 D. Zero seconds

10. What feature do you use to remove an animation from a slide?

 A. The Animations ribbon

 B. The Effect Options icon in the Animations ribbon

 C. The Design ribbon

 D. The Animation Pane

Appendix

Answers to Review Questions

Part I: Word Exam MO-100

Chapter 1: Working with Documents

1. C. Open the Find And Replace dialog box by clicking the Replace icon in the Home ribbon or by pressing Ctrl+H. Then type the existing and replacement text in the Find and Replace fields, respectively. Replace all instances of the existing text by clicking the Replace All button.

2. B. A watermark is lighter background text that conveys the document status to your readers, such as a document that's confidential and only available to certain people to read.

3. D. The header is the area between the top of the page and the top margin.

4. C. The File screen contains the Info menu option so that you can inspect documents.

5. A. When you click in a paragraph in your text and click a style that has the paragraph marker to the right of the name in the Styles list, Word applies all the formatting settings contained within the style to the selected paragraph.

6. D. A theme is a collection of styles for formatting various parts of your page, such as heading text, body text, headers, and footers.

7. B. The Share option gives you several options for sending a document either as an email attachment or on the web in a variety of formats.

8. C. In the Home ribbon, click the down arrow to the right of the Find icon, and then click Go To in the drop-down menu. (You can also press Ctrl+G.)

9. D. The Accessibility Checker inspects your document and checks to see if any potential problems exist that could keep people of different abilities from reading it.

10. B. The Compatibility Checker ensures that your document can be read by three earlier versions of Word dating back to Word 97, and it alerts you to any formatting issues that you may need to change so that all your recipients can read your document.

Chapter 2: Inserting and Formatting Text

1. C. When you click Advanced Find in the Home ribbon, the Find And Replace dialog box appears so that you can change more search options.

2. B. You can open the Find And Replace dialog box by clicking Replace in the Home ribbon and then clicking the Match Case dialog box to specify that the text you want to find has one or more letters in a different case.

3. D. Open the Symbol window from the Insert ribbon by clicking the Symbol icon and then clicking the More Symbols option in the drop-down menu. Then you can add a special character using the Special Characters tab.

4. A. To change the format of multiple selections in your document, you must first double-click Format Painter.

5. C. Word makes it easy to copy the format of a selected block of text by double-clicking the Format Painter icon. Then you can apply it to as much text in the document as you want.

6. D. Word allows you to create a maximum of three columns.

7. B. By default, Word adds a ½-inch indent to the first line of the paragraph, but subsequent lines are not indented.

8. A. Word automatically adds a new page after the one into which you inserted the page break, and you can start typing in the new page.

9. C. After you click Column in the Breaks drop-down menu, a new column appears on the page or on the next page so that you can type more text.

10. B. A section is a portion of the document that has its own formatting on the same page or a new page.

Chapter 3: Managing Tables and Lists

1. C. After you move the mouse pointer over Quick Tables, click the table style that you want to place on the page.

2. B. When you move the mouse pointer over the grid, you can highlight three columns and seven rows and then click the lower-right corner of the highlighted grid to insert the table on the page.

3. C. Sorting from Z to A is descending order. Sorting from A to Z is ascending order.

4. A. Hold down the Alt key as you click and drag on the column so that you can see the exact measurement.

5. D. The built-in AutoFit feature allows you to fit the size of your table or a column automatically to the longest block of content.

6. A. Both the Table Design and Layout menu options appear at the right side of the row of options in the menu bar.

7. B. You can use bullets from symbols, fonts, and even pictures.

8. C. You can sort by text, which is the default search type, as well as by numbers and dates in a table.

9. C. At the beginning of a new paragraph, you can start a bulleted list by pressing the asterisk (*) key, a space, and then some text. Word automatically converts the asterisk to the default bullet style.

10. D. Word gets confused when you update numbers in text and then you try to add a new number in the list. So, use the Numbering feature to keep your lists numbered correctly.

Chapter 4: Building References

1. C. When you click the References menu option, the ribbon shows you options for adding footnotes, endnotes, and more.

2. B. After you select text in the footnote, the pop-up menu appears above the footnote so that you can easily change the font, spacing, and paragraph styles.

3. C. Word automatically applies the correct citation format for the writing style that you need to use for your document, so you don't need to change the format manually.

4. A. After you click Edit Citation in the menu, add the page number in the Edit Citation dialog box and then click OK.

5. D. After you place the cursor where you want to add the placeholder, click Add New Placeholder, type the placeholder name in the Placeholder Name dialog box, and then click OK.

6. A. Word uses its built-in heading styles to determine how many times text with a certain heading style should be indented in the TOC.

7. B. You can open the Styles pane by pressing Alt+Ctrl+Shift+S to view all nine TOC styles based on all the style levels, and then modify each style as you see fit.

8. C. A TOC reflects the layout of your document when you created it, but Word doesn't update the TOC with any other text you added to the document unless you update the TOC manually.

9. C. Word applies the correct formats for your desired writing style into your bibliography, so you don't have to change any formatting manually.

10. D. When you click Bibliography in the References menu ribbon, the three built-in bibliography styles appear in the drop-down menu.

Chapter 5: Adding and Formatting Graphic Elements

1. C. When you click the Insert menu option, click Shapes to view a wide variety of shapes you can add from the drop-down menu.

2. B. When you click the SmartArt icon in the ribbon, the Choose A SmartArt Graphic dialog box opens so that you can select a prebuilt graphic from eight different categories.

3. D. A text box is useful when you want to have text that stands apart from the rest of the text, such as a sidebar, so that you can have additional information on a side of the page that doesn't interfere with the main block of text.

4. C. After you click Picture Effects, you can change an effect in one of the six effect categories.

5. A. In the SmartArt Design menu ribbon, click the Reset Design icon to clear all of your previous changes and return to the original style.

6. C. Clicking and dragging the Rotate button that appears in the middle of the selected model lets you rotate the 3D model.

7. B. After you create at least two text boxes, click in the first one. Then click Create Link in the Text section in the Shape Format menu ribbon. You can then tell Word which text box will receive overflow text.

8. D. After you right-click the shape, select Add Text from the context menu.

9. C. Placing your graphic in line with text means that the graphic is embedded at the insertion point in the text. The text above and below the graphic will stay that way, even as you add more to the document.

10. B. If you're sharing a Word document online with other people in your company who may not be able to see the graphics in your document, then Alt text is a great way to tell those people about the messages in your graphics.

Chapter 6: Working with Other Users on Your Document

1. D. The top of the comment box in the right margin tells you the name of the person who wrote the comment, shows the writer's avatar, and tells you how long ago the person wrote the comment.

2. B. Click Reply in the comment box to write your reply within the comment box.

3. C. The comment and the name of the person who wrote it are grayed out in the right margin of the document, but the comment remains in case you want to reopen it.

4. B. After you click Reopen in the comment box, the comment is restored so that you can add to your comment or reply to it.

5. D. After you click Delete All Comments in the menu, all comments and the right margin in your document disappear.

6. A. The Track Changes option is available in the Review menu ribbon.

7. B. In the Review menu ribbon, click the down arrow to the right of Simple Markup and then click All Markup. You see all of the formatting in the text as well as the change bars in the left margin.

8. C. After you click the Reject icon in the Review menu ribbon, click Reject All Changes. All of the changes made in the document disappear.

9. D. After you accept a change, click the Previous icon to go to the previous change in the document.

10. A. If you want to make sure that people do not turn off Track Changes when they make any changes to a document you've shared, add a password that only you know.

Part II: Excel Exam MO-200

Chapter 7: Managing Worksheets and Workbooks

1. A, C. A text file uses a tab character as the delimiter, and a comma-separated value file uses a comma as the delimiter.

2. B. Type the tilde (~) before the question mark to ensure that Excel finds text in cells with a question mark.

3. C. When you double-click the right edge of the column within the header, such as to the right of the B column, Excel automatically adjusts the width to the text in a cell that has the greatest width.

4. B, D. You can only add tools and commands to the Quick Access Toolbar.

5. A, B, D. You can save to PDF format, text format, and HTML, which is the language used to create web pages.

6. A, D. The Quick Access Toolbar is in the title bar by default, but you can also move it under the ribbon.

7. B. When you add a Screen Tip, a pop-up box appears when you move the mouse pointer over the link.

8. C. You can add a header and/or footer from within Page Layout view.

9. C. You must protect the worksheet by clicking the Review menu option and then clicking Protect Sheet in the Protect section in the Review menu ribbon.

10. D. Click the Page Layout menu option to open the Page Layout ribbon. Next, click Print Area in the Page Setup section and then select Set Print Area from the drop-down menu.

Chapter 8: Using Data Cells and Ranges

1. B. When you select the Formulas And Number Formatting icon from the Paste drop-down menu, Excel copies only the formatting in the formulas and any number formatting into the new cell.

2. C. When you select Merge Across from the Merge & Center drop-down menu in the Home ribbon, the selected cells merge and the data in the first column within the selected cells is left-aligned.

3. B, D. You can only start a named range with letters and underscores.

4. D. When you click a blank cell and press Ctrl+A, Excel selects all cells in the worksheet.

5. A. Place the Sparkline chart after the last column in a row to have the Sparkline collect its data from all columns within the row.

6. A, B, D. You can Auto Fill sequential information, including numbers, dates, and months of the year. You can also Auto Fill a number in one cell into one or more other cells.

7. C. When you select Format Cell Alignment from the menu, you can specify the angle in degrees.

8. C. When you click Greater, you can format cells with numbers that are greater than a specific value in the Greater Than dialog box.

9. C. A named range can be no longer than 255 characters, including spaces.

10. A, C, D. You can apply the Accounting Number style (the $ icon) for the type of currency, the Percent style (the % icon), and the Comma style for numbers larger than 999.

Chapter 9: Working with Tables and Table Data

1. C. Excel applies the formatting from your table to the cell range.

2. B, D. You can press Ctrl+Z to undo the deletion, or you can click the Undo icon in the Quick Access Toolbar if you prefer to use the mouse.

3. C. Sorting from Z to A is descending order. Sorting from A to Z is ascending order.

4. A, C, D. In the Format Cells dialog box, you can change the font, border, and fill color and pattern in the appropriate tabs.

5. D. The Count Numbers option shows you the total number of cells in the column that have numbers in them.

6. A, B, D. In the Table Design menu ribbon, the Header Row, Banded Rows, and Filter Button check boxes are checked by default.

7. A, B. The header row and filter button are two features that appear automatically in your new table.

8. C. You need to sort by column in a custom sort, and you can select the column you want to use for the sort.

9. B. Excel totals the last (or rightmost) column in a table.

10. D. Several style tiles appear in the Table Styles section within the Table Design menu ribbon that opens after you create a table.

Chapter 10: Performing Operations by Using Formulas and Functions

1. C. As you press F4 on the keyboard, the cell reference type cycles between all three types.

2. B. The COUNTA()function counts all cells in a selected range that have characters in them and returns the number of cells Excel found.

3. C. The RIGHT()function shows the last five characters, or the five characters at the right, of the text in cell A3.

4. A, C, D. You can create a mixed, relative, or absolute cell reference type in a formula.

5. D. The function does not count empty cells when you average numbers within a range of cells.

6. D. The LEFT()function treats spaces as characters, so spaces appear in the cell where you entered the LEFT() formula.

7. B. Using A2 without any $ signs in the cell reference indicates that this is a relative cell reference.

8. C. Type the equal sign before you type the left parenthesis when you start to add a formula in the Formula Bar.

9. A. The CONCAT()function combines text strings in two or more cells and does not place a space or any other characters between each string.

10. D. You need to add a comma between each cell range in the parentheses within the SUM()function.

Chapter 11: Managing Charts

1. C. When you select the All Charts tab, a list of chart categories appears at the left side of the dialog box so that you can click each category and see the different types of charts that you can add to the right of the list.

2. B. Excel uses columns for the horizontal axis when there are an equal number of columns and rows.

3. A, C. You can change styles for both shapes and WordArt.

4. A. The legend appears at the bottom of the chart area so that you know what each color in the chart represents.

5. A, C, D. The built-in styles contain options for changing the border color, text color, and/or text background color.

6. C. When you click the Chart Elements icon in the upper-right corner of the selected chart, the right arrow appears when you move the mouse pointer over the element.

7. B. A chart in a chart sheet is a fixed size, even though sizing handles appear in the bounding box around the chart.

8. C. A trendline shows you the overall trend of one specific type of data over time.

9. D. A chart layout allows you to make changes to how the data is presented, and the chart style allows you to change the look and feel of the chart.

10. B. If you're sharing an Excel workbook online with other people in your company who may not be able to see the chart in your document, then Alt text is a great way to tell those people about the messages in your chart.

Part III: PowerPoint Exam MO-300

Chapter 12: Creating Presentations

1. A, C. You can change fonts and colors in the slide layout, as well as the title, footers, and effects. You can also hide background graphics.

2. B. PowerPoint automatically displays your slideshow in Normal view.

3. B, D. PowerPoint will print slides 3 through 8, slide 10, and slide 12.

4. C. When you click the Browsed At A Kiosk (Full Screen) button in the Show Type section, the Loop Continuously Until 'Esc' check box is hidden, because when you click the button you loop the presentation automatically.

5. D. Marking a slideshow as final still gives people the ability to edit your slideshow. Adding a password turns off the ability to edit the slideshow to anyone who does not have the password.

6. C. Once you apply changes to a handout master, you will see that all pages in the handout reflect those changes.

7. A, D. Widescreen (16:9) is the default size, but you can also change your slide size to Standard (4:3).

8. B. You can select from one of nine print options for the slideshow handouts.

9. C. The bottom of the left pane tells you what slide you're on and how many slides there are in the presentation.

10. A, C. The default resolution is 1080p, but you can also choose Standard (480p), HD (720p), and Ultra HD (4K).

Chapter 13: Managing Slides

1. C. PowerPoint automatically checks to see if there is more text than a slide can manage and creates one or more additional slides to display the rest of the outline text.

2. B. You still see the hidden slide in the list, but the slide has a gray background and the slide number above the slide has a diagonal line through it.

3. D. When you click Section in the menu, select Add Sections from the drop-down menu to type the name of the new section in the Rename Section dialog box.

4. C. When you select the Keep Source Formatting check box in the Reuse Slides pane, Power-Point keeps the source formatting.

5. A, C. You can add a gradient and pattern fill to a slide background. The solid fill is selected by default. You can also hide background graphics, but PowerPoint does not classify that as a background fill.

6. D. When you press and hold the Ctrl key as you click each slide, PowerPoint selects all the slides you click on so that you can move the slides to a new location.

7. B. PowerPoint places the new slide directly below the selected slide.

8. A. A page number appears at the right side of the footer, which is the bottom-right corner of the slide.

9. C. Rename the section by clicking the Home menu option. In the Slides area in the Home section, click Section and then select Rename Section from the drop-down menu.

10. D. PowerPoint displays one slide per section within a Summary Zoom slide.

Chapter 14: Inserting and Formatting Text, Shapes, and Images

1. A. To change the format of multiple selections in your document, you must first double-click Format Painter.

2. C. PowerPoint uses the standard blue underlined text for hyperlinks in a slide.

3. C. After you click Picture Effects, you can change an effect in one of the seven effect categories.

4. D. A text box is useful when you want to have text that stands apart from the rest of the text on the slide and that doesn't interfere with the main block of text.

5. C. Selecting Send Backward from the Arrange drop-down list moves the selected object down a level in the stack of objects.

6. B, D. The Place In This Document option is selected by default. Then you have to click the numbered slide that corresponds to the Summary Zoom slide because PowerPoint does not name that slide by default.

7. A. Once you click the Home menu option, you can change the indentation and spacing in the Paragraph section in the Home ribbon.

8. D. After you right-click the shape, select Edit Text from the context menu.

9. B. If you're sharing a slideshow with other people in your company who may not be able to see the graphics in PowerPoint, then Alt text is a great way to tell those people about the messages in your graphics.

10. A, B, D. You can view guides, gridlines, and or rulers by selecting the appropriate check boxes in the View ribbon.

Chapter 15: Inserting Tables, Charts, SmartArt, 3D Models, and Media

1. C. After you move the mouse pointer over Quick Tables, click the table style that you want to place on the page.

2. B. PowerPoint uses columns for the horizontal axis when there are an equal number of columns and rows.

3. A. In the SmartArt Design menu ribbon, click the Reset Graphic icon to clear all your previous changes and return to the original style.

4. C. Clicking and dragging the Rotate icon that appears in the middle of the selected model lets you rotate the 3D model.

5. D. Press the Windows logo key, Shift, and Q at the same time to stop the video recording.

6. A. Both the Table Design and Layout menu options appear at the right side of the row of options in the menu bar.

7. C. A trendline shows you the overall trend of one specific type of data over time.

8. B. When you click the SmartArt icon in the ribbon, the Choose A SmartArt Graphic dialog box opens so that you can select a prebuilt graphic from eight different categories, including the Pyramid category.

9. B, D. You can change the height and width of the 3D model by typing those measurements in inches (and as precisely as hundredths of an inch) in the Height and Width boxes, respectively.

10. D. When you click a bookmark, you can click the bookmark dot in the playback bar timeline to jump to that spot in the audio or video clip.

Chapter 16: Applying Transitions and Animations

1. C. After you apply the transition, click Apply To All in the Timing section in the Transitions ribbon.

2. B, C. You can animate text by specifying that you can animate one letter at a time, one line at a time, or all of the text on the slide as an entire object.

3. C. After you change the duration, click Preview at the left side of the Transitions ribbon to see how long the slide stays on the screen before moving to the next one.

4. A, D. From the drop-down list of transition effects, you can choose effects from the Subtle and Exciting sections, and you can also select from the Dynamic Content section.

5. B. Click the Transitions menu option to add transition effects between slides in the Transitions ribbon.

6. A, C. When you click the Animations menu option, markers appear in the slide and show you the marker numbers in the sequence, with the largest number signifying the last animation in the sequence.

7. B. In the transition effects drop-down list, hover the mouse pointer over the effect icon for a second or two. A tooltip will pop up and tell you what the effect does.

8. B. The One by One sequence animates each shape within a SmartArt graphic. When the animation of the first shape is complete, PowerPoint animates the second shape in the graphic.

9. C. Each effect has its own default duration that you can change in the Transitions ribbon.

10. D. The Animation Pane contains a list of all animations. When you click the down arrow to the right of the animation name in the list, you can remove the animation from the drop-down menu.

Index

E

F

H

I

T

Online Test Bank

Register to gain one year of FREE access after activation to the online interactive test bank to help you study for your Microsoft Office Specialist certification exams for Word, Excel, and PowerPoint—included with your purchase of this book! All of the chapter review questions and the practice tests in this book are included in the online test bank so you can practice in a timed and graded setting.

Register and Access the Online Test Bank

To register your book and get access to the online test bank, follow these steps:

1. Go to www.wiley.com/go/sybextestprep.
2. Select your book from the list.
3. Complete the required registration information, including answering the security verification to prove book ownership. You will be emailed a pin code.
4. Follow the directions in the email or go to www.wiley.com/go/sybextestprep.
5. Find your book on that page and click the "Register or Login" link with it. Then enter the pin code you received and click the "Activate PIN" button.
6. On the Create an Account or Login page, enter your username and password, and click Login or, if you don't have an account already, create a new account.
7. At this point, you should be in the test bank site with your new test bank listed at the top of the page. If you do not see it there, please refresh the page or log out and log back in.